D1234614

Annotated Catalogue of the Papers of

CHARLES S. PEIRCE

Annotated Catalogue of the Papers of

CHARLES S. PEIRCE

BY RICHARD S. ROBIN

THE UNIVERSITY OF MASSACHUSETTS PRESS 1967

PREFACE

This is a catalogue of and guide to the Charles S. Peirce Papers which are presently housed in the Houghton Library, the rare book and manuscript library at Harvard University. The papers were for the most part received by the Harvard Philosophy Department from Peirce's widow in the winter of 1914-15, less than a year after his death. These are the papers which have been worked on over the years by several scholars, initially by Josiah Royce, who unfortunately died before much progress was made, more recently by Charles Hartshorne, Paul Weiss, and Arthur Burks, as editors of the *Collected Papers,** and most recently by Max H. Fisch, in connection with the preparation of an intellectual biography of Peirce.

The papers have been divided into two parts. Part One consists principally of manuscripts; Part Two, of correspondence. The manuscripts range over the whole of Peirce's intellectual life and include—as anyone familiar with Peirce might expect—manuscripts on logic, mathematics, metaphysics, and pragmatism. Also included are Peirce's scientific manuscripts, his manuscripts in the history of science and in linguistics, his reviews and translations, and various other manuscripts, many of biographical interest. In addition to the manuscripts, there is a considerable body of correspondence which ranges over much of Peirce's private and professional life. Placed with this correspondence, but organized separately, is the correspondence of Peirce's second wife Juliette, the correspondence among various members of Peirce's family, and some miscellaneous correspondence.

In the fall of 1960 when I began my work on the *Catalogue,* Peirce's papers had been assembled for the convenience of those who, like myself, were engaged in one or another of several Peirce projects. Although the papers were all in one place, there were, in fact, three separate sets of Peirce materials, all organized, with a catalogue for one and a catalogue of sorts for another, but none for the third. The bulk of the Peirce Collection at Harvard, consisting of sixty-one boxes and bundles, had been maintained in the Archives of Widener Library. The "Archives" material had been organized, boxed, and catalogued in 1941 by Knight W. McMahan. McMahan's ninety-nine page typewritten "Catalogue of the C. S. Peirce Manuscripts," with its description of what the boxes con-

---

* *Collected Papers of Charles Sanders Peirce,* Vols. I-VIII, Harvard University Press, 1931-1958.

tained, served well the needs of Peirce scholars who sought to examine the contents of those boxes and, although incomplete, it came as close as was possible at that time to putting Peirce's papers into some kind of final order. Later John F. Boler contributed an eleven-page addition which dealt more effectively than McMahan's catalogue had with Peirce's book reviews.

Another distinguishable part of the Peirce Collection, also sizable but of less importance than the material located in the Archives, had been maintained in Houghton Library. The "Houghton" material consisted of some nineteen boxes which had neither been classified nor catalogued until a preliminary arrangement and listing of this material was effected in 1960 by John Boler in his "Interim Catalogue," a typescript of thirteen pages.

The third distinguishable part of the Peirce Collection—the correspondence—had been kept mostly with the "Archives" material and had been partially organized by McMahan at the time he was working on his catalogue. But since then, in 1960 to be specific, the collection of family correspondence, formerly in the Benjamin Peirce Papers in the Archives had been transferred to the Charles Peirce Collection by authorization of Charles Peirce's niece, Miss Helen Ellis. Subsequently, more family correspondence found its way into the Collection, again, by authorization of Miss Helen Ellis. By this time, the whole of the correspondence had been completely reorganized.

In addition to the Peirce material noted above, there were miscellaneous manuscripts that had been listed separately in the catalogues of Widener and Houghton; various collections of articles on or by Peirce, some of the articles being annotated; annotated books from Peirce's library; public documents and photographs; and much unedited, scraplike material, to mention only some of the items which needed to be integrated with the rest. The present catalogue is the attempt to gather several collections and miscellaneous items into one collection. Unquestionably, the fact that so much of the Peirce manuscripts and correspondence had already been ordered or partially ordered, greatly facilitated my own efforts at integration. Clearly, if it were not for the fact that the cataloguing of the Peirce Papers had a history, this catalogue could not have been produced, most certainly not in the time it took to produce it.

Having noted the history of the cataloguing of the Peirce Papers, I would be remiss if I did not mention the contributions of W. F. Kernan and V. F. Lenzen.* Kernan's "List of C. S. Peirce Manuscripts," a nine-

---

* For interesting accounts of the early history of the Peirce Papers, see V. Lenzen's "Reminiscences of a Mission to Milford, Pennsylvania," *Transactions of the Charles S. Peirce Society*, I, 1 (Spring 1965) pp. 3-11 and W. F. Kernan's "The Peirce Manuscripts and Josiah Royce—A Memoir Harvard 1915-1916," *Transactions of the Charles S. Peirce Society*, I, 2 (Fall 1965) pp. 90-95.

page typescript, was prepared at the time he was assisting Royce in organizing Peirce's papers and collaborating with him on an article entitled "Charles Sanders Peirce" which appeared in the *Journal of Philosophy*, December 21, 1916, a memorial issue devoted to Peirce. Lenzen's "Notes on Papers and MSS. in The Charles S. Peirce Collection," a twenty-page typescript, is an evaluation of the contents and the physical condition of the manuscripts which, at the time (December 1917), were sorted into eighty-three boxes. The Kernan and Lenzen typescripts, along with the catalogues of Boler and McMahan, are kept with the Peirce Papers, and are available for consultation.

Needless to say, I am indebted to all those who have shared in the ordering and cataloguing of the Peirce Papers. Nor is my indebtedness limited to those who were actively engaged in cataloguing *per se*. My indebtedness extends to the several editors of the *Collected Papers* who were engaged, along with the others, in the work of identifying, classifying, and uniting papers which had become separated. With very few exceptions, the readers of this catalogue and of the microfilm edition of Peirce's papers which has recently been made available, and even the persons who may in the future use this catalogue as a guide to the original papers themselves, will get only a very inadequate sense of the years of labor that have gone into this sort of preliminary editorial work. For this and other reasons I want to record my indebtedness to those who most recently have been and still continue to be engaged in that same work of identifying, classifying, and reassembling. Besides Max H. Fisch, for whom a special word of gratitude is reserved, I wish to mention especially the contributions of Carolyn Eisele to the mathematics and the history of science sections of the *Catalogue,* of Ruth B. Fisch to the biography and correspondence sections, and of Don D. Roberts who ordered and provided a page-by-page index of the important Logic Notebook (MS. 339) and who had done considerable work on a number of logic manuscripts. Although each of the persons mentioned had areas of special interest, their efforts in behalf of the *Catalogue* were not confined only to those areas. Over the past few years earlier drafts of this catalogue were in active use, and this afforded opportunity for correction and amplification. The present catalogue is the beneficiary of both. So to those persons mentioned, I owe much of what is valuable in this catalogue; for its failures, I alone am responsible.

My major debt of gratitude is to Max H. Fisch. It is only right to point out the fact that he, along with Ruth B. Fisch, has spent an incredible amount of time on the sort of preliminary editorial work noted above. Therefore, it is not surprising that nearly every page of the *Catalogue* bears witness to his scholarship and encyclopedic knowledge of Peirce's life and works. To be more specific: McMahan's catalogue dealt reasonably well with Peirce's mathematical, philosophical, and scientific papers, but only sketchily with his correspondence and other papers of biographical interest. It was Professor Fisch's extensive work on the correspondence and these other papers which resulted, especially in the case of the correspondence, in the organization exhibited in this catalogue. Moreover, it was he, who, more than anyone else, saw the need, not only for a more adequate catalogue of Peirce's papers than existed at the time but also for the preservation of the papers themselves. So two projects—cataloguing and microfilming—were joined and brought to completion under his watchful eye.

This catalogue would not have been possible had it not been for the generosity of the Department of Philosophy of Harvard University, not only for consenting to and encouraging the cataloguing project but also for contributing very substantial financial assistance along the way. Specifically, I want to acknowledge a grant for the academic year 1960-61, wich allowed me to prepare the ground for the *Catalogue,* and other grants which enabled me to complete the project. I want also to acknowledge my gratitude to Professors Morton G. White and Donald C. Williams, who made up the Peirce Committee of the Harvard Philosophy Department, for their cordial cooperation throughout the years I was engaged on the project; to the Department for permission to quote from the unpublished manuscripts; and to the Department, again, for its generous subsidy that cleared the way for publication of the *Catalogue.*

I also wish to express my gratitude to the Henry P. Kendall Foundation for a grant-in-aid which got me through one summer and to the Mount Holyoke College Grants Committee for a research grant which helped to defray the cost of preparing the manuscript for publication. Grateful acknowledgment is made to the librarians, both at Harvard and Mount Holyoke College, whose cooperation contributed to the success of this project, but in particular to Miss Carolyn Jakeman of the Houghton Library and to Dr. William Bond, its Director. I would also like to express my thanks to Leone Barron, Director of the University of Massachusetts Press, for her unfailing enthusiasm and valuable editorial advice; to several Mount Holyoke College students for help in various ways, but principally to Miss Diane Goldberg for her help in connection with Appendix II and the General Index; and finally to my wife for her help at different stages in the preparation of the *Catalogue.*

South Hadley, Massachusetts   Richard S. Robin
June, 1967

CONTENTS

ix

CONTENTS

CONTENTS

INTRODUCTION

It had been evident for some time that an updated catalogue of the Charles S. Peirce Papers was needed, one which would survey the whole Collection, making as widely available as possible a detailed statement of what it contained and answering, so far as possible, the questions scholars raise, including those about the date of manuscripts and their relation to published versions. Indeed the manuscripts and correspondence are so voluminous and unwieldy that it is virtually impossible for anyone to deal with them successfully without benefit of the orientation which a catalogue of the kind envisioned would provide. Moreover, as the prospects of a microfilm edition of the Peirce Papers increased, so did the need for an adequate catalogue, which would reflect an orderly arrangement of the Papers and assist the users of a microfilm edition.

The catalogue which was finally produced is imperfect. It is imperfect because of the frequency of error in what already has been done. More importantly, it is imperfect because of what has not been done; that is, much remains to be done by way of identifying and describing, piecing together scattered fragments, assigning dates to undated manuscripts and letters, and the like. But, imperfect as this catalogue is, it is better than none at all, and all of us who contributed to it recognized that the needs for a comprehensive catalogue now outweighed the advantages of indefinite delay.

Organization of the Catalogue

As noted in the Preface, the *Catalogue* is divided into two parts. The first part consists of manuscripts and related material; the second part comprises the correspondence, both Peirce's and the correspondence of others. The organization of the correspondence presented no special problems, but the organization of what may be called the "subject matter" part of the *Catalogue* was another story, and a brief word concerning the problems encountered and the principle of organization finally adopted is in order.

Of the two alternative ways of organizing a man's papers—chronologically and by content—neither way, in spite of the obvious advantages of each, was easily adapted to the Peirce Collection. Consider the following problems. If the decision is made to order by chronology, what then does one do with the large quantity of undated papers? (Less than half of the 1,644 catalogue entries are dated and of the dates not supplied by Peirce himself many are conjectural.) Moreover one would have to expect that some of the material would be cut up rather badly as in those instances where Peirce comments on earlier articles. By virtue of temperament and other needs, Peirce can be described as—just as Henry James had been—an inveterate "revisionist." His tendency to rework drafts of articles and books left future editors of his manuscripts with the problem of unscrambling the various drafts, which, in some cases, had been written years apart.

Consider now the problems resulting from a decision to order the manuscripts by content. How does one handle Peirce's many digressions? Even more significant perhaps is the problem inherent in schemes that emphasize content; namely, the risk one runs of either imposing too much order or not enough order. Organization is rarely innocent, and the greater the organization the greater the risk that one's bias or interpretation will get in the way of a clear presentation of what there is. However, if one chooses to "play it safe" by arranging the manuscripts as much as possible according to content, thereby achieving a spectrum of sorts, and only then drawing the lines at the more palpable breaks, the results will tend to be nondescript. Finally, as was pointed out to me, if an index were eventually prepared, it would cancel out the need for ordering by content in the first place.

A compromise between ordering by chronology and by content seemed called for. But what compromise? One answer was provided by Boler who, at one point, submitted a plan to the Harvard Philosophy Department which seemed perfectly reasonable and promising. His plan involved six steps: (1) following Burks's bibliography of Peirce's published works (*Collected Papers,* Vol. VIII, pp. 260-321), locate and file the manuscripts for each entry; (2) place alternative drafts (and identifiable fragments) with above; (3) from the remaining unpublished material, file what is alike in content with above; (4) also, some of the remaining material, especially complete drafts and identifiable fragments, may be filed chronologically; (5) whenever possible, arrange what remains according to content; (6) finally, classify the remainder of unidentifiable fragments as such. Boler confessed that he became disillusioned about the idea that Steps 3 and 4 would take care of the bulk of the material. I too became disillusioned, and for the reasons Boler gave. But my difficulties with Boler's plan carried somewhat further.

Perhaps the decisive factor in the decision which was ultimately made to compromise while emphasizing content was the fact that the bulk of Peirce's philosophical and other manuscripts—the "Archives" material—had already been classified by content, in accordance with a scheme adopted by McMahan. The "Houghton" material which had been catalogued independently by Boler on the basis of some other scheme was from the point of view of both quantity and quality far less significant.

It was tempting, therefore, to adopt the McMahan catalogue, with its principle of organization, incorporating the "Houghton" material as best one could. In this way, the manuscripts might be consolidated, but even more important, since consolidation might be achieved in other ways, was the amount of time and work that could be saved.

The decision to adopt Peirce's own classification of the sciences (which in effect, is what McMahan did) was clearly a practical one, but only in part. Independently there are good reasons for turning to Peirce's classificatory scheme. For one thing, it has the advantage of spreading out Peirce's manuscripts in an orderly way without making the results appear nondescript and without imposing more order than is absolutely necessary. For another thing, it is Peirce's scheme, not someone else's, concocted for the occasion.

There are a number of accounts of Peirce's classificatory scheme of the sciences. In brief, his classification begins with the distinction between a theoretical and a practical science, a distinction based upon the difference of two interests—the theoretical interest in attaining knowledge for its own sake and the practical interest in attaining knowledge for the sake of something else. The theoretical branch of science is subdivided into (a) the sciences of discovery and (b) the sciences of review, with the latter dependent upon the former, since review implies the review of something which, in this case, is the information provided by the various sciences of discovery. Indeed, Peirce's own studies in classification are subsumed under (b), as one might expect.

Although Peirce did classify the practical sciences, he was chiefly concerned with the theoretical ones, especially those which fell under the heading "sciences of discovery" or, in other places, "sciences of research," and it is his classificatory scheme for those sciences which turned out to be most useful for our purposes. Below is one of several tabular listings from Peirce's papers.*

MATHEMATICS
PHILOSOPHY
    Phenomenology, or Ideoscopy
    Normative Science
        Esthetics

* This particular list is taken from a manuscript placed with the Matthew Mattoon Curtis correspondence (L107). The manuscript is an incomplete draft of a philosophical autobiography prepared in response to Curtis's request for information concerning Peirce's logical and philosophical views. For a more complete account of Peirce's classificatory scheme for the sciences, see *Collected Papers*, Vol. I, pp. 75-137. For a good summary account, see Thomas Goudge, *The Thought of C. S. Peirce* (Toronto: Toronto University Press, 1950) pp. 44-50.

    Ethics
    Logic
       Speculative Grammar
       Critic
       Methodeutic
    Metaphysics
  IDIOSCOPY, or SPECIAL SCIENCE
    Physics
       Nomological Physics
       Classificatory Physics
       Descriptive Physics
    Psychics
       Nomological Psychics   [Psychology]
       Classificatory Psychics [Ethnology]
       Descriptive Psychics   [History]

The above listing is for the sciences of discovery (research) only. It should also be clear that the listing is incomplete, for it fails to give the subdivisions of mathematics, metaphysics, and the idioscopic sciences, especially the last with its elaborate arrangement of suborders, families, and subfamilies.

The listing also fails to indicate the hierarchical character of Peirce's classificatory scheme. For Peirce, the sciences listed first are independent of those listed later. Or, if you like, when borrowing occurs, each science tends to borrow from those sciences which precede it in the classification. Thus, for example, in the case of the subdivisions of logic, methodeutic rests upon both critic and speculative grammar, critic upon speculative grammar alone vis à vis the divisions of logic, and speculative grammar upon neither, but only upon those sciences (ethics, esthetics, phenomenology, mathematics) which precede it in the hierarchy. Or, more generally, the mathematician, as such, working independently of the other scientists, seeking formal, not material, truth, traces out the necessary consequences of hypotheses which others, to be sure, may posit. Philosophy (all branches) is dependent upon mathematics, but takes precedence over all the special sciences, which follow it in the hierarchical scheme.

If one examines my table of contents, and observes the order in which Peirce's papers are catalogued, one will note the *Catalogue's* general adherence to Peirce's classificatory scheme. The *Catalogue* lists Peirce's mathematical works first, and attempts to deal with these works along the lines suggested by Peirce's division of mathematics into the mathematics of logic, of discrete series, of continua and pseudo-continua. The items listed toward the end—textbooks, recreations, computations and fragments—are conveniently placed there, and have nothing to do with the classificatory scheme for mathematics.

INTRODUCTION

If one ignores pragmatism—the next major division of the manuscripts following mathematics—and concentrates on the other divisions (phenomenology, logic, metaphysics, physics, chemistry, astronomy, geodesy, psychology, linguistics, history, sciences of review, practical science), especially the order in which they occur in the *Catalogue*, one ought to observe that the remainder of the *Catalogue* follows Peirce's classificatory scheme, although this may not be self-evident with respect to some of the divisions. Why, for example, does chemistry precede astronomy, both in Peirce's scheme and in my catalogue? The reason is that chemistry falls under classificatory physics whereas astronomy falls under descriptive physics, and classificatory physics takes precedence over descriptive physics in Peirce's scheme. Again: Why does linguistics take precedence over history? The answer is that linguistics falls under classificatory psychics, and history, as already indicated, falls under descriptive psychics. Since classificatory psychics precedes descriptive psychics in Peirce's account, linguistics takes precedence over history.

This is not to say that I have slavishly followed Peirce's scheme for the classification of the sciences. As a matter of fact, a rigid adherence to Peirce's scheme is neither required nor desirable. I have followed the scheme only so far as it proved to be advantageous to do so; I have departed from it whenever I concluded that by adhering to it the presentation of the Peirce material would be hampered. Indeed, if one observes closely the organization of this catalogue, one will observe the many liberties taken with Peirce's classificatory scheme, with perhaps the major liberty taken with respect to the manuscripts on pragmatism.

Pragmatism, as a division or heading, presents a special problem. As things stand, given Peirce's classificatory scheme, the manuscripts on pragmatism are out of order. They ought to be in closer proximity than they are now to the logical manuscripts. Pragmatism clearly cuts across the divisions of logic, and perhaps ought to have been subsumed under logic, that is, under one or more of its divisions. After all, did not Peirce come to the view that pragmatism is the logic of abduction? The justification for its present position in the *Catalogue*, as a separate division between mathematics and phenomenology, rests on the desire not to bury pragmatism among the manuscripts on logic, because of the general importance of pragmatism in Peirce's thought and of the lecture series or series of articles of which many of the manuscripts form an integral part.

There are other kinds of problems. One kind concerns the gaps in the *Catalogue*. To cite one example, Peirce's classificatory scheme calls for the ethnology of social development, one of the sciences comprising one of the many subdivisions of psychical science. The fact that there is no place or listing for it in the *Catalogue* means simply that none of the manuscripts of Peirce are concerned specifically with the ethnology of social development.

More serious, perhaps, is the failure of this catalogue to provide separate listings for, say, ethics or speculative grammar. But here the problem was not one of finding manuscripts which dealt specifically with ethical problems or the issues of speculative grammar. Indeed there are many such manuscripts. The problem was frequently that of separating units of larger works—lecture series or series of articles or chapters in a proposed book—something which this editor was reluctant to do. In such cases, the descriptions attached to catalogue entries and the general index are counted on to direct the reader's attention to subject matter for which the *Catalogue* provides no separate heading or listing.

Then there is the other kind of problem one runs into when dealing with classificatory schemes generally—the problem of how to classify this or that relative to the scheme with which one is working. For example, does this manuscript fall under logic or mathematics? Does that manuscript belong with the manuscripts on pragmatism or somewhere else? Often it is not a simple matter to decide, especially when Peirce digresses and when the digression becomes the most significant feature of the manuscript. Sometimes, usually in the case of notebooks, two quite different articles are begun, which forces the editor to decide their relative importance, with the ever present possibility of judgmental error. When confronted with problems of this kind, I have again counted on my descriptions to call attention to anomalies and the general index to bring similar but widely separated material together.

Finally, there are the outright mistakes. One of these will serve as an example. There is no excuse for separating MSS. 314 and 316, since MS. 316 continues MS. 314. In this case the error was discovered only after the microfilming of the manuscripts was completed. Undoubtedly there are errors of this and other sorts which have yet to be discovered. Work on the *Catalogue* proceeded on the expectation that errors, both of commission and omission, would be made; it also proceeded in the hope that these errors, when discovered, would be reported and collected, and then, in one way or another, made available to users of this catalogue.

THE FORM OF THE CATALOGUE

The manuscript portion of the *Catalogue* differs from the correspondence portion with respect to the form employed in presenting the relevant information concerning each entry. For the manuscript portion, each entry is presented in an arrangement of six or seven parts:

1. Title
2. Abbreviated title (Mark)
3. Type of material, whether manuscript, typescript, reprint, or other
4. Publication

5. Date
6. Pagination
7. Description of content

In the *Catalogue,* Parts 1 and 2 (title) are separated from Parts 3–6 (physical description) which in turn are separated from Part 7 (description of content).

Peirce's titles are presented without brackets or parentheses, just as they appear in the manuscripts. Title page punctuation is retained and the original spellings have been preserved in all titles without the use of *sic* to indicate deviations from the norm.

The use of brackets indicates that the title has been supplied by the editor. It goes without saying that when a title has been supplied, it is always in the absence of one provided by Peirce, either because he never provided one or because the title page is missing. In defense of supplying titles may I say that it serves as a convenient way of noting a manuscript's principal content and, in many cases, the supplied title as a brief description of the contents saves space by enabling us to dispense with a formal description at the end. May I also add that the supplied titles are sometimes less misleading than the titles which Peirce himself gives. Although Peirce's titles no doubt acquaint us with his intentions, do they also acquaint us with the manuscript's contents? Certainly not in those cases where the manuscript progresses only a few pages and where Peirce's introductory reflections have little or nothing to do with the title. Or, where the manuscript digresses from the topic indicated by the title, and the digression is the manuscript's distinctive feature.

A large number of Peirce's manuscripts have no title, but some of these possess a mark which is most often found in the upper left-hand corner of the manuscript page. When the mark occurs in conjunction with a title, it frequently stands for a short or abbreviated form of the title. It becomes a matter for conjecture when there is a mark but no title. In any event the occurrence of a mark is indicated by the use of parentheses. When the manuscript possesses both a title and a mark, the procedure is to record the title first and the mark in parentheses second. When the manuscript possesses only the mark, then the mark, distinguished from the title by the use of parentheses, serves in place of the title.

In the next parts (3–6) I was concerned with identifying the type of material, whether a manuscript or typescript, or reprint, or book, or page proof, or galley proof, or the like. I was also concerned with whether, in the case of typescripts, reprints, books, and proofs, there was any annotation or correction.

Most of the manuscripts were not published. But where publication had occurred this is noted by reference to Burks's bibliography and

Fisch's two supplements. For an explanation of both Burks's and Fisch's manner of handling bibliographical references, see my explanations of conventions on p. xxvii f. The *Catalogue* notes whether a manuscript was published in full or in part, and where publication was in part only, precisely what part was published. The only exception to notification of publication occurs in those cases where a part, or even the whole of a manuscript, was published as part of another author's publication. For example, MS. 620 was published as an appendix to one of Fisch's articles on Peirce,* but there is no indication of this publication in the description of MS. 620. This happens to be a significant publication, but, in other cases, it was difficult to say what was and was not significant, and it did not seem worthwhile to mention every publication of this kind.

When not placed within brackets or qualified in any other way, the given date is Peirce's. As a rule one date is given and this is the date which is usually recorded on the title page or, in the case of some notebooks, on the cover. Most often it is the only date. But where several dates are given, the range of dates is noted in the description.

When the date is placed in brackets, then the date, as in the case of titles, has been supplied by someone other than Peirce. Whereas I supplied the titles, various persons at different times and with varying degrees of confidence supplied the dates. When the date is placed in brackets without any other qualifying mark, then it is presumed to be accurate, derived from reliable internal evidence. A date preceded by "c." is presumed to be an accurate central locus of possible dates. A date followed by a question mark is frankly a "best guess," based on some internal evidence. When the expression "n.d." occurs, it means that for the moment not even a good guess can be made.

The pagination of a manuscript is indicated by two forms, for example, either pp. 1-5 or 5 pp. The first form signifies that the manuscript was numbered by Peirce; the second form gives the editor's count. One difficulty in determining a true page count rests with Peirce's habit of using the verso of a page of manuscript for calculations or other notes which may or may not be related to the manuscript in question. The question of whether to count a page or not sometimes proved difficult and left room for judgmental error. For additional information concerning pagination, see the guide to the use and consultation of the microfilm edition of the Peirce Papers, prepared by the Harvard University Microreproduction Service, which is reproduced in the next section of this introduction.

In 1915, a few of the manuscripts had become separated from the main Peirce Collection. These were added to the general manuscript

---

* See *Studies in the Philosophy of Charles Sanders Peirce, Second Series,* edited by Moore and Robin, University of Massachusetts Press, 1964, pp. 24-29.

collection of the Harvard University Library. They were catalogued separately, each with its own call number. Now that they have been restored to the Peirce Collection, their old call numbers have been added to the description for the purpose of identifying them.

In the interest of economy the content descriptions (Part 7) have been pared down to the bare essentials necessary for a clear indication of what there is. The descriptions tend to be topical rather than critical, serving more the function of an index than an analytical table of contents. Not all entries have descriptions, although bracketed titles are intended in all cases to emphasize the principal content of the manuscript. For the most part Peirce's own titles serve the same function. When they do not, a formal description is indicated and provided. But, in general, descriptions are provided for the important entries only, except where the lack of a description means either that, in the case of a draft of a complete or more refined version, the manuscript in question says nothing not already contained in the description of that later or refined version or contains no additional information which in the judgment of the editor is worth special notice. In any event the reader should take note of the number of pages of manuscript. If they are few, the topic or topics indicated by the title or by the formal description may not be very well developed.

Throughout the manuscript portion of the *Catalogue,* although occurring infrequently, are entry numbers for which there are no manuscripts, as distinct from those entries where a manuscript exists but is missing. These "holes" were created by the fact that the manuscripts which were originally there have been recombined with other manuscripts and that this was done after the completion of the microfilming. Rather than renumber, the entry numbers were retained, but left blank. The "holes" may even have a use someday. They might conveniently serve as the means of slipping new Peirce material into the collection, if such material is ever uncovered.

The correspondence constitutes the last portion of the *Catalogue* and is divided into four parts: the Charles S. Peirce correspondence, which contains all of Peirce's letters, both those he wrote and those he received; the Juliette Peirce correspondence, which contains all of Juliette Peirce's correspondence, except such correspondence as involves Peirce jointly and which was, for this reason, placed with his correspondence; the family correspondence, which consists of correspondence among members of Peirce's family but which does not involve Peirce or his wife Juliette directly; and miscellaneous correspondence.

The form adopted for the correspondence is the simplest possible one. For the Charles S. Peirce correspondence, the correspondents are listed alphabetically, the number of letters and letter drafts noted, and, when these are dated, the dates recorded, except when more than three of them are involved and when more than three are dated, in which case only the first and last dates are given. Where dates were lacking, an attempt was made to supply them, the procedure here being the same as for the manuscripts. Supplied dates appear in brackets, with or without "c." and with or without question marks. The remaining parts of the correspondence follow the form of the first part.

The division of the *Catalogue* into two parts—manuscripts (or, as sometimes represented, subject matter) and correspondence is a bit misleading insofar as it suggests that no correspondence is to be found in the first part and nothing which is classifiable as subject matter is to be found in the second part. On the contrary, an occasional letter draft may be found among the manuscripts; these were filmed with the manuscripts and all but those which appear on the versos of manuscript pages were subsequently placed with the correspondence, once it became clear that they belonged there. Not all of Peirce's correspondence is personal and business correspondence. There is much which can be described as professional, so much so that if the first few pages and the last were set aside, the remainder could easily be mistaken for manuscript material. Indeed, this is the principal reason why some correspondence was originally placed with the manuscripts.

Finally, a word about the four appendices. Appendix I is a supplement to my catalogue descriptions necessitated by certain discrepancies between the descriptions and what is contained in the microfilm edition of the Peirce Papers. (See the following section of this introduction for an explanation of the discrepancies and the manner of handling them.) Appendix II is a chronological listing of Peirce's manuscripts. It is hoped that this listing can be expanded some day, as scholars are able to date more of Peirce's manuscripts. Appendices III and IV are cross-reference tables. Appendix III is a cross-reference table from Burks's bibliography to my catalogue entries and Appendix IV, from McMahan's catalogue to mine. Anyone who so desires can set out from the *Collected Papers* and reach my catalogue entries through the intermediary of Burks's bibliography. See Burks's cross-reference index, pp. 325-330 of Vol. VIII of the *Collected Papers*.

THE MICROFILM EDITION

Two Peirce projects—cataloguing and microfilming—were linked almost from the beginning. The need for a new catalogue was evident; but so was the need to microfilm Peirce's manuscripts and correspondence, for the physical condition of Peirce's papers was a matter of grave concern. Although the entire collection is now kept in the Houghton Library, where temperature and air control give the papers the best chance for survival, it was feared that even with slightly more handling, given normal wear and tear, the deterioration of the papers would be rapid and alarming. With interest in Peirce mounting and with the expectation that the demand for consulting his papers would most likely increase in the years ahead, it was urged that steps be taken to microfilm them, or at least as much of them as there were funds for.

The success of the microfilming project depended in part on achieving a new arrangement of the Peirce Papers, one which would incorporate the efforts of the past, but would yield a single numerical sequence. With the present catalogue, the numbered sequence was achieved. This permitted the microfilming of Peirce's manuscripts, with all of its advantages of preserving the original manuscript collection from the wear and tear of handling, of providing a record which might serve in place of any parts of the collection that might from time to time be lost, stolen, or destroyed, and finally of making the manuscripts readily available to scholars in all parts of the world.

There are some discrepancies between what was microfilmed and my catalogue descriptions. These are few considering the number of catalogue entries and the principal reason that there are any at all is that errors were discovered in the *Catalogue* before it was printed but only after the microfilming of the manuscripts was completed. Apart from a major change or two and some minor ones, the microfilm was left untouched, mainly because of the expense involved in any extensive alteration. An asterisk placed before the catalogue entry number of the manuscript indicates that a discrepancy exists and directs attention to Appendix I "A Supplement to the Catalogue Descriptions."

A short guide to the use and consultation of the microfilm edition was prepared by the Harvard University Library Microreproduction Service in the Fall of 1964. For the benefit of those who will be working with the film and for the additional information concerning the manuscripts themselves, I reproduce the guide here.

This microfilm possesses some apparently anomalous features with which the reader ought to be acquainted to facilitate its use. The major part of the film's unusual features originates in the author's manner of composition.

First it was the author's usual practice to write on one side only of the paper. Less than 5% of the material in this microfilm contained writing on the verso of the page. In the notebooks, Peirce usually wrote only on the recto pages; accordingly, to spare unnecessary expense, only those pages of the notebooks actually bearing text have been filmed. This accounts for the fact that notebooks appear to have been filmed in irregular fashion, sometimes as a single spread and sometimes as a double spread. A similar situation prevails with the material written on loose sheets. In a few instances, both with the notebooks and the loose sheets, Peirce used the opposite sides to make routine calculations, some related and some unrelated to the main body of the work. In most instances, these routine calculations have not been filmed. Where there was doubt about routineness or where the calculations were other than ordinary arithmetic, such material was microfilmed. Some of these data may thus appear to interrupt the normal sequence of the manuscript.

Another unusual feature concerns pagination. The manuscripts follow four schemes of pagination: (1) unpaged, (2) either even-numbered or odd-numbered, (3) normal, and (4) iterated pagination. The repeated pagination almost always occurs in the notebooks when Peirce was constructing a draft. If he was dissatisfied with his first draft of page 1, he would go on to the next page, number it also "page 1," and continue with his revision until satisfied that he could carry on with page 2, and so on. It is not uncommon for a page number to be thus repeated for four or five consecutive drafts before the next sequential number.

Odd-numbered pagination only is common in the notebooks. Evidently this was Peirce's way of indicating his consciousness that he was using only the rectos, or perhaps he was saving the versos for corrections or changes. In a few instances, an explanatory target accompanies each frame of film and states that no pages are missing.

Unpaged material has been placed in sequence insofar as this was ascertainable by the editors, and, of course, insofar as the actual pages were available.

At the end of a numbered sequence of pages, there will occasionally be found a miscellany of pages consisting of broken runs or isolated pages surviving from other drafts.

Another unusual condition arises from Peirce's practice of starting some notebooks from the front, and upon reaching the center, turning the notebook upside down and beginning anew from the "back." Sometimes the separate contents of such notebooks may be unrelated although they occupy the same physical and bibliographic unit; in other instances, after the notebook was turned upside down, the same material was continued. This condition prevails in little used as well as in full notebooks. Rather than inconvenience the reader of the film with upside down images or reversed pages sequences, all such material has been filmed for normal reading sequence. In each case a notice explaining this situation is filmed at the beginning, the center, and the "end" of the item.

Peirce occasionally constructed from paper a physical device to be removed from a notebook and manipulated. An example is a doughnut-like device he constructed to elucidate a point in topology. In filming devices, a first exposure has been made with the device in place, a second with the device removed, and if necessary for clarity, a third of the device itself.

Printed editorial forms used in connection with the partial publication of this material by the Harvard University Press in the *Collected Papers* have remained with the collection, and it is possible that a few of these may have been accidentally incorporated into the microfilm. These are of course not a part of the collection and should be ignored.

POSTSCRIPT

Generally speaking, a catalogue of a man's writing stands as an impersonal record of his achievement. Standing alone it seems to cry out for some kind of personal statement, a portrait of sorts, which would complement the impersonal record. Of course it is a matter of conjecture as to what kind of personal statements or portrait of himself Peirce would have appreciated. In the introduction to a catalogue a panegyric seems somehow out of place. Perhaps it would be best to let the catalogue speak for itself. The display of prodigious intellectuality, creative genius, philosophic and scientific integrity, demonstrated therein, and, for one who knows something of the frustrations and deprivations of Peirce's personal and professional life, the sense of tragedy that pervades the whole seem to me to be intellectually stimulating and, at times, profoundly moving.

ABBREVIATIONS &
CONVENTIONS

A. autograph
CSP Charles Sanders Peirce
Collected Papers *Collected Papers of Charles Sanders Peirce*, 8 vols., Harvard
University Press, Cambridge, 1931-1958.
JP Juliette Peirce
MS., MSS. manuscript(s)
n.d. no date
n.p. no place, i.e., of publication
n.yr. no year
p., pp. page(s)
PAAAS *Proceedings of the American Academy of Arts and Sciences*
r recto
Studies in Logic *Studies in Logic, By Members of the Johns Hopkins Univer-*
sity (edited by Peirce), Little, Brown and Company, Boston,
1883.
TS. typescript
v verso
vol., vols. volume(s)

Following the established practice, all references to the *Collected Papers of
Charles Sanders Peirce* will be handled in this manner: first the volume number is given and then, after the decimal point, the paragraph number in that
volume. Thus 4.658 means Volume IV, paragraph number 658.

All bibliographical references and cross references are made with respect to
Arthur W. Burks's "Bibliography of the Works of Charles Sanders Peirce," *Collected Papers,* Vol. VIII, pp. 260-321, and to Max H. Fisch's "A First Supplement to Arthur W. Burks's Bibliography of the Works of Charles Sanders
Peirce," *Studies in the Philosophy of Charles Sanders Peirce, Second Series,*
edited by Edward C. Moore and Richard S. Robin, The University of Massachusetts Press, Amherst, 1964 and to his "Second Supplement," *Transactions of
the Charles S. Peirce Society* II, 1 (Spring 1966), pp. 51-53. Burks's bibliography
is divided into three sections: General, Items from *The Nation*, and Miscellaneous. The first two sections are arranged primarily in chronological order; the
third section is arranged alphabetically. Following the method Burks has
adopted, references and cross references to bibliographical items are as follows:
First the section is given, "G" for the General Section, "N" for *The Nation*
Section, and "M" for the Miscellaneous Section. Next come the year and the

number of the title under that year for sections "G" and "N"; only the item number for section "M." Thus "G-1883-4" refers to the fourth title under the date 1883 in the General section; "N-1901-3" refers to the third title under the date 1901 in *The Nation* section; and M-5 refers to the fifth item or name in the Miscellaneous section. Items preceded by "sup(1)" refer to Fisch's first supplement to Burks's bibliography; those preceded by "sup(2)" refer to Fisch's second supplement.

Part One

MANUSCRIPTS

MATHEMATICS

The Simplest Mathematics

*1. On the Simplest Possible Branch of Mathematics

A. MS., n.p., [c.1903?], pp. 1-9, 13, 17-33.

Brief discussion of paradisaical logic, i.e., system of logic in which only one value is supposed, provided another value (or other values) is not positively denied. The simplest kind of mathematics referred to, however, is a two-valued system of which Boole's algebra of logic is regarded as a special case. Inadequacies of Boolean algebra and some merits of secundal notation. Rules and examples for common mathematical operations in CSP's dyadic system.

2. On the Simplest Branch of Mathematics (SM)

A. MS., n.p., [c.1903?], pp. 1-2; 1-5, incomplete, with an alternative p. 5.

The pure mathematics of existential graphs, alpha and beta parts, with definitions and permissions of transformation. See MS. 512 for more of MS. 2.

3. On Dyadics: the Simplest Possible Mathematics (D)

A. MS., n.p., [c.1903?], pp. 1-2, incomplete.

Intended as the first of a series of four memoirs, with plans for further memoirs on the application of mathematical theory to deductive logic. The doctrine of multitude and a working definition of "continuity." See MS. 511.

4. Sketch of Dichotomic Mathematics (DM)

A. MS., n.p., [c.1903?], pp. 1-52 (p. 25 missing), with 11 pp. of variants.

Nominal and real definitions; definition of terms, e.g., "postulate," "axiom," "corrollary," "theorem," which are employed in mathematical or geometrical demonstration; canon of demonstration. Long digression which begins with recognition of seven schools of philosophy each determined by the emphasis placed upon one or more of the following concepts: form, matter, and entelechy. The relationship of these schools to the realist-nominalist controversy, with special attention given to the Aristotelian position. The nature of signs: sign and related notions, especially form, law, habit and entelechy; sign as having its being in the power, not act, of determining matter; sign as entelechy.

5. Dichotomic Mathematics (DM)

A. MS., n.p., [c.1903?], pp. 1-4, 1-3, 2-9, 6-11, 6-8, 10, 16-7, 45-46, with 22 pp. belonging to other drafts.

Similar in content to MS. 4, but without any of the digressions.

6. [Dyadic Value System]

A. MS., n.p., n.d., 2 pp.

The simplest of value systems serves as the foundation for mathematics and, indeed, for all reasoning, because the purpose of reasoning is to establish the truth or falsity of our beliefs, and the relationship between truth and falsity is precisely that of a dyadic value system.

Foundations of Mathematics

7. On the Foundations of Mathematics (Foundations)

   A. MS., n.p., [c.1903?], pp. 1-16, with 3 rejected pages; 17-19 of another draft.
   Mathematics as dealing essentially with signs. The MSS. below (Nos. 8-11)
   are drafts of this one, and all are concerned with the nature of signs.

8. On the Foundations of Mathematics (Foundations)

   A. MS., n.p., [c.1903?], pp. 1-4, 3-4; 4-8 of another draft.

9. [Foundations of Mathematics]

   A. MS., n.p. [c.1903?], pp. 1-5, with rejected pages.
   Vagueness, generality, and singularity.

10. [Foundations of Mathematics]

    A. MS., n.p., [c.1903?], pp. 1-2.

11. [Foundations of Mathematics]

    A. MS., n.p., [c.1903?], pp. 1-2, incomplete.

12. Notes Preparatory to a Criticism of Bertrand Russell's Principles of
    Mathematics (B. Russell)

    A. MS., n.p., February 5, 1912, pp. 1-14.

    The comments on Russell's work are as follows: ". . . true in the main" and
    "throughout, however, he betrays insufficient reflection on the fundamental
    conceptions of the subject," with the "primary difficulty . . . his not having
    begun with a thorough examination of the elements; . . . the ultimate ana-
    lytic of thought." The major part of the manuscript concerns CSP's own
    analytic of thought (theory of signs).

13. On the Logic of Quantity (L of Q)

    A. MS., n.p., [c.1895], pp. 1-13; 7-12, with an alternative p. 8 of another
    draft.

    The principal questions raised are these: Why mathematics always deals with
    a system of quantity, what the different systems of quantity are and how they
    are characterized, and what the logical nature of infinity is. The relationship
    of logic and metaphysics to the three categories of Firstness, Secondness, and
    Thirdness. Singular, dual, and plural facts. Chaldean metaphysics; chaos to
    determinacy; the evolutionary process. Postulates of mathematical logic (pp.
    7-12).

14. On Quantity, with special reference to Collectional and Mathematical
    Infinity (Quantity)

    A. MS., n.p., [c.1895], pp. 1-34.

    The nature of mathematics, pure and applied. In general, mathematics is
    concerned with the substance of hypotheses, drawing necessary conclusions
    from them; pure mathematics is concerned only with those hypotheses which
    contain nothing not relevant to the forms of deduction. The nature of quan-
    tity (real, rational, and imaginary). System of quaternions as an enlargement
    of the system of imaginary quantity. Possible grades of multitude. Spatial
    and temporal continuity. Common sense notions of continua, especially with
    regard to the flow of time. "Continuum" defined as "a whole composed of
    parts, with the parts of the whole comprising a series, such that, taking any
    multitude whatever, a collection of those parts can be discovered the multi-

4

tude of which is greater than the given multitude." Lastly, reasons are given for thinking that continuity exists beyond the evidence afforded by our natural beliefs in the continuity of space and time.

15. On Quantity, with special reference to Collectional and Mathematical Infinity (Quantity)

A. MS., n.p., [c.1895], pp. 1-29, incomplete.

Same questions raised as in MS. 14. "Mathematics" defined, with extended comments on the divisions of the sciences.

16. On the Logic of Quantity, and especially of Infinity (Logic of Quantity)

A. MS., n.p., [c.1895], pp. 1, 5-9, 7-18, 18-20.

Several definitions of "mathematics," including Aristotle's and CSP's. Mathematical proof and probable reasoning; the system and scale of quantity; the importance of quantity for mathematics. But to grasp the nature of mathematics is to grasp the three elements, which, with regard to consciousness, are feeling, consciousness of opposition, and consciousness of the clustering of ideas into sets. Recognition of the three elements in the three kinds of signs logicians employ. An analysis of the syllogism.

17. On the Logic of Quantity (Logic of Quantity)

A. MS., n.p., [c.1895], pp. 1-9; 7-10 of another draft.

This manuscript should be compared with MS. 16, to which it bears a special similarity. See also MS. 250 where CSP defines "mathematics" as "the tracing out of the consequences of an hypothesis." Five definitions of "mathematics." Benjamin Peirce's definition found acceptable with modification. "Science" defined in terms of the activity of scientists, not in terms of its content or "truths." Probable inference and certain features of mathematical proof (pp. 7-10).

18. (Logic of Quantity)

A. MS., n.p., n.d., pp. 3-4.

Defense of a modified version of Benjamin Peirce's definition of "mathematics." Cf. MS. 78.

19. Logic of Quantity (Logic of Quantity)

A. MS., n.p., n.d., pp. 1-12.

Several theorems demonstrated, e.g., that every relation included under a preference is itself a preference. Solution is offered to the following problem: Required that property which a collection must have to prevent it from proceeding from any collection of which it forms a part.

20. Logic of Quantity (Logic of Quantity)

A. MS., n.p., n.d., pp. 1-5; 1-4, 3-5; plus a single-page table of contents ("Contents") and 3 rejected pages.

Definitions, corollaries, theorems, and problems. The theorems and problems differ from those in MS. 19.

*21. Mémoire sur la Logique de la Quantité. Deuxieme Partie.

A. MS., n.p., n.d.. pp. 1-16, with 5 rejected pages.

The application of the logic of relations to quantity.

22. Systems of Quantity

A. MS., n.p., n.d., 5 pp.

Definitions of "relation," "relationship," "ring-relationship," and "quantity." Systems of logical, collectional, and total quantity distinguished.

23. [Logic of Number]

TS., n.p., n.d., pp. 2-7.

A draft of G-1881-7 (for annotated reprint of, see MS. 38). Unlimited and limited discrete simple quantity.

24. The Theory of Multitude (Multitude)

A. MS., n.p., [c.1903], pp. 1-3; 3-4 of another draft.

"Multitude" defined in terms of collection, followed by a pragmatistic definition of "collection."

25. Multitude and Number (Multitude)

A. MS., G-1897-1, pp. 1-82, with rejected or alternative pages running brokenly from p. 7 to p. 71.

Most of manuscript was published (4.170-226, except 187n[1]) but omitted were several illustrations (pp. 21-24; 34) and several proofs of theorems, among which are the following: That the collection of possible sets of units which can be taken from discrete collections is always greater than the collection of units (pp. 12-13), that the sum of an enumerable collection of enumerable multitudes is an enumerable multitude (pp. 29-32), and that there is a vast collection of indefinitely divident relations between the units of any denumerable collection (pp. 40-54).

26. On Multitude (On Multitude)

A. MS., n.p., [c.1897], pp. 1-24, with 24 pp. of rejects and/or alternatives.

An inquiry into what grades of multitude of collections are mathematically possible. This is a logical inquiry because both a strict *logica utens* and the principles of *logica docens* are required. Collection is explained but not precisely defined. Provided are three axioms relating to collections and several theorems. The inquiry concludes with a discussion of the general method of drawing conclusions by means of the above system.

27. Considerations concerning the Doctrine of Multitude

A. MS., n.p., [c.1905-07?], pp. 1-5; 23, 24, 27, 29, 30.

The nature of definition; "collection" defined; first- and second-intentional collection.

28. [On Multitudes]

A. MS., n.p., [c.1897?], pp. 23-48.

Abnumeral collection; first, second, and third denumeral multitude; princi, secundo, and tertio post-numeral multitude. Continuity and the doctrine of limits.

29. [On Multitudes]

A. MS., n.p., n.d., 10 pp.

Innumerable and inenumerable multitude. Generality and infinity.

30. Note on the Doctrine of Multitude

A. MS., n.p., [November 1903], pp. 1-6; 1-2.

Doctrine of multitude is developed in terms of dog-names and boy-names. See CSP-Josiah Royce correspondence, 11/13/03, and the CSP-E. H. Moore correspondence, 12/16/03.

31. On the theory of Collections and Multitude
    A. MS., n.p., [c.1905-07?], 2 pp.; plus 1 p. (p. 2) ("Note on Collections").

32. [On Collections]
    A. MS., n.p., n.d., pp. 1-2, incomplete.
    "Collection" defined; collection and quota distinguished.

33. [On Collections and Multitudes]
    A. MS., n.p., n.d., pp. 4-8.

34. [Collections and the Fermatian Inference]
    A. MS., n.p., n.d., 26 pp. of discontinuous fragments (nn. except for 67).

35. [Fermatian Inference]
    A. MS., n.p., n.d., 5 pp.

36. [Fragments on Collections]
    A. MS., n.p., n.d., 14 pp.

37. On the Number of Forms of Sets
    A. MS., n.p., n.d., pp. 1-3.
    Explanation of form and formality in terms of plurality and diversity of sets. Table of formalities.

38. On the Logic of Number
    Reprints, G-1881-7.
    One of the two reprints is annotated. Undated revisions in the form of marginal notes.

39. Logic of Number
    A. MS., n.p., n.d., 18 pp.
    Fundamental premises concerning number.

40. Axioms of Number
    A. MS., n.p., [c.1881?], 4 pp.
    Fifteen axioms (or assumptions) of arithmetic which provide a definition of "positive, discrete number" and from which, CSP thought, every proposition of the theory of numbers may be deduced by formal logic. Definitions of "addition" and "multiplication."

41. The Axioms of Number
    TS., n.p., n.d., 2 pp.

42. [Cardinal and Ordinal Number]
    A. MS., n.p., n.d., 10 pp.

43. [Cardinal Number]
    A. MS., n.p., n.d., pp. 36-38.
    Mathematical calculations on the versos of these pages.

44. First Definition of Ordinals (Topics)
    A. MS., G-c.1905-3 [G-1904-3], pp. 26-49, with 10 pp. of rejects and/or alternatives.
    Published, in part, as 4.331-340. Omitted: an attempt to define formally a secundal system of enumeration (pp. 38-39) and a second example (pp. 46-49).

* 45. [Second Definition of Ordinals]

A. MS., n.p., [1904], pp. 4-6; 19-22; and 1 p. (the number of which is missing).

Parenthetically: "As for the whole existing race of philosophers, —say John Dewey, to mention a relatively superior man whom you see, —why they are the sort of trash who are puzzled by Achilles and the Tortoise! Think of trying to drive any exact thought through such skulls! Royce is the only philosopher I know of real power of thought now living."

46. [Ordinals]

A. MS., n.p., n.d., pp. 6-7.

Second definition of "ordinals," and first and second ordinal definition of "addition." Also multitudinal definition of "addition."

47. Proof of the Fundamental Proposition of Arithmetic

A. MS., n.p., [1890?], pp. 1-4.

The proposition to be proved: ". . . that the order of sequence in which the things of any collection are counted makes no difference is [in] the result, provided there can be any order of counting in which the count can be completed."

48. Numeration (Num)

A. MS., n.p., n.d., pp. 1-20, with 44 pp., some of which belong to different drafts but many of which are rejected pages.

Definitions of "number" and "series." The distinction between precise and definite; vague and indefinite. Abstraction, or *ens rationis*. In what sense can it be said that *entia rationis* are real? These pages were probably intended for an arithmetic.

49. An Illustration of Dynamics (Illustration)

A. MS., n.p., [c.1901-02?], pp. 1-20, with 3 pp. of variants.

Setting out from two problems of dynamics both of which require for their solution the method of infinitesimals, CSP attempts an explanation of the method of infinitesimals, which requires, in turn, an explanation of collections and multiplicity. In addition, there is a discussion of the different modes of being, followed by a discussion of the distinction between reality and existence (for the purpose of showing that although nothing unreal can exist, something may be non-existent without being unreal).

50. (Attraction)

A. MS., n.p., [c.1901-02?], pp. 1-12, with a rejected p. 10.

Contents are similar to those of previous manuscript, but without the discussions of existence and reality and of collections.

NUMERICAL NOTATION AND ANALYSIS

51. On the Ways of Thinking of Mathematics (W of T)

A. MS., n.p., [c.1901-02?], pp. 1-4, with a rejected p. 3.

On the decimal and secundal systems of enumeration.

52. Notes on Numerical Notation

A. MS., n.p., [c.1910?], pp. 1-10, plus a rejected p. 2.

The notion of "elegance" in mathematics. The secundal system.

53. Secundal Computation
    A. MS., n.p., [c.1912?], pp. 1-6, with 2 other attempts to write p. 2.
    The notion of "elegance" in mathematics. The secundal system. Modes of reality.

54. Secundal Computation, Rules
    A. MS., n.p., [early 1912], 8 pp., with 3 rejected pages; plus 1 folded sheet ("rules for addition and subtraction").
    Notational explanation and accompanying statement of the rules for multiplication, division, addition, and subtraction. The extraction of square roots.

55. Computations for a Table of Secundal Antilogarithms
    A. MS., n.p., n.d., pp. 2-4.

56. Calculation of I.V.I. and Secundal Expression
    A. MS., n.p., n.d., pp. 1-2; plus a folded sheet ("Calc. of Table of Secundal Logarithms").

57. Essay on Secundal Augrim (SA)
    A. MS., n.p., [c. February 1905?], pp. 1-9.
    Dedicated to James Mills Peirce and concerned with the same material as MS. 54.

58. Secundal Augrim
    A. MS., n.p., n.d., 1 p.
    Calculation of fundamental antilogs by additive method. Calculation of $(10)^{01}$.

59. Secundal Augrim. Calculation of 10^{-01} by additive method continued
    A. MS., n.p., n.d., 1 p.

60. Secundal Augrim. Sheet 1
    A. MS., n.p., n.d., 1 p.

61. Secundal Numerical Notation (Secundals)
    A. MS., n.p., n.d., pp. 1-12, with variant pages 7 and 9.
    The four distinguishing characteristics of the system of secundals. CSP's version of the secundal system, with its several rules and examples of their application.

62. [Notes on Secundal Numeration]
    A. MS., n.p., [c.1905?], 1 p., with 64 pp. of secundal calculations.

63. [Secundal Notation Employed in Finding Factors]
    A. MS., n.p., n.d., 11 pp.

64. Notes for my treatise on Arithmetic
    A. MS., notebook, n.p., n.d.
    Mostly on secundals. Versos contain calculations pertinent to pendulum experiment, and two of these pages are dated Paris 1876.

65. The Binary Numerical Notation
    A. MS., n.p., n.d., pp. 1-2; 1-2 ("The Binary System of Numerical Notation").

66. Mathematics as it is to be treated in my Logic treated as Semiotics
    A. MS., n.p., [c.1892-94?], pp. 1-5.
    Binary system of notation.

67. Sextal Numeration

A. MS., notebook, n.p., n.d.

Transformation of an integer from decimal or sextal to secundal expression and back again to the decimal expression. Synthemes.

68. Note on a Series of Numbers (Series)

A. MS., n.p., [c.1903?], pp. 1-12, with variants (pp. 7, 8-12).

The series investigated is that whose first two dozen members are 2 . 3 . 3 . 4 . 5 . 5 . 4 . 5 . 7 . 8 . 7 . 7 . 8 . 7 . 5 . 6 . 9 . 11 . 10 . 11 . 13 . 12 . 9 . 9 .

69. Numerical Equations

A. MS., n.p., n.d., 1 folded sheet (2 pp.).

Method of getting all the roots when their moduli are all different.

70. Analysis of some Demonstrations concerning definite Positive Integers (N)

A. MS., G-1905-6, pp. 1-20, with 50 pp. of variants and notes.

See notes for an explanation of existential graphs. The versos of some pages contain notes for dictionary. In addition there is a draft of a letter in reply to an advertisement appearing in the *New York Herald*.

Combinatorial Analysis

71. Of the Unordered Combinations of Six Things (6 Things)

A. MS., n.p., [c.1899], pp. 1-8.

The symmetrics of combinations of six things.

72. On the Combinations of Six Things

A. MS., n.p., n.d., 1 p.

73. A Problem of Trees

A. MS., n.p., n.d., 4 pp. (incomplete or unfinished).

The problem for which a solution is offered is to find how many distinct forms there are for a row of a given number of letters (separated into two parts by a punctuation mark, and each part—not consisting of a single letter —into two parts by a subordinate punctuation mark, and so on until all letters are separated).

* 74. On the Number of Dichotomous Divisions: a problem in permutations

A. MS., n.p., n.d., pp. 1-10 (p. 7 missing); plus 17 pp. of another draft.

In the calculus of logic, a proposition is separated by its copula into two parts. The two parts may again be separated in a like manner, and so on indefinitely. One may inquire how many such propositional forms with a given number of copulas there are. Similar problem in algebra.

Algebra

75. Notes on Associative Multiple Algebra

A. MS., n.p., n.d., 23 pp.

"The main proposition of this note was presented to the American Academy of Arts and Sciences, May 11, 1875; and is published in the Proceedings of the Academy on p. 392." It is clear that this manuscript and the following two (76 and 77) belong together. See G-1875-2 and 3.150-151.

76. II. On the Relative Forms of the Algebras
    A. MS., n.p., n.d., pp. 1-7.
    A draft of G-1881-10 (Addendum 2).

77. III. On the Algebras in which division is unambiguous
    A. MS., n.p., n.d., pp. 8-14.
    A draft of G-1881-10 (Addendum 3).

78. Notes on B. Peirce's Linear Associative Algebra (LAA)
    A. MS., n.p., n.d., pp. 1-5.
    A defense of Benjamin Peirce's definition of "mathematics": Six possible objections noted and countered. Cf. G-1881-10 and MS. 18.

79. Nilpotent Algebras
    A. MS., n.p., n.d., 1 p.
    Double and triple algebras.

80. Nilpotent Algebras
    A. MS., n.p., n.d., 3 pp.

81. Notes on the Fundamentals of Algebra
    A. MS., n.p., n.d., 2 pp.
    Copula. Ligations, both simple and branching.

82. On the Application of Logical Analysis to Multiple Algebra
    A. MS., n.p., n.d., pp. 1, 3-4.
    See G-1875-2.

83. Index to Jordan's "Substitutions"
    A. MS., n.p., n.d., 8 pp.

84. [Algebraical Problems]
    A. MS., n.p., n.d., 3 pp.
    Drafts of corresponding pages of MS. 165.

85. An Algebraical Excursus
    A. MS., n.p., n.d., pp. 1-2.

86. On the Quadratic Equation (QE)
    A. MS., n.p., n.d., pp. 1-5.
    On the real, equal, or imaginary roots of quadratic equations.

87. Rough Sketch of Suggested Prolegomena to your [i.e., James Mills Peirce's] First Course in Quaternions
    A. MS., n.p., [c.1905?], pp. 1-20, 16-19, 17-26, and 20 pp. of variants.
    The mathematician's threefold task involves substituting hypotheses for less definite descriptions of real or imaginary states of affairs, then developing a point of view for making those hypotheses as comprehensible as possible, and finally employing that point of view for the purpose of solving problems. Mathematical theory is the discovery of methods of treating a broad class of problems from one general point of view. Quaternions as a particular theory of tridimensional space. Analysis of spatial and temporal relations. Listing Numbers.

88. Quaternions Applied to Probabilities
    A. MS., n.p., [1860's, early 1870?] 1 folded sheet (4 pp.).

89. Quaternions Theory of Functions

    A. MS., n.p., n.d., 7 pp.

90. [Quaternions]

    A. MS., n.p., [c.1876], 2 pp.

    Quaternion algebra. Hamilton's and Benjamin Peirce's forms interpreted geometrically.

CALCULUS OF FINITE DIFFERENCES

91. A Treatise on the Calculus of Differences (Calc. Diff.)

    A. MS., n.p., [1903-04?], pp. 1-25, with twice as many pages from other drafts.
    For "calculus of differences" CSP preferred "calculus of successions." He planned to divide treatise into four parts, but the manuscript only gets into the first part which, treating the subject generally without regard to the nature of known quantities, is occupied mainly with equations of differences. The distinction between logical and mathematical functions. Features of mathematical functionality. Definitions of "value," "universe of values," "quantity." Notational rules.

92. Note on the Notation of the Calculus of Finite Differences (NFD)

    A. MS., n.p., [1903-04?], pp. 1-4.
    The calculus of finite differences and the differential calculus compared, especially with respect to the notion of function.

93. Calculus of Finite Differences

    A. MS., n.p., n.d., pp. 1-2, with 2 pp. (of two other starts); 1 p. ("The Logic of Finite Differences"); 3 pp. ("Equations of Finite Differences"); a notebook ("Promiscuous Notes").
    The notebook from p. 17 onward is devoted to Boole's Finite Differences and related topics (Tagálog is the major subject of the first part of notebook).

BRANCHES AND FOUNDATIONS OF GEOMETRY

94. *New Elements of Geometry* by Benjamin Peirce, rewritten by his sons, James Mills Peirce and Charles Sanders Peirce.

    A. MS., n.p., n.d., pp. 1-6, 1-4 ("Preface"), 2 pp. ("Nota Bene"), pp. 1-398, (pp. 7, 31-33, 35, 69-70, 74-76, 78, 92-94, 166-168, 175, 182-183, 235 missing), with pp. xvi, xvii, xviii, xix, and pp. 37-150 from Benjamin Peirce's *Plane and Solid Geometry* mounted and ready for revision.
    Rewritten are books II-V concerned with the fundamental properties of space, topology, graphics, metrics.

95. [The Branches of Geometry; Ordinals]

    A. MS., notebook, G-1904-3 and sup(1) G-c.1905-3, pp. 1-34.
    An address delivered to the National Academy of Sciences. There is no indication of publication under G-1904-3, but this is G-c.1905-3 which is a mistake. see sup(1) G-c.1905-3.

*96. [The Branches of Geometry; Existential Graphs]

    A. MS., n.p., [c.1904-05?], 11 pp.

97. [The Branches of Geometry]

    A. MS., n.p., n.d., pp. 9-16, with 5 pp. of variants.

98. The Axioms of Geometry
    A. MS., n.p., [c.1870-71?], 2 pp., with 3 pp. of other starts.

99. The Axioms of Geometry. Attempt at enumerating them
    A. MS., n.p., [c.1875-76], 1 p.

100. First Attempt at a Geometry Logically Correct
    A. MS., notebook, n.p., September 21, 1874.

101. [Six Fundamental Properties of Space]
    A. MS., n.p., n.d., 2 pp.
    CSP's intention is to explain imaginaries in a new way, bringing them into
    the orbit of synthetic geometry by means of the principle of continuity.

ANALYTIC GEOMETRY

102. Promptuarium of Analytic Geometry
    A. MS., n.p., n.d., 5 pp. and 4 pp. of different drafts.

103. Syllabus of Plane Analytic Geometry
    A. MS., n.p., n.d., 5 pp.

104. On Real Curves
    A. MS., n.p., n.d., pp. 1-5, with variant p. 4.

105. On Real Curves. First Paper
    A. MS., n.p., n.p., n.d., 13 pp.

* 106. Four Systems of Coordinates
    A. MS., n.p., n.d., 16 pp.

EUCLIDEAN AND NON-EUCLIDEAN GEOMETRY

107. Synopsis of Euclid
    A. MS., n.p., n.d., 2 pp.

108. [Euclid's Elements; Properties of the Number 2; the Meaning of "Ra-
    tional"]
    A. MS., n.p., n.d., pp. 1-4.

109. Pythagorean Triangles (Pyth. Tri)
    A. MS., n.p., [c.1901?], pp. 1-4.

110. Note on Pythagorean Triangles
    A. MS., n.p., n.d., 1 p.

111. Formulae for Plane Triangles
    A. MS., n.p., n.d., 1 sheet.

112. Notes on Klein Icosahedron
    A. MS., n.p., n.d., 12 pp.

* 113. Icosahedron (Icosahedron)
    A. MS., n.p., n.d., 16 pp.

114. On Hyperbolic Geometry (Hyp. Geom)

A. MS., n.p., [c.1901?], pp. 1-6, 16-20, with rejected pages.

Formulae required for the projection of the hyperbolic plane upon the Euclidean. Definitions of "individual," "independence of individuals," and "collection." Fundamental theorem of multitude. (Cantor's demonstration of this theorem is thought to be fallacious.)

115. Newton's Enumeration of Cubic Curves

A. MS., n.p., n.d., 7 pp.

Hyperbolic geometry.

116. Brocardian Geometry

A. MS., n.p., n.d., 1 p.

117. The Non-Euclidean Geometry made Easy

A. MS., G-undated-7, pp. 1-8.

Published, in part, as 8.97-99. Unpublished (pp. 3-8). Denial of either the first or second of the two "natural propositions," noted in that part of manuscript which was published, leads to a non-Euclidean geometry. Both of the corresponding kinds of non-Euclidean geometry are intelligible, and a consideration of plane geometry will suffice to show this.

118. Reflections on Non-Euclidean Geometry

A. MS., n.p., n.d., pp. 1-5.

119. Non-Euclidean Geometry

A. MS., n.p., [c.1883 or later], 1 p. and 1 p. ("Notes on Non-Euclidean Geometry").

The purpose of this memoir is to find some way of treating geometry metrically by introducing the absolute synthetically. The attempt is restricted to plane non-Euclidean geometry: "Solid non-Euclidean geometry is a trifle too hard for me."

120. The Elements of Non-Euclidean Geometry. Preface

A. MS., n.p., n.d., 3 pp., plus 3 pp. which may be part of the same draft.

121. [On Non-Euclidean Geometry]

A. MS., G-undated-6, pp. 2-11; plus 4 pp. of an earlier draft.

Probably manuscript of an address to the New York Mathematical Society, November 24, 1894. Published, in part, as 8.93 n2. Was Euclid a non-Euclidean geometer? Probably! Properties of space. Evidence for thinking there is an absolute which is a real quadric surface. Newton's argument that space is an entity and its bearing on non-Euclidean Geometry. On back of p. 11: "Professor Fiske" [i.e., Thomas S. Fiske].

122. Non-Euclidean Geometry. Sketch of a Synthetic Treatment

A. MS., n.p., n.d., 32 pp. (several attempts with different titles).

123. Lobachevski's Geometry

A. MS., n.p., n.d., 3 pp.

124. Formulae

A. MS., notebook, n.p., n.d.

Notes on non-Euclidean geometry, existential graphs, and Laurent's probabilities. Solution of quadratic equation. The "formulae" of the title refers to trigonometrical formulae and formulae of analytic geometry.

Projective Geometry

125. Geometry. Book I. Projective Geometry
A. MS., n.p., n.d., pp. 1-4.
Definitions: Geometry, Body, Surface, Line, Point.

126. A Geometrico-Logical Discussion
A. MS., n.p., n.d., pp. 1-10, with 28 pp. of other drafts.
Four-ray problem (How many rays cut four given rays?) as offering best aperçus into nature of projective geometry. The impossibility of exact ideas, even in mathematics. Idea of a person; idea of a species of animal. Reality and *entia rationis*. Brief note on verso of one of the pages is dated September 16, 1906, and reads as follows: "11¼ P.M.—Fell asleep *standing* and dreamed something about a tablet in a church—In memory of my mother."

127. [Fragments on Projective Geometry]
A. MS., n.p., n.d., 61 pp.

128. [Mathematical Notion of Projection]
Amanuensis, with corrections in CSP's hand, n.p., n.d., pp. 11-12.

Metrical Geometry

129. Metrical Geometry
A. MS., n.p., n.d., pp. 1-39, with variant pages, and 155 pp. of other drafts.
Drafts for MS. 94 or 165. Foundations of linear and angular measurement. Signate, imaginary and quaternional measurement. Concept of a metron. Definitions, theorems, and demonstrations.

130. Metrical Geometry
A. MS., n.p., n.d., 27 pp.
Drafts for MS. 94 or 165. On the nature of spatial measurement.

131. [Metrical Geometry]
A. MS., n.p., n.d., 12 pp.
Drafts for MS. 94 or 165. On propositions holding true for all kinds of systems of measurement.

132. Plan of Geometry
A. MS., n.p., n.d., 28 pp.

133. [Metrical Geometry]
A. MS., n.p., n.d., pp. 1, 14-15, 17-19.
Much of the content, however, is projective geometry which is thought of as requisite for metrics.

134. [Metrical Geometry]
A. MS., n.p., n.d., pp. 27-39, plus 4 pp. of variants.
Drafts for MS. 94 or 165.

135. [Metrical Geometry]
A. MS., n.p., n.d., pp. 56-62, plus a variant p. 58.
Drafts for MS. 94 or 165.

136. [Metrical Geometry]
A. MS., G-undated-12 (Space), 1 p.

TOPICAL GEOMETRY

137. Topical Geometry (Topics)

A. MS., n.p., [1904], pp. 1-29, plus a confusion of partial drafts with pages running as high as p. 40, but with no continuous or final draft.

It is not evident that the title page goes with rest of the manuscript, which was written for *Popular Science Monthly*. The branches of geometry and their mutual relations. The branches of topics. Topics presupposes time, and time presupposes the doctrine of multitude. The topical properties of time; the hypothetically defined time of topics a true continuum; true continuity opposed to the pseudo-continuity (of the calculus). Instances of time, with the multitude of instances defined with the aid of the secundal system of enumeration. Points as possibilities, not actualized until something occurs to mark them. The dividing point between green and white is both green and white. Law of contradiction does not apply to potentialities. Census Theorem, Census Number, and Listing Numbers. On general words (signs).

138. Analysis of Time

A. MS., notebook, n.p., begun c.1904-05 with two entries dated August 13, 1908.

Four given rays may be crossed by how many rays? The analysis of the Four-ray problem requires a consideration of continuity which in its primitive, i.e., simple, sense has the form of time. Time as a determination of actuality (later—see annotation—CSP dissents). Definition of terms, e.g., instant, gradations. "I will not take up more of this book with the subject of discrete quantity—But I refer to a similar book labelled 'All Pure Quantity merely ordinal' [MS. 224] for more about it."

139. On synectics, otherwise called Topology or Topic

A. MS., n.p., n.d., 4 pp., incomplete.

Synectics as the science of spatial connections; pure synectics as the science of the connection of the parts of true continua.

140. A Treatise on General Topics (General Topics)

A. MS., n.p., n.d., pp. 1-4, plus 1 p., dated December 26, 1913, on what it means to say that a line is continuous.

141. On Topical Geometry, in General (T)

A. MS., G-undated-12, pp. 1-14, 4-8, 4-7, 5-7, 5, 9, 13.

Published, in part, as 7.524-538, except 534n[4] and 535n[6]. Omitted from publication is a discussion of the Kainopythagorean Categories centering in the view that there are but three and that there can be no element in experience not included in the three.

142. Notes on Topical Geometry

A. MS., G-undated-16 [c.1899-1900?], 6 pp., plus 2 pp. each of two other drafts having the same title as above.

Published, in part, as 8.368n[23]. Omitted from publication are definitions of "thing" and "collection," and a discussion of signs, especially icon, index, and symbol.

143. Topic (Topic)

A. MS., n.p., n.d., pp. 1-4.

Point-figures and line-figures.

144. **On General Topic (Topic)**
A. MS., n.p., n.d., pp. 1-3, incomplete.
General and special topic distinguished. Properties of a continuum.

* 145. **An Attempt to state systematically the Doctrine of the Census in Geometrical Topics or Topical Geometry, more commonly called "Topologie" in German books; Being A Mathematical-Logical Recreation of C. S. Peirce following the lead of J. B. Listing's paper in the "Göttinger Abhandlungen"**
A. MS., n.p., n.d., 12 pp.

146. **On Space-Logic**
A. MS., n.p., November 13, 1895, pp. 1-2 (with a second p. 2), incomplete.
Notation. Topical singularity of a line.

147. **On Space-Logic**
A. MS., n.p., November 14, 1895, 1 p.
Notation only.

148. **Topics of Surfaces**
A. MS., n.p., n.d., 1 p.

149. **Ch. 2. Topical Geometry**
A. MS., n.p., n.d., 1 p.
Definitions of "space," "place," "point," "particle," "line," "filament," "surface," "film," "solid," "body."

150. **[Topical Geometry]**
A. MS., n.p., n.d., 45 pp.
Draft of MS. 94 or 165. Also material on graphics (projective geometry).

151. **Topics. Chapter I. Singular Systems**
A. MS., n.p., n.d., 3 pp.
Firstness, or qualities, are positive albeit vague determinations. Vagueness and generality discriminated.

152. **Section 4. Of Topical Geometry**
A. MS., n.p., n.d., pp. 6-12; 7-8.
Kinds of multitude: numerable, innumerable, enumerable, inenumerable.

153. **On the Problem of Coloring a Map (4 Colors)**
A. MS., n.p., n.d., pp. 1-17, plus variants.

154. **On the Problem of Map-Coloring and on Geometrical Topics, in General (MC, PMC, Map)**
A. MS., n.p., [1899-1900], pp. 1-10, plus variants and many other attempts (82 pp. in all), none going beyond p. 10.
The problem of map-coloring is stated as follows: "To determine demonstratively the smallest number of colors that will suffice so as to color any map whatever which can be drawn on a given surface, that no two confine regions (that is, two regions having a common boundary-line) shall have the same color." See CSP—W. E. Story correspondence, 12/29/00.

155. **Studies in map Coloring as Starting-point for Advance into Geometrical Topics**
A. MS., notebook, n.p., [c.1897-1900?].

The first part of the notebook, the date of which is c.1870, deals with physical constants.

156. Map Coloring Vol. IV

A. MS., small notebook, n.p., n.d., plus another notebook ("Map Coloring Vol. V"), n.p., n.d.

Study of the Census Number.

* 157. [Link Coloring]

A. MS., n.p., [c.1897-1900?], 16 pp.

In how many ways, with c colors, can a simple chain of 1 links be colored, no two adjacent links being colored alike? In how may ways, with $c + 1$ colors, can a simple chain of $1 + 1$ links be colored so that all adjacent links are colored differently?

158. [Fragments on Map-Coloring]

A. MS., n.p., n.d., 32 pp. and 3 pp.

159. Notes on Listing

A. MS., n.p., [1897?], pp. 1-7.

160. A Study of Listing Numbers (Listing Numbers)

A. MS., n.p., February 3, 1897, pp. 1-5, plus 1 p. which apparently belongs here.

161. [Listing Numbers; The Census-Number; The Census Theorem]

A. MS., n.p., n.d., 5 pp.

162. [Fragments on Listing Numbers and the Census-Number]

A. MS., n.p., n.d., 8 pp.

163. [Topology; Real Curves; Astronomy; Archeology; Assorted Mathematical Notes]

A. MS., notebook, n.p., 1895 (p. 45 is dated July 1895).

MATHEMATICAL TEXTBOOKS

164. New Elements of Mathematics

A. MS., n.p., [c.1895], title page and 2 pp. ("Preface").

An introduction to a book which is designed to give the educated man all the mathematics he needs to know and which could serve as preparation for the study of higher mathematics. Brief account of the recent history of mathematics, followed by an examination of the branches of geometry.

165. Elements of Mathematics

A. MS., n.p., [c.1895], pp. 1-357 (pp. 61, 77, 93, 213, 259-273, 276-294 missing), with 23 pp. of a well-detailed "Table of Contents" and "Subject Index" and 18 pp. of another draft of Article 2, Scholium 2, of Chapter I.

Chapter I "Introduction" (pp. 1-39): Elementary account of the nature of mathematics; analysis of the game of tit-tat-too as an illustration of the process of deducing the consequences of hypotheses; definitions and the etymology of important terms. See MS. 1525 for possible early drafts of some of this material. Chapter II "Sequences" (pp. 40-76, with p. 61 missing): Sequences, both simple and complex. Chapter III "The Fundamental Operations in Algebra" (pp. 78-92, with pp. 77 and 93 missing): Fundamental operations in algebra; explicit and implicit functions; functions of several variables. Chapter IV "Factors" (pp. 94-106): Parts, divisors, and factors; prime factors; greatest common divisor of several numbers; multiples, dividends, and products; least common multiple; fundamental theorem of composition. Chapter V "Negative Numbers" (pp. 107-116): Definition and historical data. Chapter VI "Fractional Quantities" (pp. 117-130): Rational number explained; the system of rational numbers as including the values of all rational fractions except o/o. Chapter VII "Simple Equations" (pp. 131-173): Solution of linear equations; systems of simultaneous equations. Chapter VIII "Ratios and Proportions" (pp. 174-188): Ratios, proportions, anharmonic ratio. Chapter IX "Surds" (pp. 189-222, with p. 213 missing): Possibility and importance of surds; definition of "limit"; Achilles and the tortoise (p. 196); imaginary quantities; exercises and problems. Chapter X "Topical Geometry" (pp. 223-275, with pp. 259-273, 276-293 missing): Topical geometry explained; continuum; homogeneity; tridimensionality of space; singularities; topical classes of surfaces; the topical census. Long footnote on the intelligibility of infinitesimals. Chapter XI "Perspective" (pp. 294-357): Graphics; homoloidal system of places; dominant (optical) homoloids; projection; Desarques' Ten-Line theorem; the Nine-Ray theorem.

166. Elements of Mathematics

A. MS., n.p., [c.1895], pp. 44-320, with many gaps and variant pages.
Another draft of MS. 165.

167. Practical Arithmetic

A. MS., n.p., n.d., pp. 1-29 (pp. 26-27 missing), plus 2 pp.
Maxims for attaining accuracy and speed in handling numbers. Counting and measuring. The decimal names of numbers. The arabic notation.

168. Practical Arithmetic

TS. (corrected), n.p., n.d., 21 pp. of two drafts.

169. Factotal Augrim (A) (B)

A. MS., n.p., n.d., pp. 1-18 (A), 5-18 (A), plus variants; 1-4 (B).
Terminology: augrim, arithmetic, vulgar arithmetic, practical arithmetic, ciphering, and algorithm. Elementary and composite augrims. On number, including a long footnote on collections.

170. Rough List of Works Consulted for Arithmetic

A. MS., n.p., [1890-91?], 3 pp.

171. CSP's Small Inventions in Arithmetic and Logic

A. MS., n.p., n.d., 8 pp.
The arrangement of all the rational fractions, not negative, in the order of their values and without calculation.

172. Examples in Arithmetic

A. MS., n.p., n.d., 8 pp.

173. A System of Arithmetic

A. MS., n.p., n.d., 3 pp.
Rule for addition.

174. Rule for Division

A. MS., n.p., n.d., pp. 1-28 (pp. 2, 13, 15-16, 23-26 missing), plus variants and several unnumbered pages.

175. Exercises in Arithmetic
     A. MS., notebook, n.p., n.d.

176. [Elementary Arithmetic]
     A. MS., n.p., n.d., 15 pp.
     Rule for addition. Counting by threes, fours, fives, etc.

177. The Practice of Vulgar Arithmetic
     A. MS., notebook, n.p., n.d.
     Addition, multiplication, squaring a number, solving algebraic equations, Rule of False.

178. C. S. Peirce's Vulgar Arithmetic: Its Chief Features
     A. MS., notebook, n.p., [c.1890].
     Draft of a book, outlining its chief features. Shortcuts in the teaching of arithmetic.

179. Peirce's Primary Arithmetic Upon the Psychological Method
     A. MS., n.p., [1893], 52 pp.
     Teaching numeration. Addition. Multiplication.

180. Plan of the Primary Arithmetic
     A. MS., n.p., n.d., pp. 1-3.
     The contents of seventeen chapters are noted.

181. Primary Arithmetic
     A. MS., n.p., n.d., 31 pp.
     Six lessons concerned with counting.

182. Primary Arithmetic. Suggestions to Teachers
     A. MS., n.p., n.d., 12 pp.
     A teaching manual on counting.

183. Mugling Arithmetic
     A. MS., n.p., n.d., pp. 1-2.

184. [On Counting]
     A. MS., n.p., n.d., 4 pp.

185. Chapter IV. Addition
     A. MS., n.p., n.d., 6 pp.

186. Familiar Letters about the Art of Reasoning
     A. MS., n.p., May 15, 1890, pp. 1-22, plus title page and 2 pp. (unnumbered).
     In the form of a letter to Barbara (of the mnemonical verses). Card-playing as a pedagogical instrument, useful in teaching the art of reasoning.

187. [Assorted Notes for an Elementary Arithmetic]
     A. MS., n.p., n.d., 6 pp. (not all in CSP's hand).

188. [Introduction to Practical Arithmetic]
     A. MS., n.p., n.d., 2 pp.
     Discussion is somewhat advanced and may not be part of a primary or vulgar arithmetic.

189. Lydia's Peirce's Primary Arithmetic
     A. MS., notebook, n.p., [1904-05], with 65 pp. of drafts.

"Grandmother" Lydia teaches counting, making use of children's nonsense rhymes like "eeny-meeny-mony-meye," but pointing up the numerical limitations of gibberish.

190. [Notes on Square Roots, Long Division, Addition, Cyclic Numeration]
A. MS., n.p., n.d., 9 pp.

191. [Balance and Scales]
A. MS., n.p., n.d., 13 pp.
Part of a proposed book for children.

192. [On Algebra]
A. MS., n.p., n.d., pp. 2-15.
An elementary discussion possibly for a textbook.

193. Syllabus of the Elements of Trigonometry
A. MS., n.p., n.d., 4 pp., representing three different starts.

194. [Fragments on Trigonometry]
A. MS., n.p., n.d., over 100 pp.

195. Trigonometry
A. MS., n.p., n.d., pp. 1-2, plus 13 pp.

196. Sketch of a Proposed Treatise on Trigonometry
A. MS., n.p., n.d., 20 pp.

197. Elements of Geometry
A. MS., n.p., n.d., 1 p.

198. [Geometry Exercises]
A. MS., n.p., n.d., 14 pp.

MATHEMATICAL RECREATIONS

199. The Third Curiosity (MM/D)
A. MS., n.p., [1907], pp. 1-76, plus 53 rejected pages.
Numeration with a base other than 10. Sextal and secundal systems. The rules of arithmetic, e.g., rule of algebraic summation and the rule of "direct division."

200. The Fourth Curiosity (MM/E)
A. MS., G-1908-1e, pp. 1-186, plus 161 pp. (running brokenly to p. 186).
Omitted from publication in the *Collected Papers:* further discussion of the relationships of the Aristotelian pattern; definition of "pure mathematics"; numbers as *entia rationis;* first valid argument for pragmatism involves the denial of the Absolute. Kind, class, and collection. Signs and predication.

201. A Contribution to the Amazes of Mathematics (MM)
A. MS., n.p., [c.1908], 210 pp., most of which are numbered with the numbered pages running as high as p. 164 (many pages missing, however).
Rationale for two card "tricks" [The First (?) and Second Curiosities]. Abstract real (not imaginary) numbers viewed pragmatistically. Cantorian system. Cyclical system of numbers. The Fourth Curiosity. Secundal arithmetic. Reference to *Elements of Mathematics* (MS. 165), with bitter note on publishers of textbooks.

202. Some Amazements of Mathematics (Cu)

A. MS., n.p., [c.1908], pp. 1-53, plus 26 pp. of variants.

This paper begins with an analysis of the peculiarity of the number 142857. Lengthy discussion of infinitesimals. Fermat's theorem, Polynomial theorem, Rule of "direct division." Card "trick" (same as one of the two card "tricks" of MS. 201).

203. Addition (Add)

A. MS., n.p., May 24, 1908, pp. 1-5.

Alternate draft of 4.642. Does the collective system of irrational and rational quantity constitute a continuum or a pseudo-continuum? CSP says "pseudo-continuum" as against the opinions of both Cantor and Dedekind.

204. Supplement (A)

A. MS., G-1908-1b, pp. 1-17, incomplete, with variants.

The exact date of this manuscript is May 24, 1908. It was published, in part, as 7.535n[6]. Unpublished: Whether mathematicians generally, including Cantor and Dedekind, are correct in their views as to what constitutes a true continuum. The three universes of ideas, i.e., arbitrary possibilities, physical things, and minds. Reality and existence; perfect and imperfect continua.

205. Recreations in Reasoning (RR)

A. MS., G-c.1897-4, pp. 1-35, plus 22 pp. probably from another draft.

Published as 4.153-169, with the proofs of several theorems omitted.

206. Recreative Exercises in Reasoning (R)

A. MS., n.p., n.d., pp. 1-4.

Solution of the following exercise: "Required to arrange all the rational fractions (whose denominators do not exceed a given number and whose numerators do not exceed a given number of times the denominator) in the order of their values, in a horizontal row with $<$ or $=$ interposed between each successive two to state their relation of value."

207. Recreations in Reasoning (R)

A. MS., n.p., n.d., pp. 1-24, 2-5 with one rejected page and 14 pp. of variants; plus 11 pp. of notes.

Three distinguishing marks of numerical multitude. The ordering of fractions and the simplest method for calculating circulating decimals.

208. Recreations of Reasoning (RR)

A. MS., n.p., [c.1897], pp. 1, 21, 32; and 1 p.

209. Knotty Points in the Doctrine of Chances

A. MS., n.p., [c.1899], pp. 1-16.

Problem in probabilities: mathematics of the roulette table. CSP concludes whimsically: "That in an even game, say an honest roulette without zeros, all the players might make it a rule to leave off only when they had netted a winning equal to a single bet, and were their fortunes or backing unlimited, every man of them would be sure of success, while the bank, though it would not win anything, would never lose!" Now "let U.S. lend to each citizen . . ." and then allow the winnings to be taxed.

210. A Corner for Pythagoreans. Mathematical Recreations No. 1 by Pico di Sablonieri (pseudonym)

A. MS., n.p., [c.1895], pp. 1-11; plus 12 pp. and 5 pp. of other drafts.

A problem in probabilities. Content is similar to that of the preceding manuscript.

211. **A Brief Preliminary and Hasty Syllabus of a book to be entitled Calculations of Chances**
A. MS., n.p., n.d., 38 pp.; plus pp. 8, 11-18.

COMPUTATIONS AND FRAGMENTS

212. **A Trade Secret (Trade Secret)**
A. MS., n.p., n.d., pp. 1-4, with a variant p. 1.
The computing of values of a function from an infinite series: a dodge generally known among professional computers.

213. **Notes of a Computer**
A. MS., n.p., n.d., pp. 1-3, plus 1 p. ("A Device of Computation") and 1 p. ("A Computer's Device").

214. **Note on 0°**
TS., n.p., n.d., 3 pp.

215. **Integer Negative Powers of 2**
A. MS., n.p., "checked and found correct by CSP 1911, Oct. 8," 2 pp.

216. **Practical Comments on Namur's Tables of Logarithms**
A. MS., n.p., n.d., 1 p.

217. **Calc. of Nat. Log. 10**
A. MS., n.p., n.d., 1 sheet.

218. **A Short Table of Reciprocals**
A. MS., n.p., n.d., 1 sheet.

219. **Computation of the excess of $\sqrt[5]{10}$ over 1**
A. MS., n.p., n.d., 1 p.

220. **Calculation of the fractional part of $\sqrt[5]{10}$**
A. MS., n.p., n.d., 2 pp.

221. **Hints toward the invention of a Scale-Table**
A. MS., n.p., n.d., pp. 1-6; 1-3; and 9 pp. of fragments.
Table of antilogarithms and a logarithmic scale.

222. **Dedekind's Dirichlet #23**
A. MS., n.p., n.d., pp. 1-3, plus 5 pp. of two other starts.
The object of this paper is to describe a notation which reveals clearly the elementary constitution and properties of the functions connected with the GCD algorithm.

223. **Gibb's Papers. Vol. II. p. 30**
A. MS., n.p., n.d., 3 pp.
Probably a draft of G-1883-5d.

224. **All Pure Quantity merely ordinal**
A. MS., notebook, August 16, 1908.
Notes for a memoir whose purpose is "to prove that every system of signs of abstract quantities signifies nothing but that one sign denotes an object

later in one or more sequences (or later in one and earlier in another, etc.) than an object denoted by another." A study of two systems: (a) additive scheme of rational values, (b) numerative scheme of positive fractions. *Ens rationis* and feeling (monadic experience contrasted with dyadic experience, or "reaction").

225. Memorandum of How to Do Things

A .MS., notebook, n.p., n.d.

Various formulae of computation. Certain kinds of problems, e.g., drawing the best algebraic curve of a given order through any number of points, finding times of moon's rising and setting, etc., and their solutions.

226. Note to p. 378 of [Benjamin] Peirce's Analytic Mechanics

A. MS., n.p., n.d., 4 pp.

227. Theorems of Numbers

A. MS., n.p., n.d., 2 pp., incomplete.

228. Notes

A. MS., n.p., n.d., 9 pp.

Distributions of the theorems of mathematics throughout the various branches of the discipline. In addition, the notes are concerned with the theory of equations, equal roots, symmetric functions, different kinds of ratios.

229. [Logic of Number] (Lefevre)

A. MS., n.p., n.d., pp. 2-7, 16, 18, 20-21.

Definition of "mathematics" as "the science of hypotheses."

230. [Analytic Geometry]

A. MS., notebook, n.p., n.d.

Includes, in addition to the material on analytic geometry, a personal expense account, covering several days, but with no indication of the year.

231. Studies of Laws of Frequency of Occurrence of Numbers

A. MS., n.p., n.d., 1 p.

These studies are based on population figures for 1900.

232. Note on the Mouse Trap Problem

A. MS., n.p., n.d., 1 p.

233. Gauss's Rule for Easter improved

A. MS., n.p., n.d., 1 p.

234. [Arithmetical Calculations]

A. MS., notebook, n.p., n.d.

235. [Fragment on Quantity]

A. MS., n.p., n.d., pp. 15-16.

236. [Fermat's Theorem]

A. MS., n.p., n.d., 4 pp.

Draft of a postscript to an unidentified letter.

237. Formulae for Repeated Differentiations (Repeated Differentiations)

A. MS., n.p., n.d., pp. 1-2; plus 2 pp. (D^n).

238. An Apology for the Method of Infinitesimals (Apology)

A. MS., n.p., n.d., pp. 1-15.

An attempt at justifying a remark (see *Century Dictionary* s.v. limit) that the method of infinitesimals is more in harmony with advances in mathematics (1883) than the method of limits.

239. Infinitesimals
Corrected proofs, G-1900-1.

240. A Mathematical Suggestion
A. MS., n.p., n.d., 1 folded sheet (4 pp.).

241. A Mathematical Discussion
A. MS., n.p., n.d., 1 folded sheet (4 pp.).

242. [Computation of Ordinates for Points on a Probability Curve]
A. MS., n.p., n.d., 1 p.

243. The Theta Function of Probabilities
A. MS., n.p., n.d., 1 p., with 5 sheets of calculations.

* 244. [A Problem in Probabilities]
A. MS., notebook, n.p., n.d.
Solution of algebraic problems. Venn Diagrams. Calculation of the asymptotic axis of the larger atomic weights.

245. Illustrative Problem in Probabilities
A. MS., n.p., n.d., 16 pp.

246. Reflections on the Logic of Science
A. MS., n.p., January 1-7, 1889, pp. 2-22.
Evidently for a book on the philosophy of physics. The relationship between mathematics and physical theory. The Rule of False. MSS. 247-249 are presumably continuations of this one.

247. Chapter II. The Doctrine of Chances
A. MS., n.p., January 8, 1889, pp. 23-29, plus another p. 27.

248. Chapter II. Mathematics
A. MS., n.p., January 9-17, 1889, pp. 23-29.

249. Ordinal Geometry
A. MS., n.p., January 18-19, 1889, 40 pp., representing several starts.

250. Notes for Chapter of Mathematics
A. MS., n.p., November 24-25, 1901, pp. 1-4.

251. Topics of Mathematics
A. MS., n.p., n.d., 1 p.

252. [On Mathematical Reasoning]
A. MS., n.p., n.d., 22 pp.
Mathematical reasoning illustrated by means of the game tit-tat-too. The advantage, in general, of studying mathematics.

253. Logical Analysis of Some Demonstrations in High Arithmetic (D)
A. MS., n.p., June 11, 1905, pp. 1-20, incomplete, with an alternate p. 20.
Reference is made to a paper published in *The American Journal of Mathematics* (G-1881-7). Demonstrations of Fermat's and Wilson's theorems.

254. Of the Nature of Measurement
   A. MS., G-undated-4, pp. 1-26, plus 6 pp. rejected.

   Published, in part, as 7.280-312. Omitted are the demonstration and scholium in connection with the theorem on hyperbolic motion (pp. 13-17) and the corollary of the definition occurring on p. 21 and published as 7.312 (pp. 22-26).

255. Of the Nature of Measurement
   A. MS., n.p., n.d., pp. 1-8, plus variants.

256. Properties of Space
   A. MS., n.p., n.d., 11 pp. (fragmentary).

257. [On the Properties of Space]
   A. MS., n.p., n.d., 6 pp. and 5 pp. of another draft.

   The three classes of spatial properties: intrinsic, metrical, and optical.

258. [On the Properties of Mathematical Space]
   A. MS., n.p., n.d., 2 pp.

   Space is tri-dimensional and unlimited; its points are continuous; and it has the same properties everywhere, and in all directions.

259. Note on the Analytic Representation of Space as a Section of a Higher Dimensional Space
   A. MS., n.p., n.d., 1 p.

260. Note on the Utility of considering Space as a Section of a Space of more than 3 Dimensions
   A. MS., n.p., n.d., 4 pp.

261. Notes on Geometry of Plane Curves without Imaginaries
   A. MS., n.p., n.d., pp. 1-5, plus 6 pp.

262. On the Real Qualitative Characters of Plane Curves
   TS., n.p., n.d., 12 pp. of several drafts.

*263. Singularities of Pairs of Terminals
   A. MS., n.p., n.d., 2 pp.

264. On the Real Singularities of Plane Curves
   A. MS., n.p., n.d., 9 pp.

265. Topical Singularities
   A. M.S., n.p., n.d., 3 pp.

266. [Worksheets on the Nine-Ray Theorem]
   A. MS., notebook, n.p., n.d.

267. [Points, Lines, and Surfaces]
   A. MS., notebook, n.p., n.d.

268. Euclid Easy. Chapter I. A Talk on Continuity
   A. MS., n.p., n.d., pp. 1-4.

   An imaginary conversation between Thomas J. Jeffers and Euclid Easy, preparatory to a full scale discussion of the logic of continuity.

269. Notes for Theorems
   A. MS., notebook, n.p., n.d.

Various topics are listed with reference both to standard works and other writings. Topology and the four-color problem.

270. Test-Example of Mathematical Reasoning
A. MS., n.p., n.d., 6 pp.
An inquiry which presupposes points, rays, planes, and a relation called "containing."

271. Pythagorean
A. MS., n.p., n.d., 1 p.

272. Remarkable points of a triangle
A. MS., n.p., n.d., 2 pp., and 4 pp. ("Triangle").

273. [Homoloids]
A MS., n.p., n.d., 8 pp.
Discussion of the four-ray problem.

274. The Dodecanes
A. MS., n.p., n.d., 26 pp.

275. On a Geometrical Notation
TS., n.p., n.d., 2 pp., with 2 pp. of TS. (corrected) on "Notation."

276. Miscellaneous Journal
A. MS., notebook, dated entries for February 9, 11, 14-15, 20, 25, 28, 1910.
Secundal arithmetic. Probability. Petersburg problem. Justification for asserting a proposition. Analysis of the predicate "positive." Also a draft of a letter apparently to Mrs. O. H. P. Belmont.

277. The Prescott Book
A. MS., n.p., begun May 1907 and continued June 8, 1907-September 13, 1910.
On singularities, Petersburg problem, Ten-Point theorem, continuity, existential graphs. An analysis of signs, notes on phaneroscopy, and an outline of a paper for the *Hibbert Journal* on "a little known 'Argument' for the Being of God."

*278. [Unidentified Fragments]
A. MS., n.p., n.d., over 1400 pp.

PRAGMATISM

THE BASIS OF PRAGMATICISM

279. The Basis of Pragmaticism. Meditation the First (Med)
A. MS., n.p., [c.1905], pp. 1-16, with variants.
Types of readers who will not profit from this critical examination of pragmaticism. The Harvard Lectures of 1903 presented the argument which finally convinced CSP of the truth of pragmaticism. The argument of 1903 restated. Discussion of the ethics of terminology contains some amusing satire. The comparative merits of English and German; English better adapted to logic than German. A great mistake to attempt to reform English by way of German expressions out of harmony with it.

280. The Basis of Pragmaticism (Basis)

A. MS., n.p., [c.1905], pp. 1-48, plus fragments.

Of the different senses of "philosophy," preference is stated for that sense in which it is synonymous with cenoscopy, i.e., the study of common experience. The need for a technical nomenclature and terminology in the idioscopic sciences. The situation in philosophy is somewhat different. Philosophy needs to admit "into its language a body of words of vague significations with which to identify those vague ideas of ordinary life which it is its business to analyze." Logical analysis is not always adequate. Examples from the history of philosophy, especially Kant and Leibniz, of irresponsibility in logical analysis. Kant's use of "necessary" and "universal." Blunders in logical analysis inevitable until proper method (pragmaticism) is adopted. Specifically, blunders result from the failure of philosophers to understand and accept the logic of relations. Elementary discussion of existential graphs ("quite the luckiest find that has been gained in exact logic since Boole"). CSP reflects bitterly on treatment received from institutions and publishers.

281. The Basis of Pragmaticism (Basis)

A. MS., n.p., [c.1905], pp. 1-9, plus pp. 4-6.

On the senses of "philosophy" and on terminology in general. The danger of taking words from the vernacular, e.g., "light" in physics. Earlier draft of MS. 280.

282. The Basis of Pragmaticism (BP)

A. MS., G-c.1905-7, pp. 1-9.

Published as 5.497-501 with insignificant deletions.

*283. The Basis of Pragmaticism (Basis)

A. MS., G-1905-1d, pp. 1-162, with pp. 3-6 missing and with pp. 112-119 discarded (p. 120 continues p. 111), plus 210 pp. of alternative sections and single page fragments.

The following parts of this manuscript were published: p. 31 (section 8), pp. 37-45 as 1.573-574; pp. 45-59 as 5.549-554; pp. 135-148 as 5.448n (footnote to *Monist* article "Issues of Pragmaticism"). Unpublished is the argument for the truth of pragmatism based upon the argument of the Harvard Lectures of 1903 which, CSP notes, were not published in his lifetime because of the failure of a "friend" to recommend them for printing. The meaning of "science." Heuretic, practical, and retrospective science distinguished. The meaning of "philosophy." Cenoscopic and synthetic philosophy. Methods of cenoscopic research. The idea of growth, as found in Aristotle and as applied to knowledge generally. The divisions of cenoscopy, with metaphysics as the third and last division and normative science as the mid-division. The deplorable condition of metaphysics: the necessity of logic and the normative sciences generally as propaedeutic to it. The hard dualism of normative science, its distinctness from practical science, and its relationship to psychology. Action, effort, and surprise: effort and surprise only experiences from which we can derive concept of action. Doctrine of Signs. Modes of indeterminacy; indefiniteness and generality; the quantity and quality of indeterminacy. The relationship of law and existence.

284. The Basis of Pragmaticism

A. MS., two notebooks, G-c.1905-5, pp. 1-48 (one notebook); 49-91 (second notebook).

Selections from first notebook published as 1.294-299, 1.313, and 1.313n; selections from second notebook (pp. 65-69) were published as 1.350-352. Omissions from publication (First Notebook) include the disassociation of pragmaticism from some doctrines which have become associated with it; for example, the denial of the Absolute, the affirmation of a Finite God, making action (brute force) the *summum bonum*. ". . . I am one of those who say 'We believe in God, the Father Almighty, Maker of heaven and earth and of all things visible and *invisible*' where the invisible things, I take it, are Love, Beauty, Truth, the Principle of Contradiction, Time, etc. Clearly I can have but the vaguest analogical notion of the Maker of such things, and Pragmaticism, I am sure, does not require that all my beliefs should be definite." CSP thinks that Royce in *The World and the Individual* comes closer to exhibiting the meaning of pragmatism than any exposition of it given by a pragmatist other than himself. Another misrepresentation of pragmaticism is to assert that pragmatism depreciates science. The principal question for pragmaticism must be whether thought has any meaning or purport beyond the simple apprehension of the thought itself. Also omitted is a discussion of the four sects of logic: Leibnizian, Associationist, Aristotelian, and Kantian. The analogy between the indecomposable elements of thought and the atoms of the different elements. Logical terms and valencies. The indecomposable elements of the phaneron. Propositions and assertions. Omissions from publication (Second Notebook) include a discussion of the three modes of mental analysis (dissociation, precision, and discrimination). Application of these modes to primanity, secundanity, and tertianity, e.g., primanity can be prescinded though it cannot be dissociated from secundanity, but secundanity cannot be prescinded but only discriminated from primanity. Finally, the use of existential graphs to explain logical fallacy.

MONIST ARTICLES 1905-06

285. Analysis of "What Pragmatism is"

A. MS., n.p., [c.1910-11], 1 folded sheet.

An incomplete topical summary of the contents of the article entitled "What Pragmatism Is," the first of the three *Monist* articles of 1905-06. See G-1905-1a.

286. Analysis of the Issues of Pragmatism

A. MS., n.p., [c.1910-11], 2 folded sheets.

An incomplete topical summary of the contents of the article entitled "Issues of Pragmatism," the second of the three *Monist* articles of 1905-06. See G-1905-1b.

287. Analysis of Prolegomena

A. MS., n.p., [c.1910-11], 2 folded sheets.

An incomplete topical summary of the contents of the article entitled "Prolegomena to an Apology for Pragmaticism," the third of the three *Monist* articles of 1905-06. See G-1905-1c.

288. Materials for *Monist* Article: The Consequences of Pragmaticism. Vols. I and II

A. MS., two notebooks ("Vol. I" and "Vol. II"), n.p., April 27, 1905 (the first date recorded).

The material collected in both volumes is for the second article of the 1905-06 *Monist* series. Volume I: Critical Common-sensism. Pragmatism is regarded as a more critical version of a philosophy of common sense. The indubitability of propositions with indubitability associated with vagueness. The nature of doubt: the relationship of doubt to feeling, habit, and belief. The relationship of Critical Common-sensism and the normative sciences, and the relationships among the normative sciences. Volume II: Generality and vagueness. Concept of God is vague; Being of God is indefinite. Criticism of Kant: "Kant is nothing but a somewhat confused pragmatist." Ethical and logical control compared. Pragmatism connected with real possibility, with pragmatism rendered intelligible by the assertion of real possibility. Pragmatism's relationship to the normative sciences. Existence and reality: Generals are real but nonexistent.

289. Consequences of Pragmaticism (CP)

A. MS., n.p., [c.1905], pp. 1-22, plus rejected pp. 1, 5.

This paper serves as a critical commentary on the *Popular Science* article of January 1878 (G-1877-5b). Applications of the pragmatic maxim to specific questions, e.g., are the so-called "Laws of the Universe" habits of the universe in some objective sense? Question of God's objectivity. God and Demiurge are distinguished. Brief consideration of what constitutes reality and characterizes propositions.

290. Issues of Pragmaticism (CP)

A. MS., G-1905-1b, pp. 1-26, 30-63 (with no break in text); 12-28, 20-21, 27-28, 45-59; plus 9 single page variants.

Published, in part, as 5.402n (pp. 33-37). Unpublished is the mention of an early anticipation of pragmaticism in a *Journal of Speculative Philosophy* article of 1868 (G-1868-2). In that article CSP accepts two positions which underlie pragmaticism: Critical Common-sensism and Scholastic realism. Critical Common-sensism differs from the Scottish notions of common sense. Two classes of indubitable propositions noted. Acritical inferences and reasoning. *Logica docens and logica utens.* CSP finds support of Critical Common-sensism in the writings of Avicenna. Several applications of pragmaticism to the meaning of matter and time and to the notion of action at a distance. Theory of signs, especially symbols.

291. Pragmatism, Prag [4] (P)

A. MS., G-c.1905-8, pp. 2-68.

Omitted from publication (5.502-537): the footnote on pp. 20-21, which is concerned with the meaning of "to precide" as "to render precise, that is, non-vague, non-indefinite." Discussion of the derivation of the verb.

292. Prolegomena to an Apology for Pragmaticism (πλ)

A. MS., [c.1906], pp. 1-54 and pp. 29-54 of a partial draft, with 28 pp. of variants and 2 pp. ("Index to Prolegomena").

Less misleading, perhaps, to say that there are two drafts of pp. 29-54 and that it is not certain which should be counted as completing pp. 1-28. Pages 45-53 of one of these drafts were published as 1.288-292. See G-1905-1c. Not published is the first part of the manuscript which follows the third of the *Monist* articles very closely. Theory of signs. Relation among thought, thinking, and signs. Application of the type-token distinction. Diagram of thought, with some conventions for diagramming. The meaning of a conditional proposition and the revision of the tychistic hypothesis. The "second" draft is similar to the first in respect to the conventions for the diagramming of thought.

Restatement of chief purpose for constructing algebras of logic and existential graphs. Sketch of a classification of signs.

293. (PAP)

A. MS., n.p., [c.1906], pp. 1-56 (only the transition from 45-46 seems unnatural) and a sequence 10-18 marked "Keep for reference" by CSP, with 48 pp. of variants.

Anthropomorphism. The "operation of the mind" as an *ens rationis*. Genuine reasoning distinguished from reasoning which is not genuine. All necessary reasoning is diagrammatic: Diagram is an icon of a set of rationally related objects, a schema which entrains its consequences. The three modes of non-necessary reasoning: probable deduction, induction, and abduction. System of existential graphs: application of existential graphs to the phaneron; classification of the elements of the phaneron; valency; the precedence of form over matter in all natural classifications, with the distinction between form and matter applied to existential graphs. Kant's *Gesetz der Affinität*. What is meant by saying that identity is a continuous relation. Diagram variously characterized as token, as general sign, as definite form of relation, as a sign of an order in plurality, i.e., of an ordered plurality or multitude (pp. 10-18).

294. Prolegomena to an Apology for Pragmaticism (Pr)

A. MS., n.p., [c.1906], pp. 1-3, incomplete.

Stylistic problems. Should a writer be allowed to use the first person singular? Strategy for convincing the reader of the soundness of the writer's position.

295. (πλ)

A. MS., n.p., [c.1906], fragments running brokenly from p. 8 to p. 103, with 3 pp. unnumbered.

Rejected pages for the *Monist* article of 1906 (G-1905-1c). Both marking and topics treated indicate close affinity with MS. 292. Various topics discussed: kinds of signs; type-token distinction; collections and classes; the substitution of "seme," "pheme," and "delome" for "term," "proposition," and "argument," and the reason for making the substitution; several conventions of the system of existential graphs.

296. The First Part of an Apology for Pragmaticism (A₁)

A. MS., n.p., [c.1907-08 or 18 months after "Prolegomena"], pp. 1-14; 14-32, with p. 25 missing (but with no break in the text); pp. 7-16 of another draft; plus 24 pp. of variants.

This manuscript was intended as the fourth article of the *Monist* series of 1905-06, with two more articles following: The fourth article was to begin the apology, the fifth to have contained the main argument, and the sixth to have provided the subsidiary arguments and illustrations. More specifically, a rhetorical defense of the principle of pragmatism in the *Popular Science Monthly* issues of November 1877 and January 1878; system of existential graphs; the nominalism of Ockham and J. S. Mill; objective and subjective generality; Scholastic realism; the three ways in which an idea can be mentally isolated from another (dissociation, precision, and discrimination). Among the variant pages are some interesting biographical data, especially CSP's reflections on his father's "remarkable aesthetical discrimination" and his boyhood impressions of visitors, Emerson included, to the family home in Mason Street, Cambridge.

297. Apology for Pragmatism (Apol)

A. MS., n.p., [c.1907], pp. 1-7, incomplete.

Draft of G-1905-1g. CSP notes that there are three arguments favoring pragmatism of which the first "sets out from the observation that every new concept comes to the mind in a judgment." Judgment and assertion.

298. Phaneroscopy (ϕ and $\phi\alpha\nu$)

A. MS., G-1905-1h, pp. 1-36, plus 20 pp. of variants.

This article, intended for the January 1907 *Monist,* was to have followed the *Monist* article of October 1906. Published as follows: 4.534n[1] (pp. 2-3); 4.6-11 (from pp. 5-16); 4.553n[1] (pp. 18-19); 1.306-311 (pp. 26-36). Unpublished are CSP's thoughts on the relevance of existential graphs to the truth of pragmaticism; his view that existential graphs afford a moving picture of thought, and his reflections on telepathy, spiritualism, and clairvoyance. Vividness and intensity of feeling: CSP's disagreement with Hume.

*299. Phaneroscopy: Or, The Natural History of Concepts (Phy or Phaneroscopy)

A. MS., G-c.1905-4, pp. 1-37 incomplete, plus 31 pp. of variants.

Published as follows: 1.332-334 (pp. 12-18); 1.335-336 (pp. 33-37). Unpublished: definition and presuppositions of science; idioscopy and cenoscopy; mathematics and cenoscopy; the nature of experience and cognition; kinds of reasoning from experience; experience and shock (having an experience requires more than a shock).

300. The Bed-Rock Beneath Pragmaticism (Bed)

A. MS., G-1905-1e, pp. 1-65; 33-40; 38-41; 37-38; 40-43.7; plus 64 pp. of fragments running brokenly from p. 1 to p. 60.

This was to have been the fourth and ante-penultimate article of the *Monist* series. The following pages were published as indicated: 4.561n (pp. 31-39½); 4.553n[2] (pp. 37-38 of a rejected section). Omitted from publication are comments on the circumstances which led to writing the various articles of the *Monist* series. In this connection CSP notes, with some horror, the view attributed by the *New York Times* to William James that practical preference was the basis of pragmatism and considers what James probably meant to say, noting James's definition of "pragmatism" in *Baldwin's Dictionary of Psychology and Philosophy.* The truth of pragmatism and its scientific proof. CSP reveals that he "had passed through a doubt of pragmatism lasting very nearly twenty years." Discussion of the nature of doubt: the confounding of doubt with disbelief. System of existential graphs; comparison of existential graphs with chemical ones; existential and entitative graphs. Studies of modality: CSP's early views and subsequent modifications. Among the fragments one finds CSP's disagreement with Cantor on the matter of pseudo-continuity which for CSP raises a question of the ethics of terminology.

LECTURES ON PRAGMATISM

Eight Lectures delivered at Harvard from March 26 to May 17, 1903, the first seven under the auspices of the Department of Philosophy and the eighth under the auspices of the Department of Mathematics. Two of the notebooks included here are probably but not certainly part of the Harvard Lecture series.

301. Lecture I

A. MS., notebook, G-1903-1.

Published in entirety: 5.14-40.

302. Lecture II

A. MS., notebook, n.p., 1903.

A liberal education in a hundred lessons: fifty lessons devoted to the teaching of some small branch of knowledge. Of the remaining fifty lessons, thirty-six were to be devoted to logic. Lectures begin with a discussion of the different kinds of mathematics. Dichotonic and trichotonic mathematics. Logic of relatives. Incident involving Sylvester, who claimed that mathematical work shown him by CSP, who, in turn, suspected that his work reduced to Cayley's Theory of Matrices, was really nothing more than Sylvester's umbral notation. Later CSP discovers, with some satisfaction, that what Sylvester called "my umbral notation" had originally been published in 1693 by Leibniz. CSP's bitterness revealed in his remark that he can find a more comfortable way of ending his days, if nobody is interested in his efforts to gather together the scattered outcroppings of his work in logic for the purpose of a more systematic presentation of it.

303. Lecture II

A. MS., notebook, n.p., 1903.

A note appended to notebook reads: "Rejected. No time for this and it would need two if not three lectures." The history and nature of mathematics. Role of diagrams in mathematics. Algebra of logic as an attempt to analyze mathematical reasoning into its logical steps. An aside on opium's "dormitive virtue": a sound doctrine but hardly an explanation. The nature of abstraction, especially mathematical abstraction. Role played by conception of collection in mathematics. Whether pure mathematics is a branch of logic. "I am satisfied that all necessary reasoning is of the nature of mathematical reasoning." Boolean algebra.

304. Lecture II. On Phenomenology

A. MS., notebook, G-1903-1.

CSP notes "First draught" and "To be rewritten and compressed." Published: 1.322-323 (pp. 10-12). Omitted from publication is CSP's discussion of the goal of phenomenology, which is to describe what is before the mind and to show that the description is correct. Presentness (Hegel's view and CSP's contrasted). The "immediate" defined. Quality distinguished from feeling; quality as an element of feeling. Neither abstract nor complex quality is the First Category. Law of nature, with the being of law considered to be a sort of *esse in futuro*. An objection to this view of law noted and refuted. Reaction (or struggle) as the chief characteristic of experience. Content of the percept. No criticism of perceptual fact possible. Reaction is no more to be comprehended than blue or the perfume of a tea rose. Perception and imagination. Genuine and degenerate varieties of the Second Category. The Third Category (called "Mediation") and signs. First degenerate form of the Third Category.

305. Lecture II

A. MS., notebook, G-1903-1.

CSP notes: "Second Draught" and "This won't do, it will have to be rewritten." Published: 5.41-56 (pp. 7-10, 13-32). Pages 1-6 and 10-13 not published.

Classification of the various sciences and the place of philosophy among them. The three principal divisions of philosophy—metaphysics, normative science, and phenomenology—and the relation of dependence among them.

306. Lecture II

A. MS., notebook, G-1903-1.

Published: 5.59-65 (pp. 1-14). Only the first paragraph was omitted.

307. Lecture III

A. MS., notebook, G-1903-1.

This lecture is subtitled: "The Categories Continued." Published: 5.71n (p. 9); 5.82-87 (pp. 16-34). Omitted: the three categories and their degenerate forms, if any. Genuine form of the representamen is the symbol. First and second degenerate forms are the index and icon respectively. Symbol, index, and icon analyzed with regard to degenerate forms. Given the three categories, all possible systems of metaphysics are divided into seven classes, e.g., into systems which admit only one of the three categories (three systems possible), systems which admit only two of the three categories (three systems possible), and that system which admits all three categories. The history of philosophy is examined for examples of each system. Schroeder's argument against admitting the Second Category into logic deemed naive, but not Kempe's argument against the Third Category. Kempe's system of graphs.

308. Lecture III

A. MS., notebook, G-1903-1.

This lecture is subtitled: "The Categories Defended." Published: 5.66-81, except 5.71n[1] and 5.77n[1] (pp. 1-12); 5.88-92 (pp. 48-53). Omitted: whether the three categories must be admitted as irreducible constituents of thought. Objection raised against Schroeder's and Sigwart's denial of the Second Category. Discussion of Sigwart's reduction of the notion of logicality to a quality of feeling (Logical *Gefühl*). Objection raised against Kempe's denial of the irreducibility of the Third Category. Brief comparison of existential graphs with Kempe's system of graphs. Whether the categories are real, i.e., "have their place among the realities of nature and constitute all there is in nature," is a question which remains to be answered.

309. Lecture IV. The Seven Systems of Metaphysics

A. MS., two notebooks, G-1903-1.

Notebook I (pp. 1-37, of which pp. 1-4 and 12-37, with exception of 25-34, were published as 5.77n and 5.93-111 respectively). Unpublished: a discussion of the possible systems of metaphysics based on CSP's categories and their combinations. In CSP's opinion, the following philosophers were on the right track: Plato, Aristotle, Aquinas, Scotus, Reid, and Kant. Rejection of the idea attributed to the Hegelians that Aristotle belongs to their school of thought. Aristotle and the notion of *esse in futuro*. The Aristotelian distinction between existence and entelechy. Ockhamists and the rise of nominalism. Analysis of infinity (pp. 24-30). The reality of Firstness (pp. 31-35). Notebook II (pp. 38-62, of which pp. 38-45, 45-49, 49-51, 52-57, and 59-62, were published separately as 5.114-118, 1.314-316, 5.119, 5.111-113, 5.57-58 respectively). Omitted is a discussion of the reality of Secondness and a consideration of the position that feelings and laws (Firstness and Thirdness) are alone real (that to say that one thing acts upon another is merely to say that there is a certain law of succession of feelings). Experience is our great teacher; invariably it teaches by means of surprises.

310. Lecture V

A. MS., notebook, n.p., 1903, pp. 1-14.

A knowledge of logic is requisite for understanding metaphysics. The three categories are not original with CSP; they permeate human thought for all time. Statement of his own early intellectual behavior. The year 1856 is given as the year of his first serious study of philosophy. Beginning with esthetics (Schiller's *Aesthetische Briefe*) he proceeded to logic and the analytic part of the *Critic of Pure Reason*. Mentions his subsequent neglect of esthetics and his incompetence in this area. Reflections on esthetics. Is there such a quality as beauty? Is beauty the name we give to whatever we enjoy contemplating regardless of the reasons for liking it? Esthetic quality related to the three categories: It is Firstness that belongs to a Thirdness in its achievement of Secondness. Reflections on ethics.

311. Lecture V

A. MS., notebook, n.p., 1903, pp. 1-16.

The branches of philosophy. The normative sciences: the relationships among the normative sciences; the relationship between the normative sciences and the special sciences, especially psychology; the dependence of the normative sciences upon phenomenology and pure mathematics. Description of the laborious "method of discussing with myself a philosophical question."

312. Lecture V

A. MS., notebook, G-1903-1, pp. 1-50.

Published: 5.120-150 (pp. 11-50). Not published is Part I., "How I go to work in studying philosophy" (pp. 1-10), and the contents of pp. 43-47, which constitute a first draft (the published second draft is the versos of these pages) and which concern the obscurity of the relation between the three kinds of inferences and the three categories as well as CSP's attempt to achieve clarity here.

313. Lecture VI

A. MS., n.p., 1903, pp. 1-31.

Perceptual judgments as involving generality and as being beyond the power of logic to criticize, as referring to singular objects, and as relating to continuous change (time, continuity, infinity). The nature of logical goodness and the end of argumentation. Logic and metaphysics. Pragmatism: the genealogy of a born pragmatist; pragmatism and realism; the ultimate meaning of a symbol. CSP's acceptance of the term "meaning" as a technical term of logic (as referring to the total intended interpretant of a symbol). The meaning of an argument and of a proposition (rhema); the meanings of such difficult abstractions as Pure Being, Quality, Relation. Definitions, it is stated, should be "in terms of the conceptions of everyday life." CSP raises one possible objection to his formulation of the maxim of pragmatism, and ends this draft with some disparaging remarks about the state of logical studies at Harvard. The objection raised is this: If meaning consists in doing (or the intention to do), is there not a conflict with the view (to which CSP subscribes) that the meaning of an argument is its conclusion, since a conclusion is an intellectual phenomenon different from doing and presumably without relation to it?

314. Lecture VI

A. MS., notebook, G-1903-1, pp. 1-43.

This manuscript is presumably the second draft of Lecture VI. Published in entirety (5.151-179) as "Three types of Reasoning." Note on the cover reads: "first 35 pages as delivered." See MS. 316 for the continuation of Lecture VI.

315. Lecture VII

A. MS., notebook, G-1903-1, pp. 1-48.

Published: 5.180-212 (pp. 1-21). The omitted pages concern the three essentially different modes of reasoning (deduction, induction, and abduction), with the pragmatic maxim identified with the logic of abduction.

316. [Lectures on Pragmatism]

A. MS., notebook, n.p., [1903], pp. 44-60.

MS. 316 continues MS. 314, and was in fact delivered as part of Lecture VI. What is the end of a term? Distinction between term and rhema. The common noun, its late development and restriction to a peculiar family of languages. Term and index. Three truths necessary for the comprehension of the merits of pragmatism: that all our ideas are given to us in perceptual judgments; that perceptual judgments contain elements of generality (so that Thirdness is directly perceived); that the abductive faculty is a shading off of that which at its peak is called "perception." Pragmatism and the logic of abduction.

*316a. Multitude and Continuity

A. MS., notebook, n.p., 1903.

CSP notes that this is a "lecture to be delivered . . . in Harvard University, 1903 May 15." This lecture was delivered. See G-1903-1 and sup(1) G-1902-1.

PROPOSED ARTICLE ON PRAGMATISM FOR THE NATION

* 317. Topics of the Nation Article on Pragmatism (Topics)

A. MS., n.p., [c.1907], pp. 1-6, plus a variant p. 5 and a photostatic copy the original of which has been catalogued separately (HUD 3570) and can be dated by means of a letter from Paul E. More to CSP on the reverse side. The original, without the letter, was published in Philip P. Wiener's *Evolution and the Founders of Pragmatism*, p. 21. The letter is dated March 24, 190[9].

A list of sixty-three topics, with page references and the beginning of an "Index of Technical Terms."

318. Pragmatism (Prag)

A. MS., G-c.1907-1a and G-c.1907-1c, with no single, consecutive, complete draft, but several partial drafts end and are signed (Charles Santiago Sanders Peirce) on pp. 34, 77, and 86.

An article in the form of a letter to the editor of *The Nation* was published as follows: 5.11-13 (pp. 1-7); 5.464-496 (pp. 7-45 of one draft and pp. 46-87 of another; the last two sentences of 5.481 were spliced by the editors of the *Collected Papers*). Also published as 1.560-562 were pp. 20-27 of still another draft. Omitted from publication: an analysis of James's definition of "pragmatism" (pp. 10-13 of one of the alternative sections). James's pragmatism again, followed by a discussion of his own position; the two distinct opponents of pragmatism (Absolutists and Positivistic Nominalists); pragmatism and religion; law distinguished from brute fact, not, as the nominalists would have it, by being a product of the human mind, but, as the realists assert, by being a real intellectual ingredient of the universe; triadic predicates as always having an intellectual basis, the evidence for which is inductive; thoughts regarded as signs, with signs functioning triadically; three kinds of interpretants—emotional, energetic, and logical; the distinction between association and suggestion; the syllogism as an associative suggestion; "corollarial" and "theoric" reasoning, of which an example of theoric deduction is the "Ten Point Theorem" of Van Standt (pp. 10-56 of a long draft from which pp. 20-27 were published). The three kinds of interpretants of signs; ultimate intellectual interpretants; pragmatism and common sense, with the meaning of critical common sense explained (pp. 43-59 of an alternative section of the long draft numbered 10-56 and described above). Kernel of pragmatism; concepts equated with mental signs; the object and interpretant of a sign distinguished; the problem of ultimate, or "naked," meaning; existential meanings; the meaning of an intellectual concept; qualities of feeling as meanings of signs, where qualities are neither thoughts nor existential events; the distinction between real and immediate (as represented by a sign) object, with immediate objects resembling emotional meaning and real objects corresponding to existential meaning; mathematical concepts as examples of logical meaning; the relationship of logical meaning to desires and habits (pp. 11-34 of another alternative section). Object and interpretant (meaning); the different units of interpretants (meanings); pragmatic definition and a prediction that pragmatism will occupy the same position in philosophy as the doctrine of limits occupies in mathematics (pp. 14-25 of an alternative section of the one described immediately above). Kernel of pragmatism; theory of signs; by inference a sign first comes to be recognized as such; the elementary modes of inference (pp. 12-30 of an alternative section). The divisions of geometry; a problem in topics; the Census Theorem and Listing Numbers; the function of consciousness; concepts and habits; the vulnerability of James and Schiller arising from their (apparent) denial of infinity, including an infinite Being (pp. 62-77 of still another alternative section). An attempt to define "sign"; the sense in which utterer and interpreter are essential to signs; the immediate and real objects of signs; a brief note on the Census Theorem (pp. 12-90, with the exception of pp. 46-87 which were published).

319. Pragmatism (Prag)

A. MS., n.p., [c.1907], pp. 1-17, with 5 pp. of variants.

An abandoned draft of a letter to the editor of *The Nation*. After stating the purpose of the letter, CSP discusses his philosophical ancestry and the *Metaphysical Club,* of which he was a member in his youth. James's position contrasted with his own. Application of the pragmatic maxim to the problem of probability. Chance and tychism.

320. Pragmatism (Prag)

A. MS., n.p., [c.1907], pp. 1-30, incomplete, with 8 pp. of variants.

Another abandoned draft. The membership of the *Metaphysical Club.* Types of mind. Criticism of James's views on pragmatism. Application of the pragmatic maxim to philosophical questions involving chance and probability. Nominalism as a perversion of pragmatism. Criticism of J. S. Mill's attempt to eliminate necessity by regarding "law" and "uniformity" as synonymous. Affirmation of the reality of potentialities or capacities. Pragmatism as a part of methodeutic; its connection with the experimental method of the sciences. Critical Common-sensism.

321. Pragmatism (Prag)

A. MS., n.p., [c.1907], pp. 1-27, 24-30 but no continuous draft, with 13 pp. of variants.

Another abandoned draft. Notes invitation from *The Nation* to clarify pragmatism. The ancestry of pragmatism. The *Metaphysical Club*. Kant's nominalism explored. The views of James, Schiller, and CSP compared. Thought and signs. Experiences as the objects of signs, never their meanings. Mathematical concepts as examples of logical interpretants. How CSP was led to his formulation of the pragmatic maxim. Application of the maxim to the problem of ascertaining the meaning of probability.

322. (Prag)

A. MS., n.p., [c.1907], pp. 2-21, plus 3 pp. of variants.

Presumably another attempt at the article for *The Nation*. Pragmatic tendencies discovered in Kant. Definitions in Locke's *Essay Concerning Human Understanding* are pragmatistic. Tinge of pragmatic thought in Aristotle partly attributable to Socrates. Descartes is singled out as being pragmatistically blind. Characterization of some of the members of the *Metaphysical Club*, with special praise for Chauncey Wright. What pragmatism is and isn't. Pragmatism as a method of determining meaning, not a doctrine of the truth of things. A comparison of James's views on pragmatism with CSP's. Pragmatism as a rule of methodeutic. One influence of pragmatism upon metaphysics: bringing metaphysics more in line with common sense than is usually the case. The metaphysical position toward which pragmatism is favorably disposed is conditional idealism (Berkeleyanism with some modifications). Laplace and the notion of probability. Truth and error.

323. (Prag)

A. MS., G-c.1907-1b, pp. 2-12.

Apparently still another attempt at the article for *The Nation*. Published, in part: 5.5-10. In the unpublished part CSP writes of his "personal peculiarity, which prompts him to struggle against every philosophical opinion that has recommended itself to him before he definitely surrenders himself to it," and hence of his relative lack of bias in his discussions of pragmatism.

324. (Prag)

A. MS., n.p., [c.1907], pp. 1-3, incomplete, plus another draft of p. 1.

The *Metaphysical Club*, its members and its occasional visitors, e.g., Abbot and Fiske. Misunderstanding of the meaning of "pragmatism." Pragmatism is not a metaphysical doctrine. "It does not relate to what is true, *but* to what is meant." Alternative p. 1.: The *Metaphysical Club*. Of those who attended the meetings of the Club, CSP was the only one for whom Kant had an appeal. The others were inspired by the English philosophers.

MISCELLANEOUS

325. Pragmatism Made Easy (Prag)

A. MS., n.p., n.d., pp. 1-8.

A draft of a letter to the editor of the *Sun*. Associating the personal names of the discoverers with the great advances made in science is defended. The study of scientific philosophy requires a religious spirit. CSP's intellectual development. The *Metaphysical Club*. Nicholas St. John Green, a member of the Club, brought the doctrines of Bain to the attention of the other members. The correlation of the traditional threefold division of consciousness (feeling, volition, and cognition) with the threefold division of logical predicates (predicates connected with single subjects, two subjects, and more than two subjects).

326. Some Applications of Pragmaticism (SAP)

A. MS., n.p., n.d., pp. 1-21; 5-10, 11-17; 2 pp. of fragments.

Apparently a draft of a letter (see p. 13). Pages 1-21: Wundt's psychology, as exemplifying a certain kind of error in philosophy; Wundt's mistaken assumption that philosophy must be based on the results of one of the special sciences (which implies that there are no immediately indubitable facts other than those which the special sciences have uncovered); Wundt's contention that philosophy requires the results of the special sciences (or else its theories are generated from thin air) is dismissed; Wundt's confusion of cenoscopy and idioscopy. Pages 5-17: Wundt as scientist distinguished from Wundt as philosopher; Wundt's success in science contrasted with his failure in philosophy. The branches of cenoscopy, the study of those facts familiar to the whole world, and the pragmatistic variety of a philosophy of common sense.

327. Why I Am A Pragmatist (OM)

A. MS., n.p., n.d., pp. 1-8.

The meaning of abstract ideas. It would seem that either the ultimate intellectual purport of ideas conforms to the pragmatist's program or these ideas are classified with our instincts. CSP believes both to be the case. The article itself begins with a sketch of the classification of the sciences.

328. Sketch of Some Proposed Chapters on the Sect of Philosophy Called Pragmatism

A. MS., notebook, G-c.1905-6.

Published, in part, as 1.126-129 (pp. 11-17). Unpublished are the reasons why pragmatism ought to be investigated. CSP came to the position of pragmatism through the study of the following philosophers and in the order noted here: Kant, Berkeley, the other English philosophers, Aristotle, and finally the Scholastics. Whether the principle of pragmatism is self-evident. The place of philosophy among the sciences. The branches of philosophy. Pragmatism and the question of the external world. Deduction, induction and probability, and their justification.

329. Nichol's Cosmology and Pragmaticism (Carus)

A. MS., G-c.1904-3, pp. 1-6, 7½-23, with parts of several other drafts, but no continuous draft.

Nichol's book is used mainly as a point of departure for CSP's own views. An early expression of the first article of the *Monist* series of 1905-06 on pragmatism (G-1905-1a). Published, in part, as 8.194-195 (pp. 12-15). Unpublished is a description of the experimentalist's way of thinking. CSP's disagreement with Balfour on the question of a physical reality unraveled in experiments—whether a belief in a non-experiential reality is the unalterable faith of the scientist. Pragmatism, pragmaticism, and common sense. Tin doubts, toy baby scepticism. Meaning of a proper name. The pragmaticist's use of the term "real." Generality as an indispensible condition of reality. Generality and its relationship both to evolution and to the *summum bonum*. The pragmaticistic analysis of past and future.

330. The Argument for Pragmatism anachazomenally or recessively stated

A. MS., n.p., n.d., 1 folded sheet; plus 5 other folded sheets which, although lacking a title or mark, seem to be connected with the first.

The argument stated. A generalized habit of conduct is the essence of a concept, i.e., its logical interpretant. The problem of evil and CSP's solution: The evil passions are evil only in the sense that they ought to be controlled, but they are good as the only possible way that man has to reach his full and normal development. The meaning of "true" and "satisfactory"; the relationship between the true and the satisfactory. Hedonism rejected.

331. [Pragmatism and Pragmaticism]

A. MS., n.p., n.d., 5 pp.

This manuscript may possibly be a draft of a letter to *The Nation*. See note in the body of the manuscript which reads: "Say, Garrison, was not Schiller in Cornell at one time." Pragmatism, humanism, and instrumentalism. Whether the pragmatist's God must be finite. In CSP's opinion, a finite God cannot satisfy human instincts. Recommendation that the word "pragmatism" be employed for the looser sense of the term's meaning but that the word "pragmaticism" be retained for the more precise meaning.

332. [Pragmatism, Experimentalism, and Mach]

A. MS., n.p., n.d., 2 pp.

The true experimentalist is a pragmatist. Mach misses the bull's-eye by holding that general thought has no value other than its utility in economizing experience. But, although he misses the bull's-eye, Mach does hit the target.

333. [Fragments on the Fixation of Belief]

A. MS., n.p., n.d., 29 pp., plus 3 pp. (numbered 80, 81, 86) of notes and 2 pp. of a draft of 5.362-363.

The following information was supplied by Professor Max H. Fisch: "Of the present contents of this folder, some sequences of pages on the rag paper with the watermark J. Whatman 1868 may be parts of the paper read to the *Metaphysical Club* in November 1872. Others are probably, indeed almost certainly, parts of The Logic of 1873. The two slightly longer sheets of rag paper contain two pages of a draft of 'The Fixation of Belief,' probably of 1876 or 1877. The sheets of wood pulp paper numbered 80, 81, 86, or at least pages 80 and 81, probably belong to some work of the 1890's in which Peirce went over the same ground again." In connection with the numbered pages, see MS. 1002. It is of some interest to note that the earlier name for the method of tenacity was "the method of obstinacy," and instead of "authority," CSP employed the word "despotism."

334. The Fixation of Belief

Offprint from the *Popular Science Monthly* (G-1877-5a) with inserts: "A" (5 pp.), "B" (2 pp.), "C" (1 p.), "D" (pp. 1-3; 1-7), "E" (2 pp.), "F" (pp. 1-3; 1-7), "G" (2 pp.), "H" (2 pp.), "N" (2 pp.), unmarked (3 pp.).

Changes are indicated both in the margins and in the notes which were to be inserted in future editions of his earlier work. There is a clear indication where to insert some of the notes. With others (N, B, D, F, G, H, and those pages which are unmarked), there is no indication. The notes concern the fallibility of thinking, especially in mathematics (A); the distinction between definite and indefinite doubt, and the possibility of a third attitude of calm ignorance, whether conscious or unconscious, besides belief and doubt (C);

the dependence of the validity of pure mathematics and of logic upon the validity of rational instinct, and the consequences of this for evaluating the *a priori* method of fixing belief (E); on Malthus and Darwin (B); the distinction between assertion and proposition and between modal propositions and the psychological modals "can" and "would" (D); the improvement of the standards of reasoning and the inward power of growth as reflected in the development of the instinct of just reasoning, with some remarks on Malthus and Darwin (F); the ultimate appeal to instinctive feelings (G); Descartes' mythical Eldorado of absolute certainty, and the attempt to attain it by methodological scepticism (H); the development of the intellect (N), and a preface to an essay on logic and reasoning, with a digression on theology (unmarked).

335. [Fragment on the Justification of Belief]

A. MS., n.p., n.d., pp. 1-6; plus 4 pp. of another draft.

On absolute certainty: "We cannot attain absolute certainty about anything whatever, unless it be either that there are sundry seemings or something as vague as that." The proposition—twice two is four—fails as an example of perfect certainty.

PHENOMENOLOGY

336. Logic viewed as Semeiotics. Introduction. Number 2. Phaneroscopy

A. MS., notebook, G-c.1904-2.

Published, in part: 1.285-287; 1.304 (pp. 8-22). Unpublished (pp. 1-8): Definition of "phaneron" as "anything that can come before the mind in any sense whatever" and an explanation of what it means to say "before the mind."

337. Logic viewed as Semiotic. Introduction. Number 2. Phaneroscopy

A. MS., notebook, n.p., n.d.

Distinction between "manifest" and "evident." CSP claims the privilege of creating a new word, "phaneron," which is defined as "whatever is throughout its entirety open to assured observation."

338. Phanerology

A. MS., n.p., n.d., 1 p., unfinished.

Definition of "phaneron."

LOGIC

LOGIC NOTEBOOK 1865-1909

339. Logic

A. MS., notebook, n.p., November 12, 1865-November 1, 1909.

CSP kept this notebook from 1865 until his death, recording in it (and dating) many of his investigations in their first stages: "Here I write but never after read what I have written for what I write is done in the process of forming a conception." The sheets have been ordered and numbered by Professor Don Roberts, and a page by page index has been provided by him and is kept with the notebook. Among the topics included are: real definition, the categorical syllogism, intension and extension, the logic of relatives, existential graphs, collections, the theory of signs, induction and hypothesis, the history of science, scepticism and common sense, the nature of truth, liberty and necessity.

UNIVERSITY LECTURES 1865

It is not certain that all the lectures listed below belong to the University Lecture Series or that the order in which they are noted in the catalogue is the order in which they were actually given in the spring of 1865. For instance, MS. 343 duplicates, without mentioning it, the content of 342. It is conceivable that MS. 343 is Lecture V of the 351 series. Again, MS. 345 and MS. 356 begin in the same way. It is conceivable that MS. 345 is a later draft of MS. 356.

340. Lecture I

A. MS., n.p., [1864-65], pp. 1-2, 4-10 of one draft; p. 4 of another draft (all are double pages).

Preface on the reforms of science, including reform in logic. Plan of the lectures.

341. Lecture II

A. MS., n.p., [1864-65], pp. 1-12 (double pages).

Problem of induction: logical or extra-logical? The answer as suggested by Aristotle's views on induction. Distinction between premises and conclusions, and between data and inference. No induction by simple enumeration. *A posteriori* reasoning distinguished from deduction and induction. The three figures of *a priori* inference; the three principles of inference *a posteriori*. For an earlier draft of the first page, see MS. 765.

342. Lecture III

A. MS., n.p., [1864-65], 33 pp.

Theories of probabilities (Doctrine of Chances). Most of the lecture, however, concerns some peculiarities of Boole's algebra. Brief discussions of the history of logic and some sophisms.

343. Lecture V

A. MS., n.p., [1864-65], 36 pp.

The two kinds of scientific inference—induction and hypothesis—differ from the syllogistic inference as much as they do from each other. Nevertheless, the three coordinate classes of reasoning are deduction, induction, and hypothesis.

344. Lecture VI. Boole's Calculus of Logic (Boole)

A. MS., n.p., [1865-66], pp. 1-10, 11-14 (mostly double pages).

Boole's work marks an epoch in the history of logic "which in point of fruitfulness will rival that of Aristotle's *Organon*."

345. Lecture VII

A. MS., n.p., [1864-65], 34 pp., with 2 pp. of another start.

This lecture begins the second half of the lecture series. The definition of "logic." Kinds of logical systems. All deductive reasoning is merely explicatory. Direct and indirect implication. What a word denotes and what it connotes. The sphere and the content of a word. Extension and comprehension. Being (all breadth, no depth) and Nothing (all depth, no breadth). Modification of the law of the inverse proportionality of extension and comprehension. The information of a term. On the subject of induction and hypothesis, CSP writes of the slight preponderance of true over false scientific inferences, and he finds that the reason for this is the vague tendency for the whole to be like any of its parts, taken at random.

346. Lecture VIII. Forms of Induction and Hypothesis (Forms)

A. MS., n.p., [1864-65], pp. 1-14 (double pages).

The attempts to define "logic" suffer from an admixture of logic, anthropology, and psychology. Analysis of the triad of thing, representation, and form. The three kinds of representations: signs, copies, symbols. Conditions to which symbols are subject. The relationship between the syllogism and scientific inference. The proper form of induction. Induction and hypothesis distinguished. Induction increases the extension of subject; hypothesis increases the comprehension of predicate. Moreover, induction discovers a law which is a prohibition; hypothesis discovers a law which is an imposition.

347. Lecture X. Grounds of Induction (Grounds)

A. MS., n.p., [1864-65], 15 double pp. (with one double p. missing); plus pp. 1-4, incomplete, entitled "Lecture on the Grounds of Inference." Kinds of propositions: denotative, informative, connotative. Relationship of denotative, informative, connotative propositions to propositions which are simple, enumerative, and conjunctive. The peculiarities of the latter. The three kinds of inference and their ground.

348. Lecture XI (XI)

A. MS., n.p., [1864-65], pp. 1-16 (double pages).

Long recapitulation of the previous lecture. What is the probability that an induction or hypothesis is true? CSP concludes that the question is senseless both from the viewpoint of the nature of propositions and the nature of logic. Sundry comments on the views of Sir William Hamilton.

* 348a. (Bacon)

A. MS., n.p., n.d., p. 7 and 1 p.

A lecture on Bacon was promised (see MS. 340). But only two pages which may be part of that lecture have been found.

349. Lecture on Kant (Kant)

A. MS., n.p., [1864-65], pp. 1-14, with all but p. 12 being double pages.

Presumably the 12th lecture of the University Lecture Series. "Every man who wishes to vindicate his pretensions to philosophic power must display it by the discovery of an error in Kant." Most usually the critics of Kant have simply misunderstood him. Examples of misunderstanding provided. A preliminary study of Kant's *Critique of Pure Reason*, treating such topics as the *A Priori*, The Transcendental Esthetic (the objective validity of the representations of space and time), Kant on the nature of judgment.

350. Lecture on the Theories of Whewell, Mill, and Compte (Whewell)

A. MS., n.p., [1864-65], pp. 1-14 (double pages).

Presumably part of the University Lecture Series. There is a note that another lecture on Waddington, De Remusat, Graty, and others was to follow this one. Several modern theories of science treated as inseparable from the metaphysics of their authors. For example, Whewell is a Kantian. Comte is "helplessly restricted to a simple intellectual view." Criticism of Mill's logic, especially Mill's views on the ground of induction.

LOWELL LECTURES ON THE LOGIC OF SCIENCE 1866

351. Lecture I

A. MS., n.p., October 24, 1866, 39 pp.

The bad reputation of logic, with its endless controversies between realism and nominalism. Among modern logicians, CSP distinguishes the formal and the anthropological logicians. Logic as a classificatory science. The traditional syllogism, with a note that the second lecture would be concerned with the hypothetical syllogism.

352. Lecture I

A. MS., n.p., 1866, 29 pp.

The nature of logic. Kinds of arguments. The moods and figures of the categorical syllogism.

353. Lecture II

A. MS., n.p., October 27, 1866, 30 pp.

Continues MS. 351. On the hypothetical syllogism. Included here is a discussion of Zeno's paradoxes as well as a discussion of several sophisms.

354. Lecture III

A. MS., n.p., October 31, 1866, 31 pp.

Probability. Meaning of "likely" and "probable." Boole's algebra. What is the justification of induction? What are the common characters of inference in general? CSP records and then criticizes answers commonly given to these questions by mathematicians and theologians.

* 355. Lecture IV

A. MS., G-1866-2a, November 3, 1866, 34 pp. (numbered by an editor).

Published, in part, as 7.131-138 (pp. 27-32). Unpublished is the recapitulation of previous lecture and J. S. Mill's answer to the question of induction along with CSP's criticism of that answer, especially Mill's notion of the uniformity of nature.

356. Lecture VII

A. MS., n.p., delivered November 14, 1866, 6 pp.

This lecture begins the second half of the lecture series. Extention and comprehension. Digression on the intellectual superiority of Boston (CSP is pleased by the hearing he has received during the first six lectures, especially, as he says, on a subject as dry as logic). Role of philosophy in America: A promise of things to come, but as yet there is no American philosophy. Notes several traits in the Yankee character which are conducive to philosophizing.

357. Lecture IX

A. MS., n.p., [1866], 28 pp. and 8 pp. of different drafts; plus a quotation from Herbart.

First sense impressions are not representations of unknown things but those things themselves. Sensation and conception as representations. Universal conceptions: Substance and Being, with the intervening conceptions of Ground, Correlate, and Interpretant. Quality, relation, and representation. The three kinds of representations. Icon, index, and symbol. Division of symbol into term, proposition, and argument. Kinds of terms. Hamilton's views considered. The classification of the sciences.

* 358. Lecture X

A. MS., n.p., [1866-67], 3 pp. (fragmentary).

All cognition is inferred from some other cognition, i.e., there is no first premise or intuition. Some consequences of this view.

359. Lecture XI

A. MS., G-1866-2a, 29 pp. (page numbers supplied by an editor).

Published, in part, as 7.579-596 (pp. 1-22, with a single deletion). Unpublished (pp. 22-29): Symbols and the trinity of object, interpretant, and ground. Agreement between this trinity and the Christian Trinity. The interpretant is the Divine Logos. "If our former guess that a Reference to an interpretant is Paternity be right, this would also be the Son of God." The ground corresponds in its function to the Holy Spirit. A discussion of philosophical tendencies in children terminates with the conclusion that the peculiar differences of men are philosophical differences.

LOGIC OF 1873

360. Chapter I

A. MS., G-c.1873-1, 3 pp. of fragments.

7.315, 7.315n^5, and 7.316 are from these pages.

361. Chapter I (Enlarged Abstract)

A. MS., G-c.1873-1, 2 pp.

Published in entirety: 7.313-314.

362. Chapter I (Enlarge Abstract)

A. MS., n.p., [c.1873], 1 p.

363. [Fragment]

A. MS., G-c.1873-1, 1 p.

Published, in part: 7.314n^4.

364. Logic. Chapter 2. Of Inquiry

A. MS., G-c.1873-1, 1 p., incomplete; plus 9 pp. of another draft and 5 loose sheets.

Only the draft of 9 pp. was published: 7.317-325.

365. Chapter 2

A. MS., n.p., [c.1873], pp. 1, 4.

The end or purpose of inquiry is to close inquiry; its end is not its own exercise. The spirit of disputatiousness is best promoted by practical applications of reason.

366. Logic. Chapter 3. Four Methods of Settling Opinion

A. MS., n.p., [c.1873], p. 1, incomplete.

367. Logic. Chap. 4. Of Reality

Amanuensis, corrections in CSP's hand, G-c.1873-1, pp. 1-23.

Published, in part as 7.327-335 (pp. 1-17). Unpublished: reality and the final opinion upon which men are destined to agree. Reality is that thought with which we struggle to have our thoughts coincide. It can mean nothing at all to say that, in addition, some other reality exists.

368. Chapt. 4 (2nd Draft)

Amanuensis, corrections in CSP's hand, n.p., [c.1873], pp. 1-7.

Thought is regarded as a stream governed by the law of association. Independent reality is placed either at the beginning or the end of the stream. The law of association cannot account for the coherence and harmony of experience. Distinction between dreams and external experience.

369. Logic. Chap 4 (——draft)

Amanuensis, G-c.1873-1, pp. 1-6.

Published, in part, as 7.326 (pp. 1-3). Unpublished: reflections on feeling. The relationship of feeling to other feelings is such that, apart from succession in time, there are no relationships. Every feeling in itself is unanalyzable and absolutely simple.

370. [Chapter 4. Of Reality]

Amanuensis, G-c.1873-1, 11 pp.

Published in entirety: 7.336-345.

371. Logic. Chapter IV. Of Reality

A. MS., n.p., [c.1873], 18 pp. of fragments.

Investigation consists of two parts: reasoning and observation. The confusion between thought as an operation of thinking and thought as an object. Belief and the habitual connection of ideas, with belief and habit of thought being one and same thing. Fixation of belief. No genuine doubt attaches to the scientific method of fixing belief, just as no genuine doubt can attach to the belief in real things.

372. Logic. Chapter IV. Of Reality

A. MS., n.p., [c.1873], 14 pp.

Investigation involves both observation and reasoning. Reasoning as beginning with the most obvious premises and leading ultimately to one conclusion. Reality must be connected with this chain of reasoning at one extremity or the other. Nominalistic and realistic views of reality. The scientific presentation of the doctrines of logic requires the identity of the object of true knowledge with reality. The existence of things (as studied by physicists) depends upon their manifestability. Extending this conception to all real existence leads to an idealistic theory of metaphysics, once it is clearly understood that observation and reasoning are perpetually leading us toward certain final opinions whose objects may be said to have real existence.

373. Of Reality

A. MS., G-c.1873-1, pp. 1-20.

Published, in part, as 7.331n9 (p. 2) and 7.313n3 (pp. 8-9). Unpublished: investigation as involving both observation and inference, and ultimately the agreement of all investigators. How the conception of mind is acquired. Refutation of the claim that no distinction can be drawn between knowing and knowing that one knows. Does the mind have a direct experience of its own existence from the moment it is first conscious of anything? Signs and cognitions.

374. On Reality

A. MS., n.p., [c.1873], 4 pp.

What is the meaning of reality? To answer this question requires an answer to the question of meaning in general. As a start CSP asks whether a feeling can be said to have meaning. An analysis of feeling reveals its complexity.

375. On Reality

A. MS., n.p., [c.1873], 1 p.

The notion of nothing. Absurdity and unreality are two distinct cases of nothing.

376. [Time and Thought]

Amanuensis, G-c.1873-1, March 6, 1873, pp. 1-9.

Published in entirety: 7.346-353.

377. [Time and Thought]

Amanuensis, n.p., March 8, 1873, pp. 1-9.

Temporal succession of ideas as continuous. Definition of "continuum" as "something any part of which itself has parts of the same kind." Cf. MS. 376.

378. Logic. Chap. 5th

Amanuensis, G-c.1873-1, March 10, [1873], 6 pp.

Published in entirety: 7.354-357.

379. Logic. Chap. 6th

Amanuensis, G-c.1873-1, March 10, 1873, pp. 1-10; plus an exact copy (pp. 1-8) in another hand [Zina Fay Peirce?].

Published (pp. 5-6) as 7.336n. Omitted from publication: the three elements of signs. The nature of the causal connection between a thought and the thing to which it is related. Reality and figment: Reality is the most general of expressions (even a figment is a reality when considered in itself and not as the representation of something else). What is real or what exists must be an object of thought, because it is impossible to have a conception of anything which is not an object of thought. That is, the attempt to discover a word which expresses a thing that exists without, at the same time, implying that that thing is a possible object of thought results in a contradictory (or meaningless) expression.

380. Logic. Chap. 7. Of Logic as a Study of Signs

Amanuensis, n.p., March 14, 1873, 4 pp.

The three conditions for the existence of a sign.

381. On the Nature of Signs

Amanuensis, n.p., 6 pp. and 7 pp. of two drafts.

The six-page manuscript: the three conditions for the existence of a sign. The seven-page manuscript: Kant's Categories of the Understanding; Medieval logic and the division of conceptions into first and second intentions; the threefold division of representation and terms.

382. Logic. Chap. 9th

Amanuensis, n.p., March 15, 1873, 12 pp.

Ambiguity and indeterminacy. Principles of formal logic. Equiparence of the copula.

383. Chap. X. The Copula and Simple Syllogism

Amanuensis, n.p., [c.1873], 6 pp.

All reasoning is reducible to syllogistic form and is dependent upon the transitive character of the copula. Formal properties of the copula.

384. Chap. XI. On Logical Breadth and Depth

Amanuensis, n.p., [c.1873], 9 pp.

First and second intentions. "Breadth" and "depth" defined. Also defined, "informed breadth" and "informed depth." A distinction is made between essential and substantial breadth and depth.

385. Logic. Chapter ———. The List of Categories

A. MS., n.p., [c.1873], 2 pp.

Reality and Being distinguished. Doubt involves something fixed and something vague. The thing about which we doubt is fixed; what is in doubt about the thing is vague.

386. Chap. VIII. Of the Copula

A. MS., n.p., [c.1873], 3 pp., plus another page with the same title.

The properties of the copula summarized.

387. Chap. IX. Of Relative Terms

A. MS., n.p., [c.1873], 8 pp.

A study of the properties of individuals, i.e., the properties individuals would possess if they existed. General relative terms. Logic as the science of identity.

388. On Representations

A. MS., n.p., [c.1873], 3 pp.

"Representation" defined. The three things essential for having representation.

389. On Representation

Amanuensis, corrected by CSP, n.p., [c.1873], 10 pp.

The three things which are essential for representation: Representation must have qualities independent of its meaning, it must have real causal connection to its object, and it must address itself to some mind.

390. Chapter IV. The Conception of Time essential in Logic

A. MS., n.p., July 1, 1873, 4 pp.

The conception of a logical mind presupposes a temporal sequence among ideas, for every mind which passes from doubt to belief involves ideas which follow one another in time. The flow of time is not by discrete steps, but is continuous. "Continuum" defined.

391. Chapter IV. The Conception of Time essential in Logic

A. MS., n.p., July 2, 1873, 8 pp.

MS. 391 is an expanded version of MS. 390.

392. Chapter V. That the significance of thought lies in its reference to the future

A. MS., G-c.1873-1, 4 pp.

Published in entirety: 7.358-361.

393. (Pract. Logic, Lect. Logic)

   A. MS., n.p., n.d., 3 pp.

   Opinions tend toward ultimate settlement. The proposition that there is some reality which determines opinions but does not depend upon them admits of two interpretations, but on either interpretation, the real is ideal. Reality and actualities.

394. Memorandum. Probable Subjects to be Treated of

   Amanuensis, n.p., n.d., 1 p.

395. Third Lecture

   A. MS., n.p., n.d., 2 pp.

   The question, What is thought? can only be answered by means of thought.

396. [Fragments]

   A. MS., n.p., n.d., 13 pp.

   Among the topics treated here are the following: relative and absolute terms; negation; the syllogism; cognition and inconceivability; thought and signs; feelings, the continuum of feelings, and time.

GRAND LOGIC 1893
(*"How to Reason: A Critick of Arguments"*)

* 397. How to Reason: A Critick of Arguments. Advertisement

   A. MS., G-1893-5, pp. 1-12.

   Only the 1st paragraph of p. 1 was published: *Collected Papers,* Vol. 8, p. 278. Unpublished: a general summary of CSP's work in philosophy and logic, along with a short account of the significance of his efforts in logic, and a discussion of continuity as ubiquitous mediation.

398. [How to Reason: A Critick of Arguments. Advertisement]

   A. MS., G-1893-5, pp. 1-11.

   Only the last 4 paragraphs (pp. 10-11) published: *Collected Papers,* Vol. 8, pp. 278-279. Unpublished: a summary of CSP's work in philosophy and logic which is more detailed than the one found in MS. 397. Other subjects dealt with but not published are the analysis of propositions, the statistical syllogism, the conception of quantity and continuity, and the realism-nominalism issue.

399. How to Reason: A Critick of Arguments. Contents

   A. MS., G-1893-5, pp. 1-3, with variants.

   Pages 2-3 published: *Collected Papers,* Vol. 8, pp. 279-280. Only the title page was omitted.

400. Book I. Of Reasoning in General. Introduction. The Association of Ideas

   A. MS., G-1893-5, pp. 9-83, 17-19; plus two drafts (5 pp.) of "contents."

   Published in part as 7.388-450, except 392n[7]. Unpublished: pp. 14-51, with exception of proposition 3 on p. 23 which was published as 7.417n[21]. History of the doctrine of association which begins with Aristotle and continues with the English writers of the seventeenth and eighteenth centuries, e.g., Digby, Locke, Hume, Hartley, Gay, among others, and the nineteenth-century English, German, and American thinkers, e.g., James Mill, Hamilton, Bain,

LOGIC

Lewes, James, Herbart, Wundt. "Notwithstanding the writer's realism and realistic idealism, and consequent high appreciation of Schelling, Hegel, and others, and respect for German industry, he cannot but regard the English work in philosophy as far more valuable and English logic as infinitely sounder."

401. Book I. Logic in General. Introduction. The Association of Ideas
A. MS., n.p., 1893, pp. 9-11, incomplete.

402. The Association of Ideas
A. MS., n.p., 1893, pp. 2-13, with p. 3 missing.
The Principles of Association: the general rules in accordance with which one idea has a tendency to suggest another. Page 11 begins a Chapter II, which sets out to deal with the problem of time, memory, and experience.

*403. Division I. Formal Study of General Logic. Chapter I. The Categories
A. MS., n.p., 1893, pp. 16-29.
Association of ideas. Process of unification (the blending and spreading of ideas). Distinguishable grades in the process of unification. The conception of the present. Being and substance. The passage from being to substance is mediated by accident, whose threefold nature includes quality, relation, and representation. Quality is Firstness; relation, Secondness; representation, Thirdness. Primary qualities and feelings. Phenomenalism and the relativity of knowledge. The two great genera of relations: those whose ground is pre-scindible and those whose ground is not. Precision, or abstraction, distinguished from other modes of mental separation, e.g., discrimination and dissociation. Compare with "On a New List of Categories" [PAAAS series on logic (1867)]. See G-1867-1a.

404. The Art of Reasoning. Chapter II. What is a Sign?
A. MS., G-1893-5, pp. 31-46 (pp. 34, 42 missing).
Published, in part, as 2.281 (pp. 35-36), 2.285 (p. 41), 2.297-302 (pp. 43-45). Unpublished: reasoning as an interpretation of signs of some kind; the three different states of mind—feeling, reacting, thinking (pp. 31-34). Indices and icons (pp. 37-40). Reasoning as requiring a mixture of likenesses, indices, and symbols (p. 46).

405. Division II. Transcendental Logic. Chapter III. The Materialistic Aspect of Reasoning
A. MS., G-1893-5, pp. 47-54.
Published in entirety as 6.278-286.

406. Chapter IV. What is the Use of Consciousness?
A. MS., G-1893-5, pp. 55-58.
Published in entirety as 7.559-564.

407. Chapter V. The Fixation of Belief
A. MS. (and TS.), n.p., 1893, pp. 59-84; plus 1 p. ("Chapter IV. The Fixation of Belief").
A version of the article bearing the same title first published in the *Popular Science Monthly* (1877), as the first in a series of articles appearing under the general title "Illustrations of the Logic of Science." The original article of 1877 was published in the *Collected Papers* as 5.358-387, except 358n*, with revisions and notes of 1893, 1903, and c.1910. See G-1877-5a.

50

408. Division III. Substantial Study of Logic. Chapter VI. The Essence of Reasoning

A. MS., G-1893-5, pp. 85-180 (p. 163 missing) and a variant p. 85.

Published, in part, in two places: 4.21-52 (pp. 89-146, with deletions) and 7.463-467 (pp. 168-173). Unpublished: the early history and literature of logic (pp. 85-88). Experience, reality, and belief-habits; the inner and outer world of man's experience; the law of association and its principles (pp. 147-165).

409. Division III. Substantial Study of Logic. Chapter VI. The Essence of Reasoning

A. MS., G-1893-5, pp. 85-141 (pp. 109, 130 missing), with 8 pp. of variants.

Published, in part, as 4.53-56 (but not all of 56) and 4.61-79 (pp. 91-141, with deletions). The unpublished pages concern terminology mainly: term, concept, proposition, judgment, argument, and the operation of naming. As an aside, CSP's low opinion of the logical powers of the Germans.

410. Book II. Introductory. Chapter VII. Analysis of Propositions

A. MS., n.p., 1893, pp. 1-18; 1-19 (of a secretary's inaccurate copy).

Why should one want to reason? Reason versus instinct. Reasoning well requires an understanding of the theory of reasoning. The vocabulary of logic. Categorical and hypothetical propositions. "Every mother loves some child of hers" represented graphically. Nominalism and realism. Conjunctives.

411. Division I. Stecheology. Part I. Non Relative. Chapter VIII. The Algebra of the Copula

A. MS., n.p., 1893, pp. 171-234.

Material Implication. CSP introduces a new symbol $\top$ for the (his) symbol $-\!\!\!<$. All algebra based on simple definition of $\top$. On the infinite series of logical terms (logically necessary consequences). Five types of logical propositions. The crocodile paradox (dilemmatic reasoning). CSP regards logical algebra as important as an instrument for logical analysis, but of no great importance as calculus. Rules of logical aggregation and composition.

412. Division I. Stecheology. Part I. Non Relative. Chapter VIII. The Algebra of the Copula

Amanuensis, n.p.. 1893, pp. 20-84.

Second draft of MS. 411, but with no substantial changes.

413. Chapter IX. The Aristotelian Syllogistic

A. MS., G-1893-5, pp. 211-285.

Published, in part, as 2.445-460 (pp. 211-232, with deletions). Unpublished are CSP's comments on the contributions to philosophy of Hamilton, Kant, DeMorgan, and Aristotle as logicians. Importance of the syllogism, especially of the figures, in probable inference. The reduction of syllogistic forms. Natural classification of the moods. Formal fallacies, e.g., *ignoratio elenchi* and *petitio principii*. Semi-material fallacies, e.g., fallacies of ambiguity and erroneous particularization.

414. Chapter X. Extension of the Aristotelian Syllogistic

A. MS., G-1893-5, pp. 286-296.

Published as 2.532-535 with only the quotations from Hamilton on pp. 291-293 deleted.

415. De Morgan's Propositional Scheme
A. MS., n.p., 1893, pp. 297-313.

CSP improves upon De Morgan's system by expanding it and giving it graphical representation. De Morgan's views on modal logic and Christine Ladd-Franklin's scheme (from *Studies in Logic,* by Members of the Johns Hopkins University) examined. Also examined are Gilman's views on spurious propositions.

416. On a Limited Universe of Marks
A. MS., G-1893-5 and G-1883-7c, pp. 314-325.

This manuscript is a rewritten version of one of CSP's contributions (Note A: "Extension of the Aristotelian Syllogistic") to *Studies in Logic,* By Members of the Johns Hopkins University (edited by C. S. Peirce), 1883. What was published (2.517-531) is the 1883 "note," as rewritten in 1893 for Chapter X of the *Grand Logic.* The difference between the two papers is not substantial.

417. Chapter XI. The Boolian Calculus
A. MS., n.p., 1893, pp. 326-349.

Defense of "or" as allowing for "and." Definition of material implication. Examples from Mrs. Ladd-Franklin (in *Studies in Logic*). Compare with "On the Algebra of Logic: A Contribution to the Philosophy of Notation" (G-1885-3).

418. Book II. Division I. Part 2. Logic of Relatives. Chapter XII. The Algebra of Relatives
A. MS., n.p., 1893, pp. 350-372.

"If I have made any substantial improvement in logic, it is in the discovery of this manner of dealing with the imperfections of Boolians." Exhibiting and remedying imperfections of the Boolean calculus. Logic of relations, which, CSP says, he brought to essential completion in 1885 (G-1885-3). First and second intentional logic. Machines which are capable of solving problems in non-relative Boolean algebra, with an examination of the performance of one of them (Allan Marquand's, as reported in the *Proceedings of the American Academy of Arts and Sciences,* XXI. 303).

419. Chapter XIII. Simplification for Dual Relatives
A. MS., G-1893-5 and G-1883-7d, pp. 373-389, with a note that p. 376 was "struck out."

This manuscript is substantially the same as one of the contributions (Note B: "The Logic of Relatives") to the Johns Hopkins *Studies in Logic.* What was published (3.328-358) is the 1883 "note," with a marginal note and indications of the revisions of 1893 for the *Grand Logic.* New symbolism is introduced. Relatives are developed without Π or Σ.

420. Chapter XIV. Second Intentional Logic
A. MS., G-1893-5, pp. 390-394.
Published in entirety as 4.80-84.

421. Division II. Methodology. Chapter XV. Breadth and Depth
A. MS., G-1893-5 and G-1867-1e, pp. 395-438.
What was published (2.391-426) is "Upon Logical Comprehension and Extension" of *Proceedings of the American Academy of Arts and Sciences,* Vol. 7, November 3, 1867, with the revisions of c.1870 and 1893. What was pub-

lished as 2.427-430 is a supplement entitled "Terminology" (G-1893-7). In addition to being Chapter XV of the *Grand Logic*, this manuscript was also intended as Essay III of the *Search for a Method* (1893).

* 422. Methodology. The Doctrine of Definition and Division. Chapter XVI. Clearness of Apprehension

TS., G-1893-5 and G-1877-5b, pp. 439-452; A. MS., pp. 453-456, which continues 452 of TS.

What was published as 5.388-410 is the essay "How to Make our Ideas Clear" (*Popular Science Monthly*, Vol. 12, pp. 286-302, 1878), with the additions of 1893.

423. Book III. Quantitative Logic. Chapter XVII. The Logic of Quantity

A. MS., G-1893-5, pp. 1-124 (pp. 2, 102-103 missing); plus a complete and corrected copy of 125 pp., neither the copy nor the corrections in CSP's hand. Published, in part, as 4.85-152 (pp. 1-125, with omissions and with a marginal note).

424. Chapter XVIII. The Doctrine of Chances

TS., G-1893-5 and G-1877-5c, pp. 581-591.

What was published as 2.645-660 is the third article of the series "Illustrations of the Logic of Science" (*Popular Science Monthly*, Vol. 12, pp. 604-15, 1878), with corrections of 1893 and a note of 1910.

MINUTE LOGIC 1902-03

425. Minute Logic. Chapter I. Intended Characters of this Treatise (Logic)

A. MS., G-c.1902-2, pp. 1-170, with variants and a typewritten copy which differs only slightly from the original; pp. 1-50, with variants, of an incomplete first draft.

Publication (2.1-118) is from CSP's typewritten copy, with a few omissions consisting of repetitions and asides.

426. Chapter II. Prelogical Notions. Section I. Classification of the Sciences (Logic II)

A. MS., n.p., February 13, 1902, pp. 1-41, with 11 pp. of variants.

An earlier draft of MS. 427.

427. Chapter II. Prelogical Notions. Section I. Classification of the Sciences (Logic II)

A. MS., G-c.1902-2, begun February 20, 1902, pp. 1-291, with nearly 200 pp. of variants; pp. 97-125, 190-192, 196-197, 244, 271-273 from alternative drafts.

A later draft of MS. 426. Published, in part, as 1.203-283 (pp. 1-123, with omissions), 7.374n10 (pp. 125-127), 7.279 (pp. 140-142), 7.362-363 and 7.366-385 (pp. 192-242). From the alternative drafts, pp. 190-192, 196-197, 271-273 were published as 7.364, 7.365, and 7.386-387 respectively. Omitted from publication are the following: notions of family, genus, species; dynamics as a suborder of Nomological Physics; statics; theories of the constitution of matter and nature; hydrodynamics; dynamics of a particle and of rigid bodies; subfamilies of rigid dynamics; molar, molecular, and ethereal physics; cross-classification; subdivision of special nomological physiognosy; crystallography; "diagrammatic" history of astronomy; minerology; chemistry; the natural metric system; suborders of physiotaxy; families of natural history; genera of biology; physiography; physiognosy; genera and species of astronomy; geognosy. From alternative drafts, the following were omitted: the Genus language; classifications of language; races of mankind and the origin of the white race; resemblances between Polynesian and Semitic languages; the question of a common linguistic ancestor; Basque; agglutinative speech.

428. Chapter II. Section II. Why Study Logic? (Logic II, ii)

A. MS., G-c.1902-2, pp. 1-128, with 33 pp. of variants.

The second page is dated April 28, 1902; the hundred and second page, April 30, 1902. Published in entirety as 2.119-202.

429. Chapter III. The Simplest Mathematics

TS., for most part, G-c.1902-2, pp. 1-127.

Published as 4.227-323, with historical notes on signs and several theorems in algebra and logic omitted.

430. Chapter III. The Simplest Mathematics (Logic III)

A. MS., n.p., 1902, pp. 2-108 (p. 9 is missing), with many rewritten sections. Some of the pages of this manuscript are dated; page 4, for instance, is dated January 2, 1902. On postulates (footnote on the corruption of Euclid's text and the confusion between "axioms" and "postulates"). Principles of contradiction and of excluded middle. The development of Boole's logical algebra. Logical depth and breadth. Composition and aggregation: De Morgan and Jevons. Beginning with generals, logic requires notion of inference; its primary aim is criticism of inference. Definition of an "individual." Confusion of collective identity with individual identity. Algebra of the copula of inclusion. The meaning of the mathematical "is." Algebraical consequence: constituents of a consequence; standard and potential constituents; proximates of a consequence. Scriptibility. The "vital" definitions of the algebra. Distinction between collective and distributive applicability of a disjunction to "v." The distinction between several and joint applicability to "v." Close and loose combinations and their denial. Definition of the generalized copula of inclusion in five clauses. Theorems and rules of the algebra. In the alternative sections: existential graphs (pp. 14-68); explanation of CSP's notation for Boolean algebra (pp. 35-45); algebra of the copula, formal definitions of "if," "and," "or," employed in defining $\sim$; and more on consequence (pp. 56-76).

431. Chapter III. The Simplest Mathematics (Logic III)

A. MS., n.p., 1902, pp. 2-200 (p. 199 missing), including long alternative or rejected efforts.

Page 37 is dated January 5, 1902; another page, January 28, 1902. Two definitions of "mathematics" analyzed: (a) mathematics as the method of drawing necessary conclusions, and (b) mathematics as the study of the hypothetical states of things. Mathematics does not require ethics; logic does, however. Preliminary dissection of mathematics into several branches. The important rules, theorems, and demonstrations of dichotomic mathematics. Simplest mathematics is a two-valued system, but even though its subject is limited, it does enter as an element into the other parts of mathematics, and hence is important. In regard to trichotomic mathematics, it is asked, "how is the mathematician to take a step without recognizing the duality of truth and falsity?" Fundamental fact about the number three is its generative potency. Philosophical truth has its origin and rationale in mathematics. A chemical analogy. In one of the alternative sections, there is a lengthy account of CSP's dispute with Sylvester over who should receive credit for discovering the system of nonions.

432. Chapter IV. Ethics (Logic IV)
A. MS., n.p., [c.1902], pp. 1-8.
The start of a first draft. Moral virtues required in performing inductions. What constitutes a normative question? Pure ethics—philosophical ethics—regarded as a pre-normative science but of vital importance to the student of logic. Truth and reality.

433. Chapter IV. Ethics (Logic IV)
A. MS., G-c.1902-2, pp. 1-21.
Published in entirety as 1.575-584.

434. Chapter IV. Ethics (Logic IV)
A. MS., G-1902-2, pp. 12-234 (p. 12 follows the first eleven pages of MS. 433). Published, in part, as 6.349-352 (pp. 201-220). Unpublished: long footnote on the term "conscience," leading to eight rules having to do with the ethics of terminology and the governing of philosophical terminology. CSP proposes to list and examine twenty-eight conceptions or classes of supposed goods, e.g., the desirable in itself, but only gets as far as the fifteenth (all were taken from Greek philosophy, with Plato's conception of the ultimate good to have formed the basis of the fifteenth conception). At this point in the manuscript a long digression occurs which continues to the close. The digression concerns disputed points of Plato's life. In this connection, there is considerable material on the chronological order of the Platonic Dialogues as well as on Lutoslawski's researches. Sophistries in the *Sophist,* but Plato's definition of being as power approved. Various comments on the *Politicus* and *Timaeus.* For CSP, Plato's strength lies in his ethics, not in his metaphysics and logic.

DETACHED IDEAS ON VITALLY IMPORTANT TOPICS

435. On Detached Ideas in General, and on Vitally Important Topics as Such (1898)
A. MS., G-1898-1, pp. 1-35.
Lecture I: published as 1.649-677, with omissions. Discourse on admirable and contemptible qualities. The qualities most admired, e.g., devotion and courage, are instinctual; the contemptible qualities derive from reasoning. The origin and influence of the "mechanical philosophy." "But it is one of the great virtues of scientific method that the scientist need not be a deep thinker or even a cultivated mind. . . . Men of this sort believe in the mechanical philosophy."

436. Lecture I (1898)
A. MS., n.p., 1898, pp. 1-34 (pp. 6-9, 11-13, 15-26, 30, 33 missing).
Reason and instinct. The wise man in matters of greatest importance will follow, not his reason, but his heart. Reason and religion. The contention that metaphysics is a guide for the soul is humbug. Moreover, the talent for reasoning is as uncommon as the talent for music, and the cultivation of the first requires a greater effort with fewer immediate rewards. CSP's bitterness is not easily restrained. He advises against philosophy as a career, shows his

disdain of Harvard gentlemen and of publishers who refuse to publish treatises on logic on the ground that the author is not a university professor and that the work would not pay for itself.

437. Philosophy and the Conduct of Life (PL)

A. MS., G-1898-1, pp. 1-31.

Lecture I: published, in part, as 1.616-648 (pp. 1-16, 30-31). Unpublished material on the classification of the sciences and on the fact that every science grows into a more abstract science, one step higher on the classificatory scale. Asides on Plato.

438. Detached Ideas on Vitally Important Topics. Lecture II (TVI II)

A. MS., G-1898-1, pp. 1-23, incomplete, with 3 loose sheets (notes for lecture).

Selection published: 4.1-5. Deleted: pp. 1-4, 11-17, 18-22 on the relationship between philosophy and mathematics and between philosophy and the exact sciences, on the gross abuse of the word "realism," on the Peircean categories and the logic of relatives. CSP offers an explanation (suggested by a theorem of the logic of relatives that no polyads higher than triads are required to express all relations) of why his list of categories is complete. Co-discoverer, with De Morgan, of the logic of relatives, CSP introduces the reader to that logic by means of existential graphs.

439. Detached Ideas continued and the Dispute between Nominalists and Realists (NR)

A. MS., n.p., 1898, pp. 1-35, with a variant p. 24.

Peircean categories of Firstness, Secondness, Thirdness. The system of graphs is a consequence of CSP's study of the categories. Logic of relatives and the notion of generality (universality). The continuum as the true universal. Kant on continua. The question of reality. The nominalist-realist controversy. The tendency to think of nature as syllogizing, even on the part of the mechanist. But nature also makes inductions and retroductions. Infinite variety of nature testifies to her originality (or power of retroduction). That continuity is real and the significance of this fact for a philosophy of life. CSP's extreme realism lies in his acceptance of the view "that every true universal, every continuum, is a living and conscious being." On page 28, there is a marginal note signed "WJ" (William James?): "This is too abrupt along here. Should be more mediated to the common mind."

440. Detached Ideas. Induction, Deduction, and Hypothesis (DI)

A. MS., G-1898-1, pp. 1-37 (pp. 9-12 missing), plus 15 pp. of variants.

Only the four rules given on pp. 4-7 published as 7.494n[9]. The remainder concerns scientific and philosophic terminology, modern science and realism (the abuse of the term "realism"), the history of the discovery of the logic of relatives, the relationship of induction and retroduction to the syllogistic figures (induction as probable inference in the third figure; retroduction as probable inference in the second figure). A marginal note by "WJ" on p. 25.

441. Types of Reasoning (Ty)

A. MS., n.p., 1898, pp. 1-31 (p. 10 missing).

The relationship between logic and metaphysics. In order to enliven his lectures, CSP mentions his early interest in philosophy, and writes of the development of his thinking about logic. The controversy beween Philo and Diodorus. Scholastic doctrine of *Consequentia*. Hypothetical and categorical propositions and their logical equivalence. Induction, deduction, retroduction and the syllogistic forms. Induction as probable reasoning in the third figure.

442. The First Rule of Logic (FRL)

A. MS., G-1898-1, pp. 1-38, with 3 pp. of variants.

Published as 5.574-589, with omissions. Omitted were pp. 13, 18, 22-24, 36-38 on Alexandre Dumas (CSP's attitude somewhat disparaging), pure mathematics, and the notion that truth is ambiguous, e.g., that a proposition might be true in religion but false in philosophy. The theoretical and practical sense of "holding for true."

*443. Causation and Force (TC)

A. MS., G-1898-1, pp. 1-35, plus discarded pp. 13-15, 13-14, 20, 28, and 2 pp. with the titles "Time and Causation" (TC) and "Time and Causality."

Published in three places in the following order: 6.66-81; 7.518-523; 6.82-72. Only the introductory first paragraph was deleted.

444. Training in Reasoning (R)

A. MS., G-1898-1, pp. 1-9.

MSS. 444 and 445 published, with deletions and pages missing, under the title "Training in Reasoning," *The Hound and Horn* 2 (July-September 1929), 398-416. Common or liberal education and the art of reasoning. The three mental operations carried on in reasoning: observation, experimentation, and habituation (the power of taking on or discarding habit).

445. Training in Reasoning (TR)

A. MS., G-1898-1, pp. 17-39, plus 5 pp. of variants.

A discussion of the several kinds of observation and experimentation. Introspection. The categories connected with the three mental operations of feeling, willing, reasoning. The commonest fallacies in retroduction, deduction, and induction.

446. [Notes]

A. MS., n.p., [c.1898], pp. 1-7.

Possibly for the lecture on "Causation and Force." See MS. 443.

LOWELL LECTURES 1903

447. [Lecture I]

A. MS., n.p., 1903, pp. 1-2, incomplete, (from a notebook).

The beginning of an historical introduction to the subject of reasoning. Scientific form given to logic by Aristotle.

448. [Lecture I]

A. MS,. notebook, G-1903-2a, pp. 1-48.

Published as 1.591-610, with omissions. Unpublished: Present day science suffers from a malady whose source is an argument based on the notion of a "logisches Gefühl" as the means of determining whether reasoning is sound and whose conclusion is that there is no distinction between good and bad reasoning. This argument parallels another whose conclusion is that there is no distinction between good and bad conduct (pp. 1-12). Criticism of the defendant arguments and their premises—that it is unthinkable that a conclusion be found acceptable for any other reason than a feeling of logicality and that a line of conduct be adopted for any other motive than a feeling of pleasure (pp. 33-48).

449. [Lecture I]

A. MS., notebook, G-1903-2a, pp. 37-61.

Published, in part, as 1.611-615 and 8.176 (except 176n[3]) (pp. 37-49 and 51-53). Unpublished: criticism of Sigwart and the notion of "logisches Gefühl." Logic embraces methodeutic, critic, and the doctrine of signs (speculative grammar), with the ultimate purpose of the logician being the working out of a theory regarding the advancement of knowledge. Speculative grammar is neither psychology nor epistemology. *Erkenntnislehre* is mainly metaphysics. CSP agrees with those metaphysicians who insist that metaphysics must rest upon logic.

450. [Lecture I]

A. MS., notebook, n.p., 1903, pp. 1-26.

Improvement in reasoning requires, first of all, a study of deduction. For this, an unambiguous and simple system of expression is needed. The system in which reasoning is broken up into its smallest fragments by means of diagrams is the system of existential graphs, which CSP goes on to develop in terms of fourteen conventions.

451. [Lecture I]

A. MS., notebook, n.p., 1903, pp. 1-21.

Refutation of the view that there is no distinction between good and bad reasoning or, for that matter, good and bad conduct, because in both cases the distinction rests on feeling which, in turn, rests upon a confusion of the pleasure afforded by the inference with the approval of it.

452. [Lecture I]

A. MS., notebook, n.p., 1903, pp. 1-14.

The purpose of logic; the division of logic into speculative grammar, critic, and methodeutic. Why "methodeutic" as a name is preferred to "method" or "methodology." CSP's exposition begins with logical syntax.

453. [Lecture I]

A. MS., notebook, n.p., 1903, pp. 1-37.

Science hampered by the false notion that there is no distinction between good and bad reasoning. This notion related to the German idea that bases logic on feeling.

454. Lectures on Logic, to be delivered at the Lowell Institute. Winter 1903-1904. Lecture I

A. MS., notebook, n.p., 1903, pp. 1-26.

Existential graphs as a system for expressing any assertion with precision is not intended to facilitate but to analyze necessary reasoning, i.e., deduction. The system introduced by means of four basic conventions (here called "principles") and four rules ("rights") of transformation.

455. [Lecture II]

A. MS., notebook, n.p., 1903, pp. 1-31.

The first and third parts of an introduction to the alpha and beta parts of the system of existential graphs; MS. 456 is the second part.

456. Lowell Lectures. Lecture 2. Vol. 2

A. MS., notebook, n.p., 1903, pp. 40-66.

The second of a three-part introduction to the alpha and beta parts of existential graphs. For the first and third parts, see MS. 455.

457. CSP's Lowell Lectures of 1903. 1st Draught of 3rd Lecture

A. MS., notebook, n.p., begun October 2, 1903, pp. 1-10.

On a kind of decision procedure (in terms of alpha-possibility) for existential graphs. Cf. MS. 462.

458. Lowell Lectures. 1903. Lecture 3. 1st draught

A. MS., notebook, n.p., 1903, pp. 1-33.

Science, mathematics, and quantity. Pure mathematics (the science of hypotheses) is divided in accordance with the complexity of its hypotheses. Simplest mathematics is the system of existential graphs. Doctrine of multitude: Cantor's work on collections. Understanding requires some reference to the future—to an endless series of possibilities. Achilles and the Tortoise Paradox.

459. Lowell Lectures. 1903. Lecture 3

A. MS., notebook, n.p., 1903, pp. 1-41.

The words "Won't do" (by CSP) appear on the cover of the notebook. Definition of "mathematics." Denial that mathematics is reducible to logic. Alternative positions considered. Existential graphs; qualities; collection; multitude (Whitehead and Russell); substantive possibility.

460. [Lecture III]

A. MS., notebook, G-1903-2a, pp. 1-22.

Published, in part, as 1.15-26 (pp. 2-21). Gamma graphs, the third part of existential graphs, rendered intelligible by CSP's categories of Firstness, Secondness, Thirdness. And without the gamma graphs, multitude, infinity, and continuity are not easily explained. The peculiarity of gamma graphs is that they make abstractions (mere possibilities) and laws the subjects of discourse.

461. Lowell Lectures of 1903 by C. S. Peirce. Second draught of Lecture 3

A. MS., notebook, n.p., September 30, 1903, pp. 1-9; plus 2 cards which were found inserted among the unnumbered pages of the notebook.

Multitude; serial order of qualities; continuity.

462. CSP's Lowell Lectures of 1903. 2nd Draught of 3rd Lecture

A. MS., n.p., October 5, 1903, pp. 2-88 (pagination by even numbers only), incomplete.

Alpha part of existential graphs: permissible operations. The Beta part. Difference between alpha-impossibility and beta-impossibility summarized [cf. MS. 457]. The Gamma part concerns what can logically be asserted of meanings. The distinction between regulative and constitutive (in Kant). The logical doctrine called "Pragmatism." CSP claims that he has been unjustly called a sceptic, a second Hume. The "joke" about opium's dormitive virtue. Possibility and necessity (Locke's confusion). Qualities as mere possibilities. Relations are qualities of sets of subjects. Dyadic and triadic relations. All triadic relations are, more or less, thoughts. Doctrine of signs; icons, indices, and symbols.

463. Lowell Lectures of 1903. Lecture III. 2nd Draught

A. MS., notebook, n.p., 1903, pp. 11-17 (pp. 1-9 are mathematical notes and have nothing to do with the lecture).

On multitude and collection.

464. CSP's Lowell Lectures of 1903. Part 1 of 3rd draught of 3rd Lecture

A. MS., notebook, G-1903-2a, begun October 8, 1903, pp. 1-64, 68.

Published in two places: 1.324 and 1.343-349 (pp. 30-34 and 36-64 respectively). Note that part of 1.349 comes from page 68 of MS. 465, with p. 68 of that manuscript continuing p. 64 of this one. Omitted is a discussion of existential graphs, especially alpha and beta possibilities (pp. 1-30) and a discussion of the category of Firstness (pp. 34-36).

465. CSP's Lowell Lectures of 1903. 2nd Part of 3rd Draught of Lecture III

A. MS., notebook, G-1903-2a, October 12, 1903, pp. 68-126; A1-A8.

Published, in part, as 1.521-544 (pp. 68-126, with only the first and last paragraphs deleted). Pages A1-A8, unpublished, are mainly a reply to a listener's note asking, "What makes a Reasoning to be sound?" The note itself (dated November 27, 1903) has been inserted opposite p. A1. Also unpublished is material on the beta part of existential graphs.

466. Useful for 3rd or 4th?

A. MS., notebook, n.p., 1903, pp. 1-28, unfinished, with two p. 19's, both of which leave text intact.

Mathematics and logic; existential graphs introduced initially to illuminate the nature of pure mathematics, and then used in the discussion of multitude.

467. C. S. Peirce's Lowell Lectures for 1903. Lecture 4.

A. MS., 2 notebooks, G-1903-2a, pp. 1-96.

Two volumes comprise the fourth lecture, with the first volume entitled "Gamma Part of Existential Graphs." Volumes I and II (pp. 1-96) published as 4.510-529, with deletions. Deleted: brief history of exact logic, i.e., logic begun by De Morgan, including CSP's entitative and existential graphs (pp. 8-18). Opium's dormitive virtue; abstraction, including Hegel's abuse of the term (pp. 66-78).

468. CSP's Lowell Lectures of 1903. Introduction to Lecture 5

A. MS., notebook, n.p., December 4, 1903, pp. 1-9.

Gamma part of graphs continued (but quickly abandoned). Graphs of logical principles. Beta part.

469. Lowell Lectures. 1903. Lecture 5. Vol. 1

A. MS., notebook, n.p., 1903, pp. 2-74.

Doctrine of multitudes. Breadth and depth. Reference to Bertrand Russell's *Principles of Mathematics* in connection with the question, Is a collection which has but a single individual member identical with that individual or not? Cantor's system of ordinal numbers.

470. Lecture 5. Vol. 2

A. MS., notebook, n.p., 1903, pp. 76-158.

At the beginning CSP offers the following plan for his lecture series: "1. What makes a reasoning sound, 2. Existential Graphs, Alpha and Beta, 3. General Explanations, Phenomenology and Speculative Grammar, 4. Existential graphs, Gamma Part, 5. Multitude, 6. Chance, 7. Induction, 8. Abduction."

Collection and multitude; syllogism of transposed quantity; Fermatian reasoning; first and second ultranumerable multitude; continuity (pp. 78-122). Gamma graphs (pp. 124-138). The beginning of a lecture occasioned by the death of Herbert Spencer. Mentioning his personal encounters with Spencer, CSP writes on Spencer's evolutionism and his influence on philosophy generally (pp. 140-158).

471. [Lecture V]

A. MS., notebook, n.p., 1903, 10 pp.

On multitude and collection.

472. Lowell Lectures. 1903. Sixth Lecture. Probability

A. MS., 2 notebooks, G-1903-2a, pp. 2-130.

Published, in part, as 6.88-97 (pp. 8-62). Omitted: the relationship between logic and mathematics; independence of logic from metaphysics but not vice versa (pp. 2-7). Doctrine of chances: reference of the word "chance," in all its meanings, to variety; chance not a matter of ignorance but of the immense diversity of the universe; the tendency of this diversity to grow into uniformities; the conception of the "long run"; mathematical theory of probabilities; probability as requiring some objective meaning; CSP's advice to stop talking of probabilities in connection with the doctrine of chances and to talk instead of ratios of frequency; the difficulty most people have of understanding why it is not logically impossible that an event whose probability is zero should nevertheless occur; and, finally, Hume on miracles (pp. 62-130).

*473. C. S. Peirce's Lowell Institute Lectures. 1903. Seventh Lecture. Introduction Vol. I

A. MS., notebook, G-1903-2a, pp. 2-92.

Published, in part, as 7.110-130 (pp. 36-84). Omitted from publication: a discussion of deduction, induction, and abduction (pp. 2-35). The rationale of induction; Ockhamists versus Scotists; John Stuart Mill and the question of the uniformity of nature (pp. 85-92).

474. [Lecture VII]

A. MS., notebook, n.p., 1903, pp. 96-152.

Volume II of the Seventh Lecture. Law, uniformity, and variety. Critical comments on Mill's views on the uniformity of nature. For CSP it is obvious that nature is not uniform, but that variety is nature's leading characteristic. His realism is opposed to Mill's nominalism. The problem of induction, with solutions by Abbé Gratry, Laplace, and CSP.

475. C. S. Peirce's Lowell Lectures of 1903. Eighth Lecture. Abduction

A. MS., notebook, G-1903-2a, pp. 2-92 (pagination is somewhat irregular but the text is continuous).

Volume I. Published, in part, as 5.590-604 (pp. 28-92). Unpublished: the division of reasoning into deduction, induction, and abduction as deriving from Aristotle and Boole. The relationship of the three kinds of reasoning to the syllogism. A brief review of CSP's own reflections on the kinds of reasoning, noting articles he published and the errors and confusions these contain.

476. C. S. Peirce's Lowell Lectures of 1903. Eighth Lecture. Abduction. Vol. 2. Pythagoras

A. MS., notebook, G-1903-2a, pp. 94-168.

Only p. 95 published: 7.182n[7]. Unpublished are several examples of abduction. Life of Pythagoras as affording the prime example. CSP treats historical topics about which there has been considerable debate, claiming that his abductions have been verified—contrary to the expectations of historians—on five occasions.

477. Notes for a Syllabus of Logic

A. MS., notebook, n.p., June 1903, 17 pp., incomplete.

The syllabus was intended as a supplement to the Lowell Lectures of 1903. Ingredients of the phaneron. Phaneroscopic descriptions of consciousness. Aristotle's categories and predicables.

* 478. Syllabus of a course of Lectures at the Lowell Institute beginning 1903, Nov. 23. On Some Topics of Logic (Syllabus)

A. MS., G-1903-2b and G-1903-2d, pp. 1-168 (pp. 106-136 missing); a second title page; pp. 2-23 of a revised section; 69 pp. of variants; and a corrected copy of the printed syllabus.

A second version of the above title, "A Syllabus of Certain Topics of Logic," became the title of the pamphlet published by Alfred Mudge & Son, Boston, 1903. The pamphlet, however, is not an exact copy of the manuscript, several sections having been omitted. From the manuscript, pp. 1-26 and 137-149 were published in the pamphlet as pp. 1-14 and 15-20 respectively. Transformation rules for existential graphs are treated in an abridged form on pp. 20-23 of the pamphlet. For publication of the pamphlet in the *Collected Papers*, see G-1903-2b. Pages 43-46, 47-48, 48-50, and 50-89 published respectively as 2.274-277, 2.283-284, 2.292-294, and 2.309-331. Omitted from publication: sundry logical conceptions; Peircean categories of Firstness, Secondness, Thirdness; the possibility of certain kinds of separation of thought; dissociation, precision, discrimination; the categories in their forms of Firstness (phenomenology); the normative sciences and their interrelations; the division of logic into speculative grammar, logical critic, and methodeutic (pp. 27-42). Arguments as symbols; classification of arguments into deduction, induction, and abduction; etymology of deduction (pp. 89-105).

LOGICAL GRAPHS

479. On Logical Graphs (Graphs)

A. MS., G-c.1903-3, pp. 1-64; plus 30 pp. of several starts.

Published as 4.350-371, with deletions. Deleted: two complicated examples on pp. 5-8, 21-22 and some random comments, concerned chiefly with Eulerian diagrams and the history of logical graphs.

480. On Logical Graphs (Acad. Graphs)

A. MS., n.p., n.d., pp. 1-19, plus 3 pp. of variants.

Apparently an early form of what was to evolve into existential graphs. Formation and transformation rules of the system.

481. On Logical Graphs

A. MS., n.p., n.d., p. 1-10.

A system of graphs using "curves convex inwards," and presumed to be an improvement over Euler's diagrams and logical algebra.

482. On Logical Graphs

A. MS., n.p., [c.1896-98], pp. 1-30; plus 192 pp., partially ordered, but mainly a confusion of alternatives or rejects.

Includes partial drafts of several different papers (e.g., parts of an early draft of 3.468 ff.). Application of topology to logical graphs; examples and rules for interpretation; illative transformations.

483. On Existential Graphs

A. MS., n.p., [c.1901], pp. 1-9, plus 21 pp. of variants.

Several attempts to write the same pages. Basic conventions of the system of existential graphs. A reference to the *Monist* article of January 1897.

484. On Existential Graphs (F4)

A. MS., n.p., 1898, pp. 1-28; 11-15, 20.

Application of topology to logical graphs, followed by a development of the constitutive conventions of existential graphs. Remarks on the equivalence between existential graphs and familiar (ordinary) language. Elementary rules of illative transformation deduced from basic rules of existential graphs.

485. On Existential Graphs (EG)

A. MS., n.p., n.d., pp. 1-2, with at least three other attempts, none going beyond p. 2, and with another six attempts to write the same, but under the subtitle "Rules of (their) Illative Transformation."

486. Existential Graphs

Amanuensis, with marginal notes in CSP's hand, n.p., n.d., p. 1-10.

Twenty-three "Rules for their Illative (Logical) Transformation."

487. [Transformation Rules for Existential Graphs]

A. MS., n.p., n.d., 5 pp.

Seventeen rules are given, the last ten of which are derived from the first seven (or basic rules for existential graphs).

488. Positive Logical Graphs (PLG)

A. MS., n.p., n.d., pp. 1-6, plus 2 pp. of variants.

"Logical graphs" was the early name for what later became existential graphs. Definitions and conventions of the system.

489. Investigation of the Meaning $\boxed{\text{It Thunders}}$

A. MS., n.p., n.d., pp. 1-8.

An essay in which the meaning of the cut (or circle) in the example $\boxed{\text{It thunders}}$ is derived from certain basic rules for existential graphs.

490. [Introduction to Existential Graphs and an Improvement on the Gamma Graphs]

A. MS., notebook, G-1906-2.

CSP wrote on the cover of the notebook: "For the National Academy of Sci. 1906 April Meeting in Washington." Published, with omissions, as 4.573-584. Cf. MS. 480.

491. Logical Tracts. No. 1. On Existential Graphs

A. MS., n.p., [c.1903], pp. 1-12; 1-10; 1-3; 11 pp. of variants.

Logical and existential graphs (pp. 1-12). Basic definitions and principles of representation (pp. 1-10). Icon, index, symbol (pp. 1-3).

492. Logical Tracts. No. 2. On Existential Graphs, Euler's Diagrams, and Logical Algebra

A. MS., G-c.1903-2, pp. 1-141 (pp. 85 and 120 missing), with 104 pp. of variants; plus several alternative sections (pp. 3-41, with 5 pp. of variants; 18-41, with 4 pp. of variants; 19-39, with 15 pp. of variants).

Published, in part, as 4.418-509 (pp. 1-141, with omissions). Omitted: a translation of Euclid and a pair of complicated examples. From alternative sections: the relationship of symbols to past, present, and future; replicas; si signs, bi signs, and ter signs (pp. 19-39 of one section. Connexus and lines of identity; a selective connexus; phenomenology; representamens (icons, indices, symbols); si signs, bi signs, ter signs (pp. 18-41 of another section).

493. The Principles of Logical Graphics

A. MS., small red leather notebook, n.p., n.d.

Over one hundred-fifty examples of existential graphs illustrating "fundamental assumptions." Illative transformations. Rules of existential graphs: erasure and insertion, iteration and deiteration.

494. Existential Graphs: A System of Logical Expression

A. MS., standard size notebook, n.p., n.d.

A development of the existential graphs from "Constitutive Conventions" up to proofs of theorems, with good examples of graphs. Also three pages on a "Deduction of the Rule of Addition of Integers in the secundal system."

495. Logical Graphs

A. MS., small notebook, n.p., n.d.

Two attempts at a presentation of the existential graphs. Neither attempt gets beyond the "Constitutive Conventions."

496. [Notes on Graphs]

A. MS., notebook (Cyclone Composition Book), n.p., n.d.

497. [Notes on Graphs]

A. MS., small notebook, n.p., June 1897.

Note inscription on first page: "C. S. Peirce from Francis Lathrop 1897 June 15." Basic rules and commentary.

498. On Existential Graphs as an Instrument of Logical Research

A. MS., notebook (Harvard Cooperative), n.p., n.d.

Evidently prepared as an address to the American Academy. CSP mentions that existential graphs were discovered by him late in 1896, but that he was practically there some fourteen years before. The graphs were not invented to serve as a calculus, but to dissect the inferential process. Two puzzles examined with a view toward testing the system of graphs. One puzzle concerns the relation of signs to minds, and of communication from one mind to another. The other puzzle concerns the composition of concepts and the nature of judgment or, anti-psychologically speaking, propositions. Signs; reality; conventions of the system of existential graphs.

499. On the System of Existential Graphs Considered as an Instrument for the Investigation of Logic

A. MS., notebook (Harvard Cooperative), n.p., n.d.

The value of logical algebras. Logic as a calculus: CSP's minority report. The way in which the system of existential graphs serves the interest of the science of logic. Solutions suggested by the method of existential graphs to two problems, one of which concerns the relation of signs to minds and the other the composition of concepts. Existential relations of signs, from which is deduced a classification of signs and a nomenclature useful in describing existential graphs.

* 500. A Diagrammatic Syntax

A. MS., n.p., December 6-9, 1911, pp. 1-19.

A letter to Risteen on existential graphs.

501. [Worksheets on Graphs]

A. MS., n.p., n.d., 92 pp.

The worksheets are concerned mainly with two axioms: Something is scriptible and something is unscriptible.

502. Peripatetic Talks. No. 2 (PT2)

A. MS., n.p., n.d., pp. 1-4, plus 2 pp. of two other starts.

On the presuppositions of logic, e.g., that there is error, that—up to a point —it is eradicable, that there is some method of eradicating it. On the essential characteristics of belief.

503. Peripatetic Talks. No. 4 (PT4)

A. MS., n.p., n.d., pp. 1-6; 3-5.

On the five fundamental rules of existential graphs, and some of their consequences.

504. Peripatetic Talks. No. 6 (PT6)

A. MS., n.p., n.d., pp. 1-7.

On existential graphs. A defect in the system: There is no proper form for expressing the proposition that "There is some clergyman who praises every lawyer each to a doctor, so that for every possible distribution of such praises, there is a distinct clergyman who performs the praise."

505. Peripatetic Talks. No. 7 (PT7)

A. MS., n.p., n.d., pp. 1-2, with another 1 p. start.

The proposal is made to restate the fundamental principles of existential graphs in a new form. Three rules are listed and illustrated.

506. Existential Graphs

A. MS., small brown notebook, n.p., n.d.

List of rules: Rule XI— Rule XXIII. On back pages of notebook, CSP forms 62 words, beginning with the letter C, from the letters of the word "instruction," the purpose of which is not evident.

507. [Existential Graphs]

A. MS., n.p., n.d., 9 pp.

Beta and gamma graphs, with algebraic translations. Rules of transformation.

508. Existential Graphs. Rules of Transformation. Pure Mathematical Definition of Existential Graphs, regardless of their Interpretation (Syllabus B)

A. MS., n.p., n.d., pp. B1-B6.

An early draft of 4.414-417, together with some discussion of the gamma part of existential graphs.

509. Gamma Graphs
  A. MS., n.p., n.d., pp. 1-5.

510. [Notes on Graphs]
  A. MS., n.p., n.d., 12 pp.

511. (D)
  A. MS,. n.p., n.d., pp. D3-D7, with 7 pp. of variants.
  Hypotheses concerned with permissions and prohibitions and with possibility and necessity. These pages are part of MS. 3.

512. (SM)
  A. MS., n.p., n.d., 3 pp.
  These pages are part of MS. 2.

513. (FL)
  A. MS., n.p., n.d., pp. 27-98, incomplete and in some disorder, with missing sections and many alternatives and/or rejects.
  The first part of the manuscript is concerned with logical algebra. CSP's graphical method (pp. 52-78), with a note that "my cumbrous General Algebra, with all its faults, seems preferable." Pages 78 ff. present another algebraic system which is labelled the "Algebra of Dyadic Relatives" and which "seems to have fascinated Professor Schröder much more than it has me." The Algebra of Triadic Logic is mentioned ("But I have never succeeded in perfecting it").

* 514. [Fragments on Existential Graphs]
  A. MS., n.p., [1909], 53 pp.

LOGICAL ALGEBRA

515. On the First Principles of Logical Algebra (First Prin)
  A. MS., n.p., n.d., pp. 1-34, with 25 pp. of variants.
  Indecomposable transformations. Rules of transformation, with commutation and association developed from these rules. Implication; contradiction and excluded middle; aggregation and composition. Ethics of terminology applied to the case of Boole's creation of logical algebra. Transitive relations; incompossibility; identity and lines of identity. Propositions and signs; universal, particular, individual propositions; subject of propositions. Among the variants, the following topics occur: lines of identity; individual, definite, and singular terms; rules for existential graphs. Also the initial discussion of categoriology in connection with logical terms.

516. On the Basic Rules of Logical Transformation
  A. MS., n.p., n.d., pp. 1-51, plus 45 pp. of variants.
  First principles of Boolean algebra as extended by CSP to the logic of relatives with a view toward developing certain other notations. The system of symbols employed is that of existential graphs.

517. Καινὰ στοιχεῖα
  A. MS., n.p., n.d., pp. 1-85, with 81 pp. of variants.
  Part I. A reference to CSP's "New Elements of Mathematics," for which no publisher could be found, and mention of the loss of CSP's power of writing about logic in a mathematical way, which, in point of fact, he no longer

admires. Part II. On definition, postulate, axiom, corollary, theorem; signs, interpretants, entelechy; theory and practice; real relations and reactions; judgment and proposition; judgment and assertion; belief, affirmation, and judgment; doctrine of signs. Criticism of nominalism. The nature of "law"; event and fact; internal and external causes. Law signifies more than mere uniformity; it involves real connections. An improvement upon the traditional doctrine of causation. Symbols unable to exert force, but do govern things (for they are laws). A symbol signifies what it does, as in the feeling of "having been in a present situation before"—a case of accident, not of inherent necessity. Symbols as having grades of directness to the limit of being their own significations, and as having the power to reproduce themselves and to cause real facts. Reality as the limit of the endless series of symbols. Symbols and language, with language unable to provide a basis for logic. "How the constitution of the human mind may compel men to think is not the question; and the appeal to language appears to me to be no better than an unsatisfactory method of ascertaining psychological facts that are of no relevancy to logic. But if such appeal is to be made (and logicians generally do make it, in particular their doctrine of the copula appears to rest solely upon this) it would seem that they ought to survey human languages generally and not confine themselves to the small and extremely peculiar group of Aryan speech."

518. [The Regenerated Logic]

A. MS., G-1896-6a, pp. 1-29, 17-21, 25-28.

This is the manuscript of the "The Regenerated Logic" (*Monist*, Vol. 7, pp. 19-40, 1896) which was reprinted as 3.425-455.

519. Studies in Logical Algebra

A. MS., notebook, n.p., May 20-25, 1885.

520. [Schroeder's Logical Algebra]

A. MS., n.p., n.d., pp. 1-27, incomplete; 41-44; plus 5 pp. of variants.

521. Schroeder's Logic of Relatives

A. MS., n.p., n.d., pp. 1-33, with 19 pp. of variants.

* 522. Notes on Schroeder's Logic of Relatives

A. MS., small red notebook, n.p., n.d.; and 1 p. continuing the comparison of CSP's symbolism with Schroeder's begun on pp. 38-41 of the notebook.

523. Notes on Schroeder's 3rd Volume

A. MS., n.p., n.d., 2 pp.

524. [Schroeder and the Logic of Relations]

A. MS., n.p., n.d., pp. 1-9.

*525. [Fragment on Schroeder]

A. MS., n.p., n.d., p. 10.

* 526. Logic of Relatives. No. 2

A. MS., n.p., n.d., pp. 1-4; plus pp. 2-4 of Paper I.

Papers I and II are part of a series announced by the Pike County Press, Milford, Pa., 1895-96, but never published.

* 527. On the Algebra of Logic

A. MS., n.p., n.d., 5 pp. of a manuscript draft; 12 pp. of a typed draft (corrected by CSP); a reprint of "On the Algebra of Logic: A Contribution to the Philosophy of Notation" (G-1885-3); and 2 pp. of fragments.

Reprint of an article for the *American Journal of Mathematics*, Vol. 7, No. 2, 1885. Published again as 3.359-403, except 369n† (p. 230), with an undated marginal note, 384n[1].

528. On the Algebra of Logic
Reprint, G-1880-8.

Reprint of an article for the *American Journal of Mathematics*, Vol. 3, 1880. Published again as 3.154-251, except 154n[1] and 200n* (p. 128), with an editor's marginal corrections and with the revisions of 1880, c.1882, and undated.

*529. Description of a Notation for the Logic of Relatives, resulting from an Amplification of the Conceptions of Boole's Calculus of Logic
Reprints, G-1870-1.

Two reprints from *Memoirs of the American Academy of Arts and Sciences* (communicated January 26, 1870). One reprint is annotated by CSP; the other contains marginal notes, not by CSP. Published again as 3.45-149, except 45n*, with revisions from CSP's own copy.

530. A Proposed Logical Notation (Notation)
A. MS., n.p., [c.1903], pp. 1-45; 44-62, 12-32, 12-26; plus 44 pp. of shorter sections as well as fragments.
Ethics of terminology. The history of logical terms and notations, and CSP's recommendation of "the best algebraical signs for logic." On the Stoic division of hypothetical propositions. CSP's division of hypothetical propositions. Graphs, algebra of dyadic relations, linear associative algebra, nonions.

*531. Brief Account of the Principles of the Logic of Relative Terms
A. MS., n.p., n.d., 13 pp. (fragmentary).
Explanation of the three kinds of logical terms: absolute, simple relative (dyadic), and conjugative (triadic or higher). The logical copula.

532. The Logic of Relatives, Qualitative and Quantitative
A. MS., n.p., [c.1885], 13 pp. and 7 pp. of two drafts; plus 7 pp. of fragments. Two drafts distinguishable, the shorter of which has the title "The Logic of Relations, Qualitative and Quantitative." Algebraic notation explained, and principal rules of transformation, with proofs, provided. Its advantage over the Boolean algebra consists in the fact that it can do everything the Boolean algebra does without employing any superfluous symbols.

533. On the Formal Classification of Relations
A. MS., n.p., [1880's], 13 pp. (fragmentary).
Different starts on the same problem of formal classification. The classification of relatives with respect to single elements, pairs of elements, continuum of elements, and infinity of elements.

534. The Logic of Relatives
A. MS., n.p., n.d., 6 pp.
The classification of relations with respect to the two broad classes of logical and real. Under logical relations, CSP distinguishes four classes: incompossibility, identity, otherness, coexistence. Under real relations, he distinguishes the following: aliorelations, concurrencies, anti-aliorelations, anti-concurrencies, variform relations.

535. [A Boolean Algebra with One Constant]
A. MS., G-c.1880-1, 7 pp.
Published in entirety: 4.12-20.

*536. Dual Relatives
A. MS., n.p., 1889, 17 pp.
Several attempts at the same paper. Distinction between logical and real relations. The four principal logical relations and the five classes of real relations. Boolean algebra. Cf. MS. 533.

537. An Elementary Account of the Logic of Relatives
TS., n.p., n.d., 10 pp. of which some are duplicates.

538. Divisions and Nomenclature of Dyadic Relations (Dy. Rel.)
A. MS., n.p., [c.1903], pp. 1, 3-6, 9-12, 15, 19, 21-23, 29-30, and variants.
Earlier draft of MS. 539. See G-1903-2c.

539. Nomenclature and Divisions of Dyadic Relations (Syllabus)
A. MS., n.p., [c.1903], pp. 106-135 (p. 134 missing).
Modal and existential dyadic relations. See G-1903-2c.

540. Nomenclature and Division of Triadic Relations, as far as they are determined (Syllabus)
A. MS., n.p., n.d., pp. 134-155, plus 7 pp. of variants.
Provisional division of triadic relations into relations of comparison, performance, and thought. The three correlates of any triadic relation. Doctrine of signs: classes of signs.

541. (Syllabus 7)
A. MS., n.p., n.d., 1 p.

542. (Class of Dyadic Rel.)
A. MS., n.p., n.d., pp. 2-4.

543. [Triadic Relations]
A. MS., n.p., n.d., pp. 29-37 (3 folded sheets).
Reduction of tetradic relations. CSP maintains that every relation higher than triads is resolvable into a combination of triadic relations, and he conjectures that Royce holds the position that every dyadic relation is really a triadic one.

544. The Logic of Relations
A. M.S., n.p., n.d., pp. 1-9, plus 6 pp. of variants.
The three grades of clearness. Relations in their different grades of clearness.

545. [Notes on the Logic of Relatives]
A. MS., n.p., n.d., 10 pp.

546. Comments on Cayley's "Memoir on Abstract Geometry" from the point of view of the Logic of Relatives
A. MS., n.p., n.d., 5 pp.

547. Logic of Relatives
A. MS., n.p., n.d., 18 pp.
An attempt to state the main results of the work of Augustus De Morgan

and A. B. Kempe. The remainder of the paper is fragmentary but involves, in part, a statement and proof of the principles of nonrelative logic; for example, those of identity, *modus ponens,* and commutation.

548. Logic of Relatives

A. MS., notebook, n.p., n.d.

Association formulae. The external product of pairs. The converse. Relations of combination of four terms. Axioms of number. Relative of simple correspondence.

549. [Algebra of Logic]

A. MS., n.p., [c.1882-83], pp. 1-10.

Reference to a note by Mrs. Ladd-Franklin on the Constitution of the Universe (JHU *Studies in Logic,* p. 61). Principle of excluded middle. Cf. MS. 560.

550. [Algebra of Logic]

A. MS., n.p., n.d., 2 pp.

Ascertaining by algebra whether the answer to any question, as "Whether Elijah was caught up in heaven," is contained in what we already know.

551. A Problem in Testimony

TS., n.p., n.d., 4 pp.

The solution to a problem found in Boole's *Laws of Thought.* CSP's solution is, in effect, the same as Boole's though expressed differently.

552. [Relative and Non-relative Terms]

A. MS., n.p., n.d., 5 pp.

553. [On the Algebra of Relatives]

A. MS., n.p., n.d., 33 pp.

Various pages for a proposed book on logic, mostly on the algebra of relatives. Other topics covered are logical graphs, induction, deduction, and the statistical syllogism (probability).

554. [Logic of Relatives]

A. MS., n.p., n.d., 4 pp.

555. [Logic of Relatives]

A. MS., n.p., [1892?], 18 pp.

556. [Logic of Relatives]

A. MS., n.p., n.d., sections of 12 pp., 8 pp., and 3 pp.

557. [Logic of Relatives]

A. MS., n.p., n.d., 21 pp.

*558. [Logic of Relatives]

A. MS., n.p., n.d., pp. 14-28.

559. [Logical Algebra]

A. MS., n.p., n.d., 121 pp.

Notational conventions. The introduction of superfluous elements into algebra for purposes of balance and homogeneity. Rules of algebraical procedure. The three laws of thought: identity, contradiction, and excluded middle. Logic and the uses of ordinary language. Aristotle's propositional forms.

560. [Logical Algebra]
A. MS., n.p., n.d., pp. 1-27, incomplete.
Principle of excluded middle. Reference to G-1880-8 and an attempt to show that a logical algebra can be constructed without the special signs Σ and Π as quantifiers. Cf. MS. 549.

561. The Boolian Calculus
A. MS., n.p., n.d., 2 pp.
Boolean algebra and the problem of continuity.

562. Note on the Boolian Algebra
A. MS., n.p., n.d., pp. 1-4.

563. [An Improvement on Boole's Treatment of the Function]
A. MS., n.p., n.d., pp. 1-4.

564. Boolian Algebra. First Lecture
A. MS., n.p., n.d., 8 pp. (fragmentary).
Introductory remarks to a lecture on Boole with discussions of improvements (by other logicians) of the Boolean algebra.

565. Chapter II. Interpretation of Logistic
A. MS., n.p., n.d., 10 pp.

566. Chapter III. Development of the Boolian Notation
A. MS., n.p., n.d., 1 p.

567. [A Note to "On the Algebra of Logic: A Contribution to the Philosophy of Notation" (G-1885-3)]
A. MS., G-1885-3 (c.1885), 47 pp., and a crumbling copy (not in CSP's hand) on the same subject. See sup(2)G-1885-3.
Published in entirety as 3.403A-403M.

568. Chapter III. Development of the Notation, begun
A. MS., n.p., n.d., 2 pp.

569. [Algebraical. Rules to which Sign ——< is Subject]
A. MS., n.p., n.d., pp. 1-6; 1-4, with a variant p. 4.

* 570. Sketch of the Theory of Non-Associative Multiplication
A. MS., n.p., n.d., pp. 1-5, incomplete.

571. #3. Logical Addition and Multiplication
A. MS., n.p., n.d., pp. 1-6.

572. [Non-Commutative Multiplication and other Topics]
A. MS., n.p., n.d., 15 pp.

573. [Logical Algebra]
A. MS., n.p., n.d., 28 pp.
Algebra of the copula. Special modification of the Boolean algebra. The faults of ordinary language as an instrument of logic. Ordinary language is more pictorial than diagrammatic, serving well the purposes of literature but not of logic.

* 574. [Notes on Logical Algebra]
A. MS., n.p., n.d., 45 pp.
Negative and converse. Fundamental formulae of converse. Copulas.

71

575. [Notes on Logical Algebra]

A. MS., n.p., n.d., 50 pp.

These pages are devoted mainly to the copula of inclusion. Brief comments on the uses of logical algebra and on the alleged connection between logical algebra and the doctrine of the quantification of the predicate.

576. Of the Copulas of Algebra

A. MS., n.p., April 27, 1871, 8 pp.

577. Algebra of the Copula

A. MS., n.p., n.d., 7 pp., representing four starts.

578. Algebra of the Copula

A. MS., n.p., n.d., 1 p.

579. Algebra of the Copula

A. MS., n.p., n.d., 76 pp.

580. The Mathematics of Logic

A. MS., n.p., n.d., 1 p.

Various ways of expressing inclusion. CSP introduces a new sign of inclusion: $\overline{A|}$ B.

581. Notes on Logic

A. MS., notebook, n.p., 1902.

On the demonstrative part of arithmetic; the formal Boolean; haecceity.

582. Boolian Algebra

A. MS., n.p., n.d., 1 p.

583. Notes on History of Algebraical and Logical Signs

A. MS., n.p., n.d., 6 pp.

MISCELLANEOUS 1869-1913

584. Lectures on British Logicians. Lecture I. Early Nominalism and Realism

A. MS., G-1869-2, pp. 1-14; 1-17 ("Lectures on British Logicians"); 2 pp. ("List of British Logicians").

The first of a series of fifteen lectures on "British Logicians," given by CSP at Harvard during 1869-70 at the request of the President of Harvard. Published, in part, as 1.28-29 and 1.30-34 (pp. 2-4 and 6-11 respectively). Unpublished are CSP's reflections on the history of logical controversies of the medieval period and other reflections, mainly on Scotus Erigena (pp. 1, 5, 12-14). Various definitions of "logic"; distinction between psychological and logical questions; Alcuin; Aristotle's "Organon" (pp. 1-17).

585. Ockam

A. MS., notebook, n.p. [1869]; plus another notebook ("Abstract of Occam's Summa Logices").

The history of logic. Nominalism and realism, with comments on Francis Bacon and J. S. Mill.

* 586. Whewell

A. MS., notebook, n.p., [1869].

587. Notes for Lectures on Logic. To be given 1st Term. 1870-71
A. MS., notebook, n.p., 6 pp.

Problem of meaning and truth. Meaning distinguished both from the sign itself and from the thing signified. The agreement of meaning and reality. How can two things as incommensurable as meaning and reality be said to agree?

588. Preface
A. MS., G-1883-7a, 6 pp.; plus 6 pp. of an earlier draft.

The preface is to the Johns Hopkins University *Studies in Logic*.

589. The Critic of Arguments. III. Synthetical propositions a priori
A. MS., G-1892-1b, 52 pp.

This is presumably the third paper of *The Open Court* series of 1892 of which only the first two papers were published in *The Open Court*. Published, in part, as 4.187n[1] (pp. 5-8). Omitted from any publication: geometrical propositions and the notion of synthetic propositions *a priori*. CSP rejects the view that, while arithmetical propositions are analytic, geometrical ones are synthetic. Properties of number: Numbers are infinite, and the Fermatian inference is applicable to the whole collection of them. Counting.

590. The Critic of Arguments. III
A. MS., n.p., 1892, 23 pp., plus 16 pp. of another draft and 6 pp. of variants.
Mathematical propositions *a priori*.

591. [Critic of Arguments. IV]
A. MS., n.p., 1892, 11 pp.

592. A Search for a Method. Essay I
Printed Article (annotated), G-1893-6 and G-1867-1b.

This is the printed article of 1867, "On the Natural Classification of Arguments," together with photostats of the missing pages and with additions and corrections of 1893. 2.461-561 is the 1867 article with the additions and corrections of 1893; that is, Essay I of "A Search for a Method."

593. [A Search for a Method. Essay VI]
Printed Article, G-1893-6 and G-1868-2c, pp. 249-264.

This is the printed article of 1868, "Grounds of Validity of the Laws of Logic," along with the corrections found in the margins of the pages of the article. 5.318-357 is the 1868 article with the corrections of 1893; that is, Essay VI of "A Search for a Method."

594. [A Search for a Method: Fragments]
A. MS., n.p., 1893, 131 pp.

One page has the title: "The Quest of a Method. Essay I. The Natural Classifications of Arguments." Among the topics found in these pages are questions of terminology, the algebra of the copula, forms of propositions, and the analysis of reasoning.

*595. Short Logic
A. MS., G-c.1893-3, pp. 1-32, 33-38; plus 14 pp. of variants.

Selections published as follows: 2.286-291 (pp. 6-13); 2.295-296 (pp. 14-16); 2.435-443 (pp. 23-29, with the omission of p. 25); 7.555-558 (pp. 29-32). Unpublished are remarks on elementary philology and the definition of "logic," along with some historical footnotes.

596. Reason's Rules (RR)

A. MS., G-c.1902-3, pp. 1-47, with 11 pp. of variants.

Published, in part, as 5.538-545 (pp. 21-45). Omitted is a dialogue between author and reader, with an aside about the Hegelian dialectic. The various extra-firm beliefs which the reader has about reasoning and belief itself: the reader's *logica utens*. Doubt, its derivation and the psychological uneasiness associated with it. Doubt is always more or less conscious, but this is not true of belief. That a man may be quite unaware of his belief is illustrated by the Northern reaction to the South's attack upon Fort Sumter. Cf. MS. 598.

597. Reason's Rules (RR)

A. MS., n.p., [c.1902], pp. 1-6.

On what reasoning is.

598. Reason's Rules (RR)

A. MS., n.p., [c.1902], pp. 1-10, with 8 pp. of variants.

The initial or present beliefs of the reader. CSP pleads for the adoption of the principle that what is beyond control is beyond criticism or, more simply stated, do not doubt what cannot be doubted. Examples of beliefs which cannot be doubted: beliefs in what is before the eyes, the existence of persons other than oneself, memory. Cf. MS. 596.

599. Reason's Rules (RR)

A. MS., n.p., [c.1902], pp. 4-45, 31-42, and 8 pp. of fragments.

The nature of a sign. Propositions as the significations of signs which represent that some icon is applicable to that which is indicated by an index. The non-existence of propositions: propositions as merely possible. How truth and falsehood relate to propositions. Meaning as the character of a sign. Meaning and value are related: meaning as the value of a word (or the value of something for us is what that something means to us). The reference of meaning to the future.

600. (RR)

A. MS., n.p., [c.1902], 3 loose sheets, numbered 5, 35, and 36.

Critic of criticism.

601. (L)

A. MS., G-undated-13, later than the *Minute Logic,* but before 1908, pp. 1-33, with 9 pp. of variants; pp. 10-31, with 7 pp. of variants.

Published, in part, as 7.49-52 (pp. 1-9). Unpublished: the meaning of "dynamical"; the distinction between relation and relationship; speculations on the survival of the human race and on the possibility of life—similar to human life—on other planets (pp. 10-33). The classification of the sciences, based upon the distinction between theoretical and practical science (pp. 10-31).

602. On Classification of the Sciences (M)

A. MS., n.p., later than the *Minute Logic,* but before 1908, pp. 1-16.

The general classificatory scheme of the sciences. The threefold nature of inquiry. The normative sciences of esthetics, ethics, and logic. The nature of practical science.

603. (N)

A. MS., G-undated-13 [1905-06?], pp. 1-47, with 10 pp. of variants.

Published, in part, as 7.77-78 (pp. 20-29). Unpublished: the place of logic among the sciences; the fact that logic is a theoretical, not practical, science, even in respect to its methodeutic division (pp. 1-19). The relationship between logic and psychology, with CSP's opposition to the "psychological logicians" stated at some length (pp. 30-47).

604. Ch. I. Ways of Life (L)

A. MS., n.p., n.d., pp. 1-5.

Three types of men: men of sentiment (e.g., artists), practical men, and the unselfish seekers after truth.

605. Chapter II. On the Classification of the Sciences (Lii)

A. MS., n.p., n.d., pp. 1-17; plus pp. 1-2 ("Chapter II. The First Division of Science").

Distinction between theoretical and practical science. The heuretic sciences.

606. Chapter III. The Nature of Logical Inquiry (Liij)

A. MS., n.p., [1905-06?], pp. 1-29, with 2 pp. of variants.

"Maiotic" method of Socrates. The Athenian Schools and the emergence of Aristotle. Why the logical treatises of Aristotle have been called the "Organon." Discussion of the point of view that logic is a practical science, with notes on the history of this point of view. Aristotle's distinction between practical science and art. Methodeutic is not a practical science.

607. Chapter III. The Nature of Logical Inquiry (Liij)

A. MS., n.p., [1905-06?], pp. 1-9.

Aristotle's distinction between practical science and art. However, in spite of Aristotle's well-earned reputation as a philosopher, he has no conception of logic as a unitary study. Utilitarian tendencies in English logicians from Thomas Wilson to John Venn.

608. Chapter III. The Nature of Logical Inquiry (Liii)

A. MS., n.p., [1905-06?], pp. 1-3.

Dedekind and Benjamin Peirce on the relationship between logic and mathematics. Is logic mathematics?

609. Chapter I. What Logic is (Logic)

A. MS., n.p., September 23-28, 1908, pp. 1-23, plus 2 rejected pp.

The need for technical terminology. Local sign (after Lotze's "Lokal-zeichen"). Comparison of Kant and Leibniz as logicians. The first impressions of sense are caused by real external objects. CSP thinks of himself as a Berkeleyian.

610. Logic. Introduction (Logic. Introd.)

A. MS., n.p., October 24-November 28, 1908, pp. 1-10, plus 4 pp. dated October 22 and 24.

Introductory remarks to a textbook on logic, which will be concerned with both theory and practice. A discussion of literary and philosophical styles.

611. Chapter I. Common Ground (Logic)

A. MS., n.p., October 28-31, 1908, pp. 6-25.

That which is named by a noun is everything that could possibly be said of it. Definition of "nothing" as "that which is indistinct in being." Indefinite descriptions. Logical departures from grammatical usage. The term "phaneron" introduced. The nineteenth-century German logicians.

612. Chapter I. Common Ground (Logic)

A. MS., n.p., November 2-15, 1908, pp. 6-32, 32, 32-38; plus 19 pp. of variants. Phaneron. Definition of "determination." Property of word "after." Meaning as the general name of any sort of sign. Proper names.

613. Logic. Book I. Analysis of Thought. Chapter I. Common Ground. (Logic I.i)

A. MS., n.p., November 16-18, 1908, pp. 1-4.

The basis of common understanding required before an author's mind can act upon his reader's. Moral conduct: conduct that is approved upon reflection.

614. Logic. Book I. Analysis of Thought. Ch. I. Common Ground. (Logic I.i)

A. MS., n.p., November 17-20, 1908, pp. 1-12, 3, 5-6, and variants.

The common ground between author and reader: the English language and the familiar knowledge of the ordinary truths of human life. The exercise of control over our conduct: the most important business of life. The *modus operandi* of control. Psychology and observation. Not every observation about the human mind is a psychological observation. Remarks on modern science.

615. Logic. Book I. Analysis of Thought. Chapter I. Common Ground. (Logic I.i)

Λ. MS., n.p., November 28-December 1, 1908, pp. 1-29, with 8 pp. of variants.

Definition of "logic," and the pitfalls encountered on the way to a definition. Derivation of the term "science." For CSP, science refers to the collective and cooperative undertakings of men who have devoted themselves to inquiries of a general kind. Logic depends neither upon any special science nor upon metaphysics. Logic presupposes a number of truths derivable from ordinary experience or observation. These truths, handed down from the pre-scientific age as common sense, are not the truths of any special science or of science in general. Remarks on classification of the sciences.

616. An Appraisal of the Faculty of Reasoning (Reason)

A. MS., n.p., late, pp. 1-11, with a rejected p. 9.

An attempt to answer the query: Assuming the existence on another planet of a race of "high psychical development," would that race be able to reason as man does? Digressions on a defense of instinct and on testing, by means of mathematical examples, the reasoning power of superior minds apparently deficient in mathematical aptitude.

617. (Reason)

A. MS., n.p., late, pp. 4-18.

Mathematics and reasoning. Enigma: the inability of superior minds to grasp mathematical reasoning. Analysis of logical operations involved in a simple piece of mathematical reasoning. CSP notes which of these logical operations the gifted but unmathematical mind cannot perform. Exact reasoning and common sense. Should accuracy of thought give way to sound instinct and wholesome feeling?

618. Introduction (Meaning Introd.)

A. MS., n.p., March 28-29, 1909, pp. 1-3, incomplete.

This is one of several attempts by CSP in 1909 to write an introduction to a collection of his papers on pragmatism. This introduction defines "science" in terms of what it is that animates the true scientist; namely, the dedicated search for truth for its own sake. CSP rejects both the Aristotelian notion that science is syllogistically demonstrated knowledge and the notion that science is systematized knowledge. Reference to Lady Welby's "significs."

619. Studies in Meaning (Meaning)

A. MS., G-1909-1, March 25-28, pp. 1-14, with 2 rejected pp.

Only the first paragraph published, with minor editorial changes, as 5.358n*. Autobiographical material: persons with whom the Peirce family were acquainted; CSP and his father; CSP's emotional instability; CSP's early interest in chemistry and his discovery of Whately's *Logic* at the age of 13; the study of Schiller's *Aesthetische Briefe,* followed by a study of Kant's *Critique of Pure Reason* and *Prolegomena,* out of which came CSP's lifelong devotion to the study of logic. Members of the *Metaphysical Club.*

*620. Essays Toward the Interpretation of our Thoughts. My Pragmatism (Meaning Pragmatism)

A. MS., G-1909-1, April 6-May 24, 1909, pp. 1-51 (pp. 40-41 missing), with 45 pp. of variants.

Only the first sentence of the "Preface" published (7.313n[1]). CSP's intellectual autobiography: the *Metaphysical Club* and the influence of Chauncey Wright and Nicholas St. John Green on his thinking. Abbot, who attended but one meeting of the *Metaphysical Club,* heard CSP on that occasion arguing in favor of Scholastic realism. Half a generation later, Abbot, in a book entitled "Scientific Theism" urged the same opinion. CSP recalls the occasion of writing the 1877-78 articles for the *Popular Science Monthly.* Pragmatism and pragmaticism distinguished. The fallibility of human reasoning. Sound reasoning and moral virtue. The plight of university instruction in logic. Whewell and J. S. Mill. Biographical notes on Duns Scotus and Ockham. Realism versus nominalism. Nominalism, concludes CSP, leads to absolute scepticism. The meaning of "real"; the meaning of "universal."

621. (Meaning Pragmatism)

A. MS., n.p., May 24-September 1, 1909, pp. 21-36.6, with 2 rejected pp.; plus pp. 37-42.

This manuscript continues p. 20 of MS. 620. The nominalism-realism controversy. Auguste Comte and J. S. Mill.

622. (Meaning Pragmatism)

A. MS., n.p., May 26-June 3, 1909, pp. 34-70 (p. 50 missing), 42-43, 51, and fragments.

History of logic: Mill's nominalism; individualism as only one particular variety of nominalism; Bolzano's treatise on logic; Boole's logic; Augustus De Morgan; and the logicians, A. B. Kempe and Josiah Royce.

623. (Meaning Pragmatism)

A. MS., G-1909-1, June 5-7, 1909, pp. 43-50.

Published, in part, as 1.27 (pp. 48-50). Unpublished: an historical explanation of the popularity of nominalism in CSP's day. The union of humanists and Ockhamists in opposition to the position of Duns Scotus.

624. (Meaning Pragmatism)

A. MS., n.p., June 7, 1909, pp. 51-56, with a rejected p. 53.

Essence of the method of science lies in hypotheses whose predictions turn into verifications. Mill and the false doctrine of nominalism. Law of the Uniformity of Nature and Mill's attempt to justify it by induction. Doctrine of chances.

625. (Meaning Pragmatism)

A. MS., n.p., June 12-24, 1909, pp. 51-58, 58-82, incomplete.

Mill and nominalism. What makes nominalism attractive? Mill's contradictory position: he holds with Pearson and Poincaré, on the one side, and yet he stands with Whately on induction, on the other side. The Uniformity of Nature Principle. CSP regards inference as possible only because of real connections *in re*. Characteristics of mathematical reasoning.

626. (Meaning Pragmatism)

A. MS., n.p., June 12, 1909, pp. 52-56.

Alternate draft of pp. 52-56 of MS. 625.

627. (Meaning Pragmatism)

A. MS., n.p., June 14, 1909, pp. 59-65.

Probable continuation of pp. 51-58 of MS. 625.

628. Studies in the Meanings of our Thought. What is the Aim of Thinking? considered in Two Chapters. Chapter I. The Fixation of Belief (Meaning)

A. MS., n.p., March 1909, pp. 1-2, 2-5.

The aim of reasoning: "to find out, from the consideration of matters and things already known, something else that we had not before known." Good reasoning gives true conclusions from true premises.

629. Studies in the Meanings of Our Thoughts. What is the Aim of Thinking, considered in Two Chapters. Chapter I. The Fixation of Belief (Meaning)

A. MS., n.p., March 1909, pp. 1-2.

The importance of studying logic. Brief comment on the history of instruction in logic.

630. Studies of Meaning (Meaning)

A. MS., n.p., March 22-25, 1909, pp. 1, 3-6; plus an alternative p. 2 and an unnumbered page.

Reference to the *Popular Science Monthly* articles of 1877-78 and the formulation of a principle called "pragmatism." Disagreement with James who pressed the matter of pragmatism "further than Mr. Peirce, who continues to acknowledge, not the *existence,* but yet the *reality* of the Absolute, as set forth, for example, by Royce." The *Metaphysical Club* and some of its leading members. CSP's intellectual development. The purpose (and the success) of CSP's attempt to master several of the special sciences.

631. Preface (Meaning Preface to the Volume)

A .MS., n.p., August 24, 1909, pp. 1-4 (for p. 5, see MS. 632).

CSP writes of his many undertakings in science, ranging from chemistry to the history of science. He speaks of his own natural powers of mind as "rather below than above mediocrity," but mentions that his three strongest points have been "self-criticism, persistence, and logical analysis."

632. Preface (Meaning Preface to the Book)

A. MS., n.p., August 24-29, 1909, pp. 1-27, plus fragments.

CSP's estimation of his own mental powers. He speaks of having heard "the most extravagant estimates placed upon my mental powers." ". . . my principal deficiency, which is that my brain is small. This renders me incapable of thoroughly grasping together any considerable number of details; and one consequence is that I do not readily pass from one subject, or occupation of thought, to another; whence my persistency." Linguistic expression is not natural to CSP, who claims never to think in words, but always in some kind of diagram. His difficulties with foreign languages. "In college, I received the most humiliating marks for my themes. . . . My amicable teacher Professor Francis James Child . . . thought I took no pains. But I did." CSP attributes his awkwardness of linguistic expression to his left-handedness, noting that he once wrote with facility right-handed. To grasp what abstract thought is about requires more than reading about doing something—it requires actually doing it. The "literary" habit—CSP's term for it—is ruinous.

633. Preface (Meaning Preface to the volume)

A. MS., n.p., September 4-6, 1909, pp. 1.1-1.8.

Logical and psychological analysis sharply separated, without minimizing the importance of either. Logic does not rest upon psychology, although it is true to say that in the synthetical (methodeutic) part of logic, certain psychological principles ought to be considered. Logic does appeal, however, to mathematics, phenomenology, and esthetics.

634. Preface (Meaning Preface to the Book)

A. MS., n.p., September 8-17, 1909, pp. 1-27, with 3 pp. rejected; plus p. 1 of an earlier draft, dated September 7, 1909.

Criticism of the current psychological approach to logic. Ultimate assurance of the truth of the conclusion of any reasoning is faith in the governance of the universe by an Active Reason. The distinction between object of thought and the object thought about. The real object, unlike the object of thought, is not subject to the modifications of thought. Logic as general semiotic; logic considers signs in general. Relationship among object, sign, interpretant. Signs as substitutes for objects and capable of interpretation through the mind. Nothing is able to represent itself exclusively.

635. (Meaning Preface)

A. MS., n.p., September 19-October 2, 1909, pp. 2-7.7, 8-8$\frac{3}{8}$ (p. 8 following p. 7.1), 6-8 (p. 6 following p. 5 of the first sequence).

Logic and psychology. Logic is not concerned with what passes in consciousness, and no person's confidence in an argument is any sure sign of the argument's validity. Doctrine of chances serves to illustrate these points.

636. (Meaning Preface)

A. MS., n.p., September 22-30, 1909, pp. 6-31, plus 2 pp. of variants.

Whether there is any reason for absolute faith. Kant's criticism of Aristotle ("Über die falsche Spitzfindigkeit de vier syllogistischen Figuren") is deemed ludicrous. Kant makes validity of inference dependent on the manner in which facts are thought rather than on the facts themselves. The relationship between logic and psychology. The distinction between "assertion" and "urtheil."

637. (Meaning Preface)

A. MS., n.p., October 3-13, 1909, pp. 9-36, 27-30, 28-29, 31-36.

Tendency to guess right (but not necessarily on the first guess). Pure logic supports the general assertion that a cautious presumption may be credited if no contrary evidence is available. The discussion of such presumptions is relegated to methodeutic. Criticism of Kant's criticism of Aristotle (Kant's "Über die falsche Spitzfindigkeit der vier syllogistische Figuren"). Criticism of Sigwart's views that existence is the only form of reality, that any inference from thought to real objects is invalid, and that we know immediately our own thought. Unity of thought as consisting in the continuity of the life of a growing idea. An introduction to CSP's theory of signs which doesn't get beyond the elementary distinctions of the theory. Iconic, indexical, and symbolic signs.

638. (Meaning Preface)

A. MS., n.p., October 4-6, 1909, pp. 14-21.

Justification of retroduction. Pure logic encourages inquiry based on hypotheses which we accept on impulse. Practical and scientific retroduction.

639. Essays on Meaning. Preface (Meaning Preface)

A. MS., n.p., October 20, [1909], pp. 1-4.

Condemnation of present day logicians. The importance of restoring logic as the foundation of a liberal education (as was the case in medieval times).

640. Essays on Meaning. Preface (Meaning Preface)

A. MS., n.p., October 22-23, 1909, pp. 1-12 (with several other pages fitting into the sequence).

The division of logic into three studies: universal grammar, critic, and methodeutic. Mill's distinction between connotation and denotation discussed. CSP's opposition to the leading schools of logic of his day that tie rationality to human consciousness by regarding human consciousness as the author of rationality. For CSP, there is no distinction more momentous than that between "is" and "would be."

641. Significs and Logic (Significs and Logic)

A. MS., n.p., November 3-18, 1909, pp. 1-24 $25\!\frac{1}{26}$, plus 4 pp. (November 2-23).

Purpose: analysis of the relations between semeiotic (physiology of signs) and logic (theory of reasoning). Meaning of "argument." Doctrine of chances. Nominalism and realism. The meaning of the word "real." CSP refers to his review of Frazer's edition of Berkeley, in which he took the qualified realist position of Duns Scotus. Here CSP comes out for an unqualified version of realism. CSP regards himself as a disciple of Berkeley, although he is opposed to Berkeley's denial of matter as well as to his nominalism. The distinction between God's reality and God's existence. God's reality, apart from the question of God's existence, canont be doubted by anyone who meditates upon the question. Belief in God is a natural instinct. The nature of God: God is both intelligible and incomprehensible. All atheists are nominalists. Is nominalism consistent? Substance and accident. Indefiniteness: The indefinite is not subject to the principle of contradiction. Modal logic. Analogy between modes of being and modes of meaning. Biographical material: CSP writes of the conferences in Paris of leading geodesists, and he recalls an incident involving Sylvester.

642. Significs and Logic (Significs and Logic)

A. MS., n.p., November 25-28, 1909, pp. 8-25.

This manuscript continues the preceding one. The meaning of "real." The distinction between the externality and internality of fact supported by common sense. Signification of reality compared with externality of fact. Three kinds of modality. The three modes of assertion of law, of actual fact, of freedom. Principle of excluded middle does not apply to assertions of law; principle of contradiction does not apply to assertions of freedom. Both principles apply to assertions of actual fact. Sophistries of nominalism. Some of Locke's views present difficulties for CSP.

643. Studies of Logical Analysis, or Definition (Definition 1st notes)

A. MS., n.p., December 12-13, 1909, pp. 1-7, incomplete.

Purpose: discovery of the methods of dissecting the meaning of a sign. Meanings and chemical substances. The notion of valence, or attachment (the "pegs" of CSP's existential graphs). The difference between various attachments of a concept and the valences of carbon: The attachments are unlike each other; the valences are not qualitatively different. Is it the case that we always think in signs? Signs and ideas.

644. On Definition or The Analysis of Meaning (Definition: 2nd Draught)

A. MS., n.p., December 21, 1909, 1 p.

What it means to say that anything is *dependent*. What it means to say that any predicate is essentially true. Importance of the notion of "would be" for philosophy.

645. How to Define (Definition: 3rd Draught)

A. MS., n.p., December 22-January 12, 1910, pp. 1-26, with a variant p. 20.

Three studies distinguished (phaneroscopy, logic, and psychology) and their order of dependence established. Feeling, volition, and thought. In regard to feeling, Hume is in error, for he is committed to the view that vividness is an element of a sense-quality. The three modes of separating the elements of a thought-object are precision, dissociation, and discrimination. Volition and purpose. Resemblances as residing in the interpretation of secondary feelings. CSP's essential conservatism. He warns, however, that self-criticism, carried too far, leads to exaggerated distrust.

646. (Definition: 4th Draught)

A. MS., n.p., January 13-February 13, 1910, pp. 7-58, with 16 pp. of variants.

Syntax of thought. Traditional as opposed to the modern logic of relatives. An inconsistency noted in Aristotle's conception of a universal proposition. CSP's algebra of logic: Positive and negative terms are distinguished, with "positiveness" defined.

647. Definition (Definition: 5th Draught, or new, or new draught, or new work)

A. MS., n.p., February 16-26, 1910, pp. 1-26, with 22 pp. of variants.

Three grades of clearness of apprehension. Application of the pragmatic maxim to the notion of probability. Laplace's conception of probability. CSP's distinction between fact and occurrence: A fact is as much of the real universe as can be represented in a proposition; an occurrence is a slice of the universe. The failure of both Laplace and Mill to adhere to this distinction. Distinction between sciential probability and ignorantial probability. Laplacean theory of probability confuses the two.

648. Definition

A. MS., n.p., February 27-March 22, 1910, pp. 8-58, 58-60, plus 10 pp. of variants.

Page 8 of this manuscript continues p. 7 of MS. 647, and is a later draft of that manuscript. Laplace's definition of "probability." Distinction between fact and occurrence, with Laplace attributing probability to occurrences rather than facts. Probability and states of mind. Background and history of the nominalist-realist controversy. Key figures in the controversy. Scotists and Ockhamists. Humanism and nominalism. Prantl's ignorance of Scholastic logic, especially in his *Geschichte der Logik*. The first question to ask of a logician is whether he is a nominalist or a realist. Eleatic doctrines and nominalism. Epicurean theory of induction. The plight of original minds in America.

649. On Definition and Classification (Definition: 6th Draught)

A. MS., G-1910-1, May 27-April 12, 1910, pp. 1-40, with 3 pp. of variants.

Published, in part, as 1.312 (pp. 12-14). Unpublished: discussion of the three grades of clearness; an analysis of the idea of a straight line; on acquiring useful habits; the bearing of ultimate desires on the art of conduct. CSP notes that man's real self, or true nature, is revealed in how a man would act, not in haste, but after due deliberation. Pleasure and pain are signs of satisfaction and dissatisfaction; they are not the satisfactions and dissatisfactions themselves. Anesthetics and the question whether pain is at all necessary. The theological problem of evil. Faculty psychology and the distinctions among knowing, willing, and feeling.

650. Diversions of Definitions (Essays Definitions)

A. MS., n.p., July 20-August 5, 1910, pp. 1-46, 9-13, 40, 44-45.

Ordinal and cardinal numbers. Cardinal numbers, not *partes orationis*, but *orationes integrae*. System of existential graphs. Profundity of medieval Scholasticism. The three parts of the soul, with faculty psychology regarded as substantially true. Feeling (Firstness). Brute-will (Secondness). Reasoning (Thirdness).

651. Essays toward the Full Comprehension of Reasonings (Essays)

A. MS., n.p., July 1910, pp. 1-11, incomplete.

An attempt to devise a plan for the improvement of reasoning, beginning with the distinction between weak arguments and unsound ones. All sound arguments are either necessary or probable. Necessary reasoning is deductive; probable reasoning can be either inductive or retroductive.

652. Essays toward the Full Comprehension of Reasonings (Essays Preface)

A. MS., n.p., July 12-17, 1910, pp. 1-27, 16-19.

Purpose: improving the reader's power of reasoning. Criticism of German logic. Distinction between weak and unsound arguments. Necessary and probable reasoning. Probable reasoning as either inductive or retroductive. The three orders of induction are quantitative, qualitative and crude (simple enumeration). Qualitative induction mistaken for retroduction. Brief comments on the history of astronomy. CSP regards Kepler's investigation of the motions of the planets as the greatest feat of inductive reasoning ever accomplished. Fallibilism and the propositions of mathematics, logic, and ethics; fallibilism and common sense.

653. Exercises in Definition, or Analysis of Concepts (Essays and Concept Analysis)

A. MS., n.p., July 20, 1910, 1 p.

654. Essays (Essays 1st Pref.)

A. MS., n.p., August 17-19, 1910, pp. 1-7, 2-3.

Note: This manuscript was meant to serve as a "Preface," with MS. 632 serving as the "Introduction." Comments on Arnauld's *L'art de penser* and on the Port Royal Logic. All reasoning consists in interpreting signs; all thought is in signs. System of existential graphs: the simplest system capable of expressing exactly every possible assertion. Definition of "sign."

655. Quest of Quest (QQ)

A. MS., n.p., August 26-September 7, 1910, pp. 1-37.

An inquiry into the question of what makes inquiry successful. On terminology. Requirements for studying philosophy are mastery of Euclid's *Elements* and mastery of common Greek, medieval Latin, English and German. Definition of "science." The distinction between descriptive and explanatory science. The classification of the sciences. The division of the theoretical sciences into mathematics, philosophy, and idioscopy; the division of philosophy into phaneroscopy, normative science, and metaphysics. Truth and reality. Similarity of CSP's and James's viewpoints accounted for by the common acceptance of cognitionism, a position which derives from their teacher Chauncey Wright. But CSP questions James on the notion of the satisfactory. Remarks by CSP on his special talent and what it is that motivates him.

656. (Q/Q)

A. MS., n.p., September 9-10, 1910, pp. 1-7.

Note: Q/Q is the first revision of QQ (MS. 655). Terminological questions in connection with science and philosophy. The importance of definition for both philosophy and mathematics.

657. Preface (QQ Preface)

A. MS., n.p., September 16, 1910, pp. 1-6.

The author of a new book ought to give an account of himself. CSP writes of the size of his brain—"a trifle under" average—and his belief that it is unusually convoluted. He acknowledges that he is "ill adapted" for the everyday world, strong in whatever is abstract but lacking in everyday gumption.

658. The Ground Plan of Reason (G)

A. MS., n.p., October 1-3, 1910, pp. 1-6.

Man shares with the lower animals the capacity to feel. How, then, shall we describe feeling? The question is left unanswered.

659. The Rationale of Reason (G')

A. MS., n.p., October 7-22, 1910, pp. 1-41.

Feeling and effort. Faculty psychology and the division of the soul into three parts: feeling, volition, and cognition. Meaning of "faculty" as habitual possibility. Meaning of "person" as any animal that has command of some syntactical language. Problems of terminology. The law of time. Meaning of "real."

660. On the Foundation of Ampliative Reasoning (AR)

A. MS., n.p., October 24-28, 1910, pp. 1-23, incomplete.

Explicative and ampliative reasoning. Laplace and Mill on induction. Distinction between uniformity (what does happen) and law (what was compelled to happen). Criticism of Laplace's treatment of probability. CSP's views correspond to those of Venn, but derived independently. The notion of "equally possible." (Cf. "objective probability" in Venn, *Logic of Chance,* 1866.) CSP gives 1864 as the year he arrived at his conception of probability.

661. (AR_1)

A. MS., n.p., November 3-13, 1910, pp. 11-15.2, 15-19, 15-111, 110-111, 112-114.

What it means to say that all explicative reasoning is necessary and all necessary reasoning explicative. Logical critic and comments on the Aristotelian logic. Fallibilism and propositions about the meanings of words.

662. (AR_M)

A. MS., n.p., November 14-17, 1910, pp. 1-12, 4-7.
Mathematical reasoning illustrated.

663. The Rationale of Reasoning (AR_N)

A. MS., n.p., November 17-19, 1910, pp. 1-17, incomplete; plus p. 1 of another start.

The need for stricter rules of nomenclature. Meaning of the word "real." The three modes of reality are would-be's, existents, and can-be's. Berkeley's confusion of "being perceived" with "capable of being perceived." Tendency as denoting a real would-be.

664. The Rationale of Reasoning (AR)

A. MS., n.p., November 22-30, 1910, pp. 1-21, with 7 pp. of variants.

Problems of terminology. Definitions of "breadth" and "depth," both of which presuppose the definition of "proposition." Proposition and assertion. Positive truth and reality. Kant's distinction between knowledge drawn from experience and knowledge that begins in experience. Verbal knowledge.

665. The Rationale of Reasoning (AR)

A. MS., n.p., December 2-3, 1910, pp. 1-5, incomplete.

Conjunction. The origin of the term "premiss," with a reference to Sir James Murray's article in the *Oxford Dictionary.*

666. (AR)

A. MS., n.p., December 2-3, 1910, pp. 2-3, 5-6.
Earlier draft of MS. 665.

667. The Rationale of Reasoning (AR)

A. MS., n.p., December 8-12, 1910, pp. 1-11, with 3 pp. of variants.

Meaning of "reasoning," with reasoning regarded as essentially an interpretation of signs. Common sense and the soundness of reasoning. Meaning of "knowledge." Nature of probability.

668. (AR)

A. MS., n.p., n.d., pp. 1-18, 20 (possibly of another draft).

Inference and reasoning. Whether any judgment can be absolutely certain. Degrees of belief. Descartes' "Cogito ergo sum." A digression on the failure of people of wealth to support the science of reasoning.

669.   Assurance Through Reasoning (A Thr R)

A. MS., n.p., May 25-June 2, 1911, pp. 1-22, with 2 pp. of variants.

Necessary and probable deduction. Existential graphs: syntax and permissions.

670.   Assurance Through Reasoning (A Thru R)

A. MS., n.p., June 7-17, 1911, pp. 1-32, with 4 pp. of variants.

Necessary and probable deduction. Syntax of existential graphs. Essential nature of a sign.

671.   First Introduction

A. MS., n.p., [c.1911], pp. 1-20; 4-13 of another draft.

The powers of the mind are feeling, causing an action, taking on and abandoning habits. Habit explained in terms of the reality of a general fact about possible conduct; that is, in terms of the reality of would-be's. CSP lists philosophers who are opposed to his realism. Negation and contradiction.

672.   Second Essay. On the Essence of Reasoning and its Chief Varieties (II)

A. MS., n.p., [c.1911], pp. 1-6.

These pages were to supersede the 6th article of the *Popular Science Monthly* series of 1878, of which the first two articles were to appear as Part I and Part II of the "First Essay." These pages concern the false dichotomy of reason and instinct as well as the question whether animals reason. CSP thinks animals do reason, and offers two illustrations.

673.   A Sketch of Logical Critic

A. MS., G-c.1911-1, pp. 1-47, with 16 pp. of variants.

Published, in part, as 6.177-184 (pp. 21-44). Omitted: an explanation of logical critic and a definition of "reasoning." The parallel between the exercise of logical self-criticism and the exercise of moral self-criticism. Logical instinct. The triad of normative sciences. The dependence of logic upon ethics, and both upon esthetics. How habits are created. Comte's classification of the sciences. CSP's threefold division of the sciences: heuretic, tagmatic, and practical.

674.   A Sketch of Logical Critic

A. MS., n.p., [c.1911], pp. 1-15, with 6 pp. of variants.

On "criticism." Liberal education. Law of habit: CSP's hypothesis, held since 1880, that the law of habit in conjunction with events absolutely uncaused (except by a creative act of God) is all that is required to explain the universe in all its details.

675.   A Sketch of Logical Critic

A. MS., n.p., [c.1911], pp. 1-28, 12-20, and 30 pp. of variants.

"Logical critic" explained. Syllogistic recollection; unthought thought, belief and reality; belief as essentially a satisfaction, but not necessarily pleasant. The classification of the sciences and the place of logical critic among the sciences. The normative sciences; esthetics; logic as the science of symbols. The doctrine of signs and the division of signs into icons, indices, and symbols.

676.   A Sketch of Logical Critics

A. MS., n.p., [c.1911], pp. 1-6.

The meaning of "critics" and "logical critics." Definition of "sign."

677. A Sketch of Logical Critic

A. MS., n.p., [c.1911], pp. 1-5, plus 2 pp. of two other attempts to begin the essay.

Explanation of "critic." Art and science. The classification of the sciences.

678. The Art of Reasoning Elucidated

A. MS., n.p., "late in 1910" (p. 26), pp. 1-29, 14-35, with 2 pp. of variants.

Proposal to accomplish seven things in this essay, ranging from a discussion of the different kinds of reasoning to an application of reasoning to the pressing problems of the day. Love of truth as a prerequisite for reasoning well; lover of truth versus lover of knowledge; the three passions for wide knowledge, deep knowledge, and accurate knowledge equated with love of learning, love of knowledge, and love of scientific economy (pp. 1-29). Method of reasoning as man's (as opposed to woman's) way to truth; thinking as "talking" with oneself; the principles of contradiction and excluded middle; real and ratiocinative modality (pp. 14-35).

679. The Art of Reasoning Elucidated

A. MS., n.p., [1910], pp. 1-12, unfinished, with a variant p. 11.

An earlier draft of MS. 678. CSP proposes to do seven things in this essay, but the essay breaks off at this point.

680. Analysis of the Trustworthiness of the Different Kinds of Reasonings

A. MS., n.p., late, pp. 1-26, incomplete, with 18 pp. of variants.

Essay is directed toward boys between the ages of twelve and eighteen who think. The mind-body distinction. The three classes of psychical, physical, and psychophysical. The three elements in all psychical phenomena. Analysis of the state of awareness in terms of its three ingredients. Consciousness of contrast and awareness of change. Triadic distinction of actual fact, may be, and would be. History of the principles of contradiction and excluded middle. Reality of can-be's and would-be's as well as actual facts and existing things. Would-be's related to dispositions and habits.

681. A Study of How to Reason Safely and Efficiently

A. MS., n.p., 1913, pp. 1-47, with a variant p. 7.

Reasoning and sensation. Mixed and unmixed sensations. Esthetic quality attached to reasoning well. The notion of "elegance" in mathematics. Volition and attention. Awareness of acquiring a habit is the third mode of consciousness. What "habit" means. Reasoning as the process of consciously acquiring a belief from previous ones. In defense of trichotomists. CSP records that he does not know and has never inquired whether there is any connection between his own trichotomy and the Divine Trinity, but maintains there is nothing mysterious about his trichotomy. What "real" means. Long footnote on Prantl's *Geschichte der Logik im Abendlande*.

682. An Essay toward Improving Our Reasoning in Security and in Uberty

A. MS., n.p., [c.1913], pp. 1-53, with 10 pp. of variants.

Defense of final causes. Ratiocination and instinct. CSP is guided by the following maxim: Define all mental characters as far as possible in terms of their outward manifestations. This maxim is roughly equivalent to the rule of pragmatism. It can be said to aid security but not uberty of reasoning. "Yet the maxim of Pragmatism does not bestow a single smile upon beauty, upon moral virtue, or upon abstract truth, the three things that alone raise

Humanity above Animality." The science of psychology is of no help in laying the foundations of a sane philosophy of reasoning, and precisely why CSP believes this to be so.

683. **[An Essay toward Improving Our Reasoning in Security and in Uberty]**

A. MS., n.p., late, pp. 4-38, 12-28, and 16 pp. of variants.

Another version of MS. 682. Mathematical and necessary reasoning. Preference for the word "uberty" over "fruitfulness." The necessity for technical terminology. CSP's ignorance of esthetics, with Schiller's *Aesthetische Briefe* mentioned as the only book he has read on the subject. But CSP writes of his keen but uncultivated sense of beauty. To illustrate this, he notes works of literature he admires. He also notes that there is little of the artist in him, his own literary style testifying to that. The history of scientific investigation of the problems of ethics. Sir Edward Herbert, Hobbes, Cumberland. The meaning of the word "real." Modalities.

684. **A Study of Reasoning in its Security and its Uberty**

A. MS., n.p., August 26-31, 1913, pp. 1-13 (p. 8 missing), with 6 pp. of variants.

CSP planned to send copies to Royce, Dewey, Whitehead, and "even to the supercilious Bradley." Reasoning as a branch of endeavor, with an explanation of what is meant by "branch." A long digression on astronomy.

685. **The Art of Reasoning Regarded from the Point of View of A. D. 1913. Book I. The Foundations of the Art. Introduction.**

A. MS., n.p., 1913, pp. 1-29 (continuous in spite of two p. 28s).

Mathematics is a prerequisite for the study of logic. History of mathematics, especially counting. The notion of "elegance," with true elegance regarded as a variety of economy. The duties and methods of the historian. Was Boethius the author of the geometry and the theological metaphysics attributed to him?

686. **Reflexions upon Reasoning**

A. MS., n.p., late, pp. 1-9, with a variant p. 7.

"Reality," "state of things," "actuality," and "reasoning" defined. Reality is that aspect of the being of anything which is independent of the thing's being represented. The trustworthiness of immediate knowledge (sense perception) testifies only to this or that single state of things. Reasoning testifies to the truth that lies beyond our ken. CSP wonders what the eternal habits are, beyond those which involve the tridimensionality of space and the general mutability of time. Satisfactory and unsatisfactory feelings.

PRACTICAL LOGIC, NOTES, FRAGMENTS

687. **Guessing (guessing)**

A. MS., G-c.1907-2, pp. 1-35; plus pp. 2-16 of an earlier draft and 3 pp. of variants.

Published, with deletions, as 7.36-48. The manuscript was published in *The Hound and Horn* 2 (April-June, 1929) 267-282. Omitted from *Collected Papers* were pp. 8-22 (for a partial description of which see 7.40n[15]) and pp. 32-33 (the completion of a personal anecdote). Nature of pure science: questions of pure science handled differently from practical questions. For practical matters cultivate instincts! (Anecdote told in support of this advice.) Decimal and secundal systems of enumeration.

688. Guessing

A. MS., G-c.1907-2, pp. 1-22 (pp. 3-9; 16-18 missing); plus pp. 1-2 (rejected) of another start.

Only the first two sentences of p. 1 published: 7.36n[13]. This is apparently an earlier draft of MS. 690. Moreover it appears that pp. 3-9 were lifted from here and incorporated in MS. 690. This is not the case, however, with pp. 16-18, which are still missing. Personal anecdote (same as in MS. 687).

689. Surmises About Guessing (Guesses)

A. MS., n.p., n.d., pp. 1-4.

CSP gets only as far as introducing himself to his reader.

690. On the Logic of drawing History from Ancient Documents especially from Testimonies (Logic of History)

A. MS., G-1901-4, pp. 1-263 (continuous although there are no pp. 35, 137, 191), variant p. 15, a typed copy (with marginal corrections by CSP) and a lengthy (6 pp.) "Note on Collections" inserted at p. 52.

Published as 7.164-255, with the exception of 7.182n[7], which is from the Lowell Lectures of 1903 (Lecture VIII), and 7.220n[18], which is from MS. 691.

691. On the Logic of drawing History from Ancient Documents especially from Testimonies (Logic of History)

A. MS., G-1901-4, 221 pp., fragmentary, with pp. running as high as p. 238.

Published, in part, as 7.220n[18] (pp. 93-95, with one deletion). CSP added following note: "These pages are to be used in the chapter of the Logic treating Deductive Reasoning. But the theory needs completion." See MS. 1344 for what appears to be an abstract of this logic.

692. The Proper Treatment of Hypotheses: a Preliminary Chapter, toward an Examination of Hume's Argument against Miracles, in its Logic and in its History (Hist. Test.)

A. MS., n.p., 1901, pp. 1-38, 29-40, and 13 pp. of variants.

Opposition to the dualism of reason and instinct. Dogs can reason on occasions, with an example from CSP's experience. Rudimentary sense of logic (*logica utens*) and the sophisticated sense of logic (*logica docens*). Attack on modern books on logic. Precepts and hypotheses. The three stages in the life of a hypothesis, each stage governed by entirely different logical principles. Abduction, deduction, and induction.

* 693. Reason's Conscience: A Practical Treatise on the Theory of Discovery; Wherein logic is conceived as Semeiotic

A. MS., six notebooks, n.p., n.d., pp. 2-442 (even numbers mostly, but text is consecutive), including a rewritten section.

Notebook I (pp. 2-80). Purpose of book: improving the reasoning power of students. Pedagogy. Reason and instinct. Interrelations of the branches of science; ladder of the sciences, beginning with the science of discovery and ending with practical science. Notebook II (pp. 82-164). Continues the discussion of the branches of science begun in Notebook I, concentrating on phenomenology, normative science, metaphysics, general physics, and general psychology. The dependence of logic upon the other normative sciences and upon phenomenology and mathematics. The relationship of logic to metaphysics and to psychology. Sound reasoning leads to the maximum of expectation and the minimum of surprise. Notebook III (pp. 166-248). Continues the discussion of sound reasoning specifically and the relationship between logic and psychology generally. The laws of thought. Language and linguistics. The ontological argument. Mathematics and logic; the teaching of mathematics; instructions for understanding Euclidean geometry. Notebook IV (pp. 250-322). Continuation of the instructions for understanding Euclid. Discussion of existential graphs, with a note by CSP that this discussion was rewritten in Notebook V. Notebook V (pp. 278-370). The nature of mathematics. The manner in which two branches of science may support each other. CSP's speculations on the possibility of a phenomenology of esthetics, an esthetics of ethics, an ethics of logic, etc. Notebook VI (pp. 372-442). Continuation of the discussion of the usefulness of one science to another. The descriptive and classificatory sciences. The problem of knowledge: perceptual knowledge; individuality and classes; unity, singularity, and individuality distinguished; expectations.

694. **The Rules of Right Reasoning (Rules of RR or RRR)**
A. MS., n.p., n.d., pp. 1-5.
Introductory. Study of the right methods of reasoning has occupied CSP for forty-five years. Notes deficiencies as a writer. His hopes of writing a great work on logic have given way to his hope of writing a shorter, less perfect version. CSP offers his plan of simplification.

695. **A Practical Treatise on Logic and Methodology**
A. MS., n.p., n.d., 18 pp. of several attempts, none of which go beyond a few pages.
Purpose: establishing maxims for estimating validity and strength of arguments. Explanation of the use of the terms "logic" and "methodology." The function of reason. Genuine doubt and genuine investigation.

696. **Practical Maxims of Logic**
A. MS., n.p., n.d., 27 pp., of which 4 pp. are in Zina Fay Peirce's hand.
Deduction, induction, and hypothesis as practical considerations. Beware of the syllogism: everything can be explained, with the syllogism merely making our knowledge more distinct. With regard to the ontological argument, every definition implies existence of its object. Random sampling.

697. **Lessons on Practical Logic**
A. MS., n.p., n.d., 5 pp.
Concerning the definition of "logic." The investigation of consequences constitutes logic, with material and formal consequences distinguished. Suggestions of possible topics for a course in practical logic.

698. **[Maxims of Reasoning]**
A. MS., n.p., n.d., pp. 2-3, 5.
Maxim III: "The object of reasoning is to settle questions." Maxim IV: "Things are not just as we choose to think them."

699. **[Logical and Mathematical Exercises]**
A. MS. and TS., n.p., n.d., 13 pp.
Illustrations of logical doctrine.

700. **[Quiz]**
A. MS., n.p., n.d., 4 pp.

701. **[Logical Puzzles]**
A. MS., n.p., n.d., 4 pp.

702. [Logical Exercises]

A. MS., n.p., n.d., 6 pp.

703. Note (Notes on Art. III)

A. MS., G-1910-2, August 11-15, pp. 1-30 (with p. 5 missing); 6, 8-10 of another draft; and pp. 1-2 ("Notes to CSP's Third Paper in the Pop. Sci. Monthly, 1878, March").

Published in entirety as 2.661-668 and as 2.645n[1]. Article III refers to the third in the *Popular Science Monthly* series of 1877-78.

704. Notes to be added to C. S. Peirce's Third Article in Pop. Sc. Monthly (Notes No III)

A. MS., n.p., n.d., pp. 1-3.

This is a footnote to be inserted on p. 604, line 3, after the word "evident." General laws in chemistry; Vant Hoff's general law of mass-action.

705. Notes on the List of Postulates of Dr. Huntington's #2 (On Postulates)

A. MS., G-c.1904-1, pp. 1-11, 10-12, 10-11.

Published as 4.324-330 (pp. 1-11).

706. [The Concept of Probability]

A. MS., n.p., January 23-31, 1909, pp. 1-31, with 3 pp. of variants.

Remarks on the history of the concept of probability, noting incidentally that the Greeks had no idea of such a concept. Pascal's method of treating probability. Science is raised to a higher level by the "Doctrine of Chances."

*707. Note to Sylvester's Papers Vol. I p. 92

A. MS., n.p., n.d., 1 folded sheet.

System of dyadic monosynthemes of the 6th order.

708. Reply to Mr. Kempe (K)

A. MS., n.p., n.d., pp. 1-9, 5-7, and 5 pp. of another draft.

This is a reply to a short article in the *Monist* of 1897 by A. B. Kempe, which was itself, in part at least, a reply to CSP's article in the *Monist* (January 1897). See 3.468.

709. Note on Kempe's Paper in Vol. XXI of the Proceedings of the London Mathematical Society

A. MS., n.p., n.d., pp 1-6, plus 3 pp.

See MSS. 710-714 for further discussion of Kempe's paper.

710. Notes on Kempe's Paper

A. MS., n.p., n.d., pp. 1-2, plus 7 pp.

711. Notes on Kempe's Paper

A. MS., n.p., n.d., 4 pp.

712. (Kempe)

A. MS., n.p., n.d., 1 p.

713. (Kempe)

A. MS., n.p., n.d., 2 pp.

In praise of Kempe's mathematical powers and native instinct for doing logic, but critical of "his sad want of training" in logic. Specific criticism noted.

714. Notes on Kempe's Paper on Mathematical Forms
A. MS., n.p., January 15, 1889, 12 pp.

715. Kempe Translated into English
A. MS., n.p., n.d., 1 p.

716. [Fragment on Thirdness and Generality]
A. MS., G-c.1895-3, 3 pp.
Published in entirety as 1.340-342.

*717. Chapter II. The Categories
A. MS., n.p., n.d., 8 pp. (text is consecutive); plus 24 pp. (fragmentary).
Probably from the period of the *Grand Logic*. Assertions about systems of more than three subjects can be reduced to triadic assertions at most. The whole endeavor to deny the irreducibility of triadic facts is termed "nominalism." The realism-nominalism controversy. Nature of signs. Categoriology. Continuity and continuous series.

718. [On Continuous Series]
A. MS., n.p., n.d., 5 pp.
An attempt to show that the whole series of numbers, rational and irrational, does not constitute a continuous series.

719. Chapter I. Certain Fundamental Conceptions
A. MS., n.p., n.d., 5 pp.
Use of term(s) *ens (entia)*. Recourse to Scholastic usage. The first two principles of logic: (1) something or other is true of every *ens,* and (2) for everything which is true of an *ens,* something must be true of a pair of *entia* of which that is one.

720. Logic. Chapter I.
A. MS., n.p., n.d., 9 pp.
The end of logic is to form a table of categories. Proper method of deducing the categories. Qualities, relations, representations distinguished.

721. Chapter I. One, Two, Three
A. MS., n.p., n.d., pp. 1-5, plus 7 pp.
Logic begins with the analysis of the meaning of certain words of which the first is "is" (copula). *Ens (entia)* in Scholasticism. CSP then turns to the conceptions of one, two, and three before tackling the conception of independent being, but he gets only as far as a consideration of quality.

722. Chapter I. Fundamental Notions
A. MS., n.p., n.d., 2 pp.
Ens (entia) given the foremost place among logical terms. Its Scholastic usage.

723. A System of Logic. Chapter I. Syllogism
A. MS., n.p., n.d., pp. 1-6.
The historic origin of logic is the desire to test inferences. One should begin the study of logic with the syllogism; terms and propositions should be studied afterwards. Remarks on Aristotle's definition of "logic" and on Duns Scotus' views of logic.

724. Logic. Chapter I. Terms
A. MS., n.p., n.d., 4 pp. and 2 pp. of an earlier draft.

Representations, symbols, and logic. Two terms are related to each other with regard to extension, comprehension, and implication.

725. On Logical Extension and Comprehension

A. MS., notebook, n.p., n.d.

CSP comments on his own article of November 13, 1867 (G-1867-1e) and adds a 6th section entitled "Of Natural Classification," an attempt to say precisely what a natural class is.

726. An Unpsychological View of Logic to which are appended some applications of the theory to Psychology and other subjects

A. MS., n.p., [1865?], 76 pp.

An early work primarily on the intension and extension of terms which was superseded by "Upon Logical Comprehension and Extension" (G-1867-1e). Definition of "logic." Connotation, denotation, and information. The relationship of comprehension, extension, and implication summed up in the formula: Extension × comprehension = implication. Forms of induction and hypothesis.

727. [Notes on Intension and Extension]

A. MS., n.p., n.d., 2 pp.

728. Chapter 2. First Division of Symbols in Logic

A. MS., n.p., n.d., 2 pp.

Logic is a classificatory science. Its study should be preceded by a study of the science of classification.

729. Chapter II.

A. MS., n.p., n.d., 4 pp.

Logic as a classificatory science. Kinds of representation.

730. Logic. Chapter 3.

A. MS., n.p., n.d., 4 pp.

Symbols regarded as terms, propositions, and arguments.

731. Chapter II. Extension, Comprehension, Implication

A. MS., n.p., n.d., 9 pp., plus 4 pp. of an earlier attempt.

732. Introduction

A. MS., n.p., n.d., pp. 1-16.

Impressions; precision, discrimination, dissociation; substance; accident; Being; quality, relation, representation; ground, correlate, interpretant; formal objects. A note concerning a nameless philosopher of the 12th century appears on the verso of one of the pages.

733. Logic. Chapter I

A. MS., n.p., n.d., 3 pp.

Every conception is a hypothesis (supposition). Abstraction as separation in conception as opposed to separation in fact and in imagination. Conception of Being: Being distinguished from *Dasein*.

734. Logic. Chapter 2. Formal Logic

A. MS., n.p., n.d., 53 pp.

Explanation of some of the basic terms of formal logic. The objects of logic are symbols; the business of logic is the classification of symbols. Logic itself is a symbol. Symbols: terms, propositions, and arguments. The syllogism.

735. Logic. The Theory of Reasoning. Part I. Exact Logic. Introduction. What is Logic (EL)

A. MS., n.p., n.d., pp. 1-2, 1-5, 1-13, with a title page and a table of contents.

Logic is the theory of reasoning and, as such, it is not a branch of psychology (pp. 1-2). Reasoning and common sense (reasoning from the initial propositions of common sense); the relationship between hope and truth (pp. 1-5). A sect of philosophy concerned with deducing the rules of reasoning by mathematics (the achievements of this sect include CSP's contribution of the logic of continuity); Mill's logic; Sigwart and Kant; Hegel's importance to German philosophy; reasoning and signs (pp. 1-13).

736. Qualitative Logic

A. MS., G-undated-11 [1893?], 1 p. (table of contents); pp. 1-11 (preface); pp. 1-10, 2-4, 1-8 ("Chapter I. The Association of Ideas"); pp. 1-6, 1-3 ("Chapter II. The Simple Consequences"); pp. 1-11, 1-8, and a variant p. 6 ("Chapter III. The Modus Ponens"); pp. 1-48, with 24 pp. of variants ("Chapter IV. The Syllogism" and "The Traditional Syllogistic"); pp. 1-8 ("Chapter V. The Dilemma"); pp. 1-5 ("Chapter V. Dilemmatic Reasoning"); pp. 1-6, 1-2 ("Chapter VI. Logical Extension and Comprehension"); pp. 1-22, with 60 pp. of variants ("Chapter VI. The Logical Algebra of Boole"); 1 p. ("Chapter VI. Logical Algebra and Logic of Relatives"); plus 35 pp. of fragments.

Published, in part, as 7.451-457 (Chapter I, pp. 1-10) and 7.458-462 (Chapter II, pp. 1-5).

737. Memoir #4. Algebra of Copula

A. MS., n.p., n.d., 9 pp.

738. [On the Quantified Predicate]

A. MS., n.p., n.d., 4 pp.

CSP rejects the thesis that the copula of a proposition expresses primarily the identity relation, noting arguments in its favor, especially Hamilton's.

* 739. [Thought and Feeling]

A. MS., n.p., n.d., pp. 30-32.

These pages may be part of a proposed book in logic. Division of the operations of the understanding into simple apprehension, judgment, and reasoning. Distinction between objective and subjective intensity of feeling. Combination of feelings which, in some cases, is strongly suggestive of thought.

740. Appendix No. 2

A. MS., n.p., n.d., 43 pp.

The hypothetic and sensational character of simple conceptions: The Kantian position on space and time is analyzed. Difference in time is a quantitative, continuous, commutative ground of disquiparance; difference in space is a quantitative, continuous, noncommutative ground of disquiparance.

741. [Sheets from a Notebook on Logic]

A. MS., n.p., [c.1860-c.1867], 75 pp.

It is possible to distinguish the following: "On the Figures and Moods of Logic" (c.1860): induction as the middle road between *a priori* and *a posteriori* reasoning; the figures of the different kinds of inferences (7 pp. of an early draft of a work on the Aristotelian syllogism). "Induction": Aristotle's views on induction; objection to Hamilton's "logical" induction; the denotation of subjects and the connotation of predicates (Sept. 1864, 2 pp.). "Consideration of the 3rd Argument in favor of the [quantification of the] predicate" (1867, 1 p.). "On the Conversion of Quantity" (c.1867, 2 pp.). "Further Arguments for a Quantified Predicate considered" (c.1867, 1 p.). "Analogy between Logic and Algebra" (c.1865, 1 p.). "Problem. To apply algebra to logic": a numerical interpretation of Boolean concepts, e.g., $a + b = 2 \equiv a$ and b are two facts (c.1866, 4 pp.). "Propositions of Disquiparance" (c.1866, 2 pp.). "Doctrine of Conversion" (c.1860, 4 pp.). "Quality is the only Quantity belonging to the Predicate": the distinction between extension and intension (c.1866, 2 pp. and 4 pp.). "Extension, Intension, etc." (c.1867, 8 pp.). "The Course of Expression": the concrete expression of an idea requires a mode of presentation (c.1867, 2 pp.). "Quantity of the Figures" (c.1867, 2 pp.). "Notation: Considerations of the Advantages of Sir W. H.'s Analytic intended to show that mine has the same" (c.1867, 4 pp.). "Associative Principle" (c.1867, 11 pp., of which seven are in the hand of Zina Fay Peirce). The remainder are fragments and include, among other topics, notes on the syllogism and on the relation of extension, intension, and information.

742. Preliminary Sketch of Logic

A. MS., small notebook, n.p., [c.1865].

Argument; leading principle; copula; term.

743. The Rules of Logic logically Deduced

A. MS., n.p., June 23, 1860, 8 pp.

Propositions collate conceptions. Collation is comparison, and a conclusion is a comparison drawn from two comparisons. Problematical, apodictic, and assertive propositions. The application of geometry to logical doctrines.

744. Of the Distinction between *a priori* and *a posteriori*

A. MS., n.p., n.d., 10 pp., plus a folded page with the title: "Distinction between *a priori* and *a posteriori*."

Arguments in the first, second, and third figures are respectively *a priori*, *a posteriori,* and inductive. Table showing logical character of every mood. Logically *a priori* conclusions are universal, affirmative, categorical, apodictic. Logically inductive conclusions are particular, infinite, hypothetical, assertorial. Logically *a posteriori* conclusions are singular, negative, disjunctive, problematical.

745. [Plan for Sixty Lectures on Logic]

A. MS., n.p., n.d., pp. 1-25, with 17 pp. of other attempts to state the substance of the lectures.

Brief descriptions of the subjects of each lecture. The subject matter ranges widely from the physiological and psychological bases of logic (first lecture) to anthropomorphic science, physiognomy, art, and natural theology (sixtieth lecture).

746. [Introductory Remarks to a Course in Logic]

A. MS., n.p., n.d., 9 pp.

Historical notes on Aristotle and the Stoics. CSP attempts to answer the question: Is logic a science? His conclusion is that logic is the science that analyzes method.

747.   [Fragments on Logic]

A. MS., n.p., n.d., 46 pp.

These fragments may belong to the Johns Hopkins period. Among the 46 pp. are 7 pp. on the logic of relatives, one page of which reads: "Chapter IV. The Logic of Plural Relatives." The remaining pages concern the derivation of the word "logic," kinds of inferences, statistical deductions, probability.

*748.   Logic: and the Methods of Science. Book I. Formal Logic. Chapter I. The Modus Ponens

TS. (corrected), n.p., n.d., pp. 1-2 and 14 pp. of several drafts.

748a.   Logic. Chapter I. Of thinking as Cerebration

TS. (corrected), n.p., n.d., pp. 1, 1-7, 1-3, 1-2, 3, 3-6.

748b.   [Outline and First Chapter of a Book on Probability]

TS. (corrected), n.p., n.d., 1 p. ("Plan and Object of this Work"), 1 p. ("Table of Contents"), pp. 1-8 ("Part I. Descriptions. Chapter I. The Question in Probability").

748c.   [Draft of "The Observational Element in Mathematics"]

TS., n.p., n.d., pp. 4-5 and 3 unnumbered pages.

748d.   The Settlement of Opinion

TS., n.p., n.d., pp. 9-10, variant of 5.377.

749.   [What logic is]

A. MS., n.p., n.d., 10 pp.

Is logic a science or an art? Does logic have a practical aim? If so, what is that aim? The various schools of logic (transcendental, scientific, etc.).

750.   Logic I.

A. MS., n.p., n.d., pp. 1-2, incomplete.

The essence of the distinction between good and bad reasoning does not lie, as Sigwart believes, in a difference of feeling. It is a matter of fact.

751.   [Lecture on Logic]

A. MS., n.p., n.d., pp. 1-4.

Part of a lecture series. The independence of logic from psychology. Logic and artificial languages. Deduction, induction, and retroduction.

752.   [Reasoning]

A. MS., n.p., March 15, 1914, 3 pp. and 1 p.

One of the last of CSP's manuscripts, it deals with the three orders of reasoning (deduction, induction, and retroduction) and with the limits of CSP's confidence in science.

753.   [Reasoning]

A. MS., n.p., n.d., pp. 3-7 and a variant p. 5.

Draft of G-1907-1. Presumably for a lecture on the three kinds of reasoning. Examples of induction. Lutoslawski's and CSP's researches on Plato.

754.   Second Talk to the Phil. Club [and] Second Talk. On Deduction

A. MS., n.p., April 12, 1907, 2 folded sheets.

On the three kinds of reasoning (deduction, induction, retroduction). Method for the discovery of methods. Corollarial reasoning. Hypotheses of pure mathematics. The adventitious character of CSP's logical gift.

755. [On the Three Kinds of Reasoning]

A. MS., n.p., n.d., pp. 1-19, 9-23, with variants.

Drafts of beginning of CSP's "Little Book on Religion," c.1911: natural gift of understanding, common sense and self-deception, belief and conduct.

756. Retroduction (Retr)

A. MS., n.p., late, pp. 1-9, 1-5.

The three kinds or stages of inquiry illustrated.

757. What is Reasoning

A. MS., n.p., n.d., 14 pp.; plus 2 copies of 2 pp. each (not in CSP's hand) and a TS. of 7 pp.

An elementary exposition of necessary and probable reasoning.

758. (Aristotle 9, Aristotle 10)

A. MS., n.p., n.d., 4 pp., incomplete.

A lecture on inference, with all elementary inferences divided into three classes. Is the division into three classes natural?

759. (B)

A. MS., n.p., n.d., pp. 1-3.

On the modes of necessary inference.

760. [Necessary Reasoning]

A. MS., n.p., n.d., 4 pp.

761. Examples of Probable Reasoning

A. MS., n.p., n.d., 1 p.

Possibly a test question. The reader is asked to draw a conclusion (probable) from a set of four facts presented to him.

762. [Plan for a Work on Probability]

A. MS., n.p., n.d., 1 p. (plan); 1 p. of what may be the start of the proposed work; pp. 7-15 (not in CSP's hand).

763. The Doctrine of Chances

A. MS., n.p., n.d., pp. 1-3; 1-2 (New).

Introductory comments only. Ancient inquiries into the nature of probability.

*764. [Probability and Induction]

A. MS., n.p., n.d., 99 pp.

The topics of these fragments range widely from CSP's comment on his habit of thinking in the syntax of existential graphs to discussions of probability, orders of induction (crude, quantitative, qualitative), the divisions of deduction as corollarial and theorematic; introduction of the term "adduction," with a note that the adductions of Socrates were of a crude order. Also notes on the history of logic (Aristotle, Bacon, English logicians) and reflections on the meaning of "pragmatism," and its connection with signs and habits. In regard to the origins of the word "pragmatism," CSP writes: "It was about 1870—I don't think it could have been as late as 1872—that I invented the word. . . ."

765. Lecture II

A. MS., n.p., n.d., 1 folded sheet.

On the theory of induction. Hamilton and Mansel. Aristotle's notion of induction.

766. Synopsis of the Discussion of the Ground of Induction (S)

A. MS., n.p., n.d., pp. 1-3, incomplete.

Criticism of the view that the probability of inductive conclusions is calculated by inverse probabilities. CSP takes the position that "in inductive reasoning the fact stated in the conclusion does not follow from the facts stated in the premises with any definite probability, but that from the manner in which the facts stated in the premises have come to our knowledge it follows that in assigning to a certain ratio of frequency the value concluded we shall be following a rule of conduct which must operate to our advantage in the long run."

767. [Fragments on Induction and Abduction]

A. MS., n.p., n.d., 5 pp.

768. Statistical Deduction

A. M.S., n.p., n.d., 1 p.

769. Logic of Science

A. MS., n.p., n.d., 24 pp. of several starts.

Definition of "logic." Marks of the 1st, 2nd, and 3rd orders. The mark of representation is of the 3rd order.

770. The Logic of Science

A. MS., n.p., n.d., pp. 1-6, with variants.

The meaning of "logic of science." Absurdity of a common sense logic, with accompanying remarks on common sense in general. Intimate connection between reasoning and morality. On the richness of various languages, with special praise for Greek.

771. Essays on the Rationale of Science

A. MS., n.p., n.d., pp. 1-3; 1-3; 1-3, and a variant p. 2 and an unnumbered page.

Autobiographical note concerning the publication of the *Popular Science* articles of 1877-78.

772. [Physical Laws]

A. MS., n.p., [c.1873], pp. 2-7.

Draft of N-1873-1. Scientific theories and inductive processes. The way in which physicists provide definitions in terms of mass, space, and time. Law of nature is a general relation connecting measures of different quantities.

773. Third Lecture on Methodeutic

A. MS., n.p., n.d., 1 folded sheet.

CSP opens his lecture with an apology for the lecture of the previous evening and with a proof he failed to provide on that occasion. Theoric deduction as creative (its object is not an existing thing, but an *ens rationis* which is just as real). Object and interpretant of a sign. Three grades of induction.

774. Ideas, Stray or Stolen, about scientific writing. No. 1 (Rh. Sc.)

A. MS., n.p., n.d., pp. 1-16.

Semeiotics. Speculative rhetoric. A universal art of rhetoric acknowledged as an *ens in posse*. Ordinary rhetoric should be modified by way of special studies. These studies yield the various rhetorics of fine arts, speech and language, science. The rhetoric of science is subdivided into rhetorics of communication of discoveries, scientific digests, and applications of science for special purposes.

775. Jottings on the Language of Science. No. 1 or Ideas, stray or stolen, about scientific writing. No. 1 (Rh. Sc.)

A. MS., n.p., n.d., pp. 1-14.

Earlier draft of MS. 774.

776. The Rhetoric of Scientific Communications (Rhetoric of Sci or Rh of Sci)

A. MS., n.p., n.d., pp. 1-6, 4-5.

The problem of communicating discoveries. Scientific terminology. The best types of titles for scientific papers.

777. Plan of an Essay on the Rhetoric of Scientific Communication in two parts of ten of these Ms. pages each. Part I. General. Part II. Special

A. MS., n.p., n.d., 6 pp.

Semeiotics. Universal rhetoric.

778. [Late Fragments on Logic and Science]

A. MS., n.p., [c.1909], pp. 5-15.

From a rambling lecture touching on the kinds of reasoning, the classification of the sciences, nominalism and realism in medieval logic, and the lecturer's scorn for contemporary philosophy and ". . . the stupid and utterly anti-scientific doctrine that a law of nature is nothing but a fabrication of the human mind."

779. [Syllogism]

A. MS., n.p., n.d., 8 pp. of fragments.

Aristotle and the history of logic.

780. Table of Syllogisms

A. MS., n.p., n.d., 3 pp. (not in CSP's hand, with the exception of a single correction).

MSS. 780-782 may be parts of an examination.

781. Classification of Universals

A. MS., n.p., n.d., 2 pp. (not in CSP's hand).

782. Table of Contraposition

A. MS., n.p., n.d., 1 p. (not in CSP's hand).

783. [On the Syllogism]

A. MS., n.p., n.d., 4 pp.

Possibly an early draft of "Classification of Arguments."

784. Two Fallacies

A. MS., n.p., April 20, 1901, pp. 1-5.

CSP notes that Mrs. Ladd-Franklin's method of testing syllogisms, based on the inconsistency of three propositions, is very similar to the method he used for the moods of the fourth figure (but which he rejected) in his paper: "On the Natural Classification of Arguments" (see G-1867-1b).

785. Notes (to 1867 paper Vol. 3)
A. MS., n.p., n.d., 25 pp.
See G-1867-1a.

786. Notes on Mrs. Franklin's Article "Syllogism" (Syllogism)
A. MS., n.p., n.d., pp. 1-18.

*787. That Categorical and Hypothetical Propositions are one in essence, with some connected matters
A. MS., G-c.1895-1, pp. 1-49 (pp. 6-9 missing).
Published in *Collected Papers* in the following order: 2.332-339, 2.278-280, 1.564-567 (c.1899), 2.340-356.

788. Propositions of the 0 order, Propositions of the 1st order, Syllogisms of 0–0 order, Syllogisms of the 0–1 order, Syllogisms of the 1–1 order
A. MS., n.p., n.d., pp. 1-6.

789. [Elements of a Proposition]
A. MS., n.p., n.d., 6 pp. and 6 pp. (Universe).
"Universe" of a proposition is defined as "a series of possibilities to which the proposition refers but whose limits cannot be described in general terms but can only be indicated in some other way." A proposition may relate to several such universes.

790. [Fragment on Hypothetical Propositions]
A. MS., G-undated-17, 1 p.
Published in entirety as 8.380n[4].

791. #5 Analysis of the Proposition
A. MS., n.p., n.d., 1 p.

792. On the Logical Nature of the Proposition (Dicisign)
A. MS., n.p., n.d., pp. 1-2, with a rejected p. 2.
Notes confusion of proposition with statement, assertion, physical act of judging, and an act of assent. CSP proposes to state his own theory of propositions, and then he launches into a discussion of signs.

793. [On Signs]
A. MS., n.p., n.d., pp. 1-4, 10-14; plus 9 pp. of variants and 1 p. (fragment).
An attempt to define "sign" as a medium for the communication of form. Sign as essentially triadic. Application of existential graphs to signs. Speculative grammar, critic, and methodeutic. On p. 14 verso is the beginning of a letter to "Professor James."

794. Sections of Roget's Thesaurus containing words meaning signs
A. MS., n.p., n.d., 1 p.

795. [Classification of Signs on the Basis of Idea, Token, and Type]
A. MS., n.p., n.d., 1 p.

796. The Art of Reasoning. Chapter I. What is a Sign?
A. MS., n.p., n.d., 2 pp.
Introduction of terms: quality, relations, focus, ratio, a relate, reagents, terms, signification, representamen.

797. [Fragments on Signs]
A. MS., n.p., n.d., 9 pp. (but not all from the same work).

798. [On Signs]
A. MS., G-c.1897-3, 5 pp.
Published as 2.227-229 and 2.444n^1.

799. [Ten Classes of Signs]
A. MS., n.p., n.d., 3 pp.

800. P of L
A. MS., n.p., n.d., pp. 2-6, 10; plus 1 p.
On the classification of signs.

801. Logic: Regarded as a Study of the General Nature of Signs (Logic)
A. MS., n.p., n.d., pp. 1-4.
The transition from feeling to knowing. Definition of "sign." Calculations on the verso of one of the pages.

* 802. Teleological Logic
A. MS., n.p., begun May 14, 1865, 4 pp., incomplete.
Logic as the semeiotic science of representations. Division of the sciences into science of things, representations, and forms. Kinds of representations: signs, symbols, and copies.

803. [Logic and Signs]
A. MS., n.p., n.d., pp. 1-5.

* 804. [Assertion and Signs]
A. MS., n.p., n.d., pp. 22, 24, 29, 33.

* 805. [The Essential Nature of Assertions]
A. MS., n.p., n.d., pp. 18-20.

806. Of Modality
A. MS., n.p., n.d., 3 pp.
The verso of one of the pages contains a chart, dated July 12, 1908, and labelled "Divisions of Signs."

* 807. [Necessary Modality]
A. MS., n.p., n.d., pp. 16-20.
Religious instinct and the evolution of the universe. Note on the relation of mathematical abilities and music.

808. Formal Division(s) of Dyadic Relations
A. MS., n.p., n.d., 5 pp.

809. #12. Division of Formal Science
A. MS., n.p., n.d., 5 pp.
The nine prescindible references and the nine formal sciences.

810. [On the Formal Principles of Deductive Logic]
A. MS., n.p., n.d., 4 pp. and 4 pp.
An attempt to recapitulate the principles of the logic of relatives. The nature of a sign, or representation.

811. [Printed Pages of "On the Natural Classification of Arguments"]
      Printed pages (annotated), G-1867-1b (1893).
      These pages from *The Proceedings of the American Academy* (1867) contain
      CSP's revisions of 1893. See sup(1)G1867-1b. Published, again, as 2.461-516,
      with the revisions of 1893.

* 812. Logico-Mathematical Glosses
      A. MS., n.p., n.d., 8 pp. and pp. 8-9.
      Boolean algebra. Sundry misconceptions about mathematical logic (pp. 8-9).

813. [Logic and Mathematics]
      A. MS., n.p., n.d., 6 pp.
      Material on existential graphs.

814. Achilles and the Tortoise
      A. MS., n.p., n.d., pp. 1-6.

815. [Achilles and the Tortoise]
      A. MS., n.p., n.d., pp. 2-6.

816. [On Five Grades of Originality in Logic, with Illustrations from the
      History of Logic]
      A. MS., n.p., n.d., 6 pp.
      Comments on Royce as logician and metaphysician, especially in connection
      with Royce's memoir, "The Relation of the Principles of Logic to the Foun-
      dations of Geometry."

817. [Various Fragments on Indicative Words, Hypothetical Propositions,
      Truth and Satisfaction]
      A. MS., n.p., n.d., 4 pp.

818. Mr. Bertrand Russell's Paradox
      A. MS., n.p., late, 5 pp., unfinished.

819. The Conception of Infinity
      A. MS., n.p., [c.1880], 5 pp.
      De Morgan's syllogism of transposed quantity, and the inappropriateness of
      one of De Morgan's examples. Fermatian inference and the collections to
      which it does and does not apply.

820. [Fermatian Inference]
      A. MS., n.p., n.d., pp. 1-6.

821. Some Unmanageable Problems
      A. MS., n.p., n.d., 7 pp.
      Notes on Cantor's "Beiträge zur Begrundung der transfiniten Mengenlehre"
      (*Mathematische Annalen* of 1895).

822. [Hamilton and Mansel]
      A. MS., n.p., n.d., 2 pp.
      Laws of reasoning. Mansel's definitions of "absolute" and "infinite."

823. [Critic of Arguments]
      A. MS., n.p., n.d., 4 pp., consecutive but incomplete.
      An evaluation (and appreciation) of Benjamin Peirce's powers of analysis. An
      examination of Mansel's views on logic.

824. Triadic Monosynthemes of Six Monads

A. MS., notebook, n.p., n.d.

The notebook also contains a list of names (of students?) and an estimate of their abilities, but this part of the notebook is not in CSP's hand. Drafts of two letters which were in the notebook have been removed and placed with CSP's correspondence. One of these drafts was to B. E. Smith and the other to F. C. S. Schiller.

825. (FRL)

A. MS., G-c.1899-1, 3 pp.

Published in entirety as 1.135-40.

826. Some Reveries of a Dotard

A. MS., n.p., late, pp. 1-5.

Logic as the science which distinguishes bad from sound reasoning. The sense of obligation in reasoning. Reflections on psychophysics. Fallibilism.

827. [Logic and the Doctrine of "Anti-cock-sure-ism"]

A. MS., n.p., n.d., 4 pp.

Inexactitude of physical laws, e.g., law of gravitation.

828. Logic (Li)

A. MS., n.p., November 2, 1910, pp. 1-3.

An analysis of doubt as neither ignorance nor consciousness of ignorance. Doubt is treated as an emotion.

829. [Absolute Certainty]

A. MS., n.p., n.d., 2 sheets, numbered 2 and 3, incomplete.

CSP's inability to discover a single truth which seems free of doubt. Discussion of the propositions "I feel a prick" and "Twice two is four."

830. [Reasoning and Belief]

A. MS., n.p., n.d., 2 pp., incomplete; plus 1 p. of a rejected draft.

831. [Reasoning and Instinct]

A. MS., n.p., n.d., pp. 2-29, incomplete.

The fine gradations between subconscious or instinctive mind and conscious, controlled reason. Logical machines are not strictly reasoning machines because they lack the ability of self-criticism and the ability to correct defects which may crop up. Three kinds of reasoning: inductive, deductive, hypothetical. Quasi-inferences.

832. [Reason and Instinct]

A. MS., n.p., n.d., 3 pp.

Reason as inferior to instinct. Comments on the work of Zeller and other German logicians and historical philosophers.

833. [Veracity]

A. MS., n.p., n.d., 2 pp.

Signs, truth, and veracity. Perfect veracity distinct from cognizable veracity.

834. [First, Second, and Third Degrees of Knowledge]

A. MS., n.p., n.d., 1 p.

835. [Three Grades of Clearness of Thought]
A. MS., n.p., n.d., pp. 9-17, incomplete.

Absurdity of the doctrine of simple concepts.

836. [Fragments on the Normative Sciences]
A. MS., n.p., n.d., 5 pp.

837. [Various Topics in Logic]
A. MS., n.p., n.d., 27 pp.

Necessary reasoning, hypothesis, the syllogism, the logic of relatives, and the relationship between logic and evolution.

838. [Fragments on the Justification of Reasoning]
A. MS., n.p., late, 9 pp.

The fragments, all concerned with the same problem, are not from the same work. Two of the fragments are dated: April 10, 1911 and February 22, 1912.

* 839. [Fragments]
A. MS., n.p., n.d., 199 pp.

Existential graphs, the logic of relatives, logical critic, theory of signs, hypothesis and induction, belief and reasoning, generalization, rationale of science, and classification are some of the topics found here. One page is dated September 22, 1860; the remainder are undated and apparently cover several periods of CSP's career.

840. [Fragment]
A. MS., n.p., n.d., 1 p.

"Logic is a sort of tree of knowledge of good and evil which costs the loss of paradise to him who tastes of its fruit."

METAPHYSICS

RELIGIOUS METAPHYSICS

841. A Neglected Argument for the Reality of God ($\odot$)
A. MS., G-1908-2, pp. 1-64, with 11 pp. of variants.

Published in the *Hibbert Journal,* vol. 7, pp. 90-112, and again as 6.452-480.

*842. A Neglected Argument for the Reality of God (G)
A. MS., G-c.1905-1, pp. 1-134 (p. 27 and pp. 109-120 missing), with 40 pp. of variants and 1 p. ("Contents of G").

Published, in part, as 2.755-772, except 757n[1] (pp. 44-108, except 86-87). Unpublished: Dedication "to the friend of my dreams." Autobiographical notes on CSP's early interest in logic. Neglected ("Humble") argument presented. Logical critic. The nature of real doubt and inquiry. Man's tendency toward correct conjectures illustrated. Retroduction and deduction. The division of signs into iconic, indexical, and symbolic. Two kinds of deductions: definitory and ratiocinative. The correction of crude induction, e.g., argument against miracles. Scholastic realism.

843. A Neglected Argument for the Reality of God (⊙) (☉)
A. MS., n.p., n.d., pp. 1-71.

Apparently two drafts which are interwoven, with few, if any, pages missing, but with an order that is difficult to maintain. Both drafts are drafts of MSS. 841 and 842.

844. Additament to the Article A Neglected Argument for the Reality of God
A. MS., G-c.1910-1, pp. 1-8, with variants.

Published as 6.486-490 (pp. 1-8) and 6.491 (pp. 4-6 of an alternative section).

*845. Answers to Questions about my Belief in God (A)
A. MS., G-c.1906-2, pp. 1-58.

Published as 6.494-501 (pp. 1-20) and 6.502-521 (pp. 32-58).

846. Notes for my Logical Criticism of Articles of the Christian Creed
A. MS., G-c.1910-3, pp. 1-14.

Published in entirety as 7.97-109.

847. First Rough Draught of the Substance of A Logical Examination of the Christian Creed in Brief Summary
A. MS., n.p., January 23, 1911, pp. 1-7.

CSP introduces himself to his reader: autobiographical notes on ancestry and family traits. Galton's rule of inheritance.

848. First Very Rough, Hasty, and Very Summary Draught (in places requiring and admitting of Great Condensation) of A Logical Examination of the Christian Creed
A. MS., n.p., January 24, 1911, pp. 1-12.

Slight revision of MS. 847. Galton's law of inheritance. Autobiographical notes on family background and traits.

849. A Logical Criticism of Some Articles of Religious Faith
A. MS., n.p., April 9-20, 1911, pp. 1-11 (p. 2 missing; p. 11 misnumbered).
"Reasoning," "argument," and "sign," defined. Nature of signs: objects and interpretants of signs; the possibility of self-reference of signs.

850. A Logical Criticism of Essential Articles of Religious Faith
A. MS., n.p., April 22, 1911, pp. 1-3.

For a book which was to be divided into two parts, the first part relating to logical critic. CSP regrets "that the darker and more cruel parts of religious faith have not had justice done to them nor brought into so high relief as they ought."

851. Rough Draught of Preface to Logical Criticism of Essential Articles of Religious Faith
A. MS., n.p., April 23, 1911, 1 p.

The spirit of science and the spirit of religion are opposed. Religious life must begin in feeling.

*852. A Logical Critique of Essential Articles of Religious Faith
A. MS., n.p., April 25-May 21, 1911, pp. 1-15 unfinished; 6-14 of a discarded draft; plus 6 pp. also discarded.

CSP's plan to divide his book into two parts, one part concerned with logical critic and the other with the application of the principles of logical critic to religious questions. The meaning of "philosophy" as "a heuritic science of categorical truth." Philosophy based upon the common experience of all mankind. Doubt and belief opposed. Positive and negative doubt distinguished, with negative doubt regarded as the mere absence of belief. The meaning of "real"; its Latin derivation. Reality and hallucinatory experience. Common sense and critical common sense. Verbs and the Basque language (p. 15).

853. **Important Jottings for my Critique of the Articles of Religious Faith**
A. MS., n.p., April 30, 1911, 1 folded sheet.

The failure to accept common sense judgments as true has led to false metaphysics and to a rejection of common sense religious faith of the deeper kind.

854. **Notes on Logical Critique of the Essential Articles of Religious Faith**
A. MS., n.p., October 20, 1911, 1 folded sheet.
The nature of a sign: sign objects and interpretants.

855. **Contents of Rough Draught of Logical Critique of Religious Faith**
A. MS., n.p., n.d., 1 folded sheet.

Presumably an outline of the topics with which CSP's book is to be concerned. CSP's intention is to couple logical critic with the facts of human life.

856. **A Logical Criticism of the Articles of Religious Belief**
A. MS., n.p., 2 pp. of one of the alternative sections are dated April 5 and 7, 1911, pp. 1-18, with several alternative sections.

The contempt for religious faith in scientific circles reveals, not open-mindedness, but prejudice. Deduction, induction, and retroduction are the only kinds of reasoning. Deduction as either necessary or probable. Determinism and free will. Over-specialization on the part of the average scientist has made him culturally ignorant—a queer mixture of enlightenment and of what is the equivalent of superstition. Laws of nature. Miracles and ultramiracles. Two of the alternative sections contain a discussion of existential graphs.

857. **Lecture I**
A. MS., n.p., n.d., pp. 1-5, incomplete.

This is the first lecture of the course planned in MS. 876. Double purpose of lecture: (1) to determine what a reasonable mind of the day ought to think of religion and (2) to comment on the validity of reasoning in general. Three and only three kinds of reasoning. Abduction, or retroduction. CSP's objectivity on the question of God's existence. If there is an Absolute, it is nothing like God.

858. **An Essay on the Limits of Religious Thought written to prove that we can reason upon the nature of God**
A. MS., n.p., n.d., 8 pp.

There are two dates on the verso of one of the pages: April 10, 1857 and January 11, 1861. The possibility of giving intelligible definitions of things which themselves can not be comprehended. Is the definition of "infinite" possible? The three necessary modes of dependency are community, causality, and influx. The three perfect degrees of modality are possibility, actuality, and necessity. All degree admits of one of three successive degrees: nullity, positivity, and perfection. All stages have one of three temporal expressions: retrogression, contemporaniety, or succession. The three intuitions of expression. The three total quantities of intuition and the three infinite qualities of quantity. Lastly, the three influxual dependencies of quality: negation, reality, infinity.

859. Influx. Proof of the Infinite Nature of the Creator

A. MS., n.p., n.d., 1 p.

860. [Nominalism, Realism, and the Logic of Modern Science]

A. MS., G-c.1896-1, 17 pp.

From this manuscript, 6.492-493 were published. Unpublished: scientific method and the solution of philosophical problems. Misapprehensions concerning the scientific method. Nominalistic and realistic metaphysics.

861. [On Religious Belief, The Efficacy of Prayer, and Proof of God's Reality]

A. MS., n.p., n.d., 6 pp. incomplete.

The verso of one page includes a brief comment on the meaning of "real," in relation to the views of Albertus Magnus and Duns Scotus. Cf. A3 of MS. 845.

862. [On the Recognition of Divine Inspiration]

A. MS., n.p., n.d., 7 pp. (discontinuous but possibly parts of two drafts).

On the possible sources of knowledge.

863. [The Effect of Scientific Thought on Spiritual Beliefs]

A. MS., n.p., n.d., 3 pp.

864. Notes for my little book on Religion

A. MS., notebook, n.p., June 20, 1906, with a sheet of notes which seem to be part of the same project.

One page provides what is probably the topical outline of a book which would have treated the relationship between science and religion.

865. [Notes on Religious and Scientific Infallibilism]

A. MS., G-c.1897-2, 4 pp. and 7 pp.

The manuscript of 4 pp. was published as 1.8-14. The manuscript of 7 pp. was not published. Anticipated awakening of religious life, with greater simplicity of belief and greater spiritualization of the creeds. The Church's claim to infallibility is sound enough if by "infallibility" is meant practical infallibility.

866. [On the Reconciliation of Religion and Science]

A. MS., n.p., n.d., 6 pp.

The denial of mechanical infallibilism, coupled with a plea for the moderation of religious infallibilism. Agnosticism is found intolerable. The reconciliation of religion and science can not be accomplished by a religion of science.

867. [Religion, Science, and Fallibilism]

A. MS., G-c.1897-1, pp. 10-12.

Published in entirety as 1.3-7.

868. [Notes on Science and Religion]

A. MS., n.p., n.d., 4 pp., with a typed copy.

The effect of religious exercises upon morality.

869. Hume on Miracles (H on M)

A. MS., G-1901-2b, pp. 1-34, with rejected pp. 7-8.

Published in entirety as 6.522-547.

870. What is a Law of Nature (Law of Nat)

A. MS., n.p., [c.1901?], pp. 1-40, with variants.

The meaning of the phrase "Law of Nature," and the history of its usage. The Aristotelian theory of growth and potentiality. Scholastic realism and substantial forms. The anti-Aristotelianism of Ockham. The Cartesian view of "law." Seventeenth-century atheism in England. Modern nominalism.

871. What is a Law of Nature? (L of N)

A. MS., n.p., n..d, pp. 1-27 (p. 24 missing), plus several variants.

"Law of nature" as the "prognostic generalization of observations." Conception of law of nature prevalent in Hume's England. Hume's argument against miracles.

872. The Idea of a Law of Nature among the contemporaries of David Hume and among advanced thinkers of the present day (Law)

A. MS., G-1901-2a, April 19, 1901, pp. 1-29; plus 16 pp. of at least one other draft, with 1 p. bearing the title "Hume on Miracles and the Laws of Nature."

Published, in part, as 1.133-134 (pp. 4-9). Unpublished: definition of "philosophy," with philosophy and mathematics sharply differentiated. Hume and his contemporaries. Miracles and the laws of nature. How the idea of evolution has influenced philosophy. Metaphysics must be based upon a correct systematic logic. Whether philosophy should be divided into two parts (logic and metaphysics) or three parts (logic, metaphysics, and ethics).

873. Hume's Argument against Miracles, and the Idea of Natural Law (Hume)

A. MS., n.p., n.d., pp. 1-20, with variants.

Terminology: "inference," "abduction," "induction," "belief," "habit." Pragmatism as a maxim of right thinking. Hedonism and the distinction between pleasure and satisfaction. Ultimate or final ends or aims.

874. The Order of Nature

TS. (CSP's), G-1877-5e, 14 pp.

Published in entirety as 6.395-427.

*875. [On Natural Law and Chance]

A. MS., n.p., [c.1884], 36 pp.

Parts of a draft or drafts of one or more lectures delivered at The Johns Hopkins University about 1883-84, perhaps that on "Design and Chance" before the *Metaphysical Club* on January 17, 1884. Analysis of conceptions of design and intelligence. The tendencies of things toward ends. Darwin's influence upon both science and philosophy. The operation of chance.

876. Suggestions for a Course of Entretiens leading up through Philosophy to the Questions of Spiritualism, Ghosts, and finally to that of Religion

A. MS., n.p., n.d., pp. 1-11, with rejected pp. 1, 4; plus 1 p. ("Entretien1").

Sketch of a course of half-hour lectures (followed by conversation). The three basic kinds of reasoning: deduction, induction, and retroduction. The justification of reasoning.

877. Brief Sketch of a Proposed Series of Articles on the Cosmology of the Here and Hereafter

A. MS., n.p., n.d., 8 pp. (of several drafts).

Spiritualism examined; plan for four articles. On the reverse side of three of these pages are drafts of two letters, one of which is addressed to Mr. Murrian and the other unaddressed.

878. Logic and Spiritualism

TS., sup(1)G-1890-4, pp. 1-19, with corrections and additions in CSP's hand, a typed copy, and a galley proof with CSP's corrections.

Published as 6.557-587. This manuscript was intended for *The Forum* but after correcting the galleys CSP became dissatisfied with his efforts and so the article was never published.

879. Logic and Spiritualism

A. MS., n.p., n.d., pp. 1-18 (pp. 10-12 missing); pp. 1-40 (pp. 6-7 missing); a 4 pp. sequence belonging to one of the two incomplete drafts of MS. 878.

On spiritualism and scientific open-mindedness. Adequate discussion of spiritualism requires a satisfactory solution to the soul-body problem. CSP's suggestion that matter be regarded as a modification of mind rather than mind as a modification of matter.

880. [On Spiritualism, Telepathy, and Miracles]

A. MS., n.p., [c.1890-91?], 11 pp.

CSP has never attended a successful seance. He speaks of himself as "a hidebound sceptic," but admits that there is no direct argument against spiritualism and telepathy. Protestantism and Roman-Catholicism on the question of miracles.

* 881. Telepathy

A. MS., G-1903-5, pp. 1-100, plus 49 pp. of variants.

Published, in part, as 7.597-688, except $597n^3$ (pp. 1-99, with deletions).

882. [Telepathy]

A. MS., n.p., n.d., pp. 16-18 (cf. G-c.1895-4 and $7.597n^3$).

Common sense flatly denies telepathy. CSP finds the theory doubtful and rejects it provisionally.

883. [Thought Transference]

A. MS., n.p., n.d., 1 p.

Remarks on C. S. Minot's "Second Report to the American Psychical Research Society on Experimental Psychology."

884. An Examination of an Argument of Messrs. Gurney, Myers, and Podmore"

TS., n.p., 1887, 20 pp. (four drafts of 5 pp. each).

One of these drafts is a typescript of G-1887-3. An analysis of case histories of psychic phenomena in Gurney's *Phantasms of the Living*.

885. Demsis

A. MS., n.p., 1892, 5 pp.

Draft of G-1892-2.

886. Immortality in the Light of Synechism
    A. MS., G-c.1892-2, pp. 1-12.
    Published in entirety as 7.565-578.

887. [For *The Open Court* article "What is Christian Faith"]
    A. MS., G-1893-3, 7 pp.

888. [For *The Open Court* article, "Pythagorics"]
    A. MS., G-1892-1a, 4 pp., with 6 pp. addressed to the Editor of *The Open Court.*

889. [An Illustration of an Unelevated Religion: Book of Psalms]
    A. MS., n.p., n.d., 1 p.

890. [Assorted Pages on Problems of Religious Belief]
    A. MS., n.p., n.d., 2 pp. (continuous); plus 4 pp. (not continuous).
    The only solution to the problem of evil is to accept the fact that Supreme Love embraces hate, and that sin is a creation of God. "God delights in evil." Anselm's argument that God necessarily exists is rejected.

891. Private thoughts principally on the conducted life
    A. MS., notebook, n.p., 1853-March 17, 1888. Call number Am 805.
    Thirty-nine pages, being a collection of aphorisms on such subjects as genius, love, solitude, worship, prayer, heaven, impudence and grace, passion and pleasure, freedom and causation, classification of the human faculties. Sample: "Best maxim in writing, perhaps, is really to love your reader for his own sake." These aphorisms were apparently transcribed by CSP from various other writings of his on several occasions. Entry number LXX, for instance, is dated 1866 Nov. 20, and reads: "What is not a question of a possible experience is not a question of fact." This seems to be a slight revision of an entry in the Logic Notebook (MS. 339), p. 11v also dated 1866 Nov. 20: "What is not a question of what can possibly be known is not a question of fact."

892. [On Moral Necessity and the Law of Love]
    A. MS., n.p., n.d., 3 pp.

893. [Hegelianism, Christian Thought, and Morality]
    A. MS., n.p., n.d., 3 pp., with another page which may be part of the same manuscript.

894. Religion and Politics
    A. MS., G-c.1895-2, pp. 1-3.
    Published as 6.449-551, with the exception of the first paragraph and the first sentence of the second paragraph which concern the politician and his obligations to his party.

CATEGORIOLOGY

895. [Notes on the Categories]
    A. MS., G-c.1880-2, 41 pp.
    Five pages of the manuscript were published as 1.353. Omitted: application of the categories in formal logic. Logical analysis of "Cogito, ergo sum." Kantian and Peircean categories compared. The Kantian categories of total-

ity, plurality, and unity are nearly CSP's. Criticism of Kant's views on the functions of judgments.

* 896. [Fragment on the Categories]

A. MS., n.p., n.d., 1 p.

Generous and degenerate Thirdness. Entelechy as the mode of being constituted by generous Thirdness.

897. One, Two, Three: Kantian Categories

TS. (with CSP's corrections), n.p., n.d., 3 pp.

Metaphysics as an "imitation" of geometry. Both geometrical and metaphysical axioms may be doubted. Brief account of CSP's cosmology.

898. The List of Categories: A Second Essay (Cat)

A. MS., G-c.1894-1, pp. 1-4.

Published as 1.300-301, 1.293, 1.303, 1.326-329 in this order.

899. The Cenopythagorean Categories (CC)

A. MS., n.p., n.d., pp. 1-13, incomplete, with 9 pp. of variants.

Explanation of the use of the expression "Cenopythagorean." Hypothesis: The elements of the world are such that each expressly excludes the possibility of any contradiction. The whole, in this case, is such as it is by virtue of what the elements are. Some implications of this hypothesis.

900. Logic of Mathematics: An attempt to develop my categories from within (L of M)

A. MS., G-c.1896-2, pp. 5-69 (pp. 1-4 missing), with 48 pp. of variants.

Published in entirety as 1.417-520.

901. One, Two, Three: Fundamental Categories of Thought and of Nature

A. MS., G-c.1885-1, pp. 1-39, incomplete, with a variant p. 8.

Published, in part, as 1.369-372 and 1.376-378. Unpublished (pp. 20-24; 33-39): If the three categories are connected with reasoning, they must be present in the mind as innate ideas when reasoning first takes place. The three mental faculties corresponding to the three categories of logic are feeling, volition, and cognition. The three elements of consciousness must be capable of physiological explanation. Speculation as to whether the cell may contain all the fundamental elements of the universe.

902. The Author's Response to the anticipated Suspicion that he attaches a superstitious or fanciful importance to the number three, and forces Divisions to a Procrustean Bed of Trichotomy (R)

A. MS., G-1910-4, pp. 1-20, with 2 pp. of variants; plus 10 pp. of an untitled earlier draft (9/11/10).

Published, in part, as 1.568-572. Unpublished (pp. 11-20): The classification of the animal world is continued. CSP's admission of his slight acquaintance with zoology and, in spite of his study of classification under Agassiz for six months (1860), his "incapacity" for this kind of work. An examination of Huxley's classification of fish. Also unpublished (pp. R9.1-9.8): Artificial things are classified, with a view toward establishing trichotomies.

903. [First, Second, Third Categories]

A. MS., n.p., n.d., 4 pp.

Fragments of other drafts of MS. 717.

904. [Firstness, Secondness, and Thirdness]
A. MS., G-c.1875-1 [1882 or later], 4 pp., 2 pp., 1 p.

The manuscript is on paper with a watermark of 1882 and so must be dated 1882 or later. The two-page sequence was published as 1.337. The other pages offer an explanation of the three categories and touch upon the three kinds of philosophies of the absolute, namely, Epicureanism, pessimism, and evolutionism.

905. One, Two, Three
A. MS., notebook, n.p., December 7, 1907 (the earliest of several dates recorded).

Rough notes on the three categories. Digressions: stages of inquiry; kinds of induction; probability. "Unpretentious Argument for Reality of God" (April 16, 1908).

906. One, Two, Three; An Evolutionist Speculation
TS. (with corrections and additions in CSP's hand), n.p., n.d., 2 pp., with alternative drafts and carbon copies.

An attempt to explain Firstness, Secondness, and Thirdness with the use of examples.

907. [Firstness, Secondness, and Thirdness]
TS. (with corrections and additions in CSP's hand), n.p., n.d., 1 p.

The reason for not giving abstract definitions of the conceptions of Firstness, Secondness, and Thirdness. A denial that the One of Parmenides, the unity of "I think," or any other unities discussed by philosophers have anything at all to do with Firstness.

908. [The Categories]
A. MS., n.p., n.d., pp. 2-20, 6-8.

A deduction of the Categories. The breadth of pragmaticism. The elements of the phaneron.

909. A Guess at the Riddle [and] Notes for a Book to be entitled: A Guess at the Riddle
TS. (corrected), G-c.1890-1, 65 pp., including alternative drafts.

The "Notes" alone were published as follows: 1.354-368; 1.373-375; 1.379-416, with omissions.

910. Types of Third Degenerate in the Second Degree
A. MS., n.p., n.d., pp. 1-2.

911. [Degrees of Degeneracy]
A. MS., n.p., n.d., 1 folded sheet.

A triple character has two degrees of degeneracy. Degeneracy of a dual character. Nondegenerate dual relation is a real relation. Token, index, icon.

912. [The Three Categories: Primian, Secundian, Tertian]
A. MS., n.p., n.d., 6 pp.; plus 1 p. which seems to belong with the others.

913. [Firstness and Secondness]
A. MS., n.p., n.d., 4 pp.

914. [Firstness, Secondness, Thirdness, and the Reducibility of Fourthness]
A. MS., n.p., n.d., pp. 5-8.

The nature of signs.

915. [The Three Categories and the Reduction of Fourthness]
A. MS., n.p., n.d., 3 pp.

The concepts of one, two, three are inseparably connected. The concept of four (and of any higher number) is a "complication" of three. In this connection CSP's dispute with Sylvester is mentioned.

MISCELLANEOUS

916. The Modus of the It
A. MS., n.p., early, 4 pp., with a typed copy.

Three celestial worlds: manifold of sense, world of consciousness, world of abstraction. That which is in the sensible world enters the mental world by means of a revelation which is part of the abstract world. Three abstract revelations. Three kinds of absolute existence. Three kinds of necessary modes: community, causality, and influx. Three kinds of influxial derivation. Three total shapes. Three immense manifestations. The It and the Thou.

917. I, It, and Thou: A Book giving Instructions in some of the elements of Thought
A. MS., n.p., early, 2 pp., consecutive, and 2 pp. which are related.

The relationships of the three different worlds in which I, It, and Thou are discovered.

918. On the Classification of the Human Faculties
A. MS., n.p., [c.1859], 1 folded sheet (3 pp.).

Rational psychology. The seven faculties (exhibiting strong Kantian influence). Arousing regarded as a special faculty, which guarantees the intelligibility of free will. Classification of the I-impulse, It-impulse, Thou-impulse.

*919. [Fragments of Early Writings on Metaphysics]
A. MS., n.p., [c.1860], 23 pp.

Outlines for a book on metaphysics—the queen of the sciences, the supreme science. I, It, Thou. The classification of artificial objects with reference to final causes. Signs. Symbols and their objects. Leading principles. Truth. Sundry comments on life and death, heaven and hell, and on the soul. Force and power.

920. [First Four Chapters of a Treatise on Metaphysics]
A. MS., n.p., August 21, 1861 (Preface), 48 pp.

The first three chapters constitute the "Introduction" and are as follows: Chapter I, "Domain, Basis, and Fabric of Metaphysical Thought"; Chapter II, "The Insufficiency of Dialectics" (ground of dogmatical, psychological, and logical dialectics); Chapter III, "On the Uselessness of Transcendentalism." The next chapter, the first chapter of Book I, is entitled "Principles" and deals with man as the measure of all things. More generally, these chapters are concerned with metaphysics as the philosophy of primal truths; that is, whose truths are the primary conditions of all science. Fundamental distinctions of metaphysics. Metaphysics, psychology, and religion. Truth and faith. Refutation of transcendentalism. Notes on the work of Kant, Hume, and Mansel. Idealism, materialism, realistic pantheism as representing the three worlds of mind, matter, and God. These worlds mutually exclude and include each other.

921. [Fragments from a Treatise on Metaphysics]

A. MS., n.p., [1859-61], 16 pp., 4 pp., and 124 pp.

A table of contents and notes for Chapter II, "On the Insufficiency of Dialectics." Dogmatical, psychological, and logical dialectics. Examples of the necessity of diflection and ordination. Probability of error. Notes for another Chaper II, "Nature of the Perfect." Proof that there are elementary propositions and that every conception is of boundless complication. Several other titles are distinguishable of which the comprehensive title is: "Matter Preparatory to Metaphysical Meditation." Other titles are as follows: "Proper Domain of Metaphysics" (May 21, 1859); "New Names and Symbols for Kant's Categories" (May 21, 1859); "That There is No Need of Transcendentalism" (May 21, 1859); "That the Perfect is the great Subject of Metaphysics" (May 21, 1859); "Explanation of the Categories" (May 22, 1859); "Of the Stages of the Category of Modality or Chance" (May 22, 1859); "Metaphysics as a Study" (June 1859); "On the Definition of Metaphysics" (July 1859); "Comparison of our Knowledeg of God and of other Substances" (July 25, 1859); "All unthought is thought of" (July 25, 1859); "Of Realism and Nominalism" (July 25, 1859); "Sir William Hamilton's Theory of the Infinite" (July 27, 1859); "That We can Understand the Definition of Infinity" (October 23, 1859); "Two Kinds of Thinking" (October 23, 1859); "The Nature of our Knowledge of the Infinite" (October 23, 1859); "Of Objects" (October 25, 1859); "Of Pantheism" (October 25, 1859); "Why We can Reason of the Infinite" (October 25, 1859); "That Infinity is an Unconscious Idea" (October 25, 1859); "The Fundamental Distinction of Metaphysics" (June 30, 1860); "Elucidation of the Essay, headed All unthought is thought of" (June 30, 1860); "The Keystone of this System" (July 1, 1860); "The Logical and the Psychological Treatment of Metaphysics" (July 3, 1860); "The Infinite, the Type of the Perfect" (July 3, 1860); "The Orders of Mathematical Infinity" (July 13, 1860); "Summary" (December 16, 1860); "Domain of Metaphysics" (August 6, 1861); "Introductory to Metaphysics" (August 11, 1861).

* 922. [Notes for a Work on Metaphysics]

A. MS., n.p., [c.1862 with one page dated May 29, 1862], 41 pp.

The first book of this projected work would have had the title, "Principles of Metaphysical Investigation." Man as the measure of all things. Truth and the nature of faith. Refutation of transcendentalism. On language, form, and plasticity.

923. [Ten Irreducible Conceptions and their Combinations]

A. MS., n.p., 1860-62, 24 pp., with a typed copy of the page dated June 8, 1862.

924. A Treatise of the Major Premises of the Science of Finite Subjects (Nature)

A. MS., n.p., August 5, 1864, 3 pp.

All reasoning can be represented syllogistically. The major premises—the principles of science—are the subjects of metaphysics. Metaphysics as theoretically essential to science.

925. [A Treatise of the Major Premises of the Science of Finite Subjects]

A. MS., n.p., August 5, 1864, 3 pp.

Science relies on the assumption that observation has value beyond itself.

The need to discover some validity of the major premises given in sensation; otherwise assumption of the major premises is *petitio principii*.

926. **A Treatise of the Major Premisses of Natural Science**

A. MS., n.p., n.d., 3 pp.

Major premises regarded as *a priori*, i.e., logically antecedent to all science. Judgments refer predicate to subject. The subject is assumed; the predicate is experienced. All judgment is inference.

927. **Possible extensive relations of subject and predicate**

A. MS., n.p., n.d., 9 pp.

Quantities, qualities, real predicates, relations, forms of fact, reasonableness, and creative potentialities are all related. Admixture of chemical notes.

928. **Sketch of a New Philosophy**

A. MS., n.p., n.d., 15 pp.

Reasoning and experimentation essentially analogous. Philosophy is committed to the notion that the processes of nature and thought are alike. Chance, law, and continuity. Mathematical and metaphysical axioms. The monism of modern psychology is materialistic. Eleven chapters contemplated, and these are outlined briefly.

929. **[On the Study of Metaphysics]**

A. MS., n.p., n.d., 2 pp.

The training metaphysicians receive today is compared unfavorably with the training they received in the medieval universities.

*930. **[On the Meaning of "Real"]**

A. MS., n.p., n.d., 20 pp., including variants, numbered from 4-45 but not continuously.

The difference between "would be" and "actually is" ("was," or "will be"). History of word "real"; Duns Scotus and Kant on the real; CSP's definition. Mode of consciousness and the taking on of habits.

931. **Questions on Reality**

A. MS., n.p., [1868], 48 pp., with 2 pp. of an earlier draft.

The earlier draft of 2 pp. is an outline draft of G-1868-2a. Twelve questions asked and answered dogmatically. The questions are concerned with the possibility of ultimate cognitions; immediate self-consciousness; knowledge of the external world; truth and the agreement of logical conclusion with information; contradiction as not always signifying falsity; matter as not necessary to reality; thought and signs; the meaning of the "unknowable." The later draft concerns the proper method for determining how we think; self-evidentness and self-consciousness; the perceived and the imagined; our knowledge of the external world; thinking and signs; signs of the unknowable. Is there any cognition which is absolutely incapable of being known? Have we any intuitions? Some of the questions raised in the earlier draft are raised again and this time answered less dogmatically.

932. **Potentia ex Impotentia**

A. MS., n.p., [1868], 9 pp. of two drafts.

Questions concerning reality. The future of metaphysics depends upon its establishing a connection with tangible external facts. Defense of the view that no sign means anything essentially incognizable. On knowledge of things-in-themselves. Idealism and first impressions of sense.

933. [Reality, Being, and Figment]
A. MS., n.p., n.d., 7 pp. (but not continuous).
Reality and figment not equated with Being and nothing. A figment is something, and therefore comes under the heading of Being.

* 934. [Reality of the Universe]
A. MS., n.p., n.d., pp. 24-29.
Primary qualities and feelings. Phenomenalism and the relativity of knowledge. Being, accident, substance. The passage from being to substance is mediated by conception of accident. The threefold nature of accident: quality, relation, representation. Quality is firstness; relation, secondness; representation, thirdness. Relations are of two great genera: (a) those whose ground is prescindable and (b) those whose ground is not.

935. [Notes on Idealism]
A. MS., n.p., [c.1873-77?], 4 pp.
Is it possible to conceive of anything which is not an object of thought? Defense of the central position of idealism, namely, that the actual or possible object of thought is an essential part of existence.

936. [Idealism, Mind and Matter, and the Principle of Continuity]
A. MS., n.p., n.d., 3 pp.
Leibniz as the first to set forth the law of continuity, which explains how mind and matter act upon each other. Matter as effete mind which is habit bound. An elevated theory of idealism.

*937. The Connection between Mind and Matter
A. MS., G-c.1893-2, pp. 1-13, with a variant p. 8; plus an earlier draft of 10 pp.
Published in entirety as 6.272-277.

938. (Matter)
A. MS., n.p., [c.1904], pp. 1-8, with an alternative p. 8.
Comments on Balfour's British Association Address (August 17, 1904) on the constitution of matter, especially the electron theory. The experimentalist's usage of "phenomenon." The confusion between belief in a reality which is expressible in phenomenalistic terms and belief in reality which is not so expressible.

939. Notes on Portions of Hume's "Treatise of Human Nature"
A. MS., n.p., [1905], 44 pp. and 5 pp. of variants.
For the probable date of the manuscript, see S. P. Langley correspondence for a letter from CSP, dated June 1, 1905. CSP considers only Part IV, Sections 1 and 2 of the "Treatise." Criticism of Hume's analysis of reasoning leads to an exposition of his own views. Association of beliefs, acritical reasoning, and reasoning (abductive, inductive, and deductive). Reasoning as that special variety of action which is under self-control. Probability and certainty; genuine and counterfeit beliefs; indubitability of beliefs and instincts. Hume's nominalistic metaphysics in the context of the nominalist-realist dispute. Percept and perceptual judgment as well as existence and reality distinguished. Three grades of complexity of being, with the triadic mode the most complex. Three kinds of triadic relations: collectivity, energy, signs. The different kinds of signs.

940. Logic of Events (LE)

A. MS., G-1898-1, pp. 1-11.

Published in two places with minor deletions: 6.1-5; 6.214-221.

941. Notes for 8 Lectures (N⁸)

A. MS., G-1898-1, pp. 1-8.

Published with a deletion (cf. 6.222n*) as 6.222-237. These pages are to be inserted at the end of MS. 940. See the last page of "Logic of Events" for the instructions to do so.

942. Abstracts of 8 Lectures (A⁸)

A. MS., n.p., n.d., pp. 1-33, incomplete, with variants and a single sheet entitled "Bifaria for 8 Lectures" (B⁸).

The bare nothing of possibility logically leads to continuity. Continuum of possible quality. Thisness and individuality; thisness and reaction. Firstness, Secondness, Thirdness. Habit, generalization, and the laws of nature. Evolution.

943. Considerations for 8 Lectures (C⁸)

A. MS., n.p., n.d., 2 pp.; plus a typed copy.

Hegel and the logic of continuity. Specific criticism of Hegel's understanding of mathematics, for example, his view that past, present, and future are the three dimensions of time. Further criticisms of Hegel concerns the logic of events.

944. Dottings for 8 Lectures (D⁸)

A. MS., n.p., n.d., 2 pp. (two attempts); plus a typed copy.

Hegel and CSP mean nearly the same thing by existence. CSP can almost accept Hegel's definition as the immediate unity of reflection-into-self and reflection-into-another (his reservation concerns reflection). Hegel misplaces existence by putting it under the first part of his *Encyclopaedia* (Logic) and under the second division (Wesen), whereas he places time under the second part (Nature). For CSP, time would first have had to be organized before nature could have begun.

945. Mems for 8 Lectures (M⁸)

A. MS., n.p., n.d., 2 pp.

The freedom of unbounded possibility (before time and space were organized). The nothing of the not yet being distinguished from the nothing of negation. Becoming. Quality is a sleeping, potential consciousness; quale-consciousness is a potential mode of being.

946. An Outline Sketch of the Synechistic Philosophy

A. MS., n.p., n.d., 7 pp.

Explanation of the word "synechistic" and justification of its use. Its cognate opposite "diechistic."

947. [Continuity and Hegel]

A. MS., G-c.1892-1b, 2 pp.

One of the two pages was published: 1.41-42.

948. The Logic of Continuity (LC)

A. MS., G-1898-1, pp. 1-37.

This is the last of the proposed set of eight lectures of 1898. Published, in part, as 6.185-213 (pp. 7-10 and 21-37). Unpublished is material on the history of geometry (pp. 1-7). Geometrical topics; continuum; Listing Numbers (pp. 10-20).

* 949. [Continuity]

A. MS., n.p., n.d., 7 pp.

Principle of continuity as the one great desideratum in all theorizing, and the master-key of philosophy.

* 950. [Continuity, Probability, Statistical Syllogism]

A. MS., n.p., [c.1893], pp. 7-12 and 6 pp.

Ultimate continuity as a regulative principle (6 pp.). Continuity as ubiquitous mediation; its relationship to dynamics (pp. 7-12).

951. Habit (H)

A. MS., G-1898-1 [c.1898], pp. 1-10, 12-37 (MS. appears to be continuous, although there is no p. 11).

Published in entirety as 7.468-517.

952. [The Rationality of the Universe]

A. MS., n.p., n.d., 4 pp.

953. [First and Second Conversazione]

A. MS., n.p., n.d., pp. 1-8, with variants.

The three views of knowledge: Epicurean, pessimistic, and melioristic. Second *conversazione* is on the idea of clearness.

954. [Evolution]

A. MS., n.p., n.d., 5 pp. and 10 pp.

The manuscript of 5 pp. is concerned with speculation on the possibility that Darwin was influenced by Malthus and the political economists. The manuscript of 10 pp. is concerned with the three modes of evolution: Darwinian, Lamarckian, and that mode by which "the mechanical effects of external causes, which go to break up habits, especially habits of heredity, . . . make forms vary, in determinate ways." Also: spontaneity and law, with law the product of evolution; matter as mind under almost complete domination of habit; synechism and questions concerning religion, morality, and telepathy.

955. [Fallibilism, Continuity, and Evolution]

A. MS., G-c.1897-5, 57 pp.

Published, with deletions, as 1.141-175. See sup(1)G-1892-0.

* 956. The Architecture of Theories

A. MS., n.p., n.d., 65 p.

This manuscript appears to be an early draft of the *Monist* article (G-1891-1a). On the principles of evolution.

* 957. [Evolutionary Love]

A. MS., n.p., n.d., 73 pp.

Early draft of an article which appeared in the *Monist* entitled "Evolutionary Love" and reprinted as 6.287-317 (G-1891-1e).

958. Reply to the Necessitarians

A. MS., n.p., n.d., 218 pp.

Early and incomplete drafts of an article published in the *Monist* entitled

"Reply to the Necessitarians: Rejoinder to Dr. Carus" and reprinted as 6.588-618 (G-1891-1f).

959. [Fragment of "The Doctrine of Necessity Examined"]
A. MS., n.p., n.d., 1 p.

*960. [Argument Against Necessitarianism]
A. MS., n.p., n.d., 2 folded sheets (8 pp.)

961. The Law of Mind and Our Glassy Essence
A. MS., n.p., n.d., 100 pp. ("Our Glassy Essence"); 22 pp. and 2 pp. ("The Law of Mind") and a notebook "Notes for Paper on the Laws of Mind 1892 May 10."
Early drafts of G-1891-1c and G-1891-1d.

*962. A Molecular Theory of Protoplasm
A. MS., n.p., n.d., 3 pp.
See 6.239 ff.

963. Introduction. The Association of Ideas
TS. (corrected), n.p., n.d., 8 pp., with 1 p. of notes.
Principles of association: contiguity, similarity, contrast, and causality. Association is not explained by causality but causality by association. Mind is not explained by matter. Rather, matter seems to be explained by mind. Criticism of treatises on logic, based upon works passed on from the Middle Ages. See *Grand Logic* (MS. 400).

*964. The Innateness of Notions and The Innateness of Ideas
A. MS., n.p., n.d., 5 pp.
Notion and idea contrasted. "Idea" connotes the essential character of a thing.

965. Creation
A. MS., n.p., n.d., 12 pp. (with a sequence numbered 28-33).
Science strives for knowledge for its own sake, but this knowledge is not systematized. The original chaos. Feeling and the tendency to generalization which brings about attraction between objects.

966. [Reflections on Real and Unreal Objects]
A. MS., notebook, n.p., n.d.
Late notes on metaphysics; earlier jottings on mathematics of three dimensions. Definition of "object" and "real object." Abstract idea of the unreal; our inability to think of an unreal object as real.

967. [Nominalism and Realism]
A. MS., n.p., n.d., 8 pp.
Nominalism as a reductive theory. Realism as a kind of idealism.

*968. [Fragment on Metaphysical Axioms]
A. MS., G-c.1893-1, 5 pp.
Published, in part, as 1.130-132.

969. [Architectonic Character of Philosophy]
A. MS., G-c.1893-5 [c.1896], 3 pp.
Published in entirety as 1.176-179.

970. [Critique of Positivism]
A. MS., n.p., n.d,. pp. 1-18 and a 1 p. outline.
Weakness of Comtean positivism is both logical and religious. Although positivism has had a favorable influence upon science its supporters are essentially unscientific.

971. Notes on the Question of the Existence of an Eternal World
A. MS., G-c.1890-2, 5 pp., and 3 pp. of a fragmentary alternative draft.
Published, for the most part, as 1.36-39.

972. Six Lectures of Hints toward a Theory of the Universe
A. MS., n.p., n.d., 3 pp.

973. [Transcription and Translation of Plato's Defense of Socrates]
A. MS., notebook, n.p., n.d.

974. Plato's Dialogues
A. MS., notebook, n.p., n.d.
Plato's Dialogues are listed, with their length and probable date noted. There are two other lists of Dialogues, one of which is headed "probably spurious" and the other "decidedly spurious." For the rest, there is a summary and an analysis of sorts of the early Dialogues.

975. Plato
A. MS., n.p., n.d., 1 p.
List of dates of the important events in Plato's life.

976. Plato
A. MS., n.p., n.d., 2 pp.
Significant dates in the life of Plato. A note on Aristotle's references to Plato.

*977. Plato's Dialogues
A. MS., n.p., n.d., 1 folded sheet and 1 p.

978. Order of Plato's Dialogues
A. MS., n.p., n.d., 6 pp.
Chronology of Plato's Dialogues established by stylistic developments.

979. [Chronology of Plato's Dialogues]
A. MS., n.p., n.d., 6 charts.
Chronology based, in part, on Lutoslawski's data.

980. Stylistic Development of Plato's Dialogues
A. MS., n.p., November 3-5, 1901, 8 pp.

981. Conjectural Dates of Plato's Dialogues
A. MS., n.p., n.d., 1 p.

982. Lutoslawski. Plato
A. MS., n.p., n.d., 4 pp.
Notes on Lutoslawski's research on the Platonic Dialogues.

983. Lutoslawski's Recalculations
A. MS., n.p., n.d., pp. 1-3, and a single unnumbered sheet.

984. Lutoslawski's "Relative Affinities"
    A. MS., n.p., n.d., 8 pp.
    Lutoslawski's miscalculations, with a list of corrections.

985. [Lutoslawski and a Report of Diogenes Laertius]
    A. MS., n.p., n.d., 1 folded sheet (3 pp.).
    CSP takes exception to Lutoslawski's refusal to credit Diogenes Laertius's report of what Hermodorus says is the truth concerning Plato's visit to Megara after the death of Socrates.

986. Translation of the beginning of the Cratylus (Cratylus)
    A. MS., n.p., n.d., pp. 1-6.
    Commentary accompanies the translation.

987. Note to 944B Laws
    A. MS., n.p., n.d., pp. 1-2.
    This manuscript is not in CSP's hand, but a note in the right-hand corner reads: "Jowett. Pierce [sic] notes."

988. Metaphysical Axioms and Syllogisms
    A. MS., n.p., May 30, 1860, 22 pp.
    Notes on the following Platonic Dialogues: *Apology, Crito, Gorgias, Phaedo, Protagorus,* and the *Republic.*

989. [Fragments on the Platonic Dialogues]
    A. MS., n.p., n..d, 8 pp.
    These fragments are mainly concerned with chronology based on Lutoslawski's data.

990. [Plato's Philebus]
    A. MS., n.p., n.d., 1 p.
    Note on Euripedes.

991. Categories
    A. MS., n.p., n.d., 4 pp.
    The Aristotelian categories. Synonyms, homonyms, paronyms.

992. Aristotle's Notion of Priority
    A. MS., notebook, n.p., n.d.
    The first few pages of the notebook deal with the classification of the sciences into sciences of research, review, and practical application and with the relative importance of experiences, actions, and thoughts. The remaining pages are a transcription, translation, and annotation of various sections of several works of Aristotle but are primarily concerned with the notion of priority in chapters XII and XIII of the *Categories.*

993. [Aristotle's *Physics*]
    A. MS., n.p., n.d., 3 pp.

994. [Byzantine Logic and Prantl's Scholarship]
    A. MS., n.p., n.d., 2 pp. and 1 p.
    Criticism of Prantl's scholarship; "Byzantine logic" defined.

995. [Fragments on Medieval Sources]
    A. MS., n.p., n.d., 6 pp.

996. [On Boethius]
     A. MS., n.p., n.d., pp. 93, 95.

* 997. [Biographical Notes on Duns Scotus]
     A. MS., n.p., n.d., 5 pp.

998. Consequentia.
     A. MS., from a notebook, n.p., n.d., 26 pp.
     Duns Scotus (extraction and commentary). Lutoslawski's study of Plato. Phaneroscopy. Tables concerned with classification of colors.

999. Ockham's Logic
     A. MS., n.p., n.d., 2 pp.

1000. [Fragment on the History of Logic]
     A. MS., n.p., n.d., 2 pp.
     The contributions of Scotus, Ockham, Cartesianism, Bacon, Leibniz, and the Leibnizian logicians, Wolff and Lambert.

1001. Passages in Occam's Logic concerning Relations
     A. MS., n.p., n.d., 5 pp.

1002. [Fragments on the History of Philosophy]
     A. MS., n.p., n.d., pp. 41, 45, 47 (77), 73-76, 80-81.
     The *a priori* method of fixing belief: Descartes, Liebniz, Kant, and Hegel.

1003. The Axioms of Intuition. After Kant
     A. MS., n.p., n.d., 6 pp.; plus a cover with the title "Quantity."
     All intuitions are extensive quantities. Reflections on the following axioms: Space has three dimensions, a straight line is the shortest distance between two points, and two lines cannot enclose space.

1004. Notes on the Critic of the Pure Reason
     A. MS., n.p., n.d., 3 pp.
     Notes on the title of Kant's work as well as on the dedication, prefaces, and table of contents. Also notes on the distinction between pure and empirical cognition.

1005. Critic of the Pure Reason
     A. MS., n.p., n.d., 10 pp. and 24 pp.
     Translation of the *Critic* through Part I of the Introduction. Vocabulary of Kantian words and phrases (2 pp.).

1006. Critique of Pure Reason
     A. MS., n.p., n.d., 4 pp. (table of contents for CSP's translation); plus 1 p. (showing the chronological relationship of Kant's *Critique* to the works of other German philosophers).

1007. [Kant Studies: Translations]
     A. MS., n.p., n.d., 66 pp., including title page which acknowledges the aid of Miss C. E. Peirce.
     Notes and fragments of translations of *The Critique of Pure Reason*. Not all of the manuscript is in CSP's hand. Some sections are in the hand of CSP's Aunt, Charlotte Elizabeth Peirce. Translations of the First Book of the Transcendental Analytic, Chapter II, Section 2, Of the Grounds *a priori* of

the Possibility of Experience, and of the Second Book of the Transcendental Analytic, Introduction, Of the Transcendental Judgment in General. The translations are based upon the 1st German edition.

* 1008. [Kant's Treatment of Substance]

A. MS., n.p., May 21, 1911, pp. 11-14.

* 1009. [Fragments]

A. MS., n.p., n.d., 39 pp., excluding various calculations on verso of some pages.

Topics include: continuity and relativity; Anselm's proof of God's existence; feeling and consciousness; laws of nature, their growth and necessity; laws and signs; signs, symbols, propositions, and truth; relation of metaphysics to logic; cognition and inference; fallibilism and the limits of rationality; continuity and the problem of the action of matter upon mind; Kant and the confusion of logical questions with psychological ones; infinity; the final (ideal) opinion; comments on *An Essay concerning human understanding.*

PHYSICS

AERODYNAMICS

1010. A Problem in Aerodynamics

A. MS., n.p., n.d., 3 pp., with 3 pp. of variants.

Airships and wind velocity.

1011. Introduction

A. MS., n.p., n.d., 14 pp.

Probably an introduction to an article on air-sailing. Problem of mechanical flight, including an historical account of researches on the problem, beginning with the work of K. II. Schellbach.

1012. Report of the First Experimental Run of the Air-Ship of Count von Zeppelin (Z)

A. MS., n.p., n.d., pp. 1-14, with 5 pp. of variants.

An account of the preparations made in 1899 and 1900 on Lake Constance for the first airship ascension. It is quite likely that the above is a translation made for Langley of the Smithsonian.

1013. The Prospects of Air-Sailing

A. MS., n.p., [1895], pp. 1-51, with an alternate p. 28.

Hydrodynamics involved in a fish's swimming upstream. Flight of birds. Professor Langley's theory of the aerodynamics of soaring. In general, CSP treats the kinds of problems and preparation required before an airship can be successfully launched. He thought that wind should be used as motive power. Prediction of success, with commercial value foreseen.

1014. The Prospects of Sailing the Air

A. MS., n.p., n.d., pp. 1-15, 17-21, 32-34, 53-57; plus fragments.

1015. [Mathematics of Aerodynamics]

A. MS., n.p., n.d., 10 pp.

The need for research in the mathematics of aerodynamics. Reference to Professor Langley's researches.

COLOR EXPERIMENTS

1016. **Color Studies. Vol. 2. Qualitative Phenomena, Methods and Theories**
A. MS., small red notebook ("Color Miscellaneous" written on the cover), n.p., n.d., with exception of entries on p. 27 (6/9/86—6/28/87).
Fechner's Law applied to color, Spectra. Theory of Luminosity. Tables reporting the results of several experiments.

1017. **[Hue Studies]**
A. MS., small red notebook ("Hue" written on the cover), n.p., April 4, 1889, with many pages missing.

1018. **[Color Experiments]**
A. MS., small brown notebook, n.p., the notebook bought in Köln, March 6, 1876, with numerous dates throughout, the last of which (p. 71) is February 15, 1877.
Extensive notes on color experiments; brief notes on logic, specifically premises and leading principles.

1019. **[Color Experiment]**
A. MS., n.p., n.d., 7 pp. of tables.

1020. **Calc. of Wave Lengths of Maxwell's Primary Colours**
A. MS., n.p., n.d., pp. 1-3.

1021. **Scale of Maxwell's Second Colour-Box compared with Ångström's wave lengths**
A. MS., n.p., n.d., 1 p.

1022. **Memorandum of Studies to be made on Color**
A. MS., n.p., n.d., 1 p.

1023. **[Color Study]**
Small envelope containing scraps of colored ribbon numbered in order of apparent brightness as determined by CSP on a dark day.

1024. **[Fragments related to Color Experiments]**
A. MS., n.p., n.d., 10 pp.

MISCELLANEOUS

1025. **[Notes on Rates of Change of Radio-active Elements]**
A. MS., n.p., n.d., 11 pp.

1026. **The Principles of Mechanics**
A. MS., n.p., [c.1878], 1 p., 3 pp., 3 pp., 4 pp., representing at least four tentative starts.
The three independent properties of time. Isochronous oscillations. Principle of living forces.

1027. **Constants. A. Pure Physical Constants**
A. MS., n.p., [c.1880], 1 p.

1028.   Methods of Investigating the Constant of Space
        A. MS., n.p., March 24, 1891, 2 drafts, 3 pp. each.

1029.   [Fragments on Michelson-Morley Experiment on the Drift of Earth
        through the Ether]
        A. MS., n.p., n.d., 6 pp.

CHEMISTRY

1030.   Acetylene Gas (Acetylene)
        A. MS., n.p., n.d., pp. 1-16.
        The role of acetylene as an illuminating gas. Its commercial value and its
        greatest disadvantages. Way of avoiding explosions. The history of the discov-
        ery of the gas. Refutation of the claims of Berthelot, especially his theory of
        thermo-chemistry. Acetylene's importance in breaking down the barrier be-
        tween the organic and the inorganic.

1031.   Acetylene
        A. MS., n.p., n.d., pp. 1-19 (long sheets), with several pages of inserts and
        variants.
        The content of this paper is similar to that of MS. 1030, but more detailed.

1032.   Acetylene Gas (Acetylene)
        A. MS., n.p., n.d., pp. 1-6, with 2 loose first pages and a p. 47.
        Early draft of MS., 1030.

1033.   Digest of the Chemistry of Acetylene (Acetylene)
        A. MS., n.p., n.d., pp. 1-7, 1-4 (continuous), 5-20, 28-43; 5-7; plus 6 pp. of
        variants and 1 p. of logic notes.
        The history, properties, and formation of acetylene.

1034.   [Notes on Acetylene]
        A. MS., n.p., n.d., pp. 35-158 (p. 114 missing); plus one unnumbered sheet
        of calculations and one sheet dated "Astor Library 1898 Apr. 26."

1035.   [Pending Claim]
        TS., April 27, 1896, 1 p.
        Application of CSP for a generator for acetylene and other gases. Serial No.
        589239.

1036.   Argon, Helium, and Helium's Partner
        A. MS., n.p., [c.1890?], pp. 1-5.
        On the discovery of new elements, spectrum analysis, and Mendelyeev's Pe-
        riodic Law. Description of the total eclipse of 1869 in Kentucky, where CSP
        was sent as part of the Coast Survey Expedition. As an assistant to Professor
        Winlock of the Harvard College Observatory, CSP claims that he was the first
        to see argon.

1037.   Argon, Helium, and the Partner of Helium. Continued
        A. MS., n.p., [c.1890?], pp. 1-8.
        On argon.

1038. Chemistry
A. MS., n.p., n.d., pp. 1-5.
Definitions of "substance," "elementary substance," and "chemical compound." Valency and chemical graphs. Mendelyeev and the array of chemical elements.

1039. Chemistry—The Elements
A. MS., n.p., n.d. (but a reference to Clarke 1897 on p. 1), 55 pp., including a sequence pp. 1-6 (chemistry); plus fragments and mathematical jottings.
Mendelyeev's array of the elements.

1040. Notes on table of atomic weights (Notes on At. Wts.)
A. MS., n.p., n.d., pp. 1-6; plus 3 pp. of variants and 24 sheets of calculations.
Dates appear on four of the loose sheets, one of which is headed "Table of Atomic Weights compiled from very insufficient data in 1905." Another sheet reads: "Atomic Weights compiled without recent data 1908." CSP regards the table of atomic weights as one of the two most extraordinary achievements of inductive logic (Kepler's achievement is the other).

1041. Valency (Ve)
A. MS., n.p., [1905], pp. 1-26, with 6 pp. of variants.
CSP sets out to discuss "the mode of composition of ideas," developing an analogy between simple ideas and chemical elements.

1042. Valency (V) (V . . .)
A. MS., n.p., n.d., pp. 1-8, 1-12, 5-14; plus 10 pp. of variants.
Earlier draft of MS. 1041.

1043. Note . . . to be printed in small type at the end of the article
A. MS., n.p., n.d., pp. 1-5.
The article referred to here is the article on valency (MSS. 1041 and 1042, if completed). CSP favors the strict law of valency, but admits that there are some problems in connection with its application.

1044. A Proposal of a change in the Atomic Weights with a remark on the Periodicity of the Properties of the Elements
A. MS., n.p., n.d., 8 pp.
CSP proposes that the present atomic weights be multiplied by 4, and that every element whose place is set in Mendelyeev's scheme receive an ordinary number. This two-part proposal, CSP suggests, has pedagogical and mnemonic advantages.

1045. The Seventy Decanes
A. MS., n.p., n.d., 5 folded sheets (9 pp.).

1046. Chemical Curves
A. MS., notebook, n.p., n.d.
Curves of the expansion of water, of the density of mixtures of sulphuric acid and water, etc.

1047. Views of Chemistry: sketched for Young Ladies
A. MS., seven small notebooks, n.p., [c.1861].
The topics covered in the seven notebooks are as follows: kinds of matter, chemical method, qualitative analysis, salts, equivalence of force, states of aggregation, tables illustrating the equations of chemical force.

1048. [Fragments]

A. MS., n.p., n.d., 83 pp.; plus a small notebook filled with calculations pertaining to chemistry.

Among the fragments are curves of the density of the mixture of alcohol and water and of the mixture of sulphuric acid and water. Also, calculation of the axis of the upper part of the curve of residuals of atomic weights and various syntheses.

ASTRONOMY

1049. Homogeneous Light

A. MS., n.p., n.d., 2 pp.

Outline of a series of twenty experiments.

1050. [On Astronomical Magnitude]

A. MS., n.p., [1878], 28 pp.

Draft of abstract G-1878-6.

1051. [Notes on the Zodiac of Denderah]

A. MS., from a notebook, n.p., n.d., 23 pp.

1052. Zodiac (later list of Epping and Strassmaier)

A. MS., n.p., n.d., 4 pp.

1053. Outline of the Idea of an Almanac

A. MS., n.p., n.d., 1 p.; plus 2 pp. on same topic.

1054. (Gothic Period)

A. MS., n.p., n.d., pp. 1-10.

Comparison of star catalogues from Ptolemy on down.

1055. Record of C. S. Peirce's Photometric Observations

A. MS., notebook, n.p., May 4-June 10, 1872.

1056. Phyllotactic Numbers

A. MS., n.p., n.d., 25 pp.

1057. Tables to find the place of Juppiter at any given date

A. MS., n.p., n.d., 4 pp.

1058. Tracings showing our Groups of Stars 40°–50°N as they appear in Argelander

A. MS., n.p., n.d., 5 pp.

1059. [Fragments]

A. MS., n.p., n.d., over 800 pp.

Records of observation and calculations used in CSP's photometric researches and in other volumes in *The Annals of the Harvard College Observatory.*

GEODESY AND METROLOGY

1060. De l'influence de le flexibilité du trépied sur l'oscillation du pendule
à reversion
Report, 1877, pp. 1-23.
Lithographically produced manuscript distributed to the delegates of the International Geodetic Conference held at Stuttgart in 1877. The printed report
(G-1877-3) derives from this manuscript.

1061. Sur la Flexion des pieds des pendules
A. MS., n.p., n.d., 43 pp.
Draft of MS. 1060.

1062. Plan of a New Reversible Pendulum
A. MS., n.p., n.d., 13 pp.

1063. [Notes for Pendulum Research]
A. MS., two notebooks, n.p., n.d.

1064. Additional Note on the Method of Coincidences
A. MS., n.p., n.d., 6 pp., incomplete.
Additions to a report on pendulum swinging.

1065. [Records of Comparisons of Meters]
A. MS., n.p., December 25, 1878-July 19, 1879, 152 pp., of which only a small
percentage is in CSP's hand.

1066. Table of Excesses
A. MS., n.p., n.d., 3 pp., but not in CSP's hand.

1067. Table of Residuals
A. MS., n.p., n.d., 1 p., not in CSP's hand.

1068. Sheet Readings, Smithsonian
A. MS., notebook, n.p., December 1884-February 1885.
The title page is in CSP's hand but not much, if any, of the rest is. Data
for pendulum experiments.

1069. ————————————————

1070. [Coastal Survey Maps, Inventory of Instruments and Charts]
Booklet, n.p., n.d.
Page 22 of the booklet contains diagrams in CSP's hand.

1071. [Mathematical Notes on the Shape of the Earth]
A. MS., n.p., January 7-March 1914, 42 pp.

* 1072. Comparison of the Metre with a Wave-Length of Light
A. MS., n.p., n.d., pp. 1-25, 24-26, 41-83.

1073. Determination of the relative length of a wave of light and a metre bar
A. MS., n.p., [c.1879], pp. 1-7; plus single page (A1), an insert to p. 7, a
variant p. 6, and a single unnumbered page.

1074. [Notes for "Determination of the relative length of a wave of light and a metre bar"]

A. MS., n.p., [c.1879], 3 pp.; plus folded sheet.

1075. Preliminary Account of the Comparison of a Wave Length with the Metre by L. M. Rutherford and C. S. Peirce

A. MS., n.p., n.d., 4 pp.

1076. Pendulum Observations

TS., n.p., [1883], 16 pp., and A. MS., n.p., December 1-10, 1884 ("Pendulum Peirce No. 1"), 1 p.

Report on an expedition to Lady Franklin Bay. Draft of G-1883-1.

1077. [Weights and Measures of Various Countries]

TS. (with notes in CSP's hand), n.p., n.d., pp. 1-40.

1078. [Notes on Weights and Measures of Various Countries]

A. MS., notebook, n.p., n.d.

1079. [Notes on Weights and Measures]

A. MS., n.p., n.d., 6 pp. (not in CSP's hand); plus a printed report from the House of Representatives on the metric system and 1 p. (in CSP's hand).

1080. Calculation of earth's mean radius vector

A. MS., n.p., n.d., 1 p.

This calculation was made for the *Century Dictionary* (see G-1889-3).

1081. Pendulum Experiments at Stevens Institute, Hoboken, N. J.

A. MS., notebook, n.p., August 1882.

The manuscript is in E. D. Preston's hand, but CSP is listed as Chief of Party. Comparison of time pieces.

1082. Pendulum Experiments at the Observatory of McGill College, Montreal

A. MS., notebook, n.p., September 1882.

The manuscript is partly in CSP's hand and partly in Preston's. Invariable reversible pendulums.

1083. Simple Pendulum hung by an elastic string

A. MS., n.p., n.d., pp. 1-3; plus 1 p.

1084. [Record of Pendulum Experiments]

A. MS., n.p., n.d., pp. 2-13.

1085. [Metrological Notes]

A. MS., n.p., n.d., 14 pp., not all in CSP's hand, and a notebook on the history of metrology.

1086. Note de M. Chacornac and Note de M. Charcornac sur la comète de Donaté

A. MS., n.p., n.d., pp. 1-7.

1087. On the Absolute Value of Gravity

Amanuensis (Zina Fay Peirce), n.p., n.d., 6 pp.

1088. On Gravity as an Index of the Movements of the Earth's Crust

A. MS., n.p., n.d., p. 1.

1089. [On Metrology]

A. MS., n.p., n.d., 4 pp. and 7 pp., one of which contains dates (July 21-November 1, 1882).

Measurements: Egyptian, Hebrew, Greek. Metre scales compared. Determination of the length of decimetre scales.

1090. [John P. Hayford's Contributions to the Science of Geodesy]

A. MS., n.p., March 20, 1914, p. 1.

1091. ——————————————

1092. Six Reasons for the Prosecution of Pendulum Experiments

Printed article (annotated), G-1883-6b.

1093. Note on the Theory of the Economy of Research

A. MS., n.p., before June 4, 1877, pp. 1-10.

Draft of G-1879-5c.

1094. [Coast Survey Calculations]

A. MS., n.p., n.d., 61 pp.

* 1095. [Fragments on Pendulum Experiments]

A. MS., n.p., n.d., 509 pp.

A good part of what has been collected here appears to be material for a report or reports to the Coast and Geodetic Survey. Included are notes to superiors and subordinates in the Survey; a description of the Gravitation and Astronomical Station, Ebensburg, Cambria Co., Pennsylvania; pendulum readings at the Smithsonian and in Ann Arbor, Ithaca, and Madison; calculation for Gautier pendulums; the comparison of a metal decimetre with a glass decimetre; notes on a clock signal and self-switch; list of books and apparatus charged to CSP; corrections to Appendices 15 and 16 of the Report of 1884. Approximately one-hundred-fifty leaves with red and blue numbers scrawled on one side have been separated from the rest. These constitute a miscellaneous collection of worksheets, numbered by CSP in red from 1 to 2038 and in blue from 2038 to 1 (i.e., red number 1 is blue number 2038). Included here are records of pendulum observations for the Coast and Geodetic Survey, calculations, exploration of mathematical problems.

1096. [Fragments of Coast Survey Report of 1889]

TS., n.p., [1889], 18 pp., with CSP's corrections, and 2 photographs.

Among the fragments is a typescript of a report (?); various tables (calculation of atmospheric effects, coefficients of expansion of the pendulum, constants for calculating flexure effects, flexure per kilogram); descriptions and positions of the Smithsonian, Cornell, Ann Arbor, and Madison astronomical stations; deduction of the ratio of gravity between the different stations; general description of the pendulums and other equipment.

1097. [Charts]

A. MS., n.p., n.d., 4 charts.

1098. [Fragments]

A. MS., n.p., n.d., 18 pp.; plus pp. 1-7 of a typewritten report on tide elevations and 4 pp. of TS. (bibliographical notes).

PSYCHOLOGY

1099. Questions on William James's Principles of Psychology 1

A. MS., notebook, G-c.1891-1.

Forty-five questions relating to Volume I of James's *Principles of Psychology*. Questions 3, 5, 12, 14, 21-23, 29-33, 36, 41-42 were published: 8.72-90.

1100. On Small Differences of Sensation (with J. Jastrow)

TS., G-1884-10, pp. 1-15, incomplete, with 1 p. (unnumbered) and 2 duplicates; plus a reprint (*National Academy of Science*, Vol. III, 1884, pp. 3-11), corrected by CSP.

Published as 7.21-35, with corrections from the reprint.

1101. Our Senses as Reasoning Machines

A. MS., n.p., n.d., pp. 1-5, incomplete, with 7 pp. of fragments and some logical and mathematical notes on versos of some of these pages.

Instinct and reasoning. Can machines be said to reason? CSP replies that they can't; they proceed only by a rule of thumb. Quasi-inferential processes of sense.

1102. [On Sensation]

A. MS., n.p., n.d., pp. 1-3; plus 1 p.

Each of our sensations has a quality of its own.

1103. Immediate Perception

A. MS., n.p., n.d., 6 pp.

Sir W. Hamilton's definition of "common sense" stated, with CSP's criticism added. Application to the theory of perception.

*1104. On a New Class of Observations, suggested by the principles of Logic

A. MS., n.p., n.d., 5 pp.

Two metaphysical theories concerning sensation. CSP accepts the position that, although the differences between sensations can never be covered by a general description, indefinite progress toward such a description may be made.

1105. C. S. Peirce's Analysis of Creation and Analysis of Creation

A. MS., n.p., n.d., 10 pp. of several starts.

How can a modification of consciousness be produced? How can abstraction become a modification of consciousness? Abstraction combined with the manifold of sensation by means of expression. Expression as the first condition of creation. The necessity of expression. The regulation of language; the means by which meaning enters into language. Examples of the necessity of regulation.

1106. [Consciousness]

A. MS., n.p., n.d., pp. 1-12.

An attempt to define "consciousness." CSP recognizes three meanings of the word (excluding the nonphilosophical usage which occurs when a person who comes out of a faint is said to have recovered consciousness). The three meanings reflect the three categories: feeling (Firstness), effort (Secondness), and thought (Thirdness). In regard to the second mode of consciousness, CSP distinguishes the active species from the passive (or degenerate) species.

1107. [Forms of Consciousness]
A. MS., G-undated-9, pp. 1-16.
Published in entirety as 7.539-552.

1108. [Will-Reaction; Mind (Self, Ego)]
A. MS., n.p., n.d., 1 p. and 1 p.

1109. [Feeling, Reaction, Thought; Continuity]
A. MS., n.p., n.d., 5 pp.
Thought can be reduced neither to qualities of feeling nor reactions. It is characterized by generality and continuity. Generality of meaning as a special aspect of continuity.

1110. [The Threefold Division of Mind]
A. MS., G-undated-9, pp. 1-6, with a variant p. 5; plus 1 p.
Early draft of MS. 1107. Published, in part, as 7.540n[8] and 7.541n[9].

1111. [The Threefold Division of Mind]
A. MS., n.p., n.d., pp. 1-6.
Feeling, will, and knowledge. Each is analyzed in terms of the categories.

1112. [Fragment on Consciousness and Reasoning]
A. MS., G-undated-14, 3 pp.
Published in entirety as 7.553.

1113. [Fragment on Consciousness and Reasoning]
A. MS., G-undated-14, 4 pp.
Published, in part, as 7.554. Omitted: CSP's discussion of the aptness of a metaphor that he employed in the published part.

1114. [Fragment on Imagination, Sensation, and Muscular Reaction]
A. MS., n.p., n.d., 3 pp.; plus 1 p. of another draft.

1115. [Psychology and the Analysis of Feeling]
A. MS., n.p., n.d., 1 p.; plus 1 p. on the spatial continuity of feelings.

1116. Analysis of the Ego
A. MS., n.p., early, 11 pp., incomplete.
How does anything existent exist? Or, what are the conditions of subjectivity? Subject is what it is by virtue of an incarnation of a predicate. It is by quality that substance in general exists. Incarnation as a combination of carnification and materiafication.

1117. On Brain-Forcing
TS., n.p., n.d., 2 pp.
Introductory pages on the problem of how to develop a young brain, ripen the adult one, and preserve it in old age. CSP touches on the question of genius.

1118. [Fragments on the Question of Genius]
A. MS., n.p., n.d., 4 pp. and 5 pp.

1119. [Worksheets for Studies in Great Men]

A. MS., n.p., [c.1883], a model form and 50 of these forms which have been partially filled in.

An experimental project for a class in logic, devised by CSP while at Johns Hopkins. The printed forms require a good deal of data of which only a small percentage has actually been recorded. Notes on the versos of some of the forms.

1120. Materials for an Impressionistic List of 300 Great Men

A. MS., n.p., n.d., 8 pp.; plus over 250 pp. of fragments and scraps.

In addition to the list of three hundred men grouped under several headings (the first rank, provisionally admitted, doubtful, provisionally excluded), there are biographical notes, questionnaires, and other means and efforts to develop the "power of observation" through an impressionistic study of comparative biography.

1121. [Reasoning Power]

A. MS., n.p., n.d., pp. 5-20, incomplete.

The reasoning power of men in different ages. In addition, there are comments on the secundal system.

1122. [Announcement of a Lecture or Lectures on the Topic of Great Men]

A. MS., n.p., n.d., 2 pp.

1123. The Productiveness of the Nineteenth Century in Great Men

A. MS., G-1901-5b, pp. 1-32, with 8 pp. of variants and a typewritten copy. Published, with a deletion, as 7.256-261 (pp. 1-11). Unpublished: greatness and natural endowments; greatness as a function of environmental factors. Application of the doctrine of chances to the problem of greatness. Great men in several fields of endeavor and in modern history. CSP contends that the greatest men are the most human of human beings, appearances to the contrary.

1124. [The Productiveness of the Nineteenth Century in Great Men]

A. MS., G-1901-5b, pp. 1-6, with 5 pp. of variants.

Published, in part, as 7.262-266 (pp. 1-6). Unpublished: CSP's division of the nineteenth century into four eras or generations.

1125. (Great Men of the XIXth Century) (Great Men XIXth C)

A. MS., n.p., n.d., pp. 1-17, incomplete, with rejected pp. 10, 11, 11, and 16.

Great men are potentially crushed by circumstances. The nineteenth-century man of science with his lifelong devotion to the truth stands as a model for the philosopher. Generally speaking, the nineteenth century is inferior to the eighteenth in production of great practical men.

1126. Common Characteristics of the Great Men of the Past Century

A. MS., n.p., n.d., pp. 1-28, with 11 pp. of variants.

How one goes about estimating greatness in a man. The glory of the nineteenth century was its science. The spiritual conditions of nineteenth-century science exhibited in the scientist's devotion to the truth. Evaluations of the achievements of scientists in several fields. Political and artistic greatness also considered.

1127. [Preface to a Paper on Great Men in Science]

A. MS., n.p., n.d., 1 p.

1128. [Fragments on Nineteenth-Century Ideas]

A. MS., n.p., n.d., 10 pp.

In these fragments CSP argues against Dr. Osler's jocose law (men ought to be put to death at 60), by citing as counterexamples the work of Galton, Kelvin, and Mme. Curie. One of the pages bears the title, "A Brief Synopsis of C. S. Peirce's Principles of Philosophy." Apparently the first volume of the *Principles* was to have been a review of the leading ideas of the nineteenth century.

1129. [On the Nineteenth Century]

A. MS., n.p., n.d., pp. 1-9, with a rejected p. 1.

The influence of the nineteenth century was, on the whole, "hardening, narrowing, destructive of fine feeling." Division of the powers of the mind into feelings, knowing, and willing. CSP would substitute consciousness of reaction for willing and what he called "synthetic consciousness" for knowing.

1130. [On Intellectual Power]

A. MS., n.p., n.d., 4 pp.

1131. [On the Coincidence of Rainfall and Illiteracy]

A. MS., n.p., [c.1872], 2 drafts, 13 pp. (with corrections and additions by Zina Fay Peirce) and 17 pp. (not in CSP's hand).

See G-1872-3.

1132. [Intention, Resolution, and Determination]

A. MS., n.p., n.d., 1 folded sheet.

1133. An Attempted List of Human Motives (Motives)

A. MS., n.p., April 11, 1901, pp. 1-3; incomplete; plus 2 pp. of another draft.

Restatement of the enumeration of ethical classes of motives in *Popular Science Monthly* of January 1901.

1134. An Attempted Classification of Ends (Ends)

A. MS., G-c.1903-1, pp. 1-6, incomplete.

A reworking of the *Popular Science Monthly* article of January 1901. Published in entirety as 1.585-588.

LINGUISTICS

CLASSIFICATION AND SYNONYMS

1135. A Classification of Ideas and Words

A. MS., n.p., [c.1897], pp. 1-11, incomplete; plus pp. 1-11 of a second draft and 159 pp. of variants.

Worksheets for a proposed "Book of Divisions, or Index raisonée of Ideas and Words." This work was to have served the double purpose of replacing Roget's *Thesaurus* and of providing an all-in-one encyclopaedia. The worksheets contain elaborate classifications of the arts and sciences, the fountain head of which is the three categories. In connection with possible publication, CSP corresponded with B. E. Smith of the Century Company. See CSP–B. E. Smith correspondence.

1136. Classification of Words

A. MS., notebook, n.p., n.d.

Physiological terms. The principle is adopted that as many words as possible should be classified from the standpoint of their relations to human life.

1137. The Natural History of Words

A. MS., notebook, n.p., January 1859.

Words classified under the following headings: Persons (I, It, Thou); the Senses (Light, Sound, Taste, Smell, Feeling, Sight, Hearing, Optics, Acoustics); and Intuition (Space).

1138. [Classification of Words]

A. MS., notebook, n.p., n.d.

1139. [Classification of Ideas and Words]

A. MS., notebook, n.p., February 3, 1904.

Tentative studies of classification, interspersed with miscellaneous thoughts on cenoscopy. Important Latin words. Elaborate classification of German philosophers into Aristotelians, Baconians, Spinozists, etc.

1140. A Scientific Book of Synonyms in the English Language, classified according to their meanings on a definite and stated philosophy

A. MS., n.p., begun October 13, 1857, 8 pp.

The list of words includes "consciousness," "life," "soul," "intrinsicality," "essence," "existence," "substantiality," "being," "entity," and "subsistence."

1141. The Synonyms of the English Language, classified according to their meanings and a definite and stated philosophy

A. MS., n.p., begun October 13, 1857, 6 pp.

The list of words is similar to that of MS. 1140.

1142. A Scientific Book of Synonyms

A. MS., n.p., n.d., 8 pp.

Preface only. Why works similar to the kind CSP plans have failed, with specific criticism of Graham's *Synonyms* and Whateley's *Synonyms*.

DICTIONARIES

1143. A Little Dictionary of Choice English Words

A. MS., n.p., n.d., 8 folded sheets and a single half-sheet (27 pp.).

A specimen list of words, with all "inelegant and ambiguous" words excluded.

1144. [Comparative Studies of Several Dictionaries]

A. MS., n.p., n.d., 35 pp.

1145. [Annotated and Corrected Proofs for *Baldwin's Dictionary*: A–Dir]

Proofs, n.p., n.d.

These proofs were in CSP's possession. The corrections, however, are by Morsalli, another contributor to *Baldwin's Dictionary*.

1146. C. S. Peirce. Critical Notes to Baldwin's Phil. Dict. (Notes to B's D)

A. MS., n.p., n.d., pp. 1-9, with rejected pp. 2 and 3.

"Abacus" and "abduction."

* 1147. [Definitions for *Baldwin's Dictionary*]

A. MS., n.p., n.d., 471 pp., with variants.

The definitions are principally of logical words and include the following: "energy," "firstness," "image," "implicit," "information," "informed breadth," "informed depth," 'insolubilia," "involution," "kind," "knowledge," "laws of thought," "leading principle," "logic" (over 100 pp.), "logical graphs," "mathematical logic," "matter" and "form," "maxim," "metrics," "middle term," "mnemonic verses," "modality," "mood," "multiplication," "multitude," "necessity," "negation," "norm," *"nota notae,"* "numerical," *"post hoc ergo propter hoc,"* "parsimony," "power," "precision," "predicable," "predicate," "probable inference," "proof," "quantity," "relation," "signify," "simple," "sophism," "subject," "sublation," "solution," "sufficient reason," "syllogism," "symbolic logic," *"Tertium Quid,"* "theory," "truth," "uniformity," "unity," "universal," "universe," "vague," "whole."

1148. [Notes for *Baldwin's Dictionary*]

A. MS., n.p., n.d., 8 pp.

1149. [Galton's Law]

A. MS., n.p., n.d., pp. 1-9, with several discarded attempts.

For the *Century Dictionary*. Two interpretations of Galton's law of ancestral heredity, one of which conforms to Darwin's views of evolution and the other to Weissman's. Brief comments on Karl Pearson's law of ancestral heredity (in the second edition of the *Grammar of Science*).

1150. Logarithm (Copy J)

A. MS., n.p., n.d., 16 pp. of at least three drafts; plus 2 pp. on a method of solving a numerical equation.

Drafts for the *Century Dictionary*.

1151. [Planimeter]

A. MS., n.p., n.d., 6 pp.

Draft of a *Century Dictionary* article.

1152. English Color Names

A. MS., small brown notebook," n.p., May 1892.

1153. Some Color-Names

A. MS., very small thin brown notebook, n.p., May 1892.

1154. [Notes on Color Words and Words about Luminosity]

A. MS., n.p., n.d., 35 pp.

Includes notes on imperfections of the *Century Dictionary*, especially with regard to the definition of some color terms and the omission of others.

1155. [Definitions]

TS. (corrected), n.p., n.d., 9 pp.

Color and light words, for the most part. Alphabetically arranged: "capillarity" to "color-blindness." For the *Century Dictionary*, with a note to B. E. Smith.

1156. [Notes for a Philosophical Dictionary]

A. MS., notebook, n.p., [1865-69].

Extensive notes on philosophical terms from A to Z.

1157. Specimens of bad definitions in the Century Dictionary
A. MS., n.p., n.d., 2 pp.

1158. C. S. P.'s Definitions in Century Dictionary. Notes.
A. MS., n.p., n.d., 11 pp.
The list is incomplete.

1159. Funk and Wagnall's Dictionary
A. MS., notebook, n.p., n.d.
Comments on the *Dictionary,* along with notes on accented and unaccented vowels and on initial and single medial consonants. Some mathematical notes.

1160. [Notes on *Funk and Wagnall's Dictionary*]
A. MS., notebook, n.p., n.d.

1161. Omissions and Errors of Oxf. Dictionary
A. MS., notebook, n.p., n.d.
Also included are notes on unphonetic spellings as well as notes on an experimental project for a little Greek dictionary.

1162. [Criticism of *Murray's Dictionary*]
A. MS., n.p., n.d., 7 pp.

1163. C. S. P.'s contributions. Definitions written or critically examined
A. MS., n.p., n.d., 1 p.
For the *Century Dictionary.*

1164. Point, n
A. MS., n.p., n.d., 35 pp.
For the *Century Dictionary.* Examples of usage.

1165. [*Century Dictionary*]
TS., n.p., n.d., 2 pp.
List of some of the planetoids, their discoverers, and dates of discovery.

1166. [*Century Dictionary*]
TS. (annotated), n.p., n.d., 24 pp.
"Particular" to "pyrronism."

1167. [*Century Dictionary*]
TS. (annotated), n.p., n.d., pp. 1-30 (p. 3 missing); plus 1 p. on "Cologne Water."
"Earth" to "ethics."

1168. [*Century Dictionary*]
TS. (annotated), n.p., n.d., 20 pp.
List of words in P.

1169. Mathematical Definitions in Q
A. MS., n.p., [1890?], pp. 1-18, incomplete; plus pp. 20-107 of a typescript (annotated) which begins "Mathematical Words in Q; Continued."
For the *Century Dictionary.* "Quadrangle," "quadrant," "quadratic," "quadric," "quadrilateral," "quadrivium," "quantity."

1170. [Notes for Contributions to the *Century Dictionary*]
A. MS., n.p., n.d., 73 pp.
Kempe's terminology of logic. Index to Kempe's theory of mathematical form.

Definitions of "apeiry," "Cantorian," "cardinal number," "dyadic," "egoism," "eleuthercism," "empiriocriticism," "energism," "perlation," "system," "topology," among others.

1171. [*Century Dictionary* Supplement]

A. MS., n.p., n.d., 3 pp.

Definitions of "conceptual time" and "conceptual space."

1172. An English Lesson

A. MS., n.p., n.d., 1 p., incomplete.

The meaning of the word "sequestered," as illustrated in passages from Shakespeare, Pope, Cowper, and others.

1173. Copy B. Universal, n

A. MS., n.p., n.d., 1 p.

1174. Specimen of a Dictionary of the Terms of Logic and the Allied Sciences. A-ABS

A. MS., n.p., November 1867, 32 pp.

These pages spell out the dictionary for which MS. 1156 was a preliminary study.

1175. Examples of Mathematical Definitions Suitable for Imperial Dictionary

A. MS., n.p., n.d., 2 pp.

"Curve" and "continuant."

1176. [Plan for a scientific dictionary to be called "Summa Scientiae, or, Summary of Human Knowledge"]

A. MS., n.p., n.d., 32 pp.

Two outlines are actually presented. One of these is for a work whose title is tentatively given as "Synopsis, or Digest of Human Knowledge."

1177. [Fragments]

A. MS., n.p., n.d., 13 pp.

One page is labelled "Index to Peirce's Corrections to Words in A." Definitions of "collection," "normative," "evil," among others. Distinction between a liquid and a fluid.

SPELLING

1178. An Apology for Modern English

A. MS., n.p., [c.1902?], pp. 1-37.

The changes in spelling and the changes in pronunciation are independent of each other. An attempt to show that English as it is written is a dialect distinct from English as it is spoken.

1179. An Apology for English Spelling

A. MS., n.p., [c.1902?], pp. 1-30 (pp. 28-29 missing), with variants.

An earlier draft of MS. 1178.

1180. An Apology for English Spelling

A. MS., n.p., n.d., pp. 1-28 (pp. 3-5 missing), with several discarded pages.

An earlier draft of MSS. 1178 and 1179.

1181. The Editor's Manual (EM)

A. MS., n.p., n.d., pp. 1-92 (p. 47 missing), with many discarded pages; plus 4 pp. of still other attempts (Ed. Man.).

The alphabet. How English spelling is determined, with involved comparisons from Shakespeare, Pope, Crashaw, Lord Brooke, Drayton, Donne.

1182. English Spelling (Spelling)

A. MS., n.p., n.d., pp. 1-4.

Early draft of MS. 1184.

1183. English Spelling (Spelling)

A. MS., n.p., n.d., pp. 1-10.

Early draft of MS. 1184.

1184. English Spelling (ES)

A. MS., n.p., n.d., pp. 1-64, with 72 pp. of variants and worksheets.

CSP notes his forty years' study of the general subject and his first paper in the field written in collaboration with John B. Noyes and published in *North American Review,* April 1864, under the title "Shakespearian Pronunciation" (G-1864-1). Phonetics and the system of spelling. Rules for determining spelling by the sound of the vowels, with exceptions noted. Rules for doubling of consonants, with examples and exceptions to the rules.

1185. Note A

A. MS., n.p., n.d., 24 pp.

This note is referred to on p. 17 of MS. 1184. The history of the spelling of certain words as given in the *Oxford Dictionary,* showing that English spelling became relatively fixed with the multiplication of printing presses.

1186. Spelling (S)

A. MS., n.p., n.d., pp. 1-22; plus 20 pp. of earlier drafts.

Composition of the alphabet. History of the alphabet, chirography, and typography.

1187. Rules for representing the "long low back round vowel" AU in modern English Spelling

A. MS., n.p., n.d., 5 pp.

1188. Spelling of the Vowel Sounds. Short Vowels

A. MS., n.p., n.d., 26 pp.

1189. [Worksheets on Vowel Changes]

A. MS., n.p., n.d., 57 pp.

Vowel changes from Anglo-Saxon (and other languages) to modern English.

1190. Spellings of Minsheu

A. MS., n.p., n.d., 8 pp.

1191. Change of Spelling since Minsheu 1633

A. MS., n.p., n.d., pp. 1-7; plus 1 p.

1192. Spelling in *Passions of the Minde* 1604

A. MS., n.p., n.d., 4 pp.

1193. [Notes on the History of Spelling]

A. MS., n.p., n.d., 22 pp.

1194. Disputed Spellings (Disputed Spellings)
A. MS., n.p., n.d., pp. 1-7 (p. 2 missing).

1195. Peculiar (Peculiar)
A. MS., n.p., n.d., 3 pp.
Peculiar spellings.

1196. Dangers of Misspelling
A. MS., n.p., n.d., 1 p.

1197. Miscellaneous Notes (Miscellaneous)
A. MS., n.p., n.d., 2 pp.

1198. (Double L)
A. MS., n.p., n.d., pp. 1-4.

1199. (E Final)
A. MS., n.p., n.d., pp. 1-6; plus 2 pp.

1200. Words from French not traced further as to silent *e*
A. MS., n.p., n.d., 2 pp.

1201. [Worksheets]
A. MS., n.p., n.d., 31 pp.
List of words in which various sounds and letter combinations occur and in which some letters are silent.

1202. Spelling
A. MS., n.p., n.d., 20 pp., written largely on the backs of discarded pages of MS. 1184; plus a single page variant.

1203. English Spelling
A. MS., notebook, n.p., n.d.
In addition there is a single page (not from the notebook but found with it) speculating on the origin of the words "impeach" and "dispatch."

1204. [English Orthography]
A. MS., n.p., n.d., 6 pp.
Draft(s) of a letter to *The Nation,* commenting on a proposal to simplify English spelling. The proposal is contained in the enclosed circulars which bear the dates May 18, 1905 and April 30, 1907.

1205. [Notes on English Grammar and Orthography]
A. MS., n.p., n.d., 4 pp.

1206. Standard Orthography (A1)
A. MS., n.p., n.d., 1 p.
Graphical symbolization of phonetic elements.

1207. [Worksheets on Words Ending in "able"]
A. MS., n.p., n.d., 13 pp.

1208. The Principal Suffixes, and their effect upon a Final Consonant following a Single Vowel
A. MS., n.p., n.d., 40 pp., with 7 pp. of variants; plus pp. 1-60 ("Suffixes").

1209. Latin Suffixes (Latin Suffixes)
A. MS., n.p., n.d., pp. 1-5.

1210. Notes on Chemical Suffixes and Prefixes
       A. MS., n.p., n.d., 5 pp.

1211. Reply to Inquiries of Etymologists concerning scientific prefixes and suffixes
       A. MS., n.p., n.d., 2 pp.

1212. Reply to the Etymologist
       A. MS., n.p., n.d., 1 p. incomplete.

1213. [Worksheets on Affixes]
       A. MS., n.p., n.d., 15 pp.

MISCELLANEOUS

1214. [Terminology of Grammar]
       A. MS., n.p., n.d., 23 pp.
       The grammarian and the logician. Notes on the history of grammar.

1215. [Worksheets on Grammar]
       A. MS., n.p., n.d., 1 p.

1216. [Grammatical and Syntactical Notes]
       A. MS., n.p., n.d., 3 pp.
       Modes of inflection. The possessive, genitive, and instrumental. Analysis of the verb "to revolve," and a note on the reform of language.

1217. Enumeration of Tenses
       A. MS., n.p., n.d., 2 pp.

1218. Wilson's Rules for the Use of Commas
       A. MS., notebook, n.p., n.d.

1219. Jottings on Punctuation
       A. MS., n.p., n.d., pp. 1-7, with an unnumbered variant.
       On the use of the period and the comma. Examples from Goold Brown's *The Institutes of English Grammar*. CSP claims that his rules can cover every case of the use of the comma more clearly and more easily than Brown's seventeen rules and slightly fewer exceptions.

1220. Jottings on Punctuation (J on P)
       A. MS., n.p., n.d., pp. 1-17.
       The colon and semi-colon. Samples from various writers—Ruskin, Emerson, De Quincey.

1221. Jottings on Punctuation (,)
       A. MS., n.p., [c.1902?], pp. 1-27.
       On the comma. Psychological principles underlying punctuation. The necessity of keeping punctuation to the minimum.

1222. [On English Pronunciation in the Elizabethan Era]
       A. MS., n.p., n.d., 70 pp. (for the most part in the hand of John Buttrick Noyes).
       Draft of G-1864-1.

1223. The Sound of *e* in "end"

A. MS., n.p., n.d., 10 pp.; plus 10 pp. which are part of another draft which ran to at least p. 17.

1224. Notes on English Grammar

A. MS., small notebook, n.p., n.d.

1225. [Vernacular and Literary English]

A. MS., n.p., n.d., 1 p.

"It is I" and "It's me."

1226. Characteristics of Languages

A. MS., n.p., n.d., 4 pp.

A comparison of several languages (Japanese, Tibetan, Dravidian, Eskimo, etc.) in several respects. Notes on Adelaide language.

1227. [Notes on Egyptian Hieroglyphs]

A. MS., notebook, n.p., March 22, 1898.

1228. [Notes on Egyptian Hieroglyphs]

A. MS., notebook, n.p., January 21, 1893.

1229. [Miscellaneous Notes on Greek]

A. MS., n.p., n.d., 70 pp.

Index to the Introduction of C. C. Smith's *Odes to Horace*. Notes on Horace's Greek constructions. Ancient Greek pronunciation and grammar. Greek tenses and Greek names. A comparison of Greek and Indo-Germanic prepositions. Also a draft of a letter, March 16, 1904, to an unnamed and unidentified person concerning anapestic tetrameters in the *Clouds* of Aristophanes.

1230. [Notes on Greek and Latin Color Words]

A. MS., notebook, n.p., n.d.

Also included here are notes on number theory.

1231. [Table of the Occurrence and Derivation of Words in Plato's *Crito*]

A. MS., n.p., n.d., 2 pp.

1232. Pronunciation of Greek

A. MS., n.p., n.d., 1 folded sheet (3 pp.).

1233. Forms [Greek] to be remembered

A. MS., n.p., n.d., 1 folded sheet (4 pp.).

1234. Notes on Grammar, etc.

A. MS., n.p., n.d., notebook.

Notes are on German grammar exclusively.

1235. [Notes on Italian]

A. MS., n.p., n.d., 5 pp.

1236. Principles of Spanish Grammar

A. MS., n.p., n.d., 6 pp.

1237. Mnemonic Rule for the use of *à* and *de* with French infinitives following personal verbs (FV)

A. MS., n.p., n.d., pp. 1-34, with a discarded p. 1; plus an "Index to the Examples" (5 pp.) and 4 worksheets.

1238. French Verbs followed with an infinitive regime (FV)
A. MS., n.p., n.d., pp. 1-19.

1239. Regles du Régime Verbe
A. MS., n.p., n.d., 3 folded sheets (12 pp.).

1240. [On the Use of *à* and *de*]
A. MS., n.p., n.d., 2 charts.

1241. Lane's Hidden Quantities
A. MS., small notebook, n.p., n.d.; plus 8 pp. (same title).
Notes for a Latin dictionary.

1242. [Transcript from a Latin Arithmetic]
A. MS., n.p., n.d., 1 p.

1243. An Arabic Grammar
A. MS., notebook, n.p., n.d.

1244. [Fragments on Greek, Latin, Egyptian and Cuneiform]
A. MS., n.p., n.d., 72 pp.
Also includes a draft of a letter to a French journal; a note on the correct spelling of "dispatch"; and an extensive draft of a lecture on dictionaries (14 pp.).

1245. [Fragments on Arabic, Hebrew, Cuneiform (including a transliteration of the Semitic alphabet)]
A. MS., n.p., n.d., 101 pp.

1246. [The Study of Languages Based Upon Translations of the New Testament]
A. MS., n.p., April 25, 1902, January 24, 1910, and n.d., 3 pp., 3 pp., and 9 pp.
Study of an agglutinative language (3 pp.). Study of Tagalog (3 pp.). Study of several dialects—Gaelic, Welsh, etc. (9 pp.).

1247. The Beauties of Ebratum
TS. (corrected), n.p., n.d., 4 pp.
The translation of Ebratum into Hombrush. The principal rule orthography.

1248. Numerals of Many Tongues
A. MS., notebook, n.p., [c.1892-93?].

1249. The Cardinal Digets in Several Languages
A. MS., n.p., n.d., 2 pp.

*1250. [Fragments on Numbers]
A. MS., n.p., n.d., 6 pp.; plus 2 sheets.
Our present numerical figures converted into the secundal system and then given names (6 pp.). The names of numbers in different languages, principally Hungarian (2 sheets).

1251. [Fragment on Numerals]
A. MS., n.p., n.d., 3 pp.
Numerals as a class of words stand out in that, with respect to them, various languages so precisely translate each other.

1252. [Lists of Words]
A. MS., n.p., n.d., 6 pp.
"English Words of One Syllable" heads one of the lists.

1253. List of Interesting Words
A. MS., n.p., n.d., 2 pp.
From pp. 1-20 of the *Century Dictionary*.

1254. Examples of words whose meaning is affected by phrase
A. MS., n.p., n.d., 1 p.
Comments upon the words "adversity," "frosty," and "wrought."

1255. [Lines from Browning ending in the Letter K]
A. MS., n.p., n.d., 5 pp.; plus 8 pp. of a poem entitled "Friendship" by Cowper (copied out in CSP's hand).
There is no indication of the kind of study, if any, for which the quotations from Browning and the poem by Cowper were to be used.

1256. [Assorted Fragments]
A. MS., n.p., n.d., 57 pp.; plus a small notebook.
Several indices, wordlists, and a classification of words (some of which may have been intended for CSP's proposed *Thesaurus*). The notebook is titled "An Index to the Causeries du Lundi."

1257. [Index to Boswell's *Life of Johnson*]
A. MS., n.p., n.d., 33 pp.

1258. The Posthumous Papers of the Pickwick Club
A. MS., n.p., n.d., 5 pp.
Chapter by chapter notation of alcoholic consumption.

1259. [Rules for editing *A Midsummer Night's Dream*]
A. MS., n.p., n.d., 1 p.

1260. [Notes on Horace's Meter]
A. MS., n.p., n.d., 4 pp.

1261. [Fragments]
A. MS., n.p., n.d., 110 pp., of which 62 pp. of an index are not in CSP's hand.
Classification of words, wordlists, indices.

HISTORY

HISTORY OF MATHEMATICS

1262. Garrulities of a Vulgar Arithmetician (G)
A. MS., n.p., [1892-94], pp. 1-5; 1-55, plus 33 pp. of variants.
Reason for employing word "vulgar" in title. History of mathematics: the arabic system and its introduction into Europe; the chorazmian numerical system. Gerbert's life and work.

1263. Chronology of Arithmetic, with references to the collection of Mr. George A. Plimpton to the Astor Library, and to other available collections (Arithmetic)

A. MS., n.p., [1901], pp. 1-6.

History of Babylonian and Egyptian arithmetic. Pythagoras. Definitions of "arithmetic," "number," "theoretical arithmetic," "practical arithmetic," and "vulgar arithmetic."

1264. Outline of a Brief Chronology of Arithmetic

A. MS., n.p., n.d., pp. 1-7.

A list of mathematicians, their works, and significant dates. See MS. 1543.

1265. Note on Recorde's *Ground of Artes*

A. MS., n.p., n.d., 2 pp.

Speculation by CSP on the date the book was composed.

1266. [Introduction to and Translation of the Preface of an Arithmetic by Rollandus]

A. MS., n.p., n.d., 13 pp.

See G-1894-1.

1267. [Sixteenth Century Mathematics and Mechanics in Italy]

A. MS., n.p., [c.1892], 3 pp.

This manuscript may possibly be for the History of Science Lectures of 1892-93.

1268. The Chronology of Mathematics of Josephus Blancanus 1615 (Blancanus)

A. MS., n.p., n.d., pp. 1-3, 9-13.

HISTORY OF SCIENCE

1269. The History of Science (HSi)

A. MS., G-undated-5 [c.1892], pp. 1-55, with 12 pp. of variants.

Published, in part, as 7.267n8. Introductory remarks on the principles that underlie this attempt to write a history of science. CSP relies on his independent opinion in several areas, but notes deficiencies in several others including classificatory physics ("weakest spot"), mineralogy, crystallography, and biology. Candid evaluation of his knowledge of other sciences, e.g., geology and linguistics. The remaining pages concern the Egyptians and their science. The pyramids and the hypotheses of Egyptologists; failure of Egyptian mathematicians to understand fractions (errors in calculation of areas and volumes); the general stupidity of the Egyptians.

1270. (HS)

A. MS., n.p., [c.1892], pp. 1-3.

Egyptian science and the typical Egyptian.

1271. A Sketch of the General History of Science

A. MS., n.p., [c.1892], 6 pp.

Egyptian science. Two kinds of men: men who worship ideas and men who worship force.

1272. (HS)

A. MS., n.p., [c.1892], pp. 1-21; plus p. 2 of another draft.

Earlier draft of MS. 1269. Engineering as a propaedeutic to science. Egyptian science: the Great Pyramid; the lack of theoretical interest among the Egyptians reflected in their failure to advance scientific knowledge; "irrefragable" proof of Egyptian stupidity.

1273. (HS)

A. MS., n.p., n.d., pp. 2-20.

Another early draft of MS. 1269. Page 2 continues first page of MS. 1272.

1274. Lecture I. General Review of the History of Science

A. MS., n.p., [c.1892], 5 pp.: plus 1 p. of another draft.

Apparently an early draft of the introductory remarks to the twelve lectures delivered by Peirce on "The History of Science" at the Lowell Institute, 1892-93. Peirce mentions having published a memoir on the logic of relations 23 years ago. The date of this manuscript is, accordingly, c.1892.

1274a. Lecture II

A. MS., n.p., [c.1892], 7 pp., incomplete.

Lecture II recapitulates Lecture I. It praises Whewell's work in the history of science and denounces, by way of contrast, Mill's *Logic*. History of science and evolution. The question of necessitarianism.

1275. [On the Early History of Science]

A. MS., n.p., 1892, pp. 1-92.

Presumably for Lecture I or Lectures I and II of the Lowell Institute Lectures of 1892-93. The oldest scientific book in the world: Book of Aahmes. Babylonian astronomy. Thales, Anaximander, Anaximenes, Pythagoras and his school, Aristotle, Euclid, Archimedes. The development of statics. Sharp criticism of Eduard Zeller's history.

1276. Lecture III

A. MS., n.p., [c.1892], pp. 101-128, incomplete.

Presumably Lecture III of the Lowell Institute Lectures of 1892-93. Lecture II discussed the Great Pyramid. Herschel's theory accounting for the angles of slope of the entrances to the pyramid is a glorious example of bad reasoning. Lecture II seems to have closed with mention of Aahmes. Lecture III continues with some examples from Aahmes, stressing the awkwardness and stupidity of the way sums were done. Aahmes' knowledge of summation of a geometrical series. Brief comment on Egyptian chemistry and medicine.

1277. Lecture V

A. MS., G-1892-4, pp. 1-51.

Presumably Lecture V or a draft of the fifth lecture of the Lowell Institute Lectures of 1892-93. Published, in part, as 7.267n[8] (pp. 4-6). There is a reference to the preceding lecture, which concerned Chaldean astronomy. Further remarks on the Chaldees and their scientific superiority over the Egyptians. The Greek mind: sly, distrustful of induction, passion for unity. Thales and Pythagoras. CSP's criticism of Zeller's account of Pythagoras and the Pythagoreans. Cf. MS. 1275.

1278. Lecture VI

A. MS., n.p., [c.1892], 34 pp.; plus 47 pp. of notes and fragments.

Lecture VI of the Lowell Institute Lectures of 1892-93. On German historical criticism of ancient texts and the general problem of historical testimony. The ancient biographies of Pythagoras. The scientific and mathematical achievement of Pythagoras. CSP's theory of the "miracles" of Pythagoras.

1279. Lecture VIII

A. MS., n.p., [c.1892], pp. 1-35.

Lecture VIII of the Lowell Institute Lectures of 1892-93. On the life and works of Archimedes. A long digression on terminology: the words "million," "billion," etc.

1280. Lecture IX

A. MS., n.p., [c.1892], pp. 1-58, with a variant p. 14.

Lecture IX of the Lowell Institute Lectures of 1892-93. Survey of the post-Hellenic period. The failure of the Arabs to make any contribution. Semitic imagination regarded as passionate and poetical but requiring restraint in order to make scientific contributions. The beginnings of modern western science. Scientific activity is arrested by the discovery of Aristotle's nonlogical writings and the subsequent conviction that the study of Aristotle was essential to salvation. The rise of the universities. The thirteenth-century manuscript of Petrus Peregrinus (CSP claims he was the first to translate all of it).

1281. Lecture X

A. MS., n.p., [c.1892], pp. 1-14, incomplete.

Lecture X of the Lowell Institute Lectures of 1892-93. Nicholas of Cusa. Comparison of the Ptolemaic system with the heliocentric system of Copernicus. The weakness of the Copernican theory and Kepler's corrections of it. Copernicus commits a common error of rhetoric by attempting too much in one book.

1282. [Lecture XI?]

A. MS., n.p., [c.1892?], pp. 1-36, with 3 pp. of variants.

Possibly Lecture XI of the Lowell Institute Lectures of 1892-93. Galileo's life and achievements. A very rough description of Galileo's experiments, hampered by the lack of scientific log-books of that day. CSP questions how far Galileo was an experimentalist, observing that Galileo's model of logic was Archimedes.

1283. [Lecture XI?]

A. MS., n.p., [c.1892?], pp. 1-18.

A fuller treatment of the experiments of Galileo than in MS. 1282. CSP ends with an emotional appeal that the treatment accorded Galileo not be repeated. "Ah! Ladies and Gentlemen, it is a *bitter* thing to be put into the world by God to do a special great piece of work, to be hungering and thirsting to do it, and to be prevented by the jealousies and coldness of men." And: "Do not fancy that the blocking of the wheels of progress is confined to by-gone times and to strange countries."

1284. Keppler

A. MS., n.p., [c.1892?], pp. 1-16; plus drafts(s) of 8 pp. and 2 pp.

This manuscript may have been intended as a lecture to follow the one on Galileo. Reference to Kepler's curiosity, imagination, and great work on Mars.

1285. [Fragment on Kepler's work on Mars as well as the work of Copernicus and Brahe]

A. MS., n.p., n.d., pp. 1-22 (pp. 12, 14-15 missing), unfinished, with discarded pp. 3 and 7.

1286. [Concluding Remarks to Lectures on the History of Science]

A. MS., TS., G-1892-4, pp. 1-8.

Published in entirety as 7.267-275, with the exception of 7.267n[8].

1287. [The History of Science from Copernicus to Newton (1543-1686)]

A. MS., two notebooks, n.p., [1902].

Both notebooks are headed "Lecture I." In one (pp. 1-21), CSP notes that his primary interest is in the history of the doctrine of universal mechanical necessity. What follows is a discussion of the pyramids, providing, in the main, the same material as found in MS. 1269. The other notebook (dated August 1, pp. 1-29) seems to be an earlier draft of the notebook described above. The apparently later of the two notebooks is directly continued by part of MS. 1300.

1288. The Principal Lessons of the History of Science (LHS)

A. MS., G-c.1896-3 [sup(2)G-c.1896-3], pp. 1-47.

Published, in part, as 1.43-125. Unpublished: on blocking the path of inquiry; Ockham's maxim and its relationship to nominalism; an error on Carus' part concerning planetary distances and motions.

1289. The Chief Lessons of the History of Science (LHS)

A. MS., n.p., n.d., pp. 1-4.

On scientific integrity and the relationship between morality, essentially conservative, and science: "An early development of good morals, and still worse good manners, is unfavorable to science." Summaries of sections or chapters of a book.

1290. C. S. Peirce's Plan for A History of Science, in one volume (PHS)

A. MS., n.p., n.d., pp. 1-14, with 2 pp. of variants and a draft of a letter to "Dear Sir" (n.d.) on the versos of these pages.

1291. Notes toward forming Plan of A History of Science in 100,000 words

A. MS., n.p., n.d., 8 pp.

1292. How Did Science Originate?

A. MS., n.p., [c.1899], 6 pp.

Intended as an article for *Science*. Science originates in Babylon, not Egypt, as is popularly supposed. The lack of scientific interest in Egypt.

1293. On the Origins of Science

A. MS., n.p., n.d., 2 pp.

The animal repeats roughly the history of the development of the species. People (or races) in their infancy have intellectual characteristics which are similar to those of a child.

1294. Egyptian Science

A. MS., n.p., n.d., 10 pp., unfinished; plus a second draft of 13 pp.

On Egyptian characteristics, both mental and physical. The Egyptians lacked generalizing power, but possessed engineering skill, as evidenced in the construction of the Great Pyramids. Also some caustic remarks directed toward the journal *Scientific American* which carried descriptions of inventions and advised on such matters as the removal of greasepaint.

1295. Comments on Aahmes

A. MS., n.p., n.d., pp. 1-17; 1-5, 5 ("Aahmes. Table of Fractions of 2"); plus 1 p.

Criticism of Aahmes' calculations, with suggestions for improvement.

1296. Thothiana

A. MS., n.p., n.d., 7 pp.

Beginning of an article for the *Bulletin of the American Mathematical Society* on Aahmes and Egyptian mathematics. Explanation of the title of the article.

1297. [The Pyramids]

A. MS., n.p., n.d., pp. 2-7; plus 2 pp.

The Egyptian mind and character reflected in their language. An engineering people, but basically anti-scientific.

1298. [Egyptian History; Chaldean Astronomy]

A. MS., n.p., n.d., 4 pp.

1299. Babylonian Astronomy

A. MS., n.p., n.d., pp. 1-10 (p. 4 missing).

The constellation figures are of Babylonian origin. CSP attempts to prove that Aratos obtained his material from ancient Babylonian astronomical writings (the globe described by Aratos would have been the one that was visible in Babylon c.2000 B.C., not that of Greece in the 3rd century B.C.).

1300. [Notes on the "Phenomena of Aratos" and on the "Classification of the Sciences"]

A. MS., notebook, n.p., December 22-25, 1902.

The first thirteen leaves of the notebook are a direct continuation of the second of the two notebooks of MS. 1287. Additional notes on practical science and the classification of instincts.

1301. *The Phainomena or 'Heavenly Display' of Aratos* by Robert Brown

Annotations by CSP occur throughout the pages (pp. 13-55) torn from Brown's book.

1302. The Horizons of Aratos

A. MS., n.p., n.d., 1 p.; plus 3 pp. ("Phenomena of Aratus").

1303. [Random Notes on Egyptian and Babylonian Science]

A. MS., n.p., n.d., 10 pp.

Engineering interest in the pyramids, with an aside on the inability of the Egyptians to take a joke. Greek thought and humor. Burlesque as beginning with the Greeks.

1304. Analysis of the Almagest

A. MS., n.p., n.d., pp. 601-622.

Notes on several chapters of Ptolemy's work.

1305. The Constellations

A. MS., n.p., n.d., pp. 1-5, 1-2.

Star catalogues: the beginning of a discussion of Ptolemy's work.

1306. The Ptolemaic System
A. MS., n.p., n.d., pp. 1-4, incomplete; plus 11 pp. of fragments.

1307. Notes on Ptolemy
A. MS., n.p., n.d., 7 pp.

1308. [Fragments on the History of Science]
A. MS., n.p., n.d., 10 pp.
Velocity and virtual velocities. Statics and dynamical statics.

1309. Notes on Medieval Science
A. MS., notebook, n.p., n.d.

1310. Prospectus of "The Treatise of Petrus Peregrinus"
Proofs of G-c.1893-4, corrected and annotated, 18 pp.; with 61 pp. of notes and translations and with two transcriptions of the Paris MS. 7378, one in CSP's hand and the other in the hand of M. Tissier.

1311. [On the History of the Lodestone]
A. MS., n.p., n.d., pp. 2-6.

1312. Of the Age of Campanus
A. MS., n.p., 1901, 5 pp.
A draft of G-1901-3.

1313. Note on the Age of Basil Valentine
A. MS., n.p., n.d., pp. 1-16; 1, 5-16, 11, 11, 15; 1-9; a variant p. 2; 1 p.; and a memorandum from CSP to someone in the Coast Survey.
An attempt to show that Valentine was really the editor Thölde, a chemist and member of the Rosicrucian Society. Alchemy.

1314. [Fragment on Galileo and the Development of Dynamics]
A. MS., n.p., n.d., 2 pp. and 5 pp.

1315. [Fragments on Madame Curie and the Discovery of Radium]
A. MS., n.p., n.d., 3 pp.

1316. The World of Science (Science)
A. MS., n.p., n.d., pp. 1-3, incomplete.
Kelvin and Galton.

1317. [History of Logic and Scientific Progress]
TS. (corrected), n.p., n.d., 3 pp.
Two schools of logic, German and English, represented by Hegel and Mill respectively.

BIOGRAPHY

1318. Rienzi, Last of the Tribunes
A. MS., n.p., n.d., pp. 1-8; plus 10 pp. of other attempts.
CSP treats Rienzi as a kind of fourteenth-century Robespierre.

1319. Materials for the Study of Napoleon
A. MS., n.p., n.d., 1 folded sheet (2 pp.).

1320. [Notes on Arthur Levy's *Napoléon intime* (Paris: 1893)]
A. MS., n.p., n.d., pp. 1-3, 7-13, 15, 18-29; plus 28 pp. of alternatives and fragments.
See G-1893-4.

1321. [Sir William Thomson, Lord Kelvin]
A. MS., n.p., n.d., pp. 1-7.
See sup(1) N-1907-5.

1322. [Thomas Huxley]
A. MS., n.p., n.d., pp. 1-5; 5-9; plus 2 pp.

1323. [Dr. Wolcott Gibbs]
A. MS., n.p., n.d., 5 pp.

MISCELLANEOUS

1324. [On the Chronological Dissection of History]
A. MS., n.p., n.d., 5 pp.
Kinds of years: solar, lunar, lunisolar, etc. The Gregorian and Dionysian calendars. Some of this material is for the *Century Dictionary* article "Year."

1325. Ages of the World
A. MS., n.p., n.d., 3 pp.; 2 pp. ("Natural Periods of History"); 2 pp. ("Natural Divisions of History"); plus 9 pp. of other attempts to list significant dates.

1326. Note on the Gothic period
A. MS., n.p., n.d., 2 pp.

1327. History of Astronomy: Diurnal Motion
A. MS., n.p., n.d., 1 p.
Note on Ptolemy: a correction of his data.

1328. [Remarks on the History of Ideas]
A. MS., n.p., n.d., pp. 25-34, with an unfinished p. 22.

1329. (Univ)
A. MS., n.p., n.d., pp. 17, 19-20, 23, 26, 27½, 28, 30, 73, 75-82, with other pages on the same subject matter placed here.
History of the universities. From drafts of a letter to Mr. Francis Lathrop. See correspondence.

1330. [The State of Science in America]
A. MS., n.p., [1880], pp. 1-13.
An address delivered after a Fourth of July dinner in Paris. Why science in America has made such little progress. Johns Hopkins as an institution of science favorably compared with Columbia, Harvard, and Yale. The distinction between practical and theoretical men—an American distinction—for which CSP blames the colleges and the clergy.

1331. [Notes on White's *History of the Warfare of Science with Theology*]
A. MS., small notebook, n.p., June 8, 1896.
See G-1896-2. The notebook also includes notes on Basil Valentine [see G-1898-4] and some notes on acetylene gas.

1332. Note on the Earliest Work of Experimental Science

A. MS., n.p., n.d., 4 pp.

History of science. Mathematics and the inductive sciences. The relation of science to the legal profession, to theology, to art and literature, and to business and banking. The general hostility toward science.

1333. [Fragments]

A. MS., n.p., n.d., 8 pp.

History of science mainly. One page is entitled "Analysis of an induction." Material on existential graphs on the versos of several pages.

SCIENCES OF REVIEW

CLASSIFICATION OF THE SCIENCES

1334. [Adirondack Summer School Lectures]

A. MS., two notebooks, G-1905-5.

Notebook I (pp. 1-48) published, in part, as 1.284 (pp. 35-36). Unpublished: the classification of both men and the sciences in terms of prattospude (discovery for the sake of doing), taxospude (discovery for the sake of applying knowledge), heurospude (discovery for the sake of discovery). The three divisions of heurospude or pure science become mathematics, philosophy, and idioscopy. The dependence of the special sciences on philosophy: CSP's disagreement with the empirical philosophers, e.g., Comte and his followers, who make philosophy dependent upon the special sciences. The principles of common sense are indubitable; it is impossible to be consistently dissatisfied with them. The normative sciences. Esthetics, or axiagastics, treats of the ultimate aim, or the *summum bonum*. The relationship of ethics to esthetics. Ethics as the science of self-control has the double task of describing the operation of self-control (but not in psychological terms) and determining the conditions to which conduct must conform in order to be right. The second of the two tasks belongs to critical ethics which is distinguished from casuistry by reason of its avoidance of specific cases. Logic as an application of ethics to the realm of thought and as a science of signs. Logic is more than the theory of the relation of symbols to their object; it stands as the general theory of signs of all kinds. Notebook II (pp. 49-59): doctrine of signs (continued). The branches of logic: stecheology, logical critic, and methodeutic. Tritocenoscopy and taxospude.

1335. The Categories studied with reference to the English Language

A. MS., n.p., n.d., 3 pp.; plus another 3 pp. of an outline for the general classification of the sciences.

The sciences are most successfully classified on the basis of their logical dependence upon each other and their degree of specialization. Mathematics is highest on the scale of generality.

1336. Philosophy in the Light of the Logic of Relatives

A. MS., n.p., n.d., pp. 1-13, unfinished.

Classification of the sciences. Some of the ways in which CSP's classification differs from Comte's. The relationship between metaphysics and logic, on the one hand, and between metaphysics and psychics, on the other.

1337. History of Science from Copernicus to Newton

A. MS., n.p., n.d., 9 pp., unfinished.

The classification of the sciences. The division of the sciences into physics and psychics.

1338. (*Monist*)

A. MS., n.p., [c.1905-06], pp. 1-41, unfinished or incomplete, with pp. 18-19 missing and with fragments (possibly from another draft).

The entire manuscript, with the exception of some clearly marked pages concerned with Wundt on the versos, deals with the classification of the sciences. CSP sets out to clarify his *Monist* article of April 1905 (G-1905-1a).

1339. A Suggested Classification of the Sciences

A. MS., n.p., n.d., pp. 1-13; 1-6.

Some of the ways in which CSP's scheme differs from other schemes. CSP's point of departure is Comte. Division of science into its theoretical and practical parts. CSP calls for criticism, especially from taxonomists.

1340. [An Outline of the Classification of the Sciences]

A. MS., n.p., n.d., 1 double page (2 pp.); plus 2 pp. of an earlier attempt.

1341. Chapter I. Of the Classification of the Sciences (I)

A. MS., n.p., n.d., pp. 1-19, with a discarded p. 7.

Traditional classifications of the sciences: Plato's, Capella's, the Seven Liberal Arts of the Roman Schools, Schemes of the Medieval University, Bacon's.

1342. Chapter II. Of the Place of Logic among the Sciences (II)

A. MS., n.p., n.d., pp. 1-3, with 3 pp. of variants; pp. 2-3, with one discarded page, of another attempt.

Logic is a science. Before science can be characterized as "serious inquiry" (not systematized knowledge), several well-known facts must be digested, e.g., that we all have beliefs, that we are under a compulsion to believe what we do believe, etc.

1343. Of the Classification of the Sciences. Second Paper. Of the Practical Sciences (Classification of the Sci)

A. MS., G-c.1902-5, pp. 1-103, unfinished; plus 90 pp. of other drafts.

Published, in part, in the following order: 7.53-57, 7.381n[19], and 7.58 (pages 4-10, 21, 23, 75-76). Omitted: a discussion of different systems of classifying the sciences. Every natural classification is based on the purpose or quasi-purpose of the objects classified. Purpose has its root in desire. And every desire is a phase of instinct. A good classification of the instincts affords a key to purposes in general and to scientific purposes in particular. Elaborate classification of instincts.

1344. Abstract of Logic-Book. Introduction. Section 1. The Classification of the Sciences (Abstract)

A. MS., n.p., n.d., pp. 4-29, 4, 11, 20-21, with 4 other discarded pp. and 2 pp. (pp. 1 and 3) the title of which is "Abstract of a Memoir 'On the Logic of Drawing History from Ancient Documents, especially from Testimonies'" (Abstract).

1345. On the Classification of the Sciences

A. MS., n.p., n.d., 36 pp.; plus 3 pp. ("Synopsis of Logic. Chapter I. The Place of Philosophy among the Sciences") and 4 pp. ("Chapter I. Of the Place of Philosophy among the Sciences").

Threefold division of mathematics, empirics and pragmatics. Mathematics as the study of ideal forms or constructions; empirics as the study of phenomena for the purpose of correlating their forms with those studied by mathematics; pragmatics as the study of how we ought to behave in light of the truths of experience derived from empirics. The subdivision of empirics into philosophy, nomology, and episcopy. The subdivision of pragmatics into ethics, arts, and policy.

1346. [On the Classification of the Sciences]

A. MS., notebook, n.p., n.d.

Brief notes on the classification of the sciences.

* 1347. [Fragments on Classification]

A. MS., n.p., 1892 and n.d., 22 pp.

One page is dated February 13, 1892. But all the pages are concerned with classification, especially the classification of the sciences. Some of these pages may be notes or worksheets for CSP's projected *Thesaurus*.

PRACTICAL SCIENCE

BLEACHING

1348. Report on Mr. Woolf's process of Bleaching

A. MS., n.p., 1892 (but at least one item is 1894), pp. 1-18, plus 32 pp. of another draft and 25 pp. of fragments.

CARTOGRAPHY

1349. Explanation of the two Map-Projections suitable for showing the Territory and Possessions of the United States of America

A. MS., n.p., [late 1911], 1 p.

Conformal, or orthomorphic, map-projection.

1350. Formulae and tables for constructing two different Conformal Map-Projections suitable to the exhibition of all the Territory and Possessions of the United States of America

A. MS., n.p., [late 1911], pp. 1-3, with a discarded page.

Introductory statement only: an explanation of the projection.

1351. A New Map of the United States and Possessions. Explanations

A. MS., n.p., [late 1911], 1 p.

Introductory paragraphs only.

1352. A New Map of the United States and Its Possessions

A. MS., n.p., [late 1911], 1 p.

Calculations.

1353. [The Skew Mercator Map] (S M Map)

A. MS., n.p., 1894 and n.d., 35 pp.; plus 55 pp. of geographical notes.

The beginnings of several papers concerned with the mathematical theory of the map-problem. One of these papers is dated March 27, 1894, but most of them, given the shaky handwriting, would appear to be later.

1354. [Fragment on Map-Projection]

A. MS., n.p., January 7, 1914, pp. 1-2.

1355. Quincunial Projection

A. MS., n.p., n.d., 5 worksheets.

Data sheets for "A Quincuncial Projection of the Sphere," *American Journal of Mathematics* (1879), pp. 394-396.

ENGINEERING PROJECTS

1356. [The St. Lawrence River Power Plant Engineering Project]

A. MS., n.p., n.d., 4 pp.

1357. Report on the Effect of a Live Load on Mr. Morison's North River Bridge (Report on Live Loads)

A. MS., n.p., n.d., pp. 1-32, with variants; 31 pp. (Live Loads); 1-12, with variants; 1-8, with variants; plus 23 pp. of fragments and 7 pp. of typescript.

1358. Morison's Bridge

A. MS., n.p., August 3, 1898 to March 5, 1899, 244 pp.

Several drafts of a report. Among the drafts is a draft of a letter which mentions money borrowed on two jewels of Mrs. Peirce's and includes a sharp comment on appraisers.

1359. Copy of Part of my Report to Morison

A. MS., notebook, n.p., n.d.

1360. [Fragments and Scraps on Morison's Bridge Project]

A. MS., n.p., n.d., 188 pp.

MISCELLANEOUS

*1361. Characters of the International Telegraphic Code

A. MS., n.p., n.d., 7 pp.

A proposal to spell every code-word with four-mark characters, of which there will be sixteen. Sufficiency of 65,536 code-words. On secret ciphers.

1362. [Composite Photographic Process]

TS., n.p., n.d., 1 p.

The use of composite photographs as a means of forecasting the results of animal breeding and of marriages.

1363. [Description of Electrical Chronometric Device]

A. MS., n.p., n.d., 7 pp.

1364. [Rotational Displacements of Crystallography]

A. MS., n.p., n.d., 2 pp. (of two drafts).

1364a. Recipe for Cologne Water

A. MS., n.p., n.d., 7 pp.

REVIEWS

Drafts of reviews, including some notices and articles appearing in The Nation *and elsewhere, if at all. The manuscripts have been arranged chronologically and, wherever possible, Burks's designation and Fisch's supplements to Burks have been employed. For Burks's designation of review items from* The Nation *and elsewhere, see* Collected Papers, *Vol. VIII, pp. 260-317. For Fisch's first supplement, see Appendix I of* Studies in the Philosophy of Charles Sanders Peirce, Second Series, *1964. For Fisch's second supplement, see* Transactions of the Charles S. Peirce Society, II,1 *(Spring 1966), pp. 51-53.*

1365. Articles by C. S. Peirce in the Nation
A. MS., n.p., n.d., 2 pp.
An incomplete list of CSP's reviews appearing in *The Nation*.

1366. Drafts of a review of a work by Dr. Bowditch (possibly his *Growth of Children*, 1877) : pp. 2-4, 2-3.

1366a. G-1878-2 : 2 pp.

1367. Draft of a review of John Fiske's *The Idea of God as affected by modern knowledge*, 1885 : 1 p. (TS.).

1368. G-c.1885-2 (1.35) : 3 pp.

1369. G-c.1885-3 (8.39-54) : pp. 4-79, with 4 pp. of fragments.

1370. Draft of a work by Mr. Perrin (possibly *Religion of Philosophy*, 1885) : 3 pp. See N-1885-3.

1371. Fragment of what may possibly be part of a draft review of Herbert Spencer's *Essays, Scientific, Political, and Speculative* (N-1891-3) : 1 p.

1371a. N-1891-6 : pp. 1-2, incomplete.

1372. Draft of a review or notice of Tyndall's *New Fragments*, 1892 : 3 pp.

1373. N-1892-1 : 9 pp.

1374. N-1892-3 : pp. 1-9; plus 24 pp. of a second draft.

1375. N-1892-5 : 2 pp.

1376. N-1892-11 : 5 pp.

1377. N-1892-12 : 1 p.

1378. N-1892-16 : 1 p.

1379. N-1892-17 : 5 pp.

1380. Drafts of a review of Lester F. Ward's *The Psychic Factors of Civilization*, 1892 : 15 pp., 4 pp., and 2 pp.

1381. Draft of a review of Alexander Ziwet's *Elementary Treatise on Theoretical Mechanics*, 1893 : 9 pp.

1382. N-1893-3 : 4 pp.

1383. N-1893-7 : 6 pp., incomplete.

1384. N-1893-8 : 2 pp., incomplete.

1385. Draft of a review of Octavo Chanute's *Progress in Flying Machines*, 1894 : pp. 1-7, with a variant p. 7.

1386. The start of a review of G. T. Ladd's *Psychology*, 1894 : 1 p. (one sentence only).

1387. Draft of a review of Ernest Naville's *La définition de la philosophie*, 1894 : pp. 1-8.

1388. sup (1) N-1894-14.5 : 2 pp.

1389. N-1894-2 : 2 pp.

1390. N-1894-3 : 6 pp.

1391. N-1894-4 : 4 pp.

1391a. N-1894-6 : 2 pp.

1391b. sup (1) N-1894-6.5 : 2 pp.

1392. N-1894-7 : 5 pp.

1393. N-1894-9 : 1 p., incomplete.

1394. N-1894-10 : 3 pp.

1395. N-1894-11 : 5 pp.

1396. N-1894-12 : 16 pp. of draft(s).

1397. sup (1) N-1895-4 : Proof (corrected).

1398. sup (1) N-1895-5 : Proof (corrected).

1399. sup (1) N-1895-6 : 1 p.

1400. Draft of a review of Paul Stäckel, *Die Theorie der Parallellismus von Euclid bis auf Gauss*, 1895 : 1 p., incomplete.

1401. Draft of an obituary for Arthur Cayley, whose death occurred in 1895 : 4 pp.

1402. Draft of a review of William Hirsch's *Genius and Insanity*, 1896 : 7 pp

1403. sup (1) N-1896-1.5 : Proof (corrected).

1404. G-1896-2 : pp. 1-17 (with a rejected p. 3); plus pp. 1-2 of an earlier draft.

1405. N-1896-1 : 13 pp. of two drafts; plus 5 pp. of notes.

1406. N-1896-2 : 3 pp.

1406a. N-1896-3 : 2 pp.; plus page proof with marginal notes which were not incorporated in the actual review.

1407. N-1896-5 : 6 pp.

1408. N-1897-4 : 6 pp. of at least two drafts. Also a notebook containing a list of editions of Boethius, presumably in preparation for this review. In addition, the notebook contains a late [c.1910] note on propositions (possible assertions).

1409. Drafts of a review of C. R. Condor's *The Hittites and their Language*, 1898 : pp. 1-9, 1-3; plus 7 pp. of variants.
    The review which appears in *The Nation* is by J. R. S. Sherrett.

1410. Draft of a review of *The Metric System of Weights and Measures*, A. D. Risteen, compiler, 1898 : 7 pp., incomplete.

1411. G-1898-3 : pp. 1-5, with a variant p. 5.

1411a. N-1898-8 : 1 p.

1412. G-1899-2 : Cut from *The New York Evening Post* with CSP's annotations.

1413.   N-1899-2 : 5 pp.
1414.   Draft reply to Florian Cajori's letter [sup (1) N-1899-4] concerning
        CSP's review [N-1899-4] : 1 p.
1415.   N-1899-5 : 3 pp.
1416.   N-1899-6 : p. 1, incomplete.
1417.   N-1899-11 : 9 pp.
1418.   N-1899-14 : 1 p.
1419.   N-1899-15 : pp. 1-6, 1-3, 1-2, 7.
1420.   G-1900-2 : 6 pp.
1421.   N-1900-3 : 2 pp.
1422.   N-1900-4 : 1 p.
1423.   N-1900-5 : 1 p.
1424.   sup (1) N-1900-5.1 : 1 p.
1425.   N-1900-6 : pp. 1-4; plus 2 pp. of variants.
1426.   N-1900-11 : 2 pp.
1426a. N-1900-15 : pp. 1-15; plus 9 pp.
1427.   N-1900-16 : 7 pp.
1428.   N-1900-18 : 5 pp. and 1 p.
1429.   N-1900-20 : pp. 1-6; plus 12 pp. some of which belong to another draft.
1430.   N-1900-23 : 3 pp.
1431.   N-1900-25 : pp. 1-7, with 8 pp. of fragments.
1432.   N-1900-31 : pp. 1-4; plus p. 2 of another draft.
1433.   Draft of a notice (?) of a book by C. S. Hastings on the topic of light
        written for the Yale Bicentennial Publications, 1901 : 1 p.
1434.   G-1901-1 : 38 pp. of several drafts.
1435.   G-1901-9 : pp. 1-7.
1436.   N-1901-4 : 1 p.
1437.   N-1901-6 : pp. 1-8, unfinished, with 4 discarded pp.
1438.   N-1901-9 : pp. 1-5, 1-3.
1439.   N-1901-10 : pp. 1-4, 10-12.
1440.   N-1901-12 : pp. 1-15 (p. 4 missing), with variants.
1441.   N-1901-14 : pp. 7-9; plus 2 pp. of another draft.
1442.   N-1901-15 : pp. 1-5.
1443.   N-1901-16 : pp. 1-6, 4-7, 13-14.
1444.   N-1901-17 : 1 p.
1445.   N-1901-18 : 1 p., incomplete.
1446.   Draft of a review of Solon Bailey's *A Discussion of the Variable Stars
        in the Cluster ω-Centauri*, 1902: 4 pp.
1447.   Draft of a review of C. A. Schott's *The Eastern Oblique Arc*, 1902 :
        5 pp.
1448.   N-1902-3 : 21 pp. of drafts.
1449.   N-1902-4 : 2 pp.

1450. N-1902-5 : Copy of *The Nation* (with marginal notes on pp. 322 and 326). It is almost certain that the notes are in the hand of Irving Cranford Smith.

1451. N-1902-8 : pp. 1-5, 3, 6, 8-14 of at least two drafts.

1452. N-1902-11 : 1 p. On verso, draft of a letter to "Sommer."

1453. N-1902-12 : pp. 1-13.

1454. N-1902-13 : pp. 1-19 (with 3 pp. of variants); 1-14 (with 2 pp. of variants); 4-16 (with 4 pp. of variants); 1-8 (with a 1 p. variant).

1455. N-1902-14 : pp 1-9, with a variant p. 9.

1456. N-1902-16 : pp. 1-16, with 6 pp. of variants.

1457. N-1902-17 : pp. 3-4.

1458. N-1902-18 : 3 pp.

1459. N-1902-19 : 6 pp.

1460. N-1902-20 : pp. 1-8, with a variant p. 8.

1461. G-c.1902-4 : pp. 1-27, 28-30 (A)(E); 19-25 (A); 1-14 (B); 3-9, 10, 12 (C); 17-21 (D); 23-28 (F); 23, 24-27 (G); 30-31 (H); 1-4 (Royce); 7 pp. of fragments. These are, in part, manuscripts for N-1900-15 and N-1902-10.

1462. Draft of a review of Alexander Bain's *Dissertations on Leading Philosophical Topics,* 1903 : 2 pp. (unconnected).

1463. G-c.1903-6 : 15 pp., with part of a draft of N-1904-3 (MS. 1476) on the verso of one of these pages, and a single folded sheet (3 pp.) "Notes on Strong's Why the Mind has a Body."

1464. N-1903-2 : pp. 1-3.

1465. N-1903-4 : pp. 1-2.

1466. N-1903-6 : pp. 1-2, with a variant p. 2.

1467. N-1903-7 : p. 2.

1468. N-1903-9 : pp. 1-7, with variant pp. 6, 8.

1469. N-1903-10 : 32 pp. of draft(s).

1470. N-1903-11 : p. 1, incomplete.

1471. N-1903-13 : pp. 1-9, with a variant p. 7.

1472. N-1903-14 : 10 pp. of one draft; p. 10 of another.

1473. N-1903-16 : 6 pp. representing several starts.

1474. N-1903-17 : 1 p.

1475. N-1903-18 : pp. 1-2.

1476. G-c.1904-3 : pp. 1-22, with 35 pp. of variants; 10 pp. ("Notes on Nichols"), with a partially worked out definition of "conceptual space" on the verso of one of these pages.

1477. N-1904-2 : 1 p.

1478. N-1904-3 : pp. 1-4, 6-14, 2, 9 (Metre); 1-3, 3-7, 6-7 (Metric System); plus 43 pp. of variants and fragments. See MS. 1463 for one page (Metric System/5) which may belong here.

1479. N-1904-4 : 47 pp., including notes and charts.

1480. N-1904-6 : pp. 1-5, 5, 8-9, 14.

1481. N-1904-9,10 : pp. 1-3.

1482. N-1904-11 : 12 pp. of several starts.

1483. N-1904-12 : pp. 1-3; 1-6, 8-9, with a variant p. 4; 1 p.; plus 5 pp. in a notebook containing several pages of notes on existential graphs ("Studies of the Eight Systems of Existential Graphs").

1484. N-1904-13 : 2 pp.

1485. N-1904-15 : pp. 1, 3.

1486. N-1904-16 : 7 pp.

1487. N-1904-17 : 5 pp.

1488. N-1904-18 : pp. 1-3.

1488a. N-1904-20 : pp. 23, 25-28.

1489. Draft of a review of Carveth Read's *Metaphysics of Nature,* 1905 : pp. 3-8, with 3 pp. of variants.

1490. G-1905-2 : 1 p. See MS. 1476.

1491. N-1905-5 : 4 pp.

1492. N-1905-7 : 4 pp.

1493. N-1905-8 : 8 pp.

1494. N-1905-13 : pp. 1-9 (p. 2 missing). For this MS., see MS. 1497.

1495. N-1905-15 : 11 pp.

1496. N-1905-18 : pp. 1-22 (with variants) of "Notes on Ross's Foundations of Sociology"; plus 7 pp. of an earlier draft and 2 pp. (Ross) of another.

1497. N-1905-19 : pp. 2-17, the versos of which contain 8 pp. of a draft of N-1905-13 and 4 pp. of a draft of N-1905-28. For more of the Wundt manuscript, see versos of some pages of MS. 1338.

1498. N-1905-26 : 2 pp. (in the hand of Juliette Peirce).

1499. N-1905-28 : pp. 1-9, incomplete, with variant pp. 3-6; 1-6, with a variant p. 6; 1-6, with 2 variant p. 3's; 12-16, with a variant p. 13; 19-25, with 2 variant p. 20's; plus 30 pp. of notes. For another draft, see verso of MS. 1497.

1500. Draft of a review of B. Matthew's *The Spelling of Yesterday and To-morrow,* 1906 : 1 p.

1501. Draft of a review of E. E. Fournier's *Electron Theory,* 1906 : pp. 1, 2, 7, 8.

1502. N-1906-1 : pp. 1-3, 1-2, 1, 6.

1503. N-1906-2 : pp. 1-28 (pp. 6-7, 9, 11, 14-15, 22 missing) and variants.

1504. N-1906-3 : 12 pp.

1505. N-1906-8 : pp. 1-5, 4-5.

1506. N-1906-10 : pp. 1-11, 17-19, 21, with variants (Jo); 1-6, with variants (Joseph); plus 25 pp. of other drafts and notes.

1507. N-1907-1 : pp. 1-5.

1508. N-1907-2 : pp. 1-15, 1, 5-15, 15-17, and variants.

1509.   N-1907-3 : pp. 1-8 ("Notes on Baldwin's Genetic Logic"), with a variant p. 7; 21 pp. (Baldwin); 4 pp. ("Notice of Vol. II of Baldwin's Genetic Logic"); plus annotated proofs.

1510.   Draft of a review or notice of J. A. Fleming's *Recent Contributions to Cluster Wave Theory*, 1908 : pp. 2, 5-7.

1511.   Draft of a review of James McKeen Cattell's *Biographical Directory of American Men of Science*, 1910 : pp. 1, 7-11 (probably from different drafts).

1512.   Partially identified and partially dated fragments of review drafts : 43 pp.

On confidence in ancient testimony (1 p.); on metrics, with an introduction by J. M. Allen (1 p.); on a book by Burn (1 p.); on the mercator projection and Dr. Craig (1 p.); "Notes on the Ferdinand Bellows Papers" (1 p.); on D. K. Clark's *Mechanical Engineer's Pocket Book* (5th edition) and Harrison's *Mechanical Engineer's Reference Book* (1 p.); on Mervin O'Gormon's *Motor Pocket Book* (1 p.); on a poem attributed to Poe (7 pp.); on Dr. Cushman (Herbert Ernest Cushman?) (1 p.); on Nisard (a translation) (1 p.); on New-comb (reference to a volume of 1909) (8 pp.); on the Walpole letters [N-1894-3?] (2 pp.). Also the following identifiable items from *The Nation*: Draft of a review of Albert Stickney's *Organized Democracy*, 85 (12 Sept. 1907) 229 (1 p.); Draft of a review of Josiah Royce's, Joseph Le Conte's, G. H. Howison's, and Sidney E. Mezes' *The Conception of God* 65 (30 Dec. 1897) 524-527 [sup(2)N-1897-6] (1 p.); Draft of a review of Mabel Loomis Todd's *Total Eclipses of the Sun* 58 (3 May 1894) 335 [sup(2)N-1894-9.5] (1 p.); sup(1)N-1895-3 (1 p.); Draft of a review of Simon Newcomb's *Side-Lights on Astronomy and Kindred Fields of Popular Science* 83 (20 Dec. 1906) 544-545 (8 pp.) [sup(2)N-1906-11].

* 1513.   Partially identifiable fragments of review drafts : 32 pp.

Several pages are unidentifiable. Two of these pages are concerned with the theme of a future life (immortality). One page is marked (Tichener 3). The following are identifiable items from *The Nation*: N-1878-1 (1 p.); N-1892-17 (2 pp.); N-1893-3 (1 p.); N-1893-4 (1 p.); N-1893-5 (1 p.); [N-1893-6?] (1 p.); sup(1)N-1895-3 (3 pp.); sup(1)N-1898-1.5 (4 pp.); N-1898-7 (1 p.); [N-1899-9?] (1 p.); N-1905-9 (1 p.).

TRANSLATIONS

1514.   Translations of Dr. Marey's *Exhibition of Instruments and Photographs appertaining to the History of Chronophotography.*

A. MS., G-1902-5, December 12, 1901, pp. 1-45, with extensive marginal notes, including sharp criticism of the author.

1515.   Translation of Dr. Marey's "Analysis of the Motion of Animals by the Method of Muybridge," 1878.

A. MS., n.p., n.d., 2 pp.

1516.   Translation of Le Bon, ———.

A. MS., n.p., n.d., 1 p. (p. 41).

1517. Translation of William Hirsch's *Genius and Degeneration.*
A. MS., G-1896-5, pages numbered as high as 347 (incomplete), with many missing.

1518. Translation of Victor Schumann's *On the Absorption and Emission of Air and its ingredients for Light of Wave-Lengths from 250 μμ to 100 μμ,* Smithsonian Institution, Washington, 1903.
A. MS., G-1903-3, 17 pp.

1519. Translation of Henri Poincaré's *The Relation of Mathematics to Physics.*
A. MS., n.p., n.d., pp. 1-7, 11-22; 6-10, 18-22; 26.

1520. Translation of Alexandre Dumas' *Le Corricolo.*
A. MS., n.p., n.d., pp. 1-6, 1-6, with 3 pp.

MISCELLANEA

AMUSEMENTS

1521. Riddles, Conundrums, etc.
A. MS., notebook, n.p., n.d.
At the back of the notebook is part of the first scene of a drama entitled "Alfred _____ a drama."

1522. Chinese Puzzle
A. MS., n.p., n.d., 1 p.

1523. List of Jokes to be Invented
A. MS., n.p., n.d., 2 pp.

1524. Whist in Boolians
A. MS., n.p., n.d., 6 pp.

1525. Analysis of Tit-Tat-Too
A. MS., n.p., n.d., 32 pp.
A mathematical analysis of the game, prepared for Chapter I of "Elements of Mathematics" (MS. 165).

1526. Backgammon
A. MS., n.p., n.d., pp. 1-13 (p. 2 missing); plus 2 pp. of an earlier attempt.
CSP presents the rules, general idea, and nomenclature of the game as well as the mathematics involved in actual play. In response to a letter of inquiry from Professor James Woods of the Harvard Philosophy Department, Julian Masan of *The New York Evening Post* reports (December 23, 1930) that the newspaper's backgammon experts agree that the mathematical parts of this manuscript have been worked out more thoroughly since CSP's time but that, for the period it was written, the ideas contained in it are "quite remarkable."

1527. Our Chess Corner
A. MS., n.p., n.d., pp. 1-4.
Game between Pillsbury and Tarrasch (Hastings Tournament) annotated by CSP.

1528. Our Chess Corner
A. MS., n.p., n.d., 3 pp.
Game between Steinitz and von Burdeleben (Hastings 1895) annotated.

1529. [Chess]
A. MS., n.p., n.d., 4 pp., with the draft of a letter to the editor of the *Pall Mall Gazette* on the verso of one of these pages.
Letter to the Chess Editor of *The New York Evening Post,* commenting on the relative playing strength of Lasker, Steinitz, and Tschigorin.

1530. [Chess]
A. MS., n.p., n.d., 1 p.
Letter to the Chess Editor of *The New York Evening Post,* questioning a move suggested in one of the newspaper's articles on chess.

1531. [Chess]
A. MS., n.p., n.d., 1 p.
Letter to the Chess Editor of *The New York Evening Post,* commenting on a position reached by Bird and Maróczy in a game published by the *Post.*

1532. _____

1533. [Fragments on Chess]
A. MS., n.p., n.d., 3 pp.

1534. [Card Tricks]
A. MS., n.p., n.d., 13 pp.

1535. Transformation of Cards
A. MS., n.p., n.d., 3 pp.

1536. A Curious Method of Shuffling Cards (Shuffle)
A. MS., n.p., n.d., pp. 1-2.

1537. [Fragments on Games]
A. MS., n.p., n.d., 12 pp.

* 1538. [Caricatures, Doodles, Drawings, Pen Trials]
A. MS., n.p., n.d., 60 pp.

1539. Art Chirography
A. MS., n.p., n.d., 6 pp.

ANNOTATIONS, BIBLIOGRAPHIES, CATALOGUES

1540. Specimen Sketch of the Plan of a Suggested Way of Annotating the Pseudodoxia Epidemica (SS)
A. MS., n.p., n.d., pp. 1-17, with 5 pp. rejected.

1541. [Notes on a Fourteenth-Century MS.]
A. MS., n.p., n.d., 4 pp.

1542. Old Arithmetics, historically valuable (16th and 17th centuries)
A. MS., n.p., n.d., 3 pp.
Also lists of books on the history of mathematics as well as books of ancient origin.

1543. Chronology of Arithmetic
A. MS., n.p., n.d., 5 pp.
Arithmetic books in the Astor Library. Draft sheets of MS. 1264.

1544. Dutch Arithmetics
A. MS., n.p., n.d., 1 p.

1545. Copy and Notes for Arithmetic
A. MS., n.p., n.d., 12 pp.
An evaluation of some books on arithmetic.

1546. C. S. Peirce's Arithmetics. Conspectus of Copy and Notes.
A. MS., n.p., May 21, 1893, 6 pp.
Notes on arithmetics in CSP's possession. Bibliography of arithmetics, primary and advanced, used in American schools.

1547. [Notes toward a Catalogue of Plimpton's Collection of Arithmetic]
A. MS., n.p., n.d., pp. 1-46 (pp. 22-25, 43-44 missing).
Critical comments on some of the books listed.

1548. Some Arithmetical Books in Astor Library
A. MS., n.p., n.d., 5 pp. See MS. 1543.

1549. Catalogue of Books on Medieval Logic which are available in Cambridge
A. MS., notebook, n.p., January 1, 1868.

1550. [Bibliography of Books on Logic]
A. MS., n.p., n.d., pp. 86-91, with variants.
Evaluations by CSP.

1551. [Bibliography of Mathematical and Physical Treatises]
A. MS., n.p., n.d., 5 pp.
CSP's evaluation of the mathematical treatises.

1552. [Bibliography of Arithmetics]
A. MS., n.p., n.d., 2 pp.

1553. [Instructions on Bibliographical Entries]
TS., n.p., n.d., 17 pp.

* 1554. Rules for cataloguing C. S. Peirce's Books
A. MS., n.p., n.d., pp. 1-10; 9 pp.; 4 pp.; plus part of a notebook, containing a shelf list of CSP's books, n.d.

1555. Catalogue of the Library of Charles S. Peirce
A. MS., notebook, n.p., February 27, 1858.
Books are listed alphabetically.

1555a. List of all the Books in the House
A. MS., notebook, n.p., 1860.

1556. Classified List of My Books
A. MS., notebook, n.p., n.d.
Books are listed topically.

1557. [Partial Catalogue of the Library of C. S. Peirce]
A. MS., n.p., [c.1909], pp. 1-19; 12 pp. ("Books sent to Anderson's. Oct. 1909");
42 pp. ("Pamphlets for 1909 Sale").

1558. [Bibliography of Medieval Mathematical Works]
A. MS., n.p., n.d., 5 pp.
Brief comment on mathematical abbreviations in the Middle Ages.

1559. [Specimen List of Rare Books in CSP's Library]
A. MS., n.p., n.d., 8 pp.
Rare books (for possible sale) on various topics: games, puzzles, humor, science, etc.

Travels, Popular Lectures, Assorted Fragments

1560. [Notes on Travels in Turkey and Greece]
A. MS., notebook, n.p., n.d.
Notes relating to color experiments.

1560a. [Travel Information]
A. MS., notebook, n.p., n.d.
Travel advice for European trip of unidentified person.

1561. Topographical Sketches in Thessaly with Fictional Embroideries
TS., n.p., n.d., pp. 1-68 (pp. 5-6 missing), with 49-51 in CSP's hand; plus an
earlier draft of 68 pp.

Intended as a popular lecture. In the preface, CSP wrote of his desire to capture the spirit of the place and its people, resorting to as little fiction as possible.

1562. [Two Plays]
A. MS., n.p., n.d., 19 pp. and 3 pp.
The parts of two plays are copied out in CSP's hand. One of the plays is *Medea* and the other has not been identified, but has to do with a scene in an English house.

1563. [On *King Lear*]
A. MS., n.p., n.d., pp. 1-2, 4-5, incomplete; plus 2 pp. of an earlier attempt.
An introduction to what presumably will be a reading from or lecture on *King Lear*.

1564. [On Burlesque]
A. MS., n.p., n.d., 8 pp.
The introduction to a lecture.

1565. [Fragments of Humorous Verse and Prose]
A. MS., n.p., n.d., 4 pp.

1566. [Copy of Horace, *Odes,* Book I, Ode 4]
A. MS., n.p., n.d., 1 p.

1567. [Copy of Migne, *Patrologia Latina,* vol. 179, cols. 1138-40]
TS., 1 p.

1568. The Theory of Force

A. MS., n.p., n.d., 3 pp. and 4 pp. (two drafts).

The controversy over innate ideas. Is there a single elementary idea for which the mind has no special aptitude? Can we frame a clear notion of such an idea? Principle of natural selection "accounts for the possession by nearly every species of animal of instinctive and concrete notions of mechanical force." Descriptions of two experiments involving use of a flywheel.

1569. [On Political Economy]

A. MS., n.p., September 21, 1874, 8 pp.

The facts of political economy fall within three categories involving the relations of price, demand, and cost of production. The first axiom of political economy: "the desire of a person for anything has a quantity of one dimension, and a person having a choice will take that alternative which will give him the greatest satisfaction." The desirability of a thing depends on other things related to it either as alternatives or as coefficients. CSP embarks on a logical treatment of political economy based on a set of propositions which are assumed. The list of propositions is incomplete and what follows by way of discussion is fragmentary.

1570. [Lecture in Elocution]

A. MS., n.p., n.d., pp. 1-14.

Part of the first of a projected series of six lectures for ministers concerned with technique and application in the art of delivery.

* 1571. [Miscellaneous Fragments]

A. MS., n.p., n.d., 46 pp.

Included here are the following: plan of a review article on induction; a discussion of attributes; worksheets on the syllogism; an inquiry into the nature of hypotheses; Bacon's doctrine of the formal cause; notes on the definition of "logic"; bibliographical notes on the theory of logic.

* 1572. [Miscellaneous Fragments]

A. MS., n.p., n.d., 104 pp.

Metric system; truth of propositions; properties of negation, e.g., denial of a proposition; dilemma; reality of an idea; worksheets for a logic text(s).

1573. [Miscellaneous Fragments]

A. MS., n.p., n.d., 245 pp.

The topics range from coast survey material to texts for sermons. Notes on a sixteenth-century author and notes for other historical studies; bibliographical lists; dictionary materials; ethics of terminology, especially scientific terms; philosophical terminology; philosophical schools ("How many philosophers have there been"); worksheets on existential graphs; types of argument; reflections on the logic of science; mathematical notes on secundals and on a problem in percentages; metric geometry; battery formulae; "List of Books most needed."

1574. [Miscellaneous Fragments]

A. MS., n.p., n.d., over 1,000 pp.

These fragments and scraps have been partially ordered and placed in separate folders labelled as follows: "Lexicography" (notes for *Century* and other dictionaries); "Skew Mercator"; "History of Science"; "Charts and Graphs"; "Materials for Mathematics Books"; "Practical Fractions and Finite Difference"; "Study of the Census of 1880"; "Biographical" (Arisbe); "Mathematical Calculations"; "Logic Scraps."

*1575. [Miscellaneous Pages from Notebooks]
A. MS., n.p., December 26, 1913 and n.d., 41 pp.

These pages were collected for the purpose of fitting them into existent notebooks. The hope persists that at least some of these pages will eventually be placed in the notebooks from which they were removed. Only 2 pp. are dated: These pages are "on what it means to say that a line is continuous." Other topics are the following: secundal and decimal system; probability; collection; existential graphs; telegraphic code; bibliographical notes; several pages which begin "I propose to devote this book to a record of Little Ideas."

PUBLICATIONS AND PLANS FOR BOOKS, MEMOIRS, AND LECTURES

1576. List of Publications
A. MS., n.p., [c.1880], 4 pp.

1577. Logical Papers by C. S. Peirce
A. MS., n.p., [1883?], 3 pp.

1578. List of Proposed Memoirs on Minute Logic.
A. MS., n.p., n.d., 6 pp. (of three drafts).

1579. Plan of Logic.
A. MS., n.p., July 10, 1901, pp. 1-2.

1580. [For a Lecture(s) on Logic]
A. MS., n.p., n.d.(?), 3 pp.

Possibly Johns Hopkins lectures on logic. One page is stamped twice: February 7, 1884 and April 1, 1884. One page is certainly a lecture; it is so marked. The other pages were apparently written about the same time and may be lecture notes.

1581. [Announcement and Endorsements of *The Principles of Philosophy*]
A. MS., n.p., n.d., 3 pp.

The endorsements are by William James, Josiah Royce, G. Stanley Hall, Francis Abbot, Simon Newcomb, and O. C. March, one-time President of the National Academy of Science.

1582. [An Announcement of Three Lectures]
A. MS., n.p., n.d., 1 p.; plus the printed announcement, including CSP's sarcastic comment.

The titles of the three lectures are "Thessalian Topology," "The Constellations," and "The Story of Pythagoras."

1583. [Various Chapter Outlines for Books on Logic and Metaphysics]
A. MS., n.p., n.d., 2 pp. and 3 assorted pages.

One of these outlines appears to be for a volume, principally on logic, based on CSP's published papers.

MISCELLANEOUS NOTEBOOKS

These notebooks appeared after the initial microfilming of the Peirce collection had taken place. In order to accomplish the task of microfilming as much of the collection as possible with the least possible disruption, it was decided to place the notebooks here, trusting that the Index will bring together what properly belongs together. Following the notebooks, beginning with MS. 1596, are several items, some of them, perhaps, not strictly part of the "Peirce Collection," but which, nevertheless, have been given manuscript numbers for the dual purpose of calling attention to them and, at the same time, facilitating the work of the librarian who may, from time to time, be requested to make these items available.

1584. [Miscellaneous]

A. MS., notebook, n.p., 1903.

The only dated entry is December 24, 1903. There are notes on: the four-color problem; three kinds of reasoning; Schiller's Riddle of the Sphinx; Steinthal on the Stoa; rules for existential graphs; pragmatism and abduction. Inserted sheets torn out of another notebook of the same kind contain notes on the Skew Mercator and on Sylvester.

1585. [Miscellaneous]

A. MS., notebook, n.p., n.d.

Terminology; chemistry, mathematical calculations.

1586. [Miscellaneous]

A. MS., small notebook, n.p., n.d.

Chemistry; mathematical calculations.

1587. [Miscellaneous]

A. MS., small notebook, n.p., n.d.

Notes on topology; "points" of a letter.

1588. [Miscellaneous]

A. MS., notebook, n.p., n.d.

Various mathematical notes; secundals; existential graphs; notes on the Constitution (not in CSP's hand).

1589. The Rules of Existential Graphs.

A. MS., notebook, n.p., n.d. Call number Am 806.

The system of existential graphs is intended to afford a method for the analysis of all necessary reasonings into their ultimate elements. No transformations are permitted except *insertions* and *omissions*. The results of series of permissible insertions and omissions. The peculiar formal signs are the fewest with which it is possible to represent all the operations of necessary reasonings.

1590. [Quotations from Islamic Literature]

A. MS., notebook, n.p., n.d.

Number words in several languages.

1591. [List of Reference Works]

A. MS., small notebook, n.p., n.d.

1592. Library Notes

A. MS., notebook, n.p., n.d.

These notes were taken at the Astor Library.

1593. Notes Preparatory to an Index to Sainte-Beuve, *Causeries du Lundi*

A. MS., notebook, n.p., March 4, 1902.

1594. Index to Gil's *Logonomia Anglia.*
A. MS., notebook, n.p., n.d. Call number Am 806.1.

1595. [Notes for Definitions of Words Associated with Universities]
A. MS., notebook, n.p., n.d.
For the *Century Dictionary.*

*1596. [Notes]
A. MS., n.p., n.d., four large boxes filled with 3 × 5 size cards and one box filled with 2 × 5 size cards.

Reference catalogues of philosophical subjects, quotations from philosophical authors. Indices and lists of books, principally for dictionary projects.

1597. Peirce's Copy of the *Century Dictionary,* twenty-four volumes, in Houghton Library, call number 9224.15F.

Dictionary is annotated and lists CSP's more important contributions, especially "pragmatism." See G-1889-3.

1598. Marginal notes of Charles S. Peirce in his copy of Clerk Maxwell, *Theory of Heat,* 1891, tenth edition, given to Widener Library, Harvard University, June 28, 1915, by Mrs. Charles Sanders Peirce. Call number: Phys 2407.1.10.

CSP's notes are extensive and occur on pp. 95, 96, 99, 100, 112, 113, 118, 121, 122, 129, 131, 134, 139, 142, 146, 147, 149, and 306.

1599. [Bound Volumes of Peirce's Published Writings]
There are seven volumes, including two volumes of Johns Hopkins University Circulars (1879-83). Some annotation by CSP.

1600. [Peirce's Reprints and Books from his Library; Editor's Materials and Preliminary Catalogues of the Collection]
Some of the reprints contain notes and corrections by CSP. Some but not all of the corrections were reproduced in the *Collected Papers.*

BIOGRAPHICAL

AUTOBIOGRAPHICAL SKETCHES

1601. Family Record.
A. MS., notebook, n.p., begun June 1864 and later dates. Call number Am 806.5.

Genealogical information. From back end of notebook CSP wrote twenty-eight numbered pages beginning with an attempt to define "real." The page numbered 28 is dated November 5, 1909. In addition there is material on topology, theory of multitudes, secundals, existential graphs, and calculations, much of which are evidently concerned with the old map-coloring problem.

1602. My Life.
A. MS., n.p., n.d., pp. 1-5.
Earliest memories, including visits to his grandmother in Salem and moving into the new family home in 1845.

1603. [Autobiographical Sketch]

A. MS., n.p., [1903?], 2 pp. of two drafts.

Possibly for Lamb's *Biographical Dictionary of the United States*. CSP mentions that he wrote all the philosophical and mathematical definitions for the *Century Dictionary*.

1604. My reading in philosophy.

A. MS., n.p., September 1894, 5 pp.

In logic, CSP states that he has studied every important system except the second edition of Sigwart. But he is most devoted to the theory of knowledge and secondly to cosmology. Reading in esthetics, ethics, theology, and psychology. Plato read mainly in translation; Aristotle in the original. "Have read and thought more about Aristotle than about any other man." (It is difficult to tell whether this remark was meant to apply generally, since it was made in the context of his discussion of Greek philosophy.) Indeed the manuscript doesn't get beyond CSP's reading in Greek philosophy, ending with Epicureanism and atomism.

1605. A True Statement of my Reading in Philosophy.

A. MS., n.p., [1894], 2 pp.

1606. [Autobiographical Fragment]

A. MS., n.p., n.d., pp. 10-11, with an alternate p. 11.

"Although I was not a precocious child, at the age of 8 I took up of my own accord the study of chemistry, to which the following year I added natural philosophy . . ."

1607. [Autobiographical Fragment]

A. MS., n.p., [January 1] 1892, 1 p.

"My greatest trial is my inertness of mind."

1608. [Autobiographical Fragments]

A. MS., n.p., n.d., 6 pp.

1609. [List of Significant Dates]

A. MS. n.p., [1890?], 2 pp.

1610. [List of Places where Christmas was Spent]

A. MS., n.p., [1890?], 3 pp.

1611. [Biographical Form]

A. MS., n.p., [1903], 1 p.

For manuscript directory and biographical dictionary of the *Men of Science in the United States*.

1612. [Biographical Form]

A. MS., n.p., late, 2 pp.

For *Families of American Men of Science*.

1613. [Biographical Form]

A. MS., n.p., n.d., 1 p.

For the Lawrence Scientific School, Harvard University, card catalogue of graduates.

Diaries, Address and Memorandum Books

1614. [Diary]

A. MS., book, n.p., January 13, 1871.

CSP used this "Agenda," which he bought in Geneva to record the events of his European trip. The pages after February 22 have been torn out.

1615. [Diary?]

A. MS., book cover, n.p., 1876.

Activities recorded for the period August 24 to November 3. On inside cover CSP wrote: "I was said to be in N. Y. in Herald 1876 Sep 3."

1616. [Diary]

A. MS., book, n.p., 1889.

The pages after February 15 are missing.

1617. [Diary]

A. MS., book, n.p., January 1893.

1618. [Diary]

A. MS., book, n.p., January 1894.

1619. [Diary]

A. MS., book, n.p., February 1899.

1620. [Diary]

A. MS., book, n.p., December 1902.

1621. [Diary]

A. MS., book, n.p., March 1903.

1622. [Diary]

A. MS., book, n.p., December 1905.

1623. [Diaries]

A. MS., books, n.p., 1911-14.

1624. [Packet of Three Small Books]

A. MS., books, n.p., n.d.

Address, Memorandum, Cash.

1625. [Address Book]

A. MS., small book, n.p., [1870-71?].

1626. [Address Book]

A. MS., book, n.p., [1908-11].

Some addresses, but of greater interest are the lists of some of CSP's scientific journals; "My writings on the Validity of Reasoning"; notes on construction work at Arisbe; "Octavo copies of my writings in the breakfast room"; meanings of the verb "give"; "To calculate the height of Aurora according to H. A. Newton." Some undated reflections: "I like and esteem the man who knows when to resign a game of chess, and does not insist upon protracting it to a tedious and melancholy mate. I like and esteem the man who gives Death a cordial shake of the hand when the time comes, and having fought a good fight, does not finish it with a feeble, frittering, factious, fretful, futility." And: "Intellectual value lies wholly in form, not matter."

1627. [Memorandum Book]

A. MS., n.p., 1882.

The first entry lists CSP's expectations for the year which include paying off most of his debts.

JUVENILIA

1628. The Warsaw Times

A. MS., n.p., February 14, 1857, 8 pp.

A humorous replica newspaper devoted to "Society, Literature, and Business" and priced at 2 pins.

1629. [Cambridge High School and Dixwell Preparatory School Themes and Exercises]

A. MS., portfolio, n.p., 1849-54.

By his own account CSP was admitted to the Cambridge High School in 1849 and "turned out" in the Spring of 1854; after studying mathematics for six months, he entered the Dixwell School, graduating in 1855. Listed below are CSP's themes and exercises from this period: "Fine Arts" (4 pp.), "The Deserted Village" (4 pp.), "Everyman the Maker of his own Fortune" (14 pp.), "Caesar and Hannibal—their Decision of Character" (16 pp.), "The Crusades" (17 pp.), "The Parthenon" (17 pp.), "Raphael and Michael Angelo compared as men" (4 pp.), "The Strength and the Weakness of the Present Dynasty in France" (4 pp.), "Theme No. 3. Sophomore. What is your favorite virtue? etc." (2 pp.), "Translation of Part of Judith from the French of Eugene Scribe" (14 pp.), "Latin Exercises. Dixwell's" (50 pp.), "List of Poets of Whose Private History I have any Knowledge" (10 pp.), exercises in poetical meter (9 pp.), poetry (6 pp.), mathematical exercises (50 pp.).

HARVARD COLLEGE

1630. Notes to Lectures on Mathematics: 2nd Term Junior.

A. MS., notebook, n.p., 1858.

1631. Notes to the Lectures of Prof. Peirce in Mathematics delivered in the year 1858-9 A.D.

A. MS., notebook, n.p., 1858-59.

1632. [Notes on Mathematics]

A. MS., n.p., n.d.

Only the last two pages are in CSP's hand; they deal with fractional notation. The other pages, probably college notes on mathematics, are in another hand (or hands).

1633. [College Themes]

A. MS., portfolio, n.p., variously dated from 1857-59.

Thirty themes whose topics range widely. A sample list: "The Sense of Beauty never furthered the Performance of a Single Act of Duty" (an eludication of Schiller's *Aesthetische Briefe*), "The Moral and Religious Character of Coleridge," "The American Country Gentleman—The Ideal and the Reality," "The Death-Bed is a Detector of the Heart," "Some Considerations which seem to show that despotic governments are not more essentially aggressive in their policy towards other states than democracies are," "Historical Account of the Celebration of Christmas in New England."

1634. Book of Characters. My Life written for the Class-Book.

A. MS., notebook, n.p., September 10, 1860 (on first page) but parts of notebook are of a later date.

Duplicated, in part, in the appendix to T. A. Goudge's *The Thought of C. S. Peirce* and, in part, in the introduction to P. P. Wiener's edited anthology of CSP's writings, *Values in a Universe of Chance*. Both Goudge and Wiener reprinted CSP's entry in the Harvard Class-Book of 1859, written at the time of his graduation. In the "Book of Characters" we have in addition CSP's entries for the years 1859-61: "Wondered what I would do in life – – – Appointed Aid on the Coast Survey" (1859); "Came back from Louisiana and took a Proctorship in Harvard. Studied Natural History and Natural Philosophy" (1860); "No longer wondered what I would do in life but defined my object" (1861). Only the first 3 pp. are autobiographical. The balance of the notebook is given over to a financial record, covering a period of four months, most likely for the year 1863.

1635. The Class of 1859 of Harvard

A. MS., notebook, n.p., begun February 4, 1858.

CSP's evaluation of a number of fellow class members, but not all. The ones on Francis Abbot and himself are of particular interest. He described Abbot as "supremely conscientious" with "ability mediocre" and as lacking in "some elements of good taste." Of himself, he wrote: "1. Vanity 2. Snobbishness 3. Incivility 4. Recklessness 5. Laziness and Ill-tempered."

1636. Proposed New Constitution

A. MS., n.p., n.d., 7 pp.; plus 6 pp. of an earlier draft.

The constitution is for the O-K- of 1859.

1637. (Harv)

A. MS., n.p., n.d., pp. 1-3, with a rejected p. 2.

Impressions of Harvard architecture.

MISCELLANEOUS

1638. [Extracts from an Oration]

From the *Cambridge Chronicle*, November 21, 1863. The oration on the State of Civilization was delivered at the Reunion of the Cambridge High School Association, November 12, 1863.

1639. [Various Lists of Names, Addresses, and Books]

A. MS., n.p., n.d., 13 pp.

1640. [Fragment of German, French, English Dictionary]

Book, n.d.

The following appears on the flyleaf: "Juliette de Pourtalès from her friend and devoted servitor C. S. Peirce."

1641. [C. S. Peirce's Record of Juliette Peirce's Health]

A. MS., n.p., September 6-8, 1890, 2 pp.

1642. Diplomas.

1643. Photographs.

1644. Death.

Newspaper clippings; a manuscript of 9 pp., a memorial to CSP composed by Helen Peirce Ellis for a newspaper article; a brief review of CSP's life written by Richard Cobb, with an accompanying note by Benjamin Peirce Ellis; a typescript (5 pp.) of the Ellis genealogy; and a one page statement, unfinished, by Juliette Peirce of her husband's last hours: "One of our last conversations, I remonstrated with him that he could not recover physically by hard mental work, in refusing to let him have more paper to write, but when he complained that his pains were so great and writing would ease his pains, then I complied – – –"

Part Two

CORRESPONDENCE

CHARLES S. PEIRCE CORRESPONDENCE

Letters, drafts of letters, and miscellaneous items such as postal cards, tele-grams, receipts, applications, legal documents, formal invitations, notices, and even an occasional notebook. The correspondents are listed alphabetically, and of the dated entries, when there are more than three, usually the first and last dates are provided.

L 1. Abbot, Francis Ellington. One letter to CSP, January 5, 1894.

L 2. Adams, Brooks. Two letters to CSP, January 3, 1892 and January 12, 1896.

L 3. Adams, Charles K. One letter (TS.) to CSP, January 12, 1892.

L 4. Adams, George B. Two letter drafts from CSP, May 17, 1901.

L 5. Agassiz, Alexander. One letter to CSP, July 5, 1903.

L 6. Agassiz, Elizabeth C. Four letters to CSP, December 16, 1891, December 8, [1892], January 27, n. yr., and December 30, n. yr.

L 7. Agassiz, Louis. An invitation to CSP to attend a reunion of Agassiz's pupils on the one hundredth anniversary of Agassiz's birth, May 1907.

L 8. Aikens, H. Austin. One letter (with an enclosed letter to the editor of *The Nation*) to CSP, September 27, 1902; one letter draft from, n.d.

L 9. Alden, John B. One letter from CSP, August 25, 1890.

L 10. Allen, Col. Vanderbilt. One letter draft from CSP, n.d.

L 11. Alline, L. M. One letter to CSP, February 2, 1893.

L 12. American Academy of Arts and Sciences (John Trowbridge, President). One letter to CSP, n.d.

L 13. American Association for the Advancement of Science. One letter to CSP, n.d. Notice of CSP's election; August 1881.

L 14. *The American Historical Review* (Albert Bushnell Hart and J. Franklin Jameson). Nine letters to CSP, April 30, 1896–December 10, 1897; five letter drafts from, March 13 and May 17, 1901.

L 15. American Mathematical Society (Thomas S. Fiske, Secretary). One letter to CSP, October 23, 1894.

L 16. American Metrological Society (J. K. Rees, Secretary). One letter to CSP, January 20, 1885.

L 17. American Society for Psychical Research (Richard Hodgson, Secretary). One letter to CSP, October 3, 1898. One letter (T. H. Pierson, Secretary) to James H. Woods, June 3, 1931.

L 18. The American Society for the Extension of University Teaching (Willis Boughton). One letter to CSP, July 29, 1891. Notice of election, 1891.

L 19.   Anthony, Andrew V. S. (Sun and Shade, Art Department). Three letters to CSP, December 11–19, 1891.

L 20.   Anthony, R. A. (McVickar, Gaillard Realty Co.). One letter to CSP, December 20, 1905.

L 21.   Appleton, D. and Co. (William W. Appleton, William Hirsch, Ripley Hitchcock, E. Werrey, W. J. Youmans). Twenty-six letters to CSP and Juliette Peirce, May 18, [1894?]–March 9, 1900; three letter drafts from CSP, June 29, 1896 and n.d.; two letter drafts from Juliette Peirce, February 12, 1896 and n.d.

L 22.   Arisbe (The Peirce estate near Milford, Pa.). Boarding house correspondence and advertisements. Seventy-eight letters, cards, and telegrams, April 24, 1894–May 9, 1902. Placed with the Arisbe correspondence is a small notebook, with a survey in CSP's hand, January 22, 1898.

L 23.   Arisbe. Letters, drafts of letters, proposals for the sale of the property, including correspondence involving Juliette Peirce after CSP's death. Correspondence begins April 2, 1894 and concludes with a letter from the *New York Herald Tribune* of April 4, 1933.

L 24.   Arisbe. Deed, leases, and other legal business. The deed: Eleanor and Maria Quick to Juliette Peirce, May 10, 1888.

L 25.   Arnold, Constable, and Co. One letter draft from CSP, June 1911.

L 26.   Arnot, Raymond H. One letter to CSP, November 2, 1901.

L 27.   Astor, John Jacob. One letter (Astor's secretary) to CSP, November 28, 1896.

L 28.   Astor Library. Two letters to CSP, June 4, 1890 and December 6, 1895.

L 29.   *Atlantic Monthly* (the editors). One letter to CSP, June 29, 1901.

L 30.   d'Aulby, John Edward. Thirty-three letters to CSP, May 7, 1895–December 19, 1896. One letter (Francesca d'Aulby) to CSP, n.d.; incomplete letter draft from, n.d. Also: a telegram, notice of telegram, and letters to CSP from Howard Russell Butler, Adeline Lunt, William Macbeth, and E. A. Stedman, together with a copy of a release, with surrender of power of attorney, and a small notebook (CSP's), containing d'Aulby genealogy.

L 31.   Ausfeld, H. Two letters to CSP, December 23, 1872 and January 23, 1873.

L 32.   Austin, Ben W. (Secretary, Trinity Historical Society, Dallas, Texas). One letter to CSP, July 26, 1891.

L 33.   Baker, Harry T. One letter to CSP, January 20, 1897; eleven letters from CSP and Juliette Peirce, August 29, 1888–January 22, 1901.

L 34.   Baldwin, J. M. (*Dictionary of Philosophy and Psychology*). Twenty-two letters to CSP, October 9, 1900–November 8, 1902, and n.d.: nine letter drafts (one of which is not in CSP's hand) from, October 20, 1900–December 7, 1903, and n.d.

L 35.   Barnard, Augusta (Mrs. James Munson B.). Four letters to CSP and Juliette Peirce, October 22, 1896–January 12, 1906; one letter draft from CSP, n.d.

L 36. Barnet, Samuel. Fragments of letter drafts from CSP, two of which are dated, December 8, 1909 and February 16, 1910.

L 37. Barney, William. one letter to CSP, March 19, 1899.

L 38. Bartlett, John. One letter to CSP, November 23, 1894.

L 39. Becker, George Ferdinand. Twenty-two letters to CSP, November 28, 1891–March 28, 1897 and n.d.; two letter drafts from, February 22, 1897 and July 10, 1910. Also a two-page TS.; a communication to the *American Journal of Science,* Third Series, 1878, on "A Contribution to the History of Spectrum Analysis" by G. F. Becker.

L 40. Beekman, Charles K. Eleven letters to CSP and Juliette Peirce, June 20, 1898–December 7, 1900.

L 41. Bell, Alexander Graham. One letter (by Bell's secretary) to CSP, November 22, 1906; one letter draft from, March 25, 1906.

L 42. Benjamin, Park. One letter to CSP, December 6, 1895. See N-1896-1.

L 43. Benton, J. G. One letter to CSP, May 23, 1871.

L 44. Bidlack, W. W. One letter to CSP, October 12, 1888.

L 45. Bierstadt, Albert. Eleven letters to CSP, March 5, 1896–April 7, 1898. One letter (Bierstadt) to Count d'Aulby, June 21, 1896. Also CSP's receipt for an unfinished picture, May 5, 1896.

L 46. Bigler, Warren. One letter to CSP, June 28, 1911.

L 47. Billings, John Shaw. Three letters to CSP, October 22, 1900–November 5, 1910.

L 48. Billings and Stover (Pharmacy). One letter to CSP, July 31, 1904.

L 49. Blake, Francis. Five letters to CSP, May 4, 1896–February 2, 1897; two letter drafts from, April 27, 1896 and [November 2, 1896?].

L 50. Bolton, H. Carrington. One letter to CSP, March 9, 1894.

L 51. *The Bookman.* Three letters to CSP, April 18–June 23, 1900.

L 52. Boutelle, C. O. One letter to CSP, August 12, 1872.

L 53. Boston Public Library (Issue Department). One letter to CSP, September 22, 1904.

L 54. Bowen, Francis P. One letter to CSP, December 23, 1867.

L 55. Bradford, Gamaliel. One letter draft from CSP, April 16, 1904.

L 56. Bradford, J. S. and Bradford, Rosalie M. Five letters to CSP, August 4, 1872–February 11, 1873.

L 57. Brady's National Photographic Galleries. One letter to CSP, July 5, 1872.

L 58. Brennan, Alfred. Eight letters to CSP, May 8, 1890–March 24, 1904; one letter draft from, n.d.

L 59. Brentano's (Publishers). Two letters to CSP, January 13, 1896 and June 26, 1902.

L 60. Brown, Homer J. One letter to CSP, April 17, 1893.

L 61. Brownell, Eleanor Olivia (Secretary, Bryn Mawr College Philosophical Club). One letter to CSP, November 29, 1896.

L 62. Bryce, Lloyd. One letter to CSP, March 25, 1890.

L 62a. Bucherer, Alfred H. One letter to CSP, March 22, 1893.

L 63. Bull, C. W. Two letters, a card, and a telegram to CSP, August 8, 1895–July 18, 1900; one letter draft from, n.d.

L 64. Butler, George Bernard. One letter to CSP, December 8, n. yr.

L 65. Butler, Nicholas Murray. Two letters to CSP, February 15, 1892 and December 22, 1897; one letter draft (first sentence only) from, n.d.

L 66. Byerly, William E. Two letter drafts from CSP, November 17 and December 9, 1908. One letter (Byerly) to Benjamin P. Ellis, December 5, 1908.

L 67. Calderoni, Mario. One letter draft from CSP, [1905]. This is a draft of 39 pp., of which pp. 1-17 were published as 8.205-213.

L 68. Calvi, Mr. One letter draft to CSP, April 12, 1896.

L 69. Cambridge University Press. Two letters to CSP, February 17, 1911 and February 7, 1912. Memo, December 19, 1889.

L 70. Campbell, Douglas. Five letters to CSP, May 4, 1887–October 6, 1892. Also a formal wedding invitation.

L 71. Campbell, [Harriet Mumford]. One letter to CSP, May 7, 1893.

L 72. Campbell, William Wallace. One letter draft from CSP, [1908].

L 73. Cantor, Georg. Five letter drafts from CSP, December 21–23, 1900, and n.d.

L 74. Cantor, Moritz. One letter draft from CSP, November 12, 1892.

L 75. Carnegie Institution Correspondence. The principal letter of this correspondence is CSP's application for financial assistance. It is addressed to the Executive Committee of the Carnegie Institution and is dated July 15, 1902. The application, which is 76 pp. long, was published, in part, as 7.158-161 and 8.176n³ (G-1902-6). Parts of earlier drafts run as high as p. 83 and are not dated. One letter (CSP) to Ernst Schroeder contains an enclosed list of CSP's proposed memoirs and is dated July 23, 1902. One letter draft (CSP) to Dr. Weir Mitchell, n.d. Also fifty-three letters, May 3, 1901–November 21, 1906. The correspondents include CSP's brothers, H. H. D. and J. M. Peirce, and the following in alphabetical order: Marcus Baker, Richard, Cabot, J. M. Cattell, J. E. Creighton, John Dewey, George S. Fullerton, B. I. Gilman, G. Stanley Hall, O. W. Holmes, Mary Putnam Jacobi, William James, H. C. Lodge, Percival Lowell, Wayne MacVeagh, Henry Rutgers Marshall, Allan Maynard, Dickinson S. Miller, William Pepperell Montague, E. H. Moore, Edward Pickering, G. A. Plimpton, Theodore Roosevelt, Elihu Root, Josiah Royce, Wilman Henry Sheldon, Benjamin E. Smith, Albert Stickney, William E. Story, John Trowbridge, Charles Walcott, Joseph B. Warner. Some of the letters contain CSP's comments.

L 76. Carty, Thomas J. One letter to CSP, January 6, 1901.

L 77. Carus, Paul (Open Court Publishing Co.). One hundred and twelve letters (Carus, E. C. Hegeler, T. J. McCormack, Lydia Robinson, M. A. Sachsteder, F. Sigrist) to CSP, July 2, 1890–September 10, 1913; twenty-five letter drafts from, July 5, 1892–June 13, 1911, and n.d.

L 78. Cattell, J. McKeen (G. P. Putnam's Sons). Fifty-seven letters to CSP, January 6, 1898–December 7, 1911; three letter drafts from, March 31, 1898–December 18, 1903.

L 79. Century Club. One letter to CSP, August 18, 1891.

L 80. Century Company (*Century Dictionary*). Forty-seven letters to CSP and Juliette Peirce, April 12, 1890–May 18, 1932; nine letter drafts from CSP, April 10, 1901–June 20, 1909, and n.d. One letter (J. R. Buchanan) to the editor of the *Century Dictionary*, June 24, n. yr.

L 81. Chamberlin, T. C. Two letters to CSP, July 7 and September 18, 1897.

L 82. Chandler, William Henry. Two letters to CSP, January 22 and April 25, 1901.

L 82a. Chase, Pliny Earle. One letter draft from CSP, April 4, 1864.

L 83. Child, Francis J. Two letters to CSP, February 28, 1888 and April 12, 1894.

L 84. Christern, J. W. One letter to CSP, July 28, n. yr.; one letter draft from, December 3, 1900.

L 85. Civil Service Commission Correspondence (re: Application for position of Inspector of Standards, Office of Standard Weights and Measures, U.S. Coast and Geodetic Survey). Two letters from CSP, May 18 and August 12, 1899. One letter draft from CSP to John R. Procter, June 19, 1899. Two letter drafts from CSP to Cabot Lodge, November 3, 1899. Letter draft (?) of 4 pp., stating qualifications for position of Inspector of Standards, n.d. Included in the correspondence are two announcements by the United States Civil Service Commission of a new position of Inspector of Standards, mentioning the examination subjects and weights assigned to each, June 1 and July 15, 1899. Application for the examination, filled in and dated, June 1, 1889. Report of the examination averages (CSP's general average was 96.00, with 90.00 on the thesis), December 7, 1899. Draft of "Thesis on the proper functions of a National Office of Weights and Measures," with 4 pp. of earlier attempts. The following letters were sent to CSP: two letters (Ernest J. Sommer), May 14, and 19, 1899; one letter (Asaph Hall), July 1, 1899; one letter (Seth C. Chandler), July 3, 1899; two letters (John R. Procter), July 11 and 20, 1899; one letter (Simon Newcomb), July 20, 1899; one letter (Henry Cabot Lodge), November 9, 1899. The following letters have also been included in the correspondence: one letter (Henry S. Pritchett) to Henry Cabot Lodge, September 14, 1899; one letter (George A. Plimpton) to Henry S. Pritchett, October 26, 1899; one letter (George A. Plimpton) to Lyman S. Gage (Secretary of the Treasury), October 26, 1899; one letter (C. Lyman) to George A. Plimpton, November 11, 1899; one letter (George A. Plimpton) to William McKinley, President of the

United States, November 14, 1899; one letter (J. A. Porter, McKinley's Secretary) to George A. Plimpton, November 15, 1899; one letter (Henry S. Pritchett) to James Mills Peirce, November 15, 1899.

L 86. Clark, Alvan. Three letters to CSP, April 17–May 18, [1872].

L 87. Clifford, H. E. One letter to CSP, April 17, 1906; one letter draft from, n.d.

L 88. Clinton, Mr. Two letter drafts from CSP, n.d. Verso of one has draft of letter to Dr. Sommer, n.d.

L 89. Clothilde (Jeanne d'Arc Home). Forty-eight letters, thirteen postal cards, and one telegram to CSP and Juliette Peirce, September 1899–August 9, 1926; one letter draft from CSP, [1901?] and one letter draft from Juliette Peirce, February 12, 1923. Miscellaneous items: clippings, prayers, and two "Fair Books."

L 90. Coan, Titus Munson. Two letters to CSP, September 23, 1887 and January 13, 1894; one letter draft from, n.d.

L 91. Coast Survey Correspondence. Two letters (E. Mayo) to CSP, July 17, 1880 and March 23, 1882. Two letters (J. E. Hilgard) to CSP, April 17, 1882 and February 1, 1883. One letter (H. J. Chaney) to CSP, June 22, 1883. One letter (W. R. O'Neill) to CSP, February 2, 1886. Six letters (F. M. Thorn) to CSP, March 30, 1886–August 15, 1888. One letter (E. D. Preston) to CSP, May 9, 1889. Seven letters (T. C. Mendenhall) to CSP, July 17, 1889–December 24, 1891; two letter drafts from, January 20, 1892 and January 1892. One letter (W. Butler) to CSP, January 18, 1892. One letter draft from CSP to C. P. Patterson, December 29, 1878. Two letter drafts from CSP to Edwin Smith, May 25, 1882 and n.d. One letter draft from CSP to Söhmer, April 12, 1885. One letter draft from CSP to John W. Parsons, September 5, 1891. One letter draft from CSP to Henry Farguhar, n.d. Three letter drafts from CSP to an unidentified person or persons, n.d. Other correspondence includes: One letter (Julius Bein) to J. E. Hilgard, February 21, 1873. One letter (G. W. Frodsham) to J. E. Hilgard, October 16, 1873. One letter (J. M. Portin) to James Mills Peirce, November 4, 1880. One letter (C. A. Schott) to B. A. Colonne, August 13, 1885. One letter (A. Riesenberger) to F. M. Thorn, June 6, 1887. One letter (R. Faris, Acting Director) to Paul Weiss, August 10, 1931. Also: tables, instructions, vouchers, orders, circulars.

L 92. Collins, Charles. One letter to CSP, May 16, 1890.

L 93. Conger, A. B. One letter to CSP, December 27, 1872.

L 94. Cooke, Jay, and Company. Two letters to CSP, June 20, 1872 and February 25, 1873.

L 95. Cooke, Josiah P. One letter to CSP, January 17, 1894.

L 96. Cooper, Theodore. One letter to CSP, June 13, 1895.

L 97. Cooper, W. G. One letter (Cooper) to "Professor" [Benjamin Peirce?]; [August 7, 1869]. A copy in CSP's hand.

L 98. Cooper, W. W. One letter to CSP, December 16, 1872.

L 99.   Corral, F. J. del. One letter to CSP, November 18, 1889.

L 100.   Correspondence Court ("Art of Reasoning"). Sixty-six letters (students) to CSP, 1887-90; one letter (TS.) from CSP to "My dear pupil," n.d. A notebook with drafts of letters to CSP's students. Another notebook containing a list of students and an elementary explanation of Boolean algebra. Two drafts of "Boolian Algebra. First Lesson." In addition, there are handwritten and typewritten sections of the course, circulars, and an early draft of the circular.

L 101.   *Cosmopolitan Magazine* (Editorial Department). Two letters to CSP, December 10, 1897 and June 12, 1900.

L 102.   Couturat, Louis. Note or letter draft (incomplete?) from CSP, n.d.

L 103.   Craig, Thomas. One letter to CSP, May 1, 1896.

L 104.   Crofts, J. M. One letter to CSP, [c.1896]; one letter draft from, [c.1896].

L 105.   Cummings, Prentiss. Cummings' personal card, with note; n.d.

L 106.   Cupples and Schoenhof. One letter draft from CSP, December 17, 1903.

L 107.   Curtis, Matthew Mattoon. One letter to CSP, October 26, 1904. In his letter Curtis notes that he is about to rewrite the sketch of philosophy in North America for a new edition of Ueberweg-Heinze, *Geschichte der Philosophie* and requests information concerning CSP's logical and philosophical views. In response to this request CSP drafted a philosophical autobiography, pp. 1-25, with variants. This incomplete draft has been placed with the Curtis correspondence.

L 108.   Dana, Charles Anderson. Seven letters to CSP, July 8, [1872]–May 10, 1892.

L 109.   Daniel, A. T. One letter to CSP, September 26, [1894?].

L 110.   Daniells, Miss. One letter draft from CSP, September 12, 1891.

L 111.   Davidson, George. One letter to CSP, December 27, 1872.

L 112.   Davis, Charles Henry. One letter to CSP, July 1, 1872.

L 113.   Davis, Charles Henry. Ten letters to CSP, March 12, 1894–February 8, 1900, and n.d.

L 114.   Davis, Ellery W. One letter draft from CSP, April 9, 1898.

L 115.   Davis, F. du Pont. One letter to CSP, November 2, 1872.

L 116.   Davis, Louisa. One letter to CSP, n.d.

L 117.   Dean, George W. Two letters to CSP, February 15 and 20, 1873.

L 118.   Dembitz, Lewis N. One letter to CSP, November 19, 1893.

L 119.   De Morgan, Augustus. One letter to CSP, April 14, 1868.

L 120.   Denver University (F. D. Burhaus). One letter to CSP, February 26, 1894.

L 121.   De Vinne and Co., Printers. Four letters to CSP, May 5–November 11, 1893; one letter draft from, October 30, 1893.

L 122.   Devoe, F. W., and Company (J. Wyman Drummond). One letter to CSP, August 13, 1889.

L 123.   Dewey, John. Three letters to CSP, December 23, 1903, January 11, 1904, and April 11, 1905; Three letter drafts from, December 8, 1903, June 9, 1904, and n.d. One letter (Dewey) to Paul Weiss; October 1, 1931. See also Carnegie Institution correspondence.

L 124.   Dick, Joseph. One letter draft from CSP, January 6, 1900. Two letters (Dick) to the editor of *The Nation,* October 1, 1898 and January 2, 1900.

L 125.   Easton, Nelson S. Seven letters to CSP, June 6, 1896–October 4, 1898; five letter drafts from, n.d. One letter (Easton) to Count d'Aulby, July 8, 1896.

L 126.   Edmunds, James R. One letter draft from CSP; February 14, 1896.

L 127.   Eliot, Charles W. Three letters to CSP, May 23, 1872–October 4, 1895; one letter draft from, November 27, 1872.

L 128.   Elliott, E. J. One letter to CSP, October 17, 1908.

L 129.   Ellis, Helen P. Thirty-two letters to CSP, many of uncertain date; twelve letters and one postal card from, January 22, 1871–1913. In addition to the letters there is a clipping on "Our Dream-Life" which CSP's sister sent him for his comments.

L 130.   Ellis, Sally Mills (Mrs. Richard Cobb). One letter to CSP, March 12, 1901.

L 131.   Ellis, William R. One letter to CSP, August 2, 1872. A clipping from the *New York Sun,* February 26 [1895?], concerning the sale of CSP's library.

L 132.   Emery, Woodward. Two letter drafts from CSP, March 11 and 15, 1908.

L 133.   Engle, J. S. Two letters to CSP, February 24 and 25, 1905; one letter draft from, February 14, 1905.

L 134.   Errata. Printed letter by CSP, concerning the memoir, "On the Algebra of Logic" (G-1880-8), September 15, 1880.

L 135.   Esberg, L. One letter to CSP, July 8, 1872.

L 136.   Everett, William. Two letters to CSP, September 20, 1893 and February 20, 1894.

L 137.   Fahie, John Joseph. One letter draft from CSP, March 18, 1904.

L 138.   Farguhar, Henry. One postal card to CSP, March 22, [1879?].

L 139.   Fay, Charles. One letter to CSP, October 4, 1873.

L 140.   Fay, C. Norman. One letter to CSP and Zina (Harriet Melusina Fay), January 23, 1876.

L 141.   Fay, James H. One letter to CSP, April 25, 1890.

L 142.   Ferrero, Annibale. One letter to CSP, November 25, 1889.

L 143.   Fifth Avenue Bank. Two letters to CSP, August 23 and October 1, 1904; three letter drafts from, July 30, 1892–July, 1901. One letter, Fifth Avenue Bank to Juliette Peirce, March 31, 1921.

L 144.   Findlay, Mr. One letter draft from CSP, July 3, 1905.

CHARLES S. PEIRCE CORRESPONDENCE

L 145. Fine, Henry Burchard. Five letters to CSP, December 16, 1900–January 28, 1901; one letter draft from, July 17 1903.

L 146. Fiske, John. Four letters to CSP, October 12, 1891–February 6, 1894. One letter (Houghton, Mifflin and Co.) to Fiske, January 27, 1894.

L 147. Forkas (Stein-Gray Drug Co.) One letter to CSP, April 5, 1904.

L 148. Frankland, F. W. Ten letters to CSP, March 12, 1897– October 25, 1905, and n.d.; three letter drafts from, May 8, 1906, February 25, 1907, and n.d. One letter (Frankland) to Dr. Skinner, March 9, 1897.

L 149. Franklin, Fabian. Two letters to CSP, November 20, 1900 and July 10, 1901.

L 150. Fransch, Hans A. One letter draft from CSP, April 14, 1911.

L 151. Frazer, Persifor. Two letters to CSP, November 16, 1901 and July 2, 1902; one letter draft from, April 28, 1901.

L 152. Fuertes, E. A. Two letters to CSP, December 30, 1891 and May 13, 1897. One letter (Fuertes) to Juliette Peirce, 1885.

L 153. Funk and Wagnalls (Isaac K. Funk). Eleven letters to CSP, May 11, 1891–September 1, 1896; one letter draft from, July 12, 1892.

L 154. Gaillard, Alberic. Five letters to CSP, September 22, 1891–March 29, 1897.

L 155. Gallup, George H. One letter to CSP, October 28, 1911.

L 156. Gannett, Dr. One letter draft from CSP, n.d.

L 157. Gardam, Joseph. One letter to CSP and Juliette Peirce, June 19, 1911.

L 158. Gardiner, A. S. One letter to CSP, March 18, 1890.

L 159. Garrison, Wendell Phillips (*The Nation, Evening Post*). Two hundred and sixteen letters to CSP, with an occasional letter to Juliette Peirce, January 10, 1872–May 6, 1907; twenty-three letter drafts from, February 18, 1899–[c.1907-08], and n.d. Also: some correspondence between authors of books CSP reviewed and the editor of *The Nation*.

L 160. Gautier, P. Two letters to CSP, August 22, 1884 and n.d.

L 161. Gest, John M. One letter to CSP, November 27, 1901.

L 162. Gibbs, J. Willard. One letter to CSP, December 1, 1881.

L 163. Gibbs, Wolcott. Two letters to CSP, June 28, 1872 and March 14, 188–.

L 164. Giddings, Franklin H. One letter draft (possibly two) from CSP, June 11, 1910. One letter (Giddings) to W. P. Garrison, April 5, 1902.

L 165. Gill, Edith Gwynne and William Fearing. Ninety-one letters to CSP and Juliette Peirce, October 7, 1891–March 20, 1909, and n.d.; a note and the beginning of a letter from CSP, n.d. Two letter drafts (Juliette Peirce) to Gill, n.d.

L 166. Gill, J. Thompson. Four letters to CSP, October 23, 1900–February 11, 1901, and n.d.

L 167. Gilman, Benjamin Ives. Five letters to CSP, May 18, 1882–April 12, 1905, and October 28, n. yr.

L 168. Gilman, Daniel C. Three letters to CSP, April 27, 1887–February 6, 1897; one letter (copy) from, January 13, 1878, and two letter drafts from, April 18, 1895 and May 21, 1896. One letter (Mrs. D. C. Gilman) to Juliette Peirce, July 13, 1883.

L 169. Ginn and Company (G. A. Plimpton). Forty-eight letters to CSP, October 31, 1893–August 18, 1903; seven letter drafts from, May 25, 1894–November 18, 1899, and n.d. Six letters (Plimpton) to Juliette Peirce, March 14, 1895–November 9, 1898. One letter (Philbin and Beekman) to Plimpton, November 7, 1898.

L 170. Girard Trust Company. One letter draft from CSP, September 15, 1911.

L 171. Goddard, Charles H. One letter to CSP, November 24, 1903.

L 172. Goodwin, Wm. W. Two letter drafts from CSP, January 4, 1901 and September 14, 1908.

L 173. Grace, J. W. One letter to CSP, April 14, 1887.

L 174. Greely, Adolphus W. Three letters to CSP, November 30, 1888–November 10, 1902; one letter draft from, November 27, 1888; one letter (Robert Craig) to CSP, December 4, 1888.

L 175. Greenslet, Ferris. One letter draft from CSP, December 19, 1905.

L 176. Guthrie, Edwin. Two letters to CSP, June 5 and 20, 1911.

L 177. Haines, J. Harvey. Two letters to CSP, November 16 and 23, 1903.

L 178. Hall, A. One letter to CSP, May 8, 1872.

L 179. Hall, G. Stanley. Thirteen letters, one of which is from Hall's secretary, to CSP, March 17 1890–January 29, 1901.

L 180. Halsey, Frederick A. One letter to CSP, September 27, 1904; four letter drafts from, November 10, 1904–January 15, 1905, and n.d.

L 181. Halsted, George Bruce. Four letters to CSP, December 7, 1891–December 17, 1895; one letter draft from, n.d.

L 182. Harriman, Sarah F. Two letters to CSP and Juliette Peirce, March 8, 1896 and March 22, 1897; one letter draft from CSP, n.d.

L 183. Harris, William Torrey. Sixteen letters (typed from the originals) to CSP, January 1, 1868–November 29, 1869; one letter to, December 10, 1867; one letter draft from, [c.1870]. Typed copies of letters to Harris from Amos Bronson Alcott and D. C. Gilman. Two letters from Edith Davidson Harris to Max Fisch.

L 184. Harrison, A. M. One letter to CSP, October 16, 1872.

L 185. Harvard College (Class of 1859). Five letters (Class committees and class secretary), to CSP, May 15–December 11, 1872, and [1872].

L 186. Harvard College Library. A request that books borrowed from the library [for the Harvard Lectures on pragmatism (1903) and the Lowell Lectures in November and December of 1903] be returned. An accompanying list of books and the dates on which the books were borrowed.

L 187. Harvard Cooperative Society. One letter draft from CSP, January 1, 1909.

L 188. Hastings, Mr. One letter draft from CSP, February 27, 1901.

L 189. Hathaway, Philip. One letter from CSP, November 7, 1903.

L 190. Hawley, Thomas D. One letter to CSP, November 18, 1896. A card from CSP, n.d.

L 191. Hawthorne, Julian. One letter to CSP, February 10, 1909.

L 192. Heath, D. C. and Company. Two letters to CSP, October 17 and November 11, 1898.

L 193. Hein, Samuel. Three letters to CSP, November 15, 1872–February 21, 1873.

L 194. Herringshaw's *Encyclopedia of American Biography.* An advertisement, with note added that CSP is to be represented in the 2nd edition to be published in the fall of 1900.

L 195. Herschel, J. Three letters to CSP, December 29, 1884, February 11, 1886, and n.d.

L 196. Hewitt, Edward R. One letter to CSP, December 28, 1892.

L 197. Hilgard, Julius E. Four letters to CSP, June 21, 1872–January 29, 1873; three letter drafts from, February 2, 1872–March 26, 1883.

L 198. Hillebrand, W. F. One letter to CSP, September 30, 1899.

L 199. Hincourt (d'), Pierre Fourier. Personal card only.

L 200. Holden, Edward S. and Mary C. Twenty-seven letters and one postal card to CSP and Juliette Peirce, January 1, 1886–October 24, 1901; five letter drafts from CSP, January 5, 1900–July 30, 1906, and n.d. One letter (Holden) to James Mills Peirce, February 15, 1897.

L 201. Holden (Real Estate). One letter draft from CSP, n.d.

L 202. Holmes, O. W. Jr. One letter to CSP, April 20, 1908. One letter (Holmes) to Charles Hartshorne, August 25, 1927. One letter (Donald Hiss, Holmes' secretary) to Paul Weiss, May 22, 1933.

L 203. Holt, Henry. One letter to CSP, December 2, 1893. One letter (Holt) to W. P. Garrison, November 24, 1893.

L 204. Hoover, J. T. One letter to CSP, October 9, 1872.

L 205. Hopkins, Charles Jerome. Two letters to CSP, June 20 and July 3, 1872.

L 206. Horsford, Eben N. One letter to CSP, December 3, 1891; one letter draft from, December 1891.

L 207. Howe, Tracy Jr. One letter to CSP, December 31, 1872.

L 208. Huntington, Daniel. One letter to CSP, March 25, 1894.

L 209. Huntington, Edward S. Twelve letters to CSP, July 21, 1892–December 8, 1893. One letter (Julie F. Huntington) to Juliette Peirce, October 7, n. yr.

L 210. Huntington, Edward V. Three letters and two postal cards to CSP, December 11, 1903–March 1, 1904; ten letter drafts from, December 23, 1903–April 7, 1904, and n.d. One letter (Huntington) to Paul Weiss, May 20, 1929.

L 211. Huntington, Frederic Dan. Three letters to CSP, January 1897, and January 3 and 17, 1897.

L 212. Huntington, Mary. Five letters (copies) from CSP, [1903-09]; two letter drafts from CSP, January 22, 1907 and April 29, 1908. One letter draft (Juliette Peirce) to Huntington, n.d.: eight letters (Huntington) to Juliette Peirce, April 7, 1903–April 28, 1914; and one letter (MEH) to "Helen," with reminiscences of CSP, n.d.

L 213. Huntington, William Reed. Two letters to CSP, September 4, 1893 and May 12, 1897.

L 214. Husik, Isaac. Four letters to CSP, March 7–June 22, 1904; three letter drafts from, September 5, 1904 (2) and July 24, 1910. One letter (Edgar F. Smith) to CSP, March 28, 1904.

L 215. Hyatt, A. One letter to CSP, June 23, 1869.

L 216. Hyde's, J. E., Sons. One letter to CSP, January 29, 1873.

L 217. *Illustrated American.* One letter to CSP, October 12, n. yr.; one letter draft from, n.d.

L 218. *The Independent* (William Ward and Kimley Twining). Five letters to CSP, May 26, 1892–December 6, 1893; one letter draft from, May 4, 1892.

L 219. Ingraham, Andrew (?). One letter to CSP, December 10, 1903.

L 220. *International Cyclopedia (The International Year Book).* Five letters to CSP, December 29, 1900–February 1, 1901.

L 221. Jacobi, Dr. Mary Putnam. One letter and prescription to CSP, January 8, [1903?]; one letter draft from, August 6, 1898.

L 222. James, Alice H. (Mrs. William James). One letter to CSP, January 16, 1913; one letter draft from, n.d. Seventeen letters (Alice James) to Juliette Peirce, February 9, 1905–December 2, 1915. One telegram (Alice James) to Juliette Peirce, April 19, n. yr.

L 223. James, Henry, Jr. Six letters to CSP, March 30, 1911–October 4, 1912; fragments of letter drafts from, n.d., but before March 30, 1911, because HJ-CSP (3/30/11) is the reply.

L 224. James, William. One letter (fragment) to CSP, n.d.; one postal card to CSP, Rome November 26, 1900; one telegram to CSP, March 20, 1903; several letter drafts and fragments of drafts from, most of which are dated or have been dated, with the dates ranging from [April 1897] to [December 25, 1909].

L 225. Jastrow, Joseph. One letter to CSP, November 22, 1893; one postal card to, January 4, 1894; one letter draft from, December 8, 1903.

L 226. Jessurun, Edward. One letter to CSP, January 26, 1901.

L 227. Jevons, W. S. One letter draft from CSP, May 16, 1875.

L 228. Johns Hopkins University (The Board). One letter draft (fragment) from CSP, [Spring 1884].

L 229.   Johns Hopkins University (Logic Examinations). Apparently examinations written by CSP's students, probably at Johns Hopkins. One of these is by Allan Marquand, a contributor to the Johns Hopkins University *Studies in Logic*.

L 230.   Johnson, Thomas M. Six letters to CSP, December 12, 1892–August 25, 1902. One letter (Johnson) to the editor of *The Nation*, August 15, 1902.

L 231.   Kehler, J. H. One letter draft from CSP, June 22, 1911.

L 232.   Keith, Revel. Three letters to CSP, June 29–July 20, 1872.

L 232a.   Kempe, Alfred Bray. Pages from *Nature* (December 18, 1890), with a note directing CSP's attention to an article on p. 156.

L 233.   Keyser, Cassius J. Two letters to CSP, July 27 and November 12, 1908; several letter drafts from, September 29 and October 1–7, 1908, and n.d.

L 234.   Kiernan, Thomas J. One letter to CSP, September 20, 1897.

L 235.   King, Clarence. Seven letters to CSP, May 1–August 16, n. yr.; one letter draft from, n.d.

L 236.   Knight, Harry E. Three letters to CSP, May 28, 1896–April 6, 1897.

L 237.   Ladd-Franklin, Christine. Nineteen letters to CSP, December 16, 1900–November 2, 1904; one fragment, possibly in C. Ladd-Franklin's late hand, n.d.; one postal card to, April 25, 1901. In addition there are 50 pp. of notes on CSP's "On the Algebra of Logic," *American Journal of Mathematics* 3:15-57, 1880, probably made when C. Ladd-Franklin was in CSP's advanced course in logic in the fall of 1880 at the Johns Hopkins University. These notes bear CSP's comments. Seventeen letter drafts from CSP, August 29, 1891–[c.1908]. A fragment (TS., pp. 12-16) is dated [1900?]. Also included here is a manuscript of 13 pp. ("Criticism of Mrs. Franklin's Article"), [c.1900].

L 238.   LaFarge, John. One letter to CSP, n.d.

L 239.   Lafleur, Paul T. Three letters to CSP, April 16–May 14, 1901; four letter drafts from, December 7, 1900–May 11, 1901.

L 240.   Lalande, André. Three letter drafts from CSP, November 22–23, 1905. One letter (Arthur Burks) to Lalande, September 7, 1954. One letter (Lalande) to Burks, September 11, 1954, with a transcript of a letter, dated November 22, 1905, from CSP to Lalande.

L 241.   *Lamb Dictionary* (John Howard Brown). One letter to CSP, December 14, 1901. Also: proofs (*Lamb Dictionary*).

L 242.   Lane, George M. One letter to CSP, May 9, 1890.

L 243.   Larkin, Adrian H. Two letters to CSP and Juliette Peirce, June 4, 1894 and December 4, 1900; one draft from CSP, n.d.

L 244.   Lassiter, B. S. Six letters to CSP, July 12, n. yr., July 20, n. yr., October 12, n. yr., and n.d.

L 245.   Lathrop, Francis (and H. A. Hammond Smith). Twenty letters (Lathrop) to CSP, September 10, 1897–February 11, 1903; five letters (Smith) to CSP, February 16, [1901]–December 3, 1901; two letter drafts from, July 24, 1898 and n.d.

L 246. Lawrence, W. Betts. One letter to CSP, July 1, 1890.

L 247. Leidy, Joseph, Jr. One letter to CSP, January 5, 1907.

L 248. Letter copybook: 1872-73.

L 249. Letterbook Index.

L 250. Libbie, C. F. and Company (Auctioneers of Literary Property). One letter to CSP, November 13, 1908.

L 251. Library of Congress. One letter to CSP, January 22, 1904.

L 252. Lodge, A. C. M. (Mrs. Henry Cabot Lodge). Fourteen letters to CSP, [July 28, 1894]–January 5, [1900], and n.d.; one postal card to, March 2, 1900; one letter draft from, [1903?]. Two letters (A. C. M. Lodge) to Juliette Peirce, January 19, 1915 and n.d. One letter (A. C. M. Lodge) to "Helen," [April 23, 1914].

L 253. Lodge, George Cabot. An announcement of the marriage of G. C. Lodge to Matilda Davis, August 18, 1900.

L 254. Lodge, Henry Cabot. Nine letters to CSP, January 20, 1874–October 30, 1899; two letter drafts (one fragmentary) from CSP, October 30, 1899 and n.d. Another fragment of a letter draft, probably to Lodge, n.d.

L 255. Longfellow, H. W. One letter to CSP, December 12, 1872.

L 256. Lowell, A. Lawrence. One letter to CSP, February 15, 1911; two letter drafts from, December 5, 1903 and July 20, 1910, and a fragment, n.d. Personal cards of A. L. Lowell and Mrs. Lowell. One letter (A. L. Lowell) to Dr. James H. Woods, September 26, 1931.

L 257. Lowell Institute and Lowell Lectures (Augustus Lowell and W. T. Sedgwick). Five letters (Lowell) to CSP, December 8, 1891–September 21, 1892; three letter drafts from, November 28 and December 5, 1903, and n.d. Nine letters (Sedgwick) to CSP, October 3, 1903–January 1, 1904. One letter (B. E. Cotting) to CSP, November 10, 1892. Also a one-page (TS.) of a list of topics, presumably for lectures. One letter (W. H. Lawrence) to Dr. Henry Leonard, August 7, 1933. One letter (Dwyer) to Professor R. B. Perry, November 4, 1933.

L 258. Lunt, Adelaide (Mrs. George Lunt). One letter to CSP, [1896?].

L 259. Lutoslawski, Wincenty. One postal card to CSP, December 3, 1898.

L 260. MacArthur, John R. Three letters to CSP, November 5-24, 1913; one letter draft (fragment) from, n.d. One letter (J. R. MacArthur) to Juliette Peirce, April 6, 1912; one letter (Mrs. MacArthur) to Juliette Peirce, March 17, [1932]; six letters (Juliette Peirce) to Mrs. MacArthur and Mr. Neidlinger, April 2, 1924–October 19, 1932. One letter—to whom it may concern—signed "William Neidlinger," September 12, 1932.

L 261. MacColl, Hugh. One letter to CSP, May 16, 1883; one letter draft from, November 16, 1906. An announcement, August 17, 1887.

L 262. Macdonald, Duncan Black. One letter to CSP, August 3, 1904. One letter (Macdonald) to W. Garrison, July 12, 1904.

L 263. Macfarlane, Alexander. Two letters to CSP, March 29, 1881 and May 5, 1883.

L 264. Mackey, Mr. Three letters from CSP, n.d.

L 265. Macmillan and Company. Three letters to CSP, January 20, 1894–October 29, 1902.

L 266. Magown, George F. One letter to CSP, October 7, 1868.

L 267. Mann, W. E. One letter to CSP, March 12, 1896.

L 268. Maria———. One letter draft from CSP, n.d. Also a document, pertaining to Maria, n.d.

L 269. Marquand, Allan. Three letters to CSP, March 27, 1890–February 3, 1894; one letter draft from, n.d.

L 270. Marquis, *Who's Who*. One letter to CSP, September 11, 1901.

L 271. Marshall, Henry Rutgers. Two letters to CSP, November 13, 1892 and January 22, 1900.

L 272. Mayer, Alfred Marshall. Three letters to CSP, January 3, 1873–April 12, 1890.

L 273. McCallan and Gould. Three letters to CSP, May 24–December 18, 1872.

L 274. *McClure Encyclopedia*. One letter to CSP, November 29, 1899.

L 275. McCoy, L. S. One letter to CSP, June 7, 1901.

L 276. McDonald, Samuel G. Personal card of Mrs. McDonald.

L 277. McGee, William John. One letter to CSP, September 21, 1908.

L 278. McKinney, Thomas Emery. One letter to CSP, December 7, 1904.

L 279. Men of Nineteen-Fourteen. One letter to CSP, n.d.

L 280. Merritt, Thomas. One letter draft from CSP, March 27, 1911. Mortgage: Juliette Peirce to Merritt, June 5, 1922. Bond and Warrant, May 18, 1922.

L 281. Merton, S. D. Two letters to CSP, April 10, 1905 and n.d. (first page is missing).

L 282. Metcalf, L. T. One letter to CSP, June 21, n. yr.

L 283. Metropolitan Club, Washington, D. C. One letter to CSP, December 28, 1881.

L 284. Meyer, Otto. One letter to CSP, July 19, 1888.

L 285. Michaelis, Kate W. One letter to CSP, May 15, 1903.

L 286. Michaelis, O. E. Nine letters to CSP, May 6, 1872–February 7, 1873.

L 287. Michelson, Albert A. A formal invitation (award of the Copley Medal to Michelson) to CSP, January 3, 1908.

L 288. Mighill and Company. Two letters to CSP, June 2 and 29, 1900.

L 289. Miller, Charles Ransom. Three letters to CSP, March 17–May 14, 1890; two letter drafts from, March 26 and 27, 1897.

L 290. Miller, Dickinson S. Four letters to CSP, March 17, n. yr., April 6, 1897–July 17, 1902. See also Bryn Mawr.

L 291. Miller, George A. One letter to CSP, September 27, 1912.

L 292. Milwaukee Soldier's Monument. One letter to CSP, July 18, 1897.

L 293. *Mind* (Editor). Four drafts of two letters from CSP, [1896] and October 7, 1904.

L 294. Mitchell, Oscar Howard. One letter draft from CSP, December 21, 1882.

L 295. Mitchell, W. & G. One letter to CSP, July 29, 1904.

L 296. Montague, William Pepperrell. Two letters to CSP, July 6, 1898 and October 25, 1908. One letter (Henry J. Spangler, President of Ursinus College) to CSP, June 21, 1898.

L 297. Montgomery, Edmund. Three letters to CSP, May 7–October 21, 1892.

L 298. Montgomery, Thomas J. Two letters (TS., one of which is a copy) from CSP, June 18 and July 6, 1892; one letter draft from, June 15, 1892; and a "Preliminary Report upon the Woolf Process of Bleaching," June 16, 1892.

L 299. Moore, Eliakim H. Twelve letters to CSP, February 25, 1892–December 31, 1903; fifteen letter drafts, with fragments of, from, March 20, 1902–November 21, 1904, and n.d.

L 300. Morison, George Shattuck. Fifty-seven letters to CSP, February 26, 1895–January 7, 1903; three letters (carbons) from, December 14, 15, and 24, 1898; four letter drafts from, January 26, 1899–January 18, 1900. Three letters (Morison) to Juliette Peirce, June 1, 1898–February 6, 1899; one letter (Morison) to J. M. Peirce, February 13, 1895; one letter (Morison) to the Clark, Dodge and Company, May 31, 1898.

L 301. Morley, Edward Williams. One letter to CSP, December 5, 1904; one letter draft from, December 9, 1904.

L 302. Morley, Frank (*American Journal of Mathematics*). One letter to CSP, October 19, 1902.

L 303. Morris, M. F. Two letters to CSP, January 7 and February 11, 1873.

L 304. Morse, Edward Sylvester. Three letter drafts from CSP, December 16, 1905, and n.d.

L 305. Mott, S. D. Two letters to CSP, November 12, 1890 and May 29, 1901.

L 306. Mottelay, Paul Fleury. Ten letters and one postal card to CSP, July 27, 1892–October 11, 1906; one letter draft from, n.d.

L 307. Muirhead, Helen Quincy (Mrs. James Fullerton M.). One letter to CSP, February 7, [1910]; one letter draft from, March 8, 1910. One letter (M. A. De Wolfe Howe) to Paul Weiss, September 10, 1931.

L 308. Münsterberg, Hugo. Three letters to CSP, April 15, 1903–August 6, 1904.

L 309. Nagle, James F. (Dr.). Prescription and death notice.

L 310. National Academy of Sciences (George Comstock, S. F. Emmons, Arnold Hague, Ira Remsen). Eleven letters to CSP, October 20, 1893–December 1, 191–; one letter (typewritten copy) from CSP to Remsen, November 1, 1901. Diploma awarded CSP, April 18, 1877. Assorted items: invitations, list of nominees to membership, program and report.

L 311. *National Cyclopedia of American Biography.* Two letters to CSP, April 17, 1895 and July 16, 1896. One letter to Juliette Peirce, December 26, 1923. Two letters (Juliette Peirce and Mrs. Laura McLaughlin) to George Derby, Managing Editor, November 24, 1923 and n.d.

L 312. National Institute of Art, Science and Letters. A list of the members of the division of literature.

L 313. *Nautical Almanac.* Three letters to CSP, August 2, 1872–January 22, 1873.

L 314. Newcomb, Simon. Thirteen letters, including an invitation to meet the British Ambassador, to CSP, October 25, 1872–December 21, 1908; ten letter drafts from, January 17, 1889–July 28, 1892, and n.d.

L 315. Newell, William Wells. One letter draft from CSP, May 15, 1904.

L 316. Newspaper Enterprise Association. One letter to CSP, August 10, 1910.

L 317. New York and Hartford Publishing Company. One letter to CSP, April 3, 1872.

L 318. *New York Herald* (editor). One letter draft, signed "Constant Reader," [c.1906].

L 319. New York Mathematical Society. Four letters to CSP, September 7, 1891 –April 6, 1894 .

L 320. Nichols, Herbert. Seven letters to CSP, January 19, 1901–April 16, [1906?]; one letter draft from, November 22, 1905.

L 321. Norris, Howes, Jr. One letter to CSP, May 22, 1912; one letter draft from, begun May 28, 1912.

L 322. Oliver, James Edward. Three letters to CSP, April 21, 1871–February 25, 1893.

L 323. Osgood, James R. (Fields, Osgood, and Co.). Three letters and one telegram to CSP, June 2, 1869–February 20, 1873.

L 324. Osgood, William F. One letter to CSP, December 29, 1908.

L 325. Osler, William. One letter to CSP, October 24, 1904.

L 326. Otis, William K. Four letters to CSP, May 19, 1893, May 23, 1902, and n.d. One letter (Otis) to Juliette Peirce, June 13, 1891.

L 327. Palmer, Edward Henry. One letter to CSP, January 3, 1873.

L 328. Park and Tilford. Two statements, August 12, 1892 and June 6, 1894.

L 329. Passports. One letter from CSP to the Diplomatic and Consular Officers of the United States in Europe, April 13, 1880. Photostatic copy of passport and four special passports. Two letters (Passport Division) to Paul Weiss, August 19 and 27, 1931.

L 330. Patents, Commissioner of. Three letter drafts from CSP, July 20, 1894 (Bleaching Process); three letter drafts from, n.d. (Map Projections); fragments (2 pp.), n.d. An unsigned petition for *caveat,* 188– (for "certain improvements in Burners and Globes").

L 331. Peabody Institute (Baltimore). One letter to CSP, July 31, 1893.

L 332. Peck, George Mann. Draft of petition, March 1898. Also an assessment of property, 1904.

L 333. Peirce, Benjamin. Three letters and one telegram to CSP, June 25, 1872 –July 31, 1879; forty-five letters from, December 15, 1859–August 17, 1879; one letter draft from, March 20, 1873; six postal cards from, July 12, 1876–March 10, 1879.

L 334. Peirce, Benjamin Mills. Two letters from CSP, November 24 and December 18, 1859.

L 335. Peirce, Charles S. (Business and miscellaneous correspondence). One letter (E. Wright) to CSP, February 13, 1873; one letter (G. Banlina) to CSP, March 28, 1882; one letter-advertisement (W. Miller) to CSP, August 26, 1897. Two bills (J. M. Sanford and Hewins and Hollis) to CSP, April 10, 1892 and June 30, 1904 respectively. Receipt from American Express Co. and an acknowledgment of an order by J. C. Hall Co. Also Century Association Amendment, June 6, 1891; petition for the adoption of an international auxiliary language; map of the American Exhibit, London 1887 (sent to CSP by J. B. W. Bidlock).

L 336. Peirce, Charlotte Elizabeth. Six letters to CSP, September 26, [1880]– May 1, [1885?]; one letter to CSP and Juliette Peirce, May 12, n. yr.; two letters to Juliette Peirce, January 26, [1884?] and December 27, n. yr.; two letters from CSP, October 16, 1870 and September 15, 1879.

L 337. Peirce, Harriet Melusina Fay (Mrs. C. S. Peirce). One letter to CSP, [1877]; six drafts from, August 28, 1870–January 23, 1876.

L 338. Peirce, Herbert H. O. Forty-two letters to CSP, September 14, 1886– December 16, 1904; two telegrams to, October 26, 1872 and January 17, 1903; one telegram to Juliette Peirce, April 1914; ten letters or drafts of letters from CSP, August 21, 1859–November 1, 1907. Also a manuscript of 11 pp. (A21-A31), [c.1905], probably for H. H. D. Peirce. One letter (Helen J. Peirce) to Juliette Peirce, February 18, n. yr.

L 339. Peirce, James Mills. Eighty-seven letters to CSP, January 17, 1887–August 20, 1905; one telegram to, October 26, 1872; eighty-three letter drafts from, September 25, 1859–January 11, 1906, and n.d.

L 340. Peirce, Juliette (Mrs. C. S. Peirce). Four letters to CSP, n.d.; one telegram to, March 7, 1890; sixty-five letters from, March 28, 1889–June 21, 1907, and n.d.; ten letter drafts from, n.d.

L 341. Peirce, Sarah Mills (Mrs. Benjamin Peirce). Fifty-five letters to CSP, August 29, [1875]–August 30, [1887], and n.d.; one letter to CSP and Juliette Peirce, July 12, [1884]; twenty-one letters to Juliette Peirce, January 1, 1880–June 29, [1886]; forty-seven letters from CSP, May 11, 1859– April 3, 1887.

L 342. Perot, Rev. Elliston. One letter to CSP, November 28, 1905.

L 343. Perry, Bliss. One letter draft from CSP, June 24, 1907.

L 344. Perry, Thomas Sergeant. Nine letters to CSP, October 1, 1872–April 12, 1905; two letter drafts from, March 24, 1883 and n.d.

L 345. Peters, W. K. One letter to CSP, n.d.

L 346. Philosophical Society of Washington. One letter to CSP, February 24, 1873.

L 347. Pickering, Edward Charles. Seven letters to CSP, June 26, 1872–August 15, 1906; fragment of a letter draft from, n.d.

L 348. Pierce, Butler and Pierce Mfg. Co. Two letters to CSP, September 8, 1904 and October 11, 1906; two letter drafts from, September 16, 1904. Fragment, n.d.

L 349. Pierce, Josiah, Jr. One letter to CSP, May 2, 1888.

L 350. Pierpont, J. P. One letter to CSP, October 12, 1894.

L 351. Pinchot, Amos E. R. An invitation to the marriage of A. E. R. Pinchot to Gertrude Minturn, November 14, n. yr.

L 352. Pinchot, Gifford. Twelve letters to CSP, November 3, 1891–July 26, 1904; two letter drafts from, [1892] and July 26, 1905. Ten letters (Pinchot) to Juliette Peirce, June 23, 1921–August 10, 1934. One letter (Pinchot) to Alfred Marvin, June 6, 1933.

L 353. Pinchot, Gifford and Mrs. Miscellaneous: legislative letter of the Public Charities Association of Pennsylvania; letter to the Voters of Pike County; greetings; clippings.

L 354. Pinchot, James W. Three letters to CSP, May 5, 1890–March 16, 1894; one letter draft from, December 3, 1900.

L 355. Pinchot, Mrs. James W. Three letters to CSP, November 17, 1908–January 14, 1910; one letter draft from, April 22, 1897. Letter drafts from CSP and Juliette Peirce, n.d. Thirteen letters (Pinchot) to Juliette Peirce, November 1, 1908–June 22, 1914, and n.d.; one check (Juliette Peirce), August 18, 1894. A wedding invitation, Christmas card, and several personal cards.

L 356. Players Club. Three letters to CSP, June 1, 1889–November 28, 1891.

L 357. Plimpton, George Arthur. Ten letters to CSP, September 20, 1894–December 7, 1901; four letter drafts from, June 23, 1894, March 18, 1900, [1907?], and [May 12, 1903? or 1908?]. One letter (George Mann Peck) to CSP, January 5, 1901.

L 358. *Post, Evening* (New York). One letter to CSP, May 21, 1898.

L 359. Postmaster, Milford, Pa. Two letters from CSP, January 25, 1892 and February 24, 1905.

L 360. Powell, John Wesley. Two letters to CSP, June 19, 1890 and December 23, 1895.

L 361. Prang, L. and Company. One letter to CSP, March 27, 1893.

L 362. Princeton University Library. One letter to CSP, February 15, 1902.

L 363. Purdon, John E. Four letters to CSP, November 17, 1892, January 2, 1893, and n.d. Also sphygmograph tracings and "Spirit Photographs" sent to CSP by Purdon on December 2, 1892.

L 364. Putnam, G. P. Memorandum of agreement for publication of *The History of Science,* February 28, 1898.

L 365. Putnam, Herbert (Library of Congress). One letter to CSP, December 20, 1901; one postal card to, April 12, 1904.

L 366. Quincy, Josiah ("Cousin Jo"). Five letter drafts from CSP, June 25–July 15, 1909, and n.d. Fragment, n.d.

L 367. Quincy, K. M. One letter to CSP, July 7, n. yr.; one letter draft from, April 16, 1904.

L 368. Reeder, General. Empty envelope; n.d. The envelope apparently contained an introduction for CSP to General Reeder.

L 369. Remsen, Ira. One letter draft from CSP, April 28, 1906.

L 370. Repsold and Söhne. One letter to CSP, January 6, 1873; one letter (dictated) from, February 14, 1873.

L 371. Retail Merchant's Reporting Association. One letter draft from CSP, June 21, 1897.

L 372. Reyes y Prosper, Ventura. One letter to CSP, March 5, 1891.

L 373. Rice, Sallie B. One letter to CSP, n.d. One letter to Juliette Peirce, n.d.; one letter to Helen Ellis (passed on to Juliette Peirce), n.d.

L 374. Richardson, Earnest Cushing. One letter to CSP, April 29, 1902; one letter draft from, n.d.

L 375. Ricketson, John H. One letter to CSP, May 20, 1897.

L 376. Risteen, Allan Douglas. Twenty-six letters to CSP, August 4, 1887–December 17, 1911; three postal cards to, July 12, 1913, and n.d.; five letter drafts from, March 24 and July 29, 1891, and n.d. One letter (George F. Parker) to CSP, January 28, 1903.

L 377. Ritchie, E. S. and Sons. Three letters to CSP, January 25 and 29, 1873, and December 31, n. yr.

L 378. Robert, A. One letter to CSP, July 3, 1911; one letter draft (possibly two drafts) from, September 11, 1911.

L 379. Roe, William J. One letter to CSP, October 17, 1892.

L 380. Rogers, Fairman. Two letters to CSP, January 22, 1873 and October 21, 1895.

L 381. Romeike, Henry. Two letters to CSP, January 9, 1894 and June 18, 1914.

L 382. Rood, Ogden N. Six letters to CSP, November 16, 1885–March 14, 1894; one letter draft from, [1877-78].

L 383. Roosevelt, Theodore. One letter (Assistant Secretary) to CSP, April 10, 1905; one letter draft from, n.d.; two drafts (postal card) from, n.d.

L 384. Rose, Mrs. One letter draft from CSP, n.d.

L 385. Royce, Josiah. Seven letters to CSP, November 18, 1891–March 4, 1914; one letter (no apparent connection with CSP), n.d.; ten letter drafts from, January 19, 1902–August 22, 1905, and n.d. Royce's personal card with note inscribed on it. Also a single page, the heading of which reads: "Dr. Abbot accuses Professor Royce."

L 386. Russell and Erwin Mfg. Co. One letter draft from CSP, April 19, 1910.

L 387. Russell, Francis C. Thirty-three letters to CSP, January 16, 1888–December 10, 1908; two letters (copies) from, September 17, 1892 and n.d.; sixty letter drafts and three postal cards from, September 12, 1887–January 23, 1909, and n.d.; four telegrams from, February 6, 1893–May 13, 1896. One letter draft from CSP to Carus, n.d.; one letter draft from CSP to the Editor of the *Monist*, October 7, 1904. Also: a copy of a letter (Edward C. Higilen) to Russell, September 19, 1894 and Agapetos' article on religion (sent to CSP by Russell).

L 388. St. Lawrence Project (Stewart and Company: S. H. E. Stewart). Eleven letters to CSP, July 10, 1896–August 4, 1898; six letter drafts from, August 20, 1896–January 1, 1897. Fragments (5 pp.); n.d. An agreement, signed by CSP, signifying his part ownership of the St. Lawrence Power Co. and his right to one-fifth share of any stock which may be issued. One letter (H. H. Warren) to Charles R. Higgins, October 22, 1896, and a report (TS.) by John Bogart on a proposal to develop water power by the construction of a canal between the St. Lawrence and Grass Rivers in the town of Massena, St. Lawrence County, New York.

L 389. San Diego Society of Natural History. One letter to CSP, August 30, 1886.

L 390. Schiller, F. C. S. Two letters to CSP, April 30, 1905 and [May 6, 1905]; eight letter drafts from, May 12 and 23, 1905, September 10, 1906, and n.d.

L 391. Schott, Charles Anthony. Two letters to CSP, July 6 and September 10, 1872.

L 392. Schroeder, Ernst. Seven letters and one postal card to CSP, February 1, 1890–December 7, 1898; three letter drafts from, April 7, 1897 and n.d.

L 393. Schwatt, Isaac J. One letter to CSP, September 23, 1895.

L 394. *Science* (Weekly). One letter (N. C. D. Hodges) to CSP, July 20, 1892.

L 395. Scribner's, Charles, and Sons. Six letters to CSP, September 1, 1893–June 4, 1900.

L 396. Searle, Arthur. One letter to CSP, January 22, 1873.

L 397. Searle, Father George M. One letter draft (and typed copy) from CSP, August 9, 1895.

L 398. Second National Bank, New York. Two letter drafts from CSP, January 5, 1910, and n.d.

L 399. Sellers, William. One letter to CSP, February 11, 1904; one letter draft (fragment) from, February 22, 1904. One letter (A. Sellers) to Juliette Peirce, February 17, n. yr.

L 400. Sever, C. M. One letter to CSP, June 27, 1872.

L 401. Shaler, Nathaniel Southgate. One letter to CSP, July 6, 1872. Shaler Memorial Fund.

L 402. Shaw, James Byrnie. One letter to CSP, June 21, 1895.

L 403. Sheffield, Justus Pearl. One letter to CSP, April 17, 1892.

L 404. Sheldon, Wilmon Henry. One letter to CSP, April 20, 1903.

L 405. Sheltering Arms. One letter to CSP, April 13, 1904; four letter drafts from, March 13 and 14, 1904, and n.d. Two letters (Sheltering Arms) to Juliette Peirce, January 20 and September 5, 1904.

L 406. Shippen, Joseph. One letter to CSP, November 17, 1903.

L 407. Sigsbee, C. D. Two letters to CSP, March 31, 1894 and December 28, 1895.

L 408. Smith, William Benjamin. Five letters to CSP, January 6, 1908–August 1912; six letter drafts from, July 15, 1897, July 16, 1904, July 25, 1908, and n.d.

L 409. Smithsonian Institution (Hodge, Karr, Langley, Rathbun, Walcott, Winlock). Forty-five letters to CSP, January 17, 1894–February 3, 1911; six letter drafts from CSP to S. P. Langley, May 20, 1901–June 1, 1908, and n.d. One letter (Langley) to Captain Davis, January 29, 1900. Miscellaneous materials: printed matter.

L 410. Snow, Eben. Two letters to CSP, May 11, 1872 and January 9, 1873; one letter from, January 7, 1872.

L 411. Society of Arts. One letter to CSP, August 9, 1902.

L 412. Söhmer, Mr. One letter draft from CSP, n.d.

L 413. Sommer, Ernst J. Eight letters to CSP, April 10, 1902–October 21, 1902. One letter (E. J. Sommer) to Juliette Peirce, April 22, 1914. One letter (Lena Sommer) to Juliette Peirce, May 20, 1902. One letter draft (CSP for Juliette Peirce) to Mrs. E. J. Sommer, [October 1902?].

L 413a. Sommer, H. Otto. One letter draft (photostat) from CSP, n.d. Reprint of Dr. Sommer's article "The Abdomino-Sacral and other methods for the Extirpation of Rectal Cancer," *Medical Times*, July–August 1901.

L 414. Spencer, Herbert. One letter to CSP, March 5, 1894.

L 415. Stechert, G. E. One letter to CSP, July 22, n. yr.; one bill, July 1, 1891; one letter draft from, n.d.

L 416. Stedman, Edmund C. Three letters to CSP, August 15, 1898–February 7, 1900. A certificate of voucher.

L 417. Steinheil Söhne. Two letters to CSP, May 28 and July 20, 1872.

L 418. Sterneck, Robert von. Personal card with note (Sterneck's?) on reverse side, November 21, 1895.

L 419. Stevens, B. F. One letter to CSP, July 18, 1872.

L 420. Stewart, William M. One letter to CSP, October 18, 1893.

L 421. Stickney, Albert. Sixty-five letters to CSP, September 30, 1891–December 7, 1907; twenty-four letters to Juliette Peirce, February 25, 1896–

May 4, 1933; letter drafts (CSP and Juliette Peirce) to Stickney, November 12, 1906, and n.d.; three letters (Juliette Peirce) to Stickney, n.d. Also: two letters (copies) from CSP to Francis Blake, December 25 and 28, 1896. One letter (Elizabeth Stickney) to Juliette Peirce, January 4, 1904. Two letters (J. H. Van Etten) to Stickney, January 19 and 20, 1897.

L 422. Stimson, D. M., Dr. Two letters to CSP, November 20, 1890 and [April 1897]

L 423. Stokes, Sir George Gabriel. Two letters (TS.) to CSP, February 13, 1886.

L 424. Story, William Edward. Three letters to CSP, June 13, 1899–December 1, 1900; nine letter drafts from, March 22, 1896–January 26, 1909.

L 425. Stout, George Frederick. One letter to CSP, August 14, 1911; one letter draft from, October 28, 1906.

L 426. Strach, Mr. One letter draft from CSP, [1906?].

L 427. Strong, Charles Augustus. Two letters to CSP, August 2, 1903 and April 7, 1904; two letter drafts from, July 25, 1904.

L 428. Stuart, Henry W. One letter to CSP, April 12, 1905.

L 429. *Studies in Logic.* Copyright, March 22, 1883.

L 430. Subscribers: *Petrus Peregrinus.* Two letters and one postal card to CSP, January 23,–March 5, 1894.

L 431. Subscribers: "Pike County Press Series." Five letters to CSP, November 8–December 17, 1895. Also: a draft and typescript of "A New Doctrine of Reasoning" and "First Introduction."

L 432. Subscribers: *Principles of Philosophy.* Letters of thirty subscribers (1894-95). Thirteen requests for Prospectus and Syllabus.

L 433. Sullivan, Thomas Russell. One letter to CSP, June 10, 1893.

L 434. *Sun, New York* (editor). One letter (Thomas Hitchcock) to CSP, February 11, 1892; one letter draft from, n.d.

L 435. Taber, Henry. Four letters to CSP, February 23, 1892–March 13, 1895. One letter (Taber) to Paul Weiss, September 3, 1931.

L 436. Tait, Anna D. T. One letter to CSP, October 18, n. yr. Two letters (Tait) to Juliette Peirce, February 29, 1886, and n.d.

L 437. Tait, John R. One letter to CSP, November 4, 1896.

L 438. Talcott, T. W. R. One telegram to CSP, November 6, 1872.

L 439. Tatlock, John. One letter to CSP, February 8, 1907.

L 440. Thayer, William R. Two letters to CSP, November 23 and 29, 1903.

L 441. Thilly, Frank. One postal card to CSP, January 28, 1905.

L 442. Thomas, R. and Son. One letter to CSP, July 24, 1872.

L 443. Thurston, Robert Henry. One letter to CSP, February 2, 189(?).

L 444. *Times, New York* (editor). One letter draft from CSP, December 1, 1908.

L 445. Todd, David Peck. One letter to CSP, July 10, 1889.

L 446. Toller, Samuel. One letter to CSP, January 16, 1901.

L 447. Trevor, Joseph Ellis. One letter to CSP, September 21, 1909.

L 448. University of the South. One letter to CSP, February 27, 1894.

L 449. Vailati, Giovanni. Empty envelope, n.d.

L 450. Van Etten, J. H. Two letters to CSP, December 3, 1895 and July 11, 1898. Three letters (Van Etten) to Juliette Peirce, March 14, 1895–November 9, 1895. One letter (Van Etten) to Albert Stickney, May 25, 1896.

L 451. Van Nostrand, D. Co. (W. H. Farrington). Three letters to CSP, October 31, 1888, January 24, 1889, and March 7, 18—; two letters (dictated by Speirs) to CSP, May 15, 1902 and November 5, 1903. Three statements, December 8, 1888–January 23, 1889.

L 452. Venable, Richard M. One letter to CSP, April 24, 1883.

L 453. Wake, C. Staniland. One letter to CSP, December 10, 1892.

L 454. Walcott, Charles D. Three letters to CSP, January 5-29, 1897, the last of which contains an enclosed letter (C. R. Van Hise) to the Director, U.S. Geological Survey (January 24, 1897); one letter draft (37 pp. on the problem of slaty cleavage) from CSP, January 1897.

L 455. Walker, F. Amasa. One letter to CSP, September 20, 1893.

L 456. Water, Leo. Bill (?) signed Benjamin Vannoy and statement of the account of Leo Water, March 2, 1895 and n.d.

L 457. Walters, Henry G. Six letters to CSP, October 8, 1908–January 3, 1914; one letter to CSP and Juliette Peirce, March 4, 1914.

L 458. Ward, H. B. One letter to CSP, January 20, 1873.

L 459. Waring, M. E. (Atlantic Lyceum Bureau). Two letters to CSP, February 3 and 17, 1894.

L 460. Waterbury Clock Company. One letter to CSP, November 15, 1906.

L 461. Watson, John. One letter to CSP, April 18, 1895.

L 462. Webster, Arthur G. One letter draft from CSP, August 13, 1910.

L 463. Welby, Lady Victoria. Eighteen letters to CSP, May 24, 1903–June 27, 1911; two postal cards to, November 20 and December 17, 1903; three letters to Juliette Peirce, October 18, 1909–February 25, [1912], the last of which is from Maria L. H. Welby, daughter-in-law of Lady Welby; thirteen letter drafts from CSP, May 4, 1904–March 14, 1909, and n.d.; one letter draft (Juliette Peirce, but in CSP's hand), n.d. Fragment, n.d. (February 9, 1909 in upper right corner applies to some independent calculations). One letter (Open Court) to CSP, November 1, 1898. Two letters (J. W. Slaughter) to CSP, August 20, 1909 and April 25, 1911.

L 464. Westermann, B., and Company. One letter to CSP, June 28, 1872.

L 465. Weston, Stephen F. One letter to CSP, July 27, 1905.

L 466. White, James T. (*National Cyclopedia of American Biography*). Two letters to CSP, December 13, 1895 and April 14, 1896.

L 467. Whiton-Stuart, J. P. One letter to CSP, June 14, 1904.

L 468. Wilder, Bunt S. One letter to CSP, December 5, 1887.

L 469. Wilson, J. Cook, One postal card to CSP, April 30, 1905.

L 470. Wilson, Louis N. One letter to CSP, March 9, 1906.

L 471. Winchester, W. L. Two letters to CSP, May 22 and 27, 1887.

L 472. Winlock, Joseph. Nine letters to CSP, January 16, 1872–February 2, 1873; three letter drafts from, December 10, 1871–October 12, 1873.

L 473. Winsor, Justin. One letter to CSP, March 15, 1894.

L 474. Withers, John W. One letter to CSP, January 6, 1904.

L 475. Wolf, C. One letter to CSP, July 9, 1876.

L 476. Woodbridge, Frederick J. E. One letter to CSP, December 12, 1903.

L 477. Woods, Frederick Adams. One letter to CSP, October 10, 1913; five letter drafts from, July 26, 1911–Christmas 1913. One letter to Albert Edward Wiggam, February 12, n. yr. One letter to James H. Woods, August 22, 1931. Fragments, n.d.

L 478. Wundt, Wilhelm. One letter to CSP, May 2, 1867.

L 479. Yoder, A. H. One letter to CSP, April 2, 1894.

L 480. Young, Charles Augustus. Three letters to CSP, May 7 and 23, 1872, and May 16, n. yr.

L 481. Zumbrack, A. One letter to CSP, February 24, 1873.

L 482. Unidentified Correspondents. Five letters to CSP and Juliette Peirce, April 15, 1881–June 19, 1911; one postal card to CSP, June 13, 1895; eleven letter drafts from CSP, April 4, 1864–Christmas 1913. Fragments, n.d.

L 483. Unidentified Correspondents. Letter drafts (CSP) to editors of unidentified newspapers.

L 484. Unidentified Correspondents. Fragments of letters to CSP, n.d.

JULIETTE PEIRCE CORRESPONDENCE

All correspondence involving Juliette Peirce directly or indirectly, except such correspondence as was placed in the C. S. Peirce correspondence. Also miscellaneous items, such as newspaper clippings and pamphlets, have been included.

L 485. Aitken, Son and Co. One letter to JP, July 19, 1905.

L 486. Aldridge, Adele. One letter to JP, April 11, [1928].

L 487. Alexandre, Nathalie (Mrs. J. Joseph Alexandre). Personal card, with note, n.d.

L 488. Alger, Luise (Mrs. Ellice M. Alger). Two letters to JP, April 10, 1906, and n.d.

L 489. Almer, John. One letter to JP, May 5, 1925.

L 490. Appleyard, Amanda. One letter to JP, n.d. Statement of Mrs. Appleyard at the Pike County Court, October 9, 1933.

L 491. Balch, Mrs. Franklin. Photographs [1930?].

L 492. Barckley, Ethel Noyes. One letter to JP, October 14, 1927.

L 493. Barnes, Elsie. Three letters to JP, June 10–August 1, 1925.

L 494. Buchanan, Annie R. Four letters to JP, October 30 and November 25, 1932, January 20, n. yr., and n.d.

L 495. Bull, George R. Three letters to JP, April 28, 1922–November 10, 1933. Also copy of an affidavit by Paul Hoffmaster concerning Bull.

L 496. Bunnell, Mrs. P. M. and "sister." Four letters to JP, September 1925–October 22, 1926.

L 497. Calef, Mrs. John H. Two letters to JP, December 3, 1917 and January 10, 1918.

L 498. Carter, Marian. One letter to JP, September 1922.

L 499. Cholerton, Margie. One letter to JP, January 5, 1934; one letter draft from, n.d.

L 500. Cobb, Sally Mills. Three letters to JP, March 12 and May 7, 1901, and n.d.

L 501. Coulter, Leonie. Three letters to JP; two are postmarked November 20 and December 2, 1929, and one is dated June 12, [1930?].

L 502. Cron, Minerva. One postal card to JP, January 16, 1933.

L 503. Custard, Leila R. One letter to JP, September 9, 1934.

L 504. Darbie, Louise. One letter to JP, November 4, 1914. A list of CSP's books given by Juliette Peirce to the Rev. Mr. Darbie.

L 505. Davis, Elizabeth. Two letters to JP, October 31 and November 1, 1923.

L 506. Dessimoz, Auguste. One letter to JP, April 23, 1921.

L 507. Dewitt, A. J. One letter to JP, February 20, 1933.

L 508. Dietz, Ida R. One letter to JP, n.d.

L 509. Draper, Anna P. One letter to JP, February 16, 1905.

L 510. Dubreuil, Mr. One letter draft, with revisions by CSP, from JP, n.d.

L 511. DuFais, John. Two letters to JP, April 19–May 5, 1898.

L 512. Ellis, Benjamin P. Three letters (and telegram) to JP, January 12–February 29, 1932. One letter (R. B. Perry) to Benjamin Ellis, May 14, 1935.

L 513. Ellis, Elizabeth (Mrs. Benjamin P. Ellis). Two letters to JP, June 22 and August 15, 1915. One postal card to, n.d.

L 514. Ellis, Helen Peirce. Twenty-six letters to JP, many of uncertain date; four telegrams to, April 21–23, 1914; two letters from, August 28, 1916 and January 2, n. yr.; one letter draft by CSP for Juliette, n.d.; one postal card from JP, April 18, 1919.

L 515. Elston, boys. Deposition and notes concerning Harold and Charles Elston, sons of a neighbor of Juliette Peirce, 1927. Newspaper clippings.

L 516. Felton, Mary. One letter to JP, [December 1892?].

L 517. Financial matters. Statement of a loan from Gifford Pinchot. One letter draft to Gifford Pinchot from JP, n.d. One letter (Birkbeck Investment Savings and Loan Co.) to JP, May 11, 1895. Three statements of Judgment, September 1922–January 25, 1925. One letter (Maitland Coppell and Co.) to JP, April 26, 1927. Three letters (The National City Bank of New York) to JP, August 31, 1927–April 6, 1934. Deposit slips (The First National Bank), February 25, 1921–September 1, 1927. Deposit slips (The Second National Bank), September 11, 1917–July 18, 1921. Notice of overdrawn account (The Second National Bank), December 20, 1913. Two receipts (*Milford Dispatch*).

L 518. Fitze, Mrs. Elizabeth. One letter to JP, July 10, 1929.

L 519. Flaherty, M. H. One letter to JP, October 27, 1898.

L 520. Floor, Sophie. One letter to JP, September 15, 1931.

L 521. Foster, Charles A. One letter to JP, July 22, 1931. One letter (Foster) to Claude Shull, August 6, 1931.

L 522. Fouquet, Docteur. One letter, with attached card, to JP, [January 24, 1890].

L 523. Fox, Mrs. Beauvais. One letter to JP, September 22, 1928.

L 524. Funk, William. One letter to JP, n.d.

L 525. Gardner, Constance. Four letters to JP, April 18, 1916–October 27, 1923.

L 526. Gassmann, Charles. Check from JP, August 7, 1901.

L 527. General Hospital (Stroudsburg). One letter to JP, December 19, 1928. Two receipts, December 15, 1928 and January 11, 1930.

L 528. Ginsheim, Louise de. Two letters to JP, October 29, 1901 and March 14, 1903; two postal cards to, November 13 and December 18, 1901.

L 529. Goudy, Florence. Seventy-two letters and postal cards to JP, March 26, 1896–June 8, 1934; one letter draft from, n.d.

L 530. Gregory, Algernon. One letter to JP, May 8, 1933.

L 531. Homer, Charlotte M. One letter to JP, n.d.

L 532. Hopkins, Ellen M. (Mrs. Dunlap). Twenty letters to JP, March 1890–January 29, 1893; one postal card to, January 11, 1898. Miscellaneous items: clippings from the *New York World,* pamphlet of the New York School of Applied Design, and a memorandum.

L 533. Howland, Henry E. One letter to JP, March 5, 1889.

L 534. Huddy, Xenophon P. Six letters to JP, July 11, 1922–January 11, 1933; two cards to, n.d. One letter (George R. Bull) to Huddy, September 2, 1922. Legal notice, Juliette Peirce (the complainant) and Marie Emilie Steiner (the defendant).

L 535. James, Henry, Jr. Thirty-three letters and two telegrams to JP, over half of which have the years omitted [1914-23?]; six letter drafts from JP, n.d. One letter (James) to Madame Steiner, February 11, 1921; two letters (James) to George Bull, December 2 and 14, 1921; one letter (George Bull) to James, December 12, 1921. Draft outline of a lease from Juliette Peirce to Madame Bour. Copies of letters (Juliette Peirce) to Madame Bour.

L 536. Johnstone, Lady. Thirteen letters to JP, September 29, [1887?]–August 1932; one letter (copy) from, August 3, 1932.

L 537. Joseph, J. P. M. One letter to JP, January 23, 1897.

L 538. Keiper, Steward. One letter to JP, September 14, 1931.

L 539. Knopf, Dr. S. A. Instructions for JP, April 29, 1902.

L 540. Linthicum, Cadwallader E. One letter to JP, November 10, 1897. Business cards.

L 541. Ludwig, Frank P. and Mrs. One letter to JP, n.d. Newspaper clipping concerning an attempted robbery of the Peirce home.

L 542. MacKaye, Steele and Mary. Five letters to JP, June 11, 1887–November 21, 1888.

L 543. Martha Washington Hotel. One letter to JP, November 17, 1903.

L 544. Marvin, Alfred. Four letters to JP, April 20, 1914–April 18, 1934. Two letters (Dorothy Marvin) to Juliette Peirce, n.d. One letter (A. Marvin to Gifford Pinchot, June 3, 1933. One letter (G. Pinchot) to Marvin, June 6, 1933. Two letters (A. Marvin) to Hon. Samuel E. Shull, April 10 and August 14, 1934. One letter (S. E. Shull) to Marvin; April 12, 1934.

L 545. Merritt, Victoria. Two letters to JP, June 12, 1923, and n.d.

L 546. Milford, Pa. Volunteer Fire Department. Three letters to JP, September 28, 1926–December 10, 1928. Also miscellaneous items.

L 547. Moulton, Lillie Greenough. One letter to JP, n.d.

L 548. Noll, J. E. (M. D.) Note for JP, May 1, 1933.

L 549. Otto, Max C. One letter to JP, September 16, 1926.

L 550. Palmer, L. Osma. Two letters to JP, October 20 and 27, 1917.

L 551. Peirce, James Mills. Nine letters and one postal card to JP, September 11, 1888–October 29, 1905.

L 552. Phillips, William J. Bill and receipt, April 24, 1903.

L 553. Pinchot, Cornelia B. Fifteen letters to JP, September 11, 1919–January 8, 1934, and n.d.

L 554. Pinchot, Gifford. Nine letters to JP, June 23, 1921–August 10, 1934. One letter (Pinchot) to Alfred Marvin, June 6, 1933.

L 555. Pinchot, Gifford and Mrs. Fifteen letter drafts from JP, November 16, 1919–September 4, 1934. Other drafts from, n.d. one letter (J. H. Cole) to Juliette Peirce, n.d.

L 556. Public Charities Association. Five letters to JP, February 21, 1929–March 2, 1931.

L 557. Quincy, Helen Fanny (Mrs. Josiah Phillips Quincy). One letter to JP, n.d.

L 558. Red Cross Correspondence. Six letters to JP, November 20, 1917–January 23, 1918. One letter (Alfred Marvin) to Albert W. Staub, November 20, 1917. One letter (Charles Scott, Jr.) to Albert Tamblyn, December 27, 1917.

L 559. Robinson, Guilford Allen (M. D.) Bill, December 2, 1924.

L 560. Sawyer, Mrs. F. P. One letter to JP, January 2, 1925.

L 561. Schuler, William. One letter from JP, n.d.

L 562. Shull, Samuel, Judge. Five letters (three of them copies) from JP, January 26, 1929–June 14, 1934; two letter drafts from, 1934 and n.d.

L 563. Shull and Shull. Four letters to JP, August 5, 1932–September 26, 1934; one letter (copy) from, May 31, 1934; nine letter drafts from, [December 3, 1932], February 15, 1933, and n.d.

L 564. Smith, Irving C. Two letters to JP, December 5, 1918 and June 12, 1919. A note from Putnams, December 18, 1916.

L 565. Steiner, Marie. Twenty-one letters to JP, March 5, 1920–April 15, 1921.

L 566. Stratton, Mrs. Leslie C. Personal card. A copy of "The Stratton Annual," December 25, 1927.

L 567. Stroyan, Peter. Three letters to JP, September 20, 1930, April 25, n. yr., and n.d.; eight letter drafts from, n.d. Memos. A note (George Fisher).

L 568. Thorp, Anna G. Two letters to JP, January 20, 1890 and December 28, n. yr.

L 569. Tuscano, A. H. One letter to JP, n.d.

L 570. Van Auken, D. M. One letter to JP, November 16, 1895.

L 571. Van Etten, Louise. One letter to JP, September 22, 1926.

L 572. Van Tassell, M. P. Twenty-five bills and receipts, October 14, 1909–July 31, 1919.

L 573. Wadman, Nellie P. One letter to JP, August 2, 1933; two letter drafts from, May 24, 1932, and n.d.

L 574. Weiss, Paul. One letter to JP, January 3, 1931; one letter draft from, May 24, 1932.

L 575. Werner, Eva Mary. One letter to JP, July 27, 1925.

L 576. Wucher, Père. One letter to JP, January 14, 1916.

L 577. Wylie, W. Gill, Dr. Three letters to JP, March 26, 1901, January 1, 1902, and December 5, 1906.

L 578. Unidentified Correspondents. Three letter drafts from JP, n.d.

L 579. Miscellaneous: clippings (concerned with the late years of Juliette Peirce's life); passport to Egypt (1890); handcopy of the parts of *Medea*.

FAMILY CORRESPONDENCE

Letters, principally, to and from members of CSP's family, exclusive of those letters which were incorporated in the Charles S. Peirce and Juliette Peirce correspondences. Also noted here are letters and assorted items found with the family correspondence but, strictly speaking, not part of it.

L 580. Adams, Mrs. Brooks (Evelyn Davis). One letter to Helen P. Ellis, March 25, 1916.

L 581. Anthony, Joseph. One letter to Captain Ichabod Nichols, August 13, 1798.

L 582. Anthony, Joseph and Co. One letter to John Nichols, October 25, 1797.

L 583. Arnold, E. S. (?). One letter to Benjamin Mills Peirce, July 29, 1861.

L 584. Bache, Alexander Dallas. Three letters to Cousin Sarah [Sarah Mills Peirce], January 27, [1857]–February 6, 1857. One letter to Benjamin Peirce, April 5, 1860. One letter to Michael Faraday, March 26, 1860.

L 585. Blake genealogy. MS, 2 pp., May 24, 1790, possibly in the hand of Sarah Mills Peirce.

L 586. Blake, Harrison Gray Otis. One letter to James Mills Peirce, June 16, 1881.

L 587. Bombay Missionaries. One letter to Salem supporters (subscribers) and via them to Mrs. Benjamin Peirce, Sr., 1822.

L 588. Bowditch, Charles P. One letter to Charlotte Elizabeth Peirce, [November 18 or 19, 1884].

L 588a. Bray, Mary. One letter to Mr. Ellis, October 17, 1949.

L 589. Brown, Moses. One letter to Captain Ichabod Nichols, April 22, 1811.

L 590. Burney, Charles M. Jr. One letter to Benjamin Mills Peirce, n.d.

L 591. Cabot, James Elliot. One letter to Sarah Mills Peirce, n.d.

L 592. Catlin, M. One letter to Benjamin Peirce, August 1, 1842.

L 593. Choate, Rufus. One letter to Benjamin Peirce, Sr., February 16, 1831. Benjamin Peirce's reply, February 21, 1831.

L 594. Cornwell, H. One letter to Benjamin Peirce, n.d.

L 595. Crowinshield, Clara. One letter to Lydia Ropes Peirce, October 22, [1836].

L 596. Curtiss, Erastus. One letter to Benjamin Peirce, January 16, 1848.

L 597. Darwin, Sarah Sedgwick. One letter to [Sarah Mills Peirce], March 27, 1879.

L 598. Davis, Anna Cabot Mills. One letter to Benjamin Mills Peirce, September 27, 1868.

L 599. Davis, Harriette Mills. One letter to Sarah Mills Peirce, n.d.

L 600. Derby, Mary Jane. One letter to Charlotte Elizabeth Peirce, October 17, 1820.

L 601. Dexter, Mrs. Lucy W. One letter to Helen Peirce Ellis, March 26, [1906].

L 602. Eliot, Charles W. One letter to William R. Ellis, n.d.

L 603. Ellis, Francis. One letter to Benjamin P. Ellis, April 13, 1926.

L 604. Ellis, Gertrude. One letter to Sarah Mills Peirce, December 24, 1885. One letter to James Mills Peirce, March 2, [1887?].

L 605. Ellis, Helen P. One letter to Sarah Mills Peirce [1874]. Also, Helen P. Ellis's plan for a children's calendar.

L 606. Ellis, Rufus. One letter (signed "R. E.") to Helen Peirce Ellis, August 31, 1879. Two letters (signed "R. E.") to William R. Ellis, June 9, n. yr. and n.d. Private scrapbook.

L 607. Ellis, William R. One letter to Charlotte Elizabeth Peirce, December 25, 1867. One letter to Helen P. Ellis, August 22, 1883.

L 608. Emory, W. H. One letter to James Mills Peirce, June 11, 1866.

L 609. Farrar, Eliza. One letter to Mrs. Charles Sanders, June 16, 1831.

L 610. Fay, Charles Norman. One letter to James Mills Peirce, n.d.

L 611. Filippi and Figli. Two letters to Captain Ichabod Nichols, June 13, 1806 and December 20, 1807.

L 612. Fishley, Ennis. One letter to Mrs. Lydia Ropes Nichols, July 10, 1822.

L 613. Frank, T. One letter to Benjamin Mills Peirce, May 28, 1864.

L 614. Frazier, M. Fragment of a letter to Lydia Ropes Nichols, n.d.

L 615. French, Rev. J. W. Two letters to Lydia Ropes Nichols, July 5, 1820 and February 1, 1821.

L 616. Frodsham, Charles. Bill to United States Coast Survey, November 2, 1870.

L 617. Gill, —. Two letters to Benjamin Peirce, December 14, 1841 and March 6, n. yr. Solution to a mathematical problem (4 pp.).

L 618. Gould, B. A. One letter to James Mills Peirce, May 19, 1881.

L 619. Greenough, Louisa. One letter to Sarah Mills Peirce, July 27, n. yr.

L 620. Haagensen, J. One letter to Benjamin Peirce, October 27, 1879.

L 621. Hall, A. One letter to James Mills Peirce, September 28, 1900.

L 622. Hantz, J. M. One letter to Benjamin Peirce, December 7, 1872.

L 623. Higginson, H. L. Two letters to James Mills Peirce, January 14, 1894 and January 28, 1903.

L 624. Hornblower, Bryne and Taylor. Nine letters to James Mills Peirce, January 19–March 15, 1895. One telegram to James Mills Peirce, February 12, 1895.

L 625. Hosmer, James K. One letter to James Mills Peirce, October 7, 1867.

L 626. Huntington, Charles P. One letter to Benjamin Peirce, n.d.

L 627.   Huntington, Helen Mills. Three letters to Sarah Mills Peirce, March 29, [1835]–January 8, [1843].

L 628.   Huntington, Mary Ellis. One letter to Helen Peirce Ellis, October 6, [1885].

L 629.   Johnson, John. One letter to Benjamin Mills Peirce, May 8, 1867.

L 630.   Jones, E. C. S. (Caty). One letter to Charlotte Elizabeth Peirce, June 6, 1845.

L 631.   Jones, Mary Anna. One letter to Charlotte and Charles H. Peirce, September 1835. Four letters to Lydia Ropes Peirce, February 5 and October 29, 1835, and n.d.

L 632.   Jones, Judge Samuel. One letter to Bradley Martin, September 12, 1836. One letter to Lydia Ropes Peirce, February 8, 1934.

L 633.   Jones, Sarah. One letter to Charlotte Elizabeth Peirce, January 20, n. yr. Verses, July 9, 1835.

L 634.   Kerr, John B. One letter to Benjamin Peirce, Sr., December 21, 1829.

L 635.   Lamb, Harriet. One letter to Helen P. Ellis, [October 1880].

L 636.   Lee, Mrs. Hannah F. (Hannah Sawyer). Three letters to Lydia Ropes Peirce, June 18, 1855, and n.d. One letter to Charlotte Elizabeth Peirce, n.d.

L 637.   Lee, Mary Anna. Seven letters to Charlotte Elizabeth Peirce, March 17, 1826, and n.d.

L 638.   Manning, Charles Henry. One letter to Benjamin Mills Peirce, July 6, 1862.

L 639.   Mifflin, George H. One letter to Benjamin Peirce, August 7, 1865. Six letters to Benjamin Mills Peirce, August 17, 1866–March 19, 1870.

L 640.   Mills, Charles Henry. Two letters to Sarah Mills Peirce, January 31, 1866 and August 18, [1871?].

L 641.   Mills, Elijah Hunt, Jr. One letter to Sarah Mills Peirce, August 4, 1829.

L 642.   Mills, Harriet. Nine letters to Charles Sanders and to her relatives, January 27, 1827–April 25, [1880's].

L 643.   Mills, Sarah Hunt. One letter to Mrs. Charles P. Huntington (Helen Sophia Mills), August 26, 1828.

L 644.   Mitchell, P. M. One letter to Benjamin Peirce, July 9, 1846.

L 645.   Monackjer, Nasservanji. Four letters to Ichabod Nichols, Sr., April 22, 1800–January 10, [1811].

L 646.   Nichols, Benjamin. One letter to brother (John Nichols), April 30, [1797].

L 647.   Nichols, George. One letter to Benjamin Peirce, Sr., July 7, 1831, with Benjamin Peirce, Sr.'s reply of July 11, 1831. One letter to sister [Lydia Nichols], November 26, 1800. One letter to Nasservanji Monackjer, [1800].

L 648.   Nichols, Henry. One letter to his brothers, July 20, 1813.

L 649. Nichols, Captain Ichabod. One letter to George Nichols, May 7, 1796. Five letters to John Nichols, December 20, 1788–April 27, 1797. One letter to Charlotte (Sanders), March 15, 1811. Two letters to Lydia Ropes (Peirce), December 16, 1803, and n.d. Two letters to Ichabod Nichols (later Rev.), March 12, 179– and July 30, 1812. Four letters to Benjamin Peirce, Sr., April 20, 1801–November 2, 1803. One letter to Joseph Story, March 27, 1801.

L 650. Nichols, Ichabod, Rev. One letter to Lydia Nichols (sister), March 7, 1800. One letter to his sister, May 3, 1832. One letter to his nephew, July 31, 1832. One letter to Benjamin Peirce, April 18, 1842.

L 651. Nichols, John. Two letters to Benjamin Peirce, August 14 and December 25, 1832. Fifteen letters and letter drafts to Lydia Ropes Nichols, July 18, 1793–August 21, 1832. One letter to Joseph Anthony and Co., September 1797.

L 652. Nichols, Lydia Ropes (Mrs. Ichabod Nichols). Eight letters to John Nichols, May 1794–May 6, 1797, and n.d. One letter to her daughter, Lydia Ropes Nichols Peirce (Mrs. Benjamin Peirce, Sr.), October 22, 1826.

L 653. Nichols, Martha. Two letters to Helen Ellis, July 30 and December 12, 1916.

L 654. Nichols, M. S. (Mrs. Rev. Ichabod Nichols). One letter to Mrs. Lydia Nichols, May 30, 1832.

L 655. Palfrey, John C. One letter to James Mills Peirce, May 28, 1872.

L 656. Parsons, Thomas William. One letter to Benjamin Peirce, September 24, [1867].

L 657. Patterson, C. P. One letter to Benjamin Peirce, December 13, 1867.

L 658. Peabody, M. J. Two letters to "Friend" [Charlotte Elizabeth Peirce?], July 5, [1885?] and [1885?].

L 659. Peirce Genealogy. MS., 2 pp., unsigned.

L 660. Peirce, Benjamin, Sr. One letter to Jacob Abbot, February 26, 1805. One letter to Rufus Choate, February 21, 1831. One letter to John Forrester, September 16, 1826. One letter to John Thornton Kirkland, President of Harvard, August 15, 1826. Two letters to George Nichols, September 1797 and July 11, 1831. Two letters to Captain Ichabod Nichols, April 22, 1801 and October 29, 1803. Twelve letters to Lydia Ropes Nichols, August 31, 1797–August 20, 1826. One letter to Lydia Ropes Nichols (copied by Benjamin Peirce Ellis), n.d. Two letters to Benjamin Peirce, Jr., September 11, 1824 and January 11, 1825. One letter to Charles Henry Peirce, August 3, 1831. Two letters to Elizabeth Peirce, his sister, August 26, 1798 and February 14, 1799. Nine letters to Jerathmeel Peirce, his father, September 20, 1796–May 1801. Two letters to Sarah Peirce, his sister, February 26 and April 7, 1798. One letter draft (?) to Gamaliel Hodges, February 1831.

L 661. Peirce, Benjamin, Sr. Lease of Warren Street house in Salem from Pickering Dodge.

L 662. Peirce, Benjamin, Sr. Mill Dam Papers.

L 663. Peirce, Benjamin, Sr. College compositions and other manuscripts. Newspaper clippings.

L 664. Peirce, Benjamin, Jr. Two letters to A. D. Bache, 1860 and 1863. One letter to Rufus Ellis, February 28, 1868. One letter (copy) to Joseph Henry, with a copy of Joseph Henry's reply, January 29, 1869. One letter (copy) to Mrs. C. P. Huntington, December 27, 1832. One letter to Charles P. Huntington, April 2, 1844. Fourteen letters to Benjamin Mills Peirce, May 6, 1867–March 1, 1870. One letter to Charles H. Peirce, August 3, 1831. Two letters to Charlotte Elizabeth Peirce, June 29, 1874 and n.d. One letter to Helen, his daughter, 1865. One telegram to James Mills Peirce, April 25, 1870. Eight letters to Sarah Mills Peirce, December 7, 1855–October 2, 1879. One letter to unidentified person, February 14, 1845. Fragment of a letter to unidentified person, November 14, 1801.

L 665. Peirce, Benjamin, Jr., and Mrs. Benjamin Peirce. One letter to Charlotte Elizabeth Peirce, December 11, 1874. One letter to James Mills Peirce, March 11, 1867.

L 666. Peirce, Benjamin, Jr. Miscellaneous manuscripts and other items: A report on the progress and abilities of some of his mathematics students (July 3, 1848); "On the Uses and Transformations of Linear Algebras," 8 pp., incomplete; "The Perturbations of Uranus," 2 pp.; fragments of a draft concerning analytic mechanics, pp. 2-3, 4, 8-13; Almanac (1860), with some entries; college diploma; diploma of American Academy of Arts and Sciences (January 29, 1834); typescript of a biography of Benjamin Peirce, written by either James Mills Peirce or CSP (probably the former), an abridged version of which appeared in *Lamb's Biographical Dictionary*, Vol. VI, 1903, pp. 196-8; printed letter of Charles W. Eliot on the death of Benjamin Peirce; newspaper clippings.

L 667. Peirce, Benjamin Mills. Ten letters to Constant Davis, July 19, 1857–January 28, 1863. Seven letters to Benjamin Peirce, July 29, 1853–September 16, 1869, and n.d. One letter to Charlotte Elizabeth Peirce, n.d. Seven letters to James Mills Peirce, July 12, [1854?]–October 11, 1865. Nineteen letters (with a letter from Helen Peirce to her mother enclosed in the first of these) to Sarah Mills Peirce, May 2, 1858–April 2, 1870, and n.d. Five letters to Perry [TS.], October 8, 1867–May 11, 1869. Two letters to Mrs. Charles Sanders, n.d. Two letters to Frederick Ware, [September 24, 1857]–July 1861. Also a notebook of letters to Fanny L. Porter, copied by F. L. Porter and presented to Helen Peirce Ellis as a memorial on the death of Benjamin Mills Peirce: eighteen letters, November 19, 1865–June 12, 1866.

L 668. Peirce, Benjamin Mills. Private scrapbook of mounted letters. One letter (E. L. Arnold), March 9, 1863. One letter (A. D. Bache), January 28, 186(?). One letter (John S. Blatchford), July 14, 1864. Two letters (Charles B. Bowen), [March 7, 1863?] and July 11, 1863. Two letters (Thomas Brownell; both torn out), n. yr. One letter (Charles Warren

Clifford), April 30, 1863. One letter (George Wales Dillaway), July 14, 1864. Five letters (Walter Henry Dorr), March 5–June 11, 1863. Twelve letters (Charles James Ellis), March 2, 1863–February 4, 1864. One letter (Amy Fay), July 18, 1863. One letter (C. A. Garten), February 3, 1863. Three letters (Frank Bunker Greene), February 17–August 6, 1863. One letter (H. S. Greenough), November 2, 1863. Three letters (Frank Merrick Hollister), February 16–May 16, 1863. Ten letters (Charles H. Manning), February 23, 1863–February 16, 1864. One letter (George Harrison Mifflin), July 22, 1864. Two letters (Ferdinand G. Morrill), October 1, 1862 and August 12, 1863. One letter (C. C. Ogden), November 11, 1863. Six letters (Benjamin Peirce), February 22, 1858–June 24, 1863. One letter (Helen H. Peirce), April 10-12, 1863. One letter (Charlotte Elizabeth Peirce), March 9, 1863. Two letters (Herbert Henry Davis Peirce), April 12 and May 17, 1863. Two letters (James Mills Peirce), March 6 and 10, 1863. Twenty-one letters (Sarah Mills Peirce), February 22–June 21, 1863. Two letters (Zina Fay Peirce), March 10 and April 11, 1863. Three letters (William Peters), March 5–[December 1, 1863]. Two letters (Charles Arthur Rand), July 25 and 29, 1864. One letter (Cami Bell Rogers), May 24, 1864. Seven letters (William Rotch), July 22, 1862–August 30, 1863. Two letters (Cabot J. Russell), April 19 and May 11, 1862. One letter (George Briggs Russell), October 1, 1863. Four letters (Charles J. Train), March 4, 1863–February 16, 1864. Five letters (Frederick Ware), March 1–July 29, 1863. Two letters (Anna A. Whitney), April 9, 1862–February 12, 1863.

L 669. Peirce, Benjamin Mills. Business correspondence (Mining, Peat). Twelve letters, December 12, 1865–March 25, 1870. A set of instructions for establishing and running a peat mill. A circular of The Vulcan Peat Manufacturing Co.

L 670. Peirce, Benjamin Mills. A journal, kept while at North Conway, New Hampshire, July 1859.

L 671. Peirce, Benjamin Mills. "Function Hall Journal."

L 672. Peirce, Benjamin Mills. *The Hen-Keeper's Manual.* A journal (notebook), July 16, 1865 (the first recorded date). Also: Sermon by BMP, May 23, 1852; Harvard Class Day Program, June 23, 1865; Diary (notebook) for 1870; poetry; photographs; a note from Grandmother Mills.

L 673. Peirce, Benjamin Osgood. Minute on the life and services of Professor Benjamin Osgood Peirce (CSP's third cousin).

L 674. Peirce, Charles Henry. Two letters to Charlotte Elizabeth Peirce, January 1, 1832 and May 18, 1837. A note on the death of his father.

L 675. Peirce, Charles Henry. A. MS., Pharmacopoeia, n.p., n.d., 403 pp., with two notes by CSP and his copy of part of the section on opium.

L 676. Peirce, Charlotte Elizabeth. One letter to Benjamin Peirce Ellis, Christmas 1884. Two hundred and thirteen letters to Helen P. Ellis, April 5, [1879?]–February 3, 1888. One letter to Mrs. Rufus Ellis, January 14, 1887. One letter to Charles Huntington, March 22, 1885. Two letters to her mother (Lydia Ropes Nichols), February 17, 1832 and n.d. Two letters to her aunt, March 9, 1830 and June 5, 1834. One hundred and thirty-eight letters to Salem aunt (Nichols), [Early June 1831?]–January 27, [1887?]. Seventeen letters to cousins, [Early June 1831]–January 7, 1887. Two letters to Mrs. George Nichols (Elizabeth Peirce), n.d. Four letters to her grandparents (Nichols), May 11, 1833–April 6, 1834. Five letters to Benjamin Peirce, July 7, 1832–August 28, 1873. Two letters to Benjamin Peirce and Sarah Mills Peirce, September 19, 1875 and n.d. Thirteen letters to Mrs. Benjamin Peirce (Sarah Mills Peirce), August 13, [1840]–August 11, [1887], and n.d. Eleven letters to Benjamin Mills Peirce, September 25, 1865–August 2, 1868. Thirty-seven letters to James Mills Peirce, December 13, 1840–September 9, [1887]. Miscellaneous: notes on Aunt Sanders' will and a remembrance, May 12, 1865 and April 1872 respectively.

L 677.   Peirce, Elizabeth. One letter to Mrs. Ichabod Nichols, n.d. Eight letters to Benjamin Peirce, Sr., December 4, 1796–September 30, 1799, and September 5, n. yr.

L 678.   Peirce, Helen Huntington. Ten letters to Benjamin Mills Peirce, October 3, 1862–May 26, 1869, and n.d.

L 679.   Peirce, Henry. Four letters to Benjamin Peirce, Sr., September 14, 1826–July 17, 1827.

L 680.   Peirce, Herbert H. D. Two letters to Helen P. Ellis, April 21, 1914 and April 1914. One letter to Benjamin Peirce, January 31, 1874. Six letters to James Mills Peirce, November 24, 1885–May 11, 1903. Poetry.

L 681.   Peirce, James Mills. One letter and telegram to Byrne (Hornblower, Byrne and Taylor), January 11 and February 13, 1895. One letter to Helen P. Ellis, August 16, 1874. Part of a letter to Helen P. Peirce, copied by Benjamin Peirce Ellis and with his note, August 13, 1905. Three letters to William James, February 27–June 23, 1903. Three letters to Benjamin Peirce, February 25, [1847]–May 25, 1859. Four letters to Benjamin Mills Peirce, January 16, 1866–August 15, 1869, and n.d. One letter to Sarah Mills Peirce, November 19, 1863.

L 682.   Peirce, James Mills. Miscellaneous: "Adventures of a Pin" (June 9, 1845); triangulation of the observatory (May 8, 1950); sermon [1859–60]; Game of Poetry (December 20, 1846); bill; statues of Harvard University; a copy of the Sylvester Medal; copyright; tables of logarithmic and trigonometric functions (October 4, 1871).

L 683.   Peirce, Jerathmeel. One letter to Mrs. Ichabod Nichols, April 4, 1787. Twenty-six letters to Benjamin Peirce, Sr., September 5, 1796–March 7, 1801. One letter (Mrs. Jerathmeel Peirce) to Lydia Ropes, June 3, 1780.

L 684.   Peirce, Lydia Ropes Nichols (Mrs. Benjamin Peirce, Sr.). One letter to Mrs. Hannah Lee (Hannah F. Sawyer), December 20, 1821. One letter to Mrs. Benjamin R. Nichols, January 24, 1833. One letter to Charlotte Nichols, n.d. Two letters to George Nichols, January 16, [1827] and March 19, 1864. One letter to Mrs. George Nichols, December 19, 1853. One letter to Mr. and Mrs. George Nichols, January 15, 1860 [this letter was attached to the end of a letter from Charlotte Peirce to her Aunt Elizabeth and Uncle George Nichols (1/15/60) which has been placed with the Charlotte Elizabeth Peirce correspondence]. One letter to Henry Nichols, November 3, 1833. Two letters to Ichabod Nichols, April 11, 1800 and n.d. Twelve letters to Captain and Mrs. Ichabod Nichols, July 19, 1812–December 1, 1833, and n.d. Four letters to Mrs. Ichabod Nichols, July 19, 1812–April 12, 1832. Seven letters to John Nichols, July 22, 1793–May 4, 1797. One letter to Sarah P. Nichols, March 15, 1833. Thirty letters to Benjamin Peirce, Sr., September 18, 1797–August 11, 1830, and n.d. Two letters to Benjamin Peirce, Jr., April 21, 1832 and January 19, [1834]. Four letters to Benjamin Peirce, Jr. and Charles Henry Peirce, April 29–November 6, 1832. Twenty-two letters to Charlotte Elizabeth Peirce, April 29, 1832–August [1836?]. One letter to Elizabeth Peirce, March 1, 1846. One letter to James Mills Peirce, August 10, 1845. Six letters to Charlotte Sanders (Mrs. Charles Sanders), April 6, 1834–January 1, 1850. One letter ("Harriet") to Joseph Story ("Henry"), n.d. One draft to the Treasurer of the Savings Institution of Cambridge, Massachusetts, June 25, 1863.

L 685. Peirce, Lydia Ropes Nichols. Miscellaneous: Journal, September 1–October 10, 1824; Will of Lydia R. Peirce, December 26, 1856; notes on an early religious experience.

L 686. Peirce, Sarah. Eleven letters to Benjamin Peirce (brother), September 20, 1796–September 7, 1799.

L 687. Peirce, Sarah Mills. One letter to Benjamin P. Ellis, n.d. Forty letters to Helen P. Ellis, August 5, [1861?]–October 19, [1885], and n.d. Five fragments of letters to Helen P. Ellis, n.d. Fifty-eight letters to Benjamin Peirce, Jr., Sept. 2, 1840–July 30, [1871], and n.d. Ninety letters to Benjamin Mills Peirce, April 17, 1859–April 18, [1870], and n.d. Five letters to Charlotte Elizabeth Peirce, April 18, [1869]–October 7, [1874]. One letter to H. H. D. Peirce, July 24, 1864. Thirty-five letters to James Mills Peirce, January 1, 1867–July 16, [1883?], and n.d. One letter to her children, December 4, 1867. One letter to an unidentified person, n.d. Poetry (5 pp.).

L 688. Peirce, Zina Fay. One letter to Helen P. Ellis, April 8, 1919.

L 689. Pickering, John. Three letters to Benjamin Peirce, September 15, 1826–July 21, 1827. Two letters to Lydia Ropes Peirce (Mrs. Benjamin Peirce, Sr.), September 15, 1826-May 26, 1832.

L 690. Pickman, Dudley Leavitt. One letter to Lydia Nichols, n.d.

L 691. Putnam, Mary. One letter to Charlotte Elizabeth Peirce, March 6, n. yr.

L 692. Robbins, E. H. One letter or part of a letter to an unidentified person, n.d.

L 693. Rogers, Mrs. (Salem Schoolmistress). One letter to Charlotte Nichols, March 11, n. yr. Six letters to Lydia Nichols (later Mrs. Benjamin Peirce, Sr.), April 8, 1798 and n.d. One note (unaddressed), n.d. Poetry.

L 694. Root, O. One letter to Benjamin Peirce, January 24, 1842.

L 695. Ropes, Joseph. One letter to David Nichols (cousin), April 12, 1814. One letter to Lydia Nichols (aunt), June 6, 1814.

L 696. Ropes, W. One letter to an unidentified person, November 1842.

L 697. Rotch, William. One letter to Benjamin Mills Peirce, August 17, 1866.

L 698. Sanders, Charles. One letter to Charlotte Nichols, June 7, 1808.

L 699. Sanders, Charlotte Nichols (Mrs. Charles Sanders). Early will (before 1868).

L 700. Sawyer, Hannah. Nine letters to [Lydia Nichols], June 8, 1798 and n.d. These letters were copied by Benjamin Peirce Ellis. Thirty letters to Lydia Ropes Nichols, June 18, [1798]–April 11, 1801.

L 701. Schuyler, Louisa Lee. One letter to [James Mills Peirce], September 16, n. yr.

L 702. Schuyler, Robert. Two letters to Mrs. George Lee (aunt), December 25, 1853 and July 28, 1854. Five letters to Charlotte Elizabeth Peirce, April 29, 1837 and n.d. One letter to John Ostrem, September 12, 1836.

L 703. Sharpe, James. One letter to Captain Ichabod Nichols, February 27, 1807.

L 704. Smyrna Committee. One letter to Rufus Ellis, June 24, 1881.

L 705. Story, Joseph ("Henry"). Six letters to Lydia Ropes Nichols, March 3, 1803 and n.d. Also "Lines to L. Nichols," subsequently published in *The Power of Solitude and other Poems.*

L 706. Stuart, Rev. M. One letter to Mrs. Charles Sanders, December 25, 1824.

L 707. Sylvester, John Joseph. One letter to Benjamin Peirce, Jr., August 6, 1852.

L 708. Tracy, H. D. One letter to Captain Ichabod Nichols, October 30, 1823.

L 709. Walker, Timothy. One letter to Benjamin Peirce, Sr., October 11, 1830.

L 710. Ward, Elizabeth. One letter to Lydia Nichols, n.d.

L 711. Ware, Frederick. One letter to Benjamin Mills Peirce, September 4, 1866.

L 712. Willard, Joseph. One letter to Benjamin Peirce, Sr., June 16, 1804.

L 713. Unidentified letters.

L 714. Miscellaneous. Clipping; small notebook, July 12-22, 1824; diary of one of the Nichols.

MISCELLANEOUS CORRESPONDENCE

L 715. Babbidge, Benjamin. One letter to the President and Directors of the Salem Bank, March 19, 1810.

L 716. Barton, Elizabeth. One letter to O Rourke (or A. Rourke), February 25, 1923.

L 717. Boole, Mary E. One letter to the editor of *The Nation,* March 3, 1905.

L 718. Breed, W. J. One letter to the editor of *The Nation,* April 17, 1895.

L 719. Brown, F. Tilden, M.D. One letter to Governor William E. Russell, November 25, 1892.

L 720. Chadwick, John W. One postal card to W. P. Garrison, 1862.

L 721. Choate, Joseph H. One letter (of introduction for CSP) to John Jacob Astor, November 19, 1896.

L 722. *International Monthly, The* (F. A. Auchenchloss). One letter to G. Stanley Hall, March 6, 1900.

L 723. James, Henry. One letter (Joseph Jastrow) to James, November 23, 1934. One letter (with an enclosed copy of the CSP–Juliette Peirce marriage certificate) from James to Henry S. Leonard, October 2, 1936. One letter (A. Lawrence Lowell) to James, May 16, 1932; one letter (carbon) from, May 17, 1932. Four letters (Alfred Marvin) to James, November 3, 1934–March 11, 1936; six letters (carbons) from, November 2, 1934– March 18, 1936. One letter and telegram (Gifford Pinchot) to James, October 8 and 22, 1934; one letter (carbon) from, May 20, 1935. One letter (Paul Weiss) to James, November 5, 1934; two letters (carbons) from, November 2 and 7, 1934. One letter from James to the Girard Trust Company, October 31, 1934. A memorandum concerning Juliette Peirce dictated by James on December 27, 1921, with a note added to the memorandum the following day.

L 724. Storer, D. Humphreys. One letter to Bowditch, [December?] 9, 1884.

L 725. Vanderbilt, Cornelius. One letter from Edith ———, April 11, 1892.

L 726. Wedderburn, Joseph Henry Maclagan. One letter to Flexner, February 13, 1932.

L 727. Weiss, Paul. Three letters (J. S. Ames, President of Johns Hopkins University) to Weiss, August 1, 5, and 24, 1931. One letter (David Bailey) to Weiss, August 27, 1931. One letter (J. A. Brearley) to Weiss, August 26, 1931. One letter (Irving Smith Cranford) to Weiss, January 9, 1932. One letter (Weiss) to W. P. Durfee, August 26, 1931. Two letters (R. L. Faris) to Weiss, August 10 and 25, 1931. One letter (J. C. Fields) to Weiss, November 25, 1931. One letter and memorandum (Edwin Hall) to Weiss, August 28, 1931. One letter (Edwin B. Holt) to Weiss, October 7, 1931. One letter (Weiss) to W. W. Jacques (with Jacques's reply of September 9, 1931), August 26, 1931. One letter (William James, Jr.) to Weiss, September 12, 1931. One letter (Dumas Malone) to Weiss, August 22, 1931. One letter (Charles A. Perkins) to Weiss, September 25, 1931. One letter (Weiss) to Ralph Barton Perry, October 13, 1932; three letters from Perry, May 24, 1933–February 25, 1934. One letter (Alfred C. Potter) to Weiss, July 6, 1931. One letter (Carl A. Richmond) to Weiss, May 25, 1937. One letter (Acting Director of the Treasury Department) to Weiss, August 21, 1931. One letter (A. A. Veblen) to Weiss, October 9, 1931. One letter (Charles R. Whiteford) to Weiss, December 18, 1931. Notes (biographical data, etc.).

L 728. Wiggam, Albert E. One letter to Donald C. Williams, May 15, 1951. Two letters (Secretary, Harvard Philosophy Department) to Wiggam, May 22 and June 20, 1951.

L 729. Woods, James H. One letter to Charles Hartshorne, June 3, 1928. One letter to Albert E. Wiggam, January 27, 1933.

APPENDICES

APPENDIX I

A Supplement to the Catalogue Descriptions

The greater part of the Peirce Collection, exclusive of the correspondence, was microfilmed in 1963-64. Upon completion of the microfilming, errors in cataloguing were discovered. Because any extensive revision of the microfilm was prohibited by the expense involved, the microfilm, apart from a very few changes, was left alone. Asterisks placed before manuscript numbers have called attention to discrepancies between what was filmed and the revised catalogue descriptions, except where an entire manuscript was removed from the folder reserved for it, in which case, for the sake of convenience, the catalogue description and the microfilm correspond.

MS. 1	Six pages added from MS. 1250 (a p. 14 continuing p. 13; pp. 14, 14, 15, 16, 18 of one or more drafts); 1 p. from MS. 525.
MS. 21	Two pages added from MS. 278.
MS. 45	Contents removed to L299.
MS. 74	Two pages added from fragments.
MS. 96	Contents removed to MS. 145.
MS. 106	Sixteen pages removed to MS. 1095, of which they form leaves numbered in red 1263-1278 and in blue 776-761.
MS. 113	Four pages added from fragments.
MS. 145	Eleven pages added from MS. 96.
MS. 157	Seven pages added from fragments; one page from MS. 839.
MS. 244	Four pages added from fragments.
MS. 263	One page added from fragments.
MS. 278	Two pages removed to MS. 21; two pages removed to MS. 531; one page removed to MS. 881; one page removed to MS. 1147.
MS. 283	One page (p. 20) overlooked in the microfilming.
MS. 299	A single-page variant added from MS. 1572.
MS. 316a	The notebook is missing. It was not filmed.
MS. 317	The photostat has been misplaced; it belongs with MS. 620.
MS. 348a	For the film of these pages, see film of MS. 1571.
MS. 355	Two pages added from MS. 358.
MS. 358	Two pages removed to MS. 355.
MS. 397	Six pages (pp. 7-12) added from MS. 950.
MS. 403	Six pages added from MS. 934. For pp. 24-29, see film of MS. 934.
MS. 422	Only the typescript was filmed. The manuscript (pp. 453-456) was added subsequently.

MS. 443	Two pages added.
MS. 473	One page (p. 2) overlooked in the microfilming.
MS. 478	One page (p. 8) overlooked in the microfilming.
MS. 500	Contents removed to L376.
MS. 514	One section (pp. 9-40) and several unnumbered folded sheets from prior drafts were added to L 231.
MS. 522	One page added from fragments which continues the comparison of CSP's symbolism with Schroeder's begun on pp. 38-41 of the notebook.
MS. 525	One page removed to MS. 1.
MS. 526	Three pages (pp. 2-4 of Paper I) added from MS. 839
MS. 527	Two pages added from fragments.
MS. 529	CSP's annotated copy has been placed here.
MS. 531	Two pages (one double page) added from fragments; two pages added from MS. 278; and two pages removed to L183.
MS. 536	Two pages added from MS. 839.
MS. 558	One page (p. 15) added from MS. 1572.
MS. 570	Two pages (pp. 2 and 4) were overlooked in the microfilming.
MS. 574	One page added from fragments.
MS. 586	The notebook is missing, but a positive of it was made by Carolyn Eisele so its contents have been preserved.
MS. 595	Pages 23, 30-32, 38 are rejects of MS. 787. These pages, together with the contents of MSS. 804 and 805, yield some consecutive runs and give some idea of the extent of revision in the final draft of MS. 787. See also below notes to MSS. 717 and 787.
MS. 620	A photostat, formerly part of MS. 317, has been placed here.
MS. 693	One page added to Vol. 3; one page added to Vol. 6.
MS. 707	One folded sheet removed to L340.
MS. 717	Among the fragmentary pages are pp. 2-3, 8, 21-24 and discarded pp. 8 and 24. These pages are from a draft of the Short Logic (MS. 595). Also MS. 1214 contains partial drafts of MS. 595, and MS. 739 contains pp. 30-32 which are continued by pp. 33-34 of MS. 595. It is likely that other parts of the Short Logic have been scattered throughout the section on Logic. See MS. 903 for fragments of other drafts of MS. 717.
MS. 739	Pages 30-32 are continued by pp. 33-34 of the Short Logic (MS. 595).
MS. 748	This MS. was filmed as if it were a single work. Subsequently it was determined that it actually consisted of several different parts which, because of their importance, have been catalogued under MS. numbers 748a–d.
MS. 764	Seven folded sheets (28 pp.) added to L231; two folded sheets (8 pp.) added to L256.

MS. 787   See MSS. 804 and 805 for rejected pages of MS. 787. These pages, together with pages numbered 23, 30-32, and 38 in MS. 595 (which are also rejects from MS. 787), yield some consecutive runs and give some idea of the extent of revision in the final draft of MS. 787. See also MS. 812 for two missing pages (pp. 8-9).

MS. 802   One page added from MS. 1347.

MS. 804   Rejected pages of MS. 787.

MS. 805   Rejected pages of MS. 787.

MS. 807   Pages 16-20 continue a letter draft from CSP to Lady Welby, probably of a letter draft of December 14, 1908.

MS. 812   The two numbered pages (pp. 8-9) are two of the missing pages in MS. 787.

MS. 839   Three pages removed to MS. 526; two pages removed to MS. 536; one page removed to MS. 937; and one page removed to MS. 157.

MS. 842   One page ("Contents") added.

MS. 845   Pages 21-31 added from L338.

MS. 852   Pages 11-14 added from MS. 1008.

MS. 875   Three pages removed to MS. 962.

MS. 881   The final page (p. 100) added from MS. 278.

MS. 896   The single page is part of MS. 339 and has been removed to that place as a14r and inserted between pp. 108 and 109. MS. 339 has been refilmed with the inserted page.

MS. 919   Two pages removed to MS. 922.

MS. 922   Two pages added from MS. 919; five pages added from MS. 964.

MS. 930   Three pages added from fragments.

MS. 934   Pages 24-29 removed to MS. 403.

MS. 937   One page (alternative p. 8) added from MS. 839.

MS. 949   Two pages added from fragments.

MS. 950   Pages 7-12 combine with and complete MS. 397.

MS. 956   See MS. 968 for part of this draft.

MS. 957   One page added from fragments.

MS. 960   Eight pages removed to L307.

MS. 962   Three pages added from MS. 875.

MS. 964   Contents removed to MS. 922.

MS. 968   Part of draft of *The Architecture of Theories*. For the remainder see MS. 956.

MS. 997   One page added from fragments.

MS. 1008   Contents removed to MS. 852.

MS. 1009   One page removed to L463.

MS. 1072   Page 5 was not filmed. It is blank except for the number.

MS. 1095	Sixteen pages added from MS. 106.
MS. 1104	One page added from fragments.
MS. 1147	One page added from MS. 278.
MS. 1250	Six pages removed to MS. 1. See note to MS 1.
MS. 1347	One page removed to MS. 802.
MS. 1361	One page added from MS. 1575.
MS. 1513	Sixteen pages, most of them identifiable items for *The Nation,* added from fragments.
MS. 1538	Two pages added from fragments.
MS. 1554	Part of a notebook, containing a list of CSP's books by shelves, added.
MS. 1571	Two pages removed to MS. 348a.
MS. 1572	One page removed to MS. 299; one page removed to MS. 558.
MS. 1575	One page moved to MS. 1361.
MS. 1596	Two letters removed to L62a and L70.

APPENDIX II

A Chronological Listing of Peirce's Manuscripts

The chronological listing includes not only those manuscripts which Peirce himself dated but also those manuscripts which the several editors of Peirce's manuscripts have dated with varying degrees of confidence. For precise information concerning the dates, both Peirce's and the editors', the reader is referred to the manuscript statements themselves. A word of caution: When more than one year is indicated for a manuscript, as in the case of the Logic Notebook (MS. 339), which covers a period of over forty years, the first year alone is noted in the chronology.

Year	Manuscript Number
Early	916-917, 1116
1849	1629
1853	891
1857	1140-1141, 1628, 1633
1858	1555, 1630-1631, 1635
1859	921, 1137
c.1859	918
1860	743, 923, 988, 1555a, 1634
c.1860	741, 919
1861	920
c.1861	1047
c.1862	922
1863	1638
1864	340-350, 924-925, 1601
1865	339, 344, 726, 802, 1156
c.1865	742
1866	351-359
1867	421, 592, 811, 1147
1868	593, 931-932, 1549
1869	584-586
1870	529, 587, 1625
c.1870	88, 98
1871	576, 1614
1872	1055
c.1872	1131
1873	376-380, 382, 390-391
c.1873	360-375, 383-389, 392, 772, 935
1874	100, 1569

c.1875	99
1876	1018, 1615
c.1876	90
1877	334, 422, 424, 874, 1060, 1093
c.1877	1366
1878	1050, 1065, 1366a, 1513, 1515
c.1878	1026
c.1879	1073-1074, 1355
1880	528, 1330
c.1880	533, 535, 819, 895, 1027, 1576
1881	38
c.1881	40
1882	1081-1082, 1089, 1627
c.1882	549
1883	416, 419, 588, 1076, 1092, 1577
c.1883	119, 1119
1884	1068, 1076, 1100
c.1884	875, 1580
1885	519, 1367, 1370
c.1885	532, 567, 901, 1368-1369
1886	1016
1887	884
1889	246-249, 536, 714, 1017, 1096, 1616
1890	47, 170, 186, 878, 971, 1169, 1609-1610, 1641
c.1890	178, 880, 909, 1036-1037
1891	1028, 1317, 1371a
c.1891	1099
1892	555, 589-591, 885, 888, 961, 1152-1153, 1262, 1275, 1277, 1286, 1347-1348, 1372-1380, 1513, 1607
c.1892	66, 886, 947, 1248, 1267, 1269-1272, 1274, 1274a, 1276, 1278-1284
1893	179, 397-424, 592-594, 736, 811, 887, 1228, 1381-1384, 1513, 1546, 1617
c.1893	595, 811, 937, 950, 968-969, 1310, 1513
1894	1353, 1385-1396, 1512, 1604-1605, 1618
c.1894	898, 1512
1895	146-147, 163, 1013, 1397-1400, 1512-1513
c.1895	13-17, 164-166, 210, 716, 787, 894, 1401
1896	518, 1035, 1331, 1402-1407, 1517
c.1896	482, 860, 900, 969, 1288
1897	25, 159-160, 497, 1408, 1512
c.1897	26, 28, 155, 157, 205, 208, 798, 865, 867, 955, 1135, 1512
1898	435-445, 484, 940-941, 948, 1034, 1227, 1358, 1409, 1411, 1411a, 1513
c.1898	446, 951, 1410

1899	154, 1412-1419, 1619
c.1899	71, 142, 209, 825, 1292, 1414, 1513
1900	239, 1420-1432
1901	114, 250, 690-692, 784, 869, 872, 980, 1123-1124, 1133, 1263, 1312, 1433-1445, 1579
c.1901	49-51, 109, 483, 870
1902	426-431, 434, 581, 635, 1246, 1287, 1300, 1446-1460, 1514, 1593, 1620
c.1902	425, 429, 432-433, 596-600, 1178-1179, 1221, 1461
1903	30, 91-92, 301-315, 447-478, 881, 1462, 1464-1475, 1518, 1584, 1603, 1611, 1621
c.1903	1-11, 24, 68, 479, 491-492, 530, 538-539, 1134, 1463
1904	45, 95, 137, 189, 1139, 1477-1488a
c.1904	96, 138, 329, 336, 705, 938, 1476
1905	70, 95, 253, 283, 288, 290, 298, 300, 603, 606-607, 939, 1040-1041, 1334, 1489-1493, 1495-1499, 1513, 1622
c.1905	27, 31, 44, 57, 62, 87, 95, 279-282, 284, 289, 291, 299, 328, 608, 842, 1338
1906	490, 864, 1500-1506, 1512
c.1906	292-295, 845, 1512
1907	199, 277, 754, 905, 1507-1509
c.1907	296-297, 317-324, 687-688, 1512
1908	138, 200, 203-204, 224, 609-615, 841, 1040, 1510, 1626
c.1908	201-202, 1510
1909	514, 618-644, 706
c.1909	514, 778, 1557
1910	276, 645-667, 678-679, 703, 828, 902, 1246, 1511
c.1910	52, 285-287, 844, 846
1911	215, 500, 669-670, 838, 847-854, 856, 1008, 1349-1352, 1623
c.1911	671-677, 755
1912	12, 54, 838, 1623
c.1912	53
1913	681, 684-685, 1575, 1623
c.1913	682
1914	752, 1071, 1090, 1354, 1624
Late	616-617, 680, 683, 686, 756, 818, 826, 838

APPENDIX III

CROSS-REFERENCE INDEX: BIBLIOGRAPHICAL ENTRIES

Although for many of Peirce's published writings no manuscripts are extant, there are among his papers some which were published in the Collected Papers *and elsewhere. The purpose of this index is to enable the reader who has a bibliographical item in mind to determine at a glance whether there is a corresponding catalogue entry. Only catalogue entries which involved some publication either in whole or in part are noted. The principal exception concerns Peirce's drafts of reviews, which, for the most part, are incomplete and fragmentary, although a few of them were published. The bibliographical items are Burks's, supplemented by Fisch's, and the omission of any item means that there is nothing among Peirce's papers corresponding to it.*

Bibliography Item	Catalogue Number
GENERAL	
G-1863-2	1638
G-1866-2a	355, 359
G-1867-1b	592, 811
G-1867-1e	421
G-1868-2a	931
G-1868-2b	932
G-1868-2c	593
G-1869-2	584
G-1870-1	529
G-c.1873-1	360-361, 363-364, 367, 369-370, 373, 376, 378-379, 392
G-1875-2	75
G-c.1875-1	904
G-1877-5a	334
G-1877-5b	422
G-1877-5c	424
G-1877-5e	874
G-1878-2	1366a
G-1878-6	1050
G-1879-5c	1093
G-1880-8	528
G-c.1880-1	535
G-c.1880-2	895
G-1881-7	38
G-1881-10	76-77
G-1883-1	1076
G-1883-6b	1092
G-1883-7a	588

ITEMS FROM *The Nation*

APPENDIX IV

CROSS-REFERENCE INDEX: McMAHAN CATALOGUE

Until very recently all references to Peirce's unpublished materials, or at least to those portions of the unpublished materials which had been maintained separately in the Archives of Widener Library at Harvard University, were by citations to Knight W. McMahan's "Catalogue of the C. S. Peirce Manuscripts." A Considerable number of such references appear in the Collected Papers and elsewhere. This index serves the purpose of connecting the McMahan catalogue with this one. Citations of McMahan tend to be cumbersome because that catalogue is tied to the manner in which the Peirce materials were boxed. Indeed the citations frequently note the number of the boxes, which are marked as belonging to one or another of the several divisions which McMahan adopted for the purpose of cataloguing. As already noted in the Introduction to this catalogue, the McMahan divisions correspond roughly to Peirce's classification of the sciences, as is evident from the following:

    I. Sciences of Discovery
        A. Mathematics
        B. Philosophy
            1. Pragmatism and the Categories
            2. Normative Sciences (Logic)
            3. Metaphysics
        C. Idioscopy
            1. Psychognosy
                a. Psychology
                b. History
                c. Linguistics
            2. Physiognosy
                a. Physics
                b. Chemistry
                c. Astronomy; Miscellaneous
   II. Science of Review: Classification of the Sciences
  III. Practical Sciences and Miscellaneous
   IV. Book Reviews
    V. Life and Letters
       Unclassified: Vα, Vβ, . . . Vξ
       A. Biography
       B. Correspondence

Most of the entries in the McMahan catalogue fall under Division I. Divisions IV and V are the least developed parts, with only nine pages of the ninety-nine page typescript devoted to Peirce's reviews, biography, and correspondence. Accordingly, this cross-reference table does not extend beyond Division III of the McMahan catalogue. But this should be of no particular concern to the reader because the biographical and correspondence portions of the present catalogue are clearly laid out and, therefore, there should be no great difficulty in locating published manuscripts originally cited in Mc-Mahan.

McMahan Catalogue	Robin Catalogue
I. A. archive box, § 1(a)	1
I. A. archive box, § 1(b)	2
I. A. archive box, § 1(c)	4
I. A. archive box, § 2	49-50
I. A. archive box, § 3	238
I. A. archive box, § 4	24
I. A. archive box, § 5	68
I. A. archive box, § 6	51
I. A. archive box, § 7	12
I. A. archive box, § 8	7
I. A. archive box, § 9	47
I. A. archive box, § 10	40
I. A. archive box, § 11(a)	13
I. A. archive box, § 11(b)	14
I. A. archive box, § 11(c)	15
I. A. archive box, § 11(d)	16
I. A. archive box, § 11(e)	19
I. A. archive box, § 11(f)	17
I. A. archive box, § 11(g)	20
I. A. archive box, § 11(h)	21
I. A. archive box, § 12	75
I. A. archive box, § 13	76
I. A. archive box, § 14	39
I. A. archive box, § 15	72, 268
I. A. wooden box, § 1	137
I. A. wooden box, § 2	94
I. A. wooden box, § 3	94
I. A. wooden box, § 4	139
I. A. wooden box, § 5	1575
I. A. wooden box, § 6	141-142
I. A. wooden box, § 7	143-144
I. A. wooden box, § 8	146
I. A. wooden box, § 9	127
I. A. wooden box, § 10	126
I. A. wooden box, § 11	125
I. A. wooden box, § 12	154
I. A. wooden box, § 13	117-119
I. A. wooden box, § 14	159-160
I. A. wooden box, § 15	109
I. A. wooden box, § 16	112-113
I. A. wooden box, § 17	104, 261
I. A. wooden box, § 18	106
I. A. wooden box, § 19	275
I. A. wooden box, § 20	114
I. A. wooden box, § 21	108
I. A. wooden box, § 22	546
I. A. wooden box, § 23	164
I. A. wooden box, § 24	165

I. C. 1b. box marked IC1ab, § 1	1600
I. C. 1b. box marked IC1ab, § 2	1126
I. C. 1b. box marked IC1ab, § 3	1123
I. C. 1b. box marked IC1ab, § 4	1125
I. C. 1b. box marked IC1ab, § 5	1323
I. C. 1b. box marked IC1ab, § 6	1322
I. C. 1b. box marked IC1ab, § 7	1321
I. C. 1b. box marked IC1ab, § 8	1319-1320
I. C. 1b. box marked IC1ab, § 9	1318
I. C. 1b. box marked IC1ab, § 10	1129
I. C. 1b. box marked IC1ab, § 11	1128
I. C. 1b. box marked IC1ab, § 12	953
I. C. 1b. box marked IC1ab, § 13	1119
I. C. 1b. box marked IC1ab, § 14	1120
I. C. 1b. box marked IC1b, § 1(a)	1262
I. C. 1b. box marked IC1b, § 1(b)	1263
I. C. 1b. box marked IC1b, § 1(c)	1264
I. C. 1b. box marked IC1b, § 1(d)	1265
I. C. 1b. box marked IC1b, § 2	1269-1273
I. C. 1b. box marked IC1b, § 3(a)	1274
I. C. 1b. box marked IC1b, § 3(b)	1275
I. C. 1b. box marked IC1b, § 3(c)	1276
I. C. 1b. box marked IC1b, § 3(d)	1277
I. C. 1b. box marked IC1b, § 3(e)	1278
I. C. 1b. box marked IC1b, § 3(f)	1279
I. C. 1b. box marked IC1b, § 3(g)	1280
I. C. 1b. box marked IC1b, § 3(h)	1281
I. C. 1b. box marked IC1b, § 3(i)	1282-1283
I. C. 1b. box marked IC1b, § 3(j)	1284-1285
I. C. 1b. box marked IC1b, § 3(k)	1286
I. C. 1b. box marked IC1b, § 4	1287
I. C. 1b. box marked IC1b, § 5(a)	1288
I. C. 1b. box marked IC1b, § 5(b)	1289
I. C. 1b. box marked IC1b, § 6	1290
I. C. 1b. box marked IC1bc, § 7(a)	1294
I. C. 1b. box marked IC1bc, § 7(b)	1295
I. C. 1b. box marked IC1bc, § 7(c)	1296
I. C. 1b. box marked IC1bc, § 7(d)	1304
I. C. 1b. box marked IC1bc, § 7(e)	1306
I. C. 1b. box marked IC1bc, § 7(f)	1305
I. C. 1b. box marked IC1bc, § 7(g)	1299
I. C. 1b. box marked IC1bc, § 7(h)	1292
I. C. 1b. box marked IC1bc, § 8	1310
I. C. 1b. box marked IC1bc, § 9	1312
I. C. 1b. box marked IC1bc, § 10(a)	1313
I. C. 1b. box marked IC1bc, § 10(b)	1313
I. C. 1b. box marked IC1bc, § 10(c)	1313
I. C. 1b. box marked IC1bc, § 11(a)	1036-1037
I. C. 1b. box marked IC1bc, § 11(b)	1330
I. C. 1b. box marked IC1bc, § 11(c)	1431
I. C. 1c. § 1	1135

I. C. 1c. § 2	1143
I. C. 1c. § 3(a)	1222
I. C. 1c. § 3(b)	1223
I. C. 1c. § 4(a)	1219
I. C. 1c. § 4(b)	1220
I. C. 1c. § 4(c)	1221
I. C. 1c. § 5(a)	1178
I. C. 1c. § 5(b)	1179
I. C. 1c. § 5(c)	1180
I. C. 1c. § 5(d)	1181
I. C. 1c. § 5(e)	1182-1184
I. C. 1c. § 5(f)	1185
I. C. 1c. § 5(g)	1186
I. C. 1c. § 5(h)	1187
I. C. 1c. § 5(i)	1188
I. C. 1c. § 5(j)	1189-1199
I. C. 1c. § 6(a)	1213
I. C. 1c. § 6(b)	1208
I. C. 1c. § 6(c)	1209
I. C. 1c. § 6(d)	1201
I. C. 1c. § 6(e)	1207
I. C. 1c. § 7	1237
I. C. 1c. § 8(a)	1249
I. C. 1c. § 8(b)	1258
I. C. 1c. § 8(c)	1225
I. C. 2a. § 1(a)	1010
I. C. 2a. § 1(b)	1011
I. C. 2a. § 1(c)	1012
I. C. 2a. § 1(d)	1013
I. C. 2a. § 1(e)	1014
I. C. 2a. § 1(f)	1015
I. C. 2a. § 2	1072-1073
I. C. 2a. § 3	1025
I. C. 2a. § 4	1598
I. C. 2a. § 5	L85
I. C. 2a. § 6	1093
I. C. 2a. § 7	1026
I. C. 2a. § 8	1027
I. C. 2b. § 1(a)	1030
I. C. 2b. § 1(b)	1031
I. C. 2b. § 1(c)	1032
I. C. 2b. § 1(d)	1033
I. C. 2b. § 1(e)	1034
I. C. 2b. § 2	1038
I. C. 2b. § 3	1600
I. C. 2b. § 4	1045
I. C. 2b. § 5(a)	1039
I. C. 2b. § 5(b)	1040
I. C. 2b. § 5(c)	1041-1043
I. C. 2b. § 5(d)	1044
I. C. 2b. § 6	1211
I. C. 2b. § 7	1047

I. C. 2c. Bundles of papers and notes on
   (a) Pendulum Experiments   See Geodesy: 1060-1098
   (b) Astronomy   See Astronomy: 1049-1059
   (c) Color   See Physics: 1016-1024

II. § 1	1334
II. § 2	1335
II. § 3	1336
II. § 4	1337
II. § 5	1338
II. § 6(a)	1339
II. § 6(b)	1339
II. § 7	1341
II. § 8	1342
II. § 9	1340
II. § 10	1343
II. § 11	1344
III. A. § 1	1348
III. A. § 2(a)	1349-1352
III. A. § 2(b)	1353
III. A. § 2(c)	153
III. A. § 2(d)	L330
III. A. § 3	1514
III. A. § 4	L675
III. A. § 5	1556, L388
III. A. § 6	1357-1360
III. B. § 1	1539
III. B. § 2(a)	1559
III. B. § 2(b)	1541
III. B. § 3(a)	1524
III. B. § 3(b)	1525
III. B. § 3(c)	1527-1531
III. B. § 3(d)	1526
III. B. § 3(e)	1534
III. B. § 4	1361
III. B. § 5	1562
III. B. § 6(a)	1561, 1582
III. B. § 6(b)	1582
III. B. § 6(c)	1582

GENERAL INDEX

GENERAL INDEX

An index of the Catalogue, *exclusive of the correspondence, with the numbers referring to manuscripts, not to pages.*

A posteriori 341, 741, 744
A priori 334, 349, 741, 744, 926
  see also Belief, fixation of
Aahmes 1275-1276, 1295-1296
Abbot, Francis Ellingwood 324, 620
Abduction 293, 315, 470, 473, 475-476, 478, 692, 767, 857, 873, 939, 1147
  and pragmatism 1584
  see also Hypothesis; Retroduction
Abnumerable
  see Collections
Absolute, the 119, 121, 200, 284, 318, 630, 822, 857, 904
Abstraction 48, 402, 467, 733, 916, 1105
Absurdity 375
Accident 403, 641, 732, 934
Acetylene 1030-1035
  generator for 1035
Achilles and Tortoise 45, 165, 814-815
Action 283-284, 290, 939, 992
Actuality 138, 303, 393, 686, 858, 930
  see also Existence; Fact; Secondness
Addition 40, 46, 173, 176-177, 179, 185, 190
  logical 571
Adduction 764
Adirondack Summer School Lectures 1334
Aerodynamics 1010-1015, 1385, 1456
  air-sailing 1011, 1013-1014
  airship ascension, Lake Constance 1012
  airship of Count von Zeppelin 1012
  commercial value of 1013
  Langley's theory of soaring 1013
  mathematics of 1015
  mechanical flight 1011
  problem in 1010
Aesthetische Briefe (Schiller) 310, 619, 683
Affirmation 517, 744
Agassiz, Louis 902
Aggregation 430, 515, 1047

Agnosticism 866
Albertus Magnus 861
Alchemy 1313
Alcuin 584
Algebra 75-90, 165, 177, 192, 199
  notation and signs of 532, 583
  theorems of 430
  theories of 429
  see also Boolean algebra; Logic
Algorithm 169
Aliorelations 534
Almagest 1304
Almanac 1503
Alpha graphs
  see Graphs, existential
Alphabet 1181
  history and composition of 1186
  Semitic 1245
Ambiguity 382, 413
Ampliative reasoning
  see Reasoning
Amusements 1521-1539
  backgammon 1526
  chess 1527-1531, 1533
  riddles, puzzles, jokes 1521-1523
  tit-tat-too 1525
  whist and other card games 186, 202, 1388, 1524, 1534-1536
Anaximander 1275
Anaximenes 1275
Anesthetics 649
Anglo-Saxon 1189
Animal breeding 1362
Anselm, Saint 890, 1009
Anthropomorphism 293, 745
Anti-aliorelations 534
Anti-cock-sure-ism 827
Anti-concurrencies 534
Antilogarithms 221
Apprehension 422, 647, 739
Aquinas, Saint Thomas 309
Aratos, *Phainomena* or *Heavenly Display of* 1299-1302

247

Belmont, O. H. P. (Mrs.)   276

Bentham, Jeremy   816

Berkeley, George   328, 641, 663, 816-817
  Frazer's edition of   641, 1439

Berkeleyianism   322, 609

Berthelot, Pierre Eugene Marcelin, refutation of   1030

Beta graphs
  see Graphs, existential

Bibliography   1408, 1542-1553, 1558, 1571, 1573, 1575

Biography   1318-1323
  comparative   1120

Biology, genera of   427

Birds, flight of   1013

Blancanus, Josephus   1268

Bleaching process   1348

Body
  definition of   125
  dynamics of   427
  and mind (soul)   680, 879

Boethius   685, 996, 1408

Bolzano, Bernard   622

Book of Psalms   889

Boole, George   93, 280, 475, 551, 563, 622, 816

Boolean algebra   303, 342, 344, 354, 417-418, 430, 515-516, 529, 532, 535-536, 561-564, 566, 573, 581-582, 736, 741
  inadequacies of   1
  whist in   1524

Boswell, James, *Life of Johnson*   1257

Bradley, Francis H.   684

Brahe, Tycho   1285

Brain-forcing   1117

Breadth   384, 421, 430, 469, 664
  informed   384, 1147

Brooke, Lord   1181

Brown, Gould, *The Institutes of English Grammar*   1219

Brown, Robert, *The Phainomena* or *'Heavenly Display' of Aratos*   1301

Brute force
  see Secondness

Brute will   650

Burlesque   1303

Business (banking)
  and science   1332

Byzantine logic   994

Calculus, differential   92, 237

Calendars
  Dionysian   1324
  Gregorian   1324

Campanus, age of   1312

Can-be   334, 663, 680

Cantor, Georg   114, 201-204, 300, 458, 469, 816, 821

Cantorian   1170

Capacities   320

Cardinal number
  see Number

Carnification   1116

Cartesianism   1000

Cartography   1349-1355

Carus, Paul   958, 1288

Casuistry   1334
  see also Ethics

Categories   13, 307-310, 312, 385, 403, 438, 515, 717, 720, 744, 895-915, 991-992, 1111, 1135, 1335
  Aristotelian   477, 991-992
  kainopythagorean   141
  Kantian   895, 897, 921
  see also Firstness; Secondness; Thirdness

Causality   379, 858, 916, 963

Causation   891
  and force   443, 446
  see also Determinism; Necessitarianism

Cause
  external and internal   517
  final   682, 919
  formal   1571

Causeries du Lundi   1256, 1593

Cayley, Arthur   302, 546, 806, 1401

Celestial worlds   916

Cell   901

Cenoscopy   280, 283, 299, 326, 1139

Census
  doctrine of   145
  study of   1574

Census number   137, 156, 161-162

Census theorem   137, 161, 318

Century Dictionary, CSP's definitions for
  see Dictionary, *Century*

Certainty   334-335, 668, 829, 939

Chaldean   1277
  astronomy   1298
  metaphysics   13

Chance
  see Tychism

Chances, doctrine of
  see Probability

rules for doubling 1184
and suffixes 1208
Constants, physical and spatial 1027-1028
Constellations 1299
   star catalogues 1305
   lecture on 1582
   see also Astronomy; Stars
Containing, relation of 270
Contemporaneity 858
Continuity 3, 101, 137-138, 268, 277, 313, 316a, 397-398, 460-461, 470, 561, 717, 735, 928, 942, 948-950, 955, 1009, 1109, 1575
   Aristotle's notion of 816
   common sense notions of 14
   existence of 14
   and feeling 1115
   and Hegel 943, 947
   law of 936
   and the doctrine of limits 28
   pseudo 203, 300
   and relativity 1009
   spatial 14, 1115
   temporal 14
   see also Continuum; Synechism; Thirdness
Continuum 14, 139, 144, 165, 203-204, 377, 390, 439, 948
   and Kant 439
   perfect and imperfect 204
Contiguity 963
Contradiction, principle of 137, 430, 515, 559, 641-642, 671, 678, 680
   see also Laws of thought
Contraposition 782
Contrast 680, 963
Converse 574
Conversion 741
Coordinates 106
Copernicus 1281, 1285
Copies 346, 802
Copula, algebra of 382-383, 386, 411-412, 430, 517, 531, 573-579, 594, 721, 737-738, 742
Correlate 357, 732
Correspondence (simple), relative of 548
Cosmology 329, 877, 879
Counting 167, 169, 181-182, 184, 589, 685
Cowper, William 1172, 1255
Crashaw, Richard 1181
Creation 965, 1105

Creator
   see God
Critic, logical 449, 452, 478, 640, 661, 673-677, 793, 839, 842, 850, 852, 855, 1334
   and religion 852
   see also *Logica docens*
Critical common-sensism 290, 320, 852
   see also Common sense
Criticism 600, 674
Critique of Pure Reason, CSP's translation and notes
   see Kant
Crystallography 427, 1364
Cumberland, Richard 683
Cuneiform 1244-1245
Curie, Marie 1128, 1315
Curiosities 201
   see also Mathematical recreations
Curves
   algebraic 225
   cubic 115
   plane 261-262, 264
   real 104-105, 163
   see also Chemistry, curves of

Darwin, Charles 334, 875, 954, 1149, 1383
Dasein 733
Data
   and inference 341
Death 919
Decanes 1045
Decimal system 51, 67, 167, 207, 687, 1575
Decimetres 1095
Dedekind, J. W. R. 203-204, 222, 608
Deduction 293, 315, 328, 343, 440-441, 443, 450, 454, 473, 475, 553, 651, 669-670, 692, 696, 747, 751-752, 754, 764, 810, 831, 842, 856, 876, 939, 1411a
   corollarial 764
   definitory 842
   etymology of 478
   necessary 669-670, 856, *see also* Necessity
   probable 764, 856, *see also* Probability
   statistical 747, 768, *see also* Probability
   theorematic 764, 773
   see also Reasoning
Definite
   and precise 48

Hayford, John P. 1090
Heaven 877, 891, 919
Hedonism 330, 816, 873
   see also Pleasure
Hegel, Georg W. F. 304, 400, 467, 596,
   735, 943-944, 947, 1002, 1317, 1383,
   1457, 1467
Hegelians 309, 893
Helium 1036
Helmholtz, H. L. F. von 1395
Herbart, Johann Friedrich 357, 400
Herbert, Sir Edward 683
Heredity 954, 1149
Hermodorus 985
Herschel, J. F. W. 1276
Heurospude 1334
History 476, 685, 690-691, 1324, 1573
   great men in 1119-1127, 1373
   of ideas 1328
   periods of 1325-1326
   of words 1137
   see also Astronomy, history of; Logic,
     history of; Mathematics, history
     of; Science, history of
Hittites 1409
Hobbes, Thomas 683, 1418, 1477
Homogeneity 165
Homoloids 165-166, 273
   dominant 165
   optical 165
   system of places 166
Homonyms 991
Hope
   and truth 735
Horace 1229, 1260
Humanism 331, 623, 648
Hume, David 298, 400, 472, 645, 692,
   816, 869, 871-873, 920, 939
Hungarian 1250
Huntington, Edward V. 705, 816
Huxley, Thomas H. 902, 1322, 1389
Hydrodynamics 427, 1013
Hypothesis 78, 339, 343, 345-346, 348,
   440, 692, 696, 726, 733, 747, 837, 839,
   1571
   see also Abduction; Induction

I 917-919
   see also It; Thou
Icon 142, 307, 357, 404, 491-492, 599,
   637, 675, 842, 911
   see also Signs, classification of
Icosahedron 112-113

Idealism 322, 816, 920, 932, 935-936,
   967, 1468
   see also Mind
Ideas 126, 204, 643, 964, 1572
   abstract 327
   association of 284, 318, 368, 390, 400-
     403, 408, 515, 548, 736, 741, 963
   classification of 1135, 1139
   innate 1572
Identity 293, 515, 534
   individual and collective 430
   lines of 492, 515
   principle of 547, 559, *see also* Laws
     of thought
Idioscopy 299, 326, 655, 1334
Ignoratio elenchi 413
Illiteracy 1131
Imaginaries 101
Imagination 304, 931, 1114
Immediacy 304
Immortality 886
Implication 345, 515, 724, 726, 731
   material 411, 417
Implicit 1147
Impression 732
Impulse
   see I; It; Thou
Inclusion 580
   copula of, *see* Copula, algebra of
Incompossibility 515, 534
Inconceivability 396
Indefiniteness 48, 283, 641
Indeterminacy 283, 382
   see also Chance; Possibility; Tychism
Index 142, 307, 316, 357, 404, 462, 491-
   492, 599, 637, 675, 842, 911
   see also Signs
Indicative words 817
Indices
   Sainte-Beuve, *Causeries du Lundi*
     1593
   Logonomia Anglia 1594, 1596
Individual, and Individuality 114, 387,
   430, 622, 693, 942
   see also Index; Subject
Indubitability 288
   see also Common sense; Critical com-
     mon-sensism
Induction 293, 315, 328, 339, 341, 343,
   345, 348, 354, 440-441, 445, 470, 473-
   475, 478, 553, 624, 648, 652, 660,
   692, 696, 726, 741, 744, 747, 751,
   753-754, 758, 764-767, 773, 831, 839,

Reality 126, 204, 289, 367-368, 370-375,
379, 393, 408, 439, 498, 517, 637, 663,
852, 858, 931-934, 938-939, 1572
and Being 385
and belief 675
definition of 686
and *ens rationis* 48
and existence 49, 288
of God 641, 841-844, 861, 905
and meaning 587
physical 329
and truth 655, 664
Reason 410, 435-436, 617, 622, 658-660,
672, 693, 695, 831-832
active 634
and instinct 672
and religion 857
Reasoning 186, 290, 293, 299, 314-315,
334, 345, 371-372, 400, 404, 408-409,
441, 444-445, 447-448, 450-451, 453-
454, 465, 470, 475, 594, 596-599, 616-
617, 620, 628, 641, 650-652, 654, 661-
673, 678-686, 693-694, 698, 735, 739,
741, 750, 752-755, 757, 770, 778, 796,
822, 826, 830-831, 837-839, 849, 857,
876, 901, 924, 928, 939, 1101, 1112-
1113, 1121, 1584
acritical 939
ampliative 660
corollarial 318, 754
dilemmatic 736
explicative 661
foundation of 6
materialistic aspect of 405
mathematical 617, 625, 662, 683
necessary 293, 651-652, 661, 669-670,
683, 757, 760, 837, 856
probable 757, 761, *see also* Probability
recreations of 205-208
theoric 318
uberty of 682-684
see also Abduction; Deduction; Induction; Inference; Inquiry; Logic;
Thinking
Recollection 675
Recorde, Robert, *Ground of Artes* 1265
Recreation
see Amusements; Reasoning, recreations of
Reference works 1591, 1596
Reid, Thomas 309

Relation 22, 313, 357, 403, 517, 720,
732, 796, 911, 927, 934, 1001, 1147
distinguished from relationship 601
dyadic 419, 462, 513, 530, 536, 538-
539, 542-543, 808
plural 747
tetradic 543, 548
triadic 462, 540-541, 543, 939
Relations, spatial and temporal 87
Relationship 22, 601
Relatives, logic of 19, 21-22, 302, 339,
418-419, 438, 440, 515-516, 521-522,
524, 526, 529, 532-537, 544-545, 547-
548, 553-558, 646, 736, 747, 810, 837,
839, 1274, 1336, 1406a
Relativity
and continuity 1009
of knowledge 934
Religion 325, 841-894, 920, 954, 1440
and faith 849-856
and fallibilism 867
and infallibilism 865
and instinct 807, 853
and politics 894
and pragmatism 318
and reason 436, 857
and science 851, 856, 863-864, 866-868
Replicas 492
Representamen 307, 492, 796
see also Sign
Representation 346, 357, 381, 388-389,
403, 491, 720, 724, 729, 732, 769, 802,
810, 934
see also Meaning; Sign; Thirdness
Research, theory of the economy of 1093
Resemblances 645
see also Icon; Likeness
Resolution 1132
Retroductions 439-441, 445, 638, 652,
751-752, 754, 756, 842, 856-857, 876
see also Abduction
Retrogression 858
Revelations, abstract 916
Reviews, CSP's, principally for *The Na-
tion* 1365-1513
Rhema 313, 316
see also Proposition
Rhetoric 774, 776-777
speculative, *see* Methodeutic
Risteen, Arthur D. 500, 1403, 1410
Roget's Thesaurus 749
Rollandus 1266
Roman Catholicism 880

Roman schools, seven liberal arts of 1341

Rosicrucian Society 1313

Roulette 209-210
see also Probability

Royce, Josiah 45, 284, 543, 622, 630, 684, 816, 1369, 1426a, 1461, 1465, 1487, 1512

Ruskin, John 1220

Russell, Bertrand 12, 459, 469, 818

Satisfaction 330, 649, 655, 817
and feelings 686
and pleasure 873
and truth 817

Scales 191, 221, 1089

Scepticism 329, 334, 339, 620

Schellbach, K. H. 1011

Schelling, Friedrich 400

Schiller, F. C. S. 318, 321, 331, 824, 1584

Schiller, Friedrich 310, 619, 683

Scholastic 328
logic 648
realism 296, 620, 842, 870

Scholasticism 650, 721-722

Schroeder, Ernst 307-308, 520-525, 1406a

Science 280, 283, 340, 438, 440, 485, 614-615, 624, 673, 678, 687, 693, 745, 809, 839, 856, 863, 926, 1211, 1289, 1330, 1332, 1335, 1421, 1484
classification of 327, 357, 427, 437, 601-602, 605, 615, 655, 675, 677, 693, 728-729, 778, 1334-1347
definition of 17, 283, 299, 615-624, 655
dictionary of 1174, 1176
and fallibilism (infallibilism) 865, 867
heuritic 283, 605, 673, 852
history of 339, 1127, 1267, 1269-1317, 1333, 1337, 1574, *see also* Astronomy, history of; Mathematics, history of
logic of 246, 343, 345-346, 407, 435, 603, 647, 769-771, 778, 860, 1573
and metaphysics 350, 924
practical 283, 673, 693, 1339, 1348-1364a
and religion 851, 856, 863-864, 866-868
rhetoric of 774, 776-777
theoretical 655, 1339

Sciences of review
see Sciences, classification of

Scotists 473, 648

see also Duns Scotus

Scotus Eregena 584

Seance 880

Secondness 13, 284, 304, 307-310, 403, 439, 460, 478, 650, 721, 897, 901, 903-907, 912-915, 934, 942, 1106
see also Categories; Effort; Reaction

Secundal system of enumeration 1, 44, 51-67, 137, 199, 201, 276, 494, 687, 1121, 1250, 1573, 1575, 1588, 1601

Self 1108

Self-consciousness 931

Self-control 939, 1334

Self-criticism 673, 831

Self-deception 755

Self-evidence 931

Self-switch 1095

Seme 295
see also term

Semeiotics 336-337, 634, 641, 693, 774, 777
see also Sign

Sensation 357, 681, 925, 1100, 1102, 1104, 1114

Sense(s) 1137
impression 932
manifold of 916
perception 686
as reasoning machine 1101

Series 48
continuous 717-718
geometrical 1276

Sermons, texts for 1573

Sets, forms of 37

Sextal system of enumeration 67, 199

Shakespeare, William 1172, 1259

Shock 299

Significs, and logic 618, 641-642

Signify, and Signification 642, 796, 1147

Skew mercator
see Map

Sign(s) 4, 7-12, 137, 142, 200, 224, 277, 283, 292-293, 295, 304, 318, 321, 346, 373, 379-381, 396, 404, 429, 449, 462, 492, 498-499, 515, 517, 541, 599, 634, 637, 643, 654, 667, 670, 675, 717, 735, 764, 773, 792-804, 806, 810, 833, 839, 842, 849, 854, 911, 914, 919, 931-932, 939, 1009
classification of 16, 292, 795, 799-800
definition of 654, 793, 801, 849
and logic 569, 583, 609, 801, 803
and mathematics 7, 583